Abraham Dieffenbachers
Book

Z. Taylor

PRESIDENT OF THE UNITED STATES.

CERRA GORDO
CHURUBUSCO
CHEPULTEPEC
SCOTT
PALO ALTO
RESACA DE LA PALMA
BUENA VISTA
TAYLOR
VERA CRUZ
MONTEREY
MEXICO

HISTORY OF THE WAR

BETWEEN THE

UNITED STATES AND MEXICO,

FROM THE

COMMENCEMENT OF HOSTILITIES

TO THE

RATIFICATION OF THE TREATY OF PEACE.

BY JOHN S. JENKINS,

AUTHOR OF "THE GENERALS OF THE LAST WAR WITH GREAT BRITAIN," ETC. ETC. ETC.

AUBURN.
DERBY & MILLER,
1850.

THOMAS B. SMITH, STEREOTYPER,
216 WILLIAM STREET, N. Y.

This Work is Dedicated

TO

THE AMERICAN ARMY,

BOTH REGULARS AND VOLUNTEERS,

WHOSE GALLANTRY AND INTREPIDITY WERE SO OFTEN MANIFESTED DURING THE PROGRESS OF THE WAR WITH MEXICO; AND THE RECORD OF WHOSE ACHIEVEMENTS WILL CONSTITUTE, THROUGH ALL FUTURE TIME, ONE OF THE MOST ATTRACTIVE FEATURES OF OUR MILITARY AND NATIONAL HISTORY.

PREFACE.

The War with Mexico constitutes an episode, and, by no means, an unimportant one, in the history of the American Union. Its brilliant scenes, and stirring incidents, have attracted unusual attention, and they must long continue to be remembered. The honor of the nation, and the triumph of her arms, are so closely allied, in the estimation of our citizens, that the permanent record of these events cannot be devoid of interest.—The military annals of the world present no higher, or more enduring evidences, of the skill and courage of any other soldiery. Each arm of the service,—cavalry, artillery,* and infantry,—has gained imperishable renown; and the navy, too, ever famed for its gallantry and heroism, though necessarily participating, to a less extent, in the active operations of the war, is entitled to no small share of the laurels which have been won.

Since the commencement of hostilities, there has certainly

* It will be borne in mind, by the reader, that the artillery regiments in the American service, are equipped, and act, as infantry; with the exception of those detached companies serving with batteries, and designated by the names of their commanding officers.

been no great dearth of publications, having reference, directly or indirectly, to the prosecution of the war. Biographical sketches of our most distinguished officers, and numerous compilations, glancing at the more important achievements of the army, have been issued;—but, at the moment of writing this Preface, I am not aware of the publication of any complete history of the collision between the two great republics on this Continent, which is now happily terminated. Such a work must naturally be desired, and these pages have been written, with a view of satisfying, in some degree, the public expectation.

In the preparation of this volume, my main reliance, for the facts and details connected with the military operations, has been upon the official reports of the officers of the army, —as well those occupying subordinate positions, as those at the head of columns or divisions. The narrative, proper, of the war, is preceded by a review of its origin and causes, written after a careful examination of the diplomatic correspondence, and the various publications, of a public or private character, that have appeared from time to time, calculated to throw any light on the subject.

Most of the works which have been of service to me, in preparing the volume, are cited in the text, or notes. Among those not so cited, are,—Newell's History of the Revolution in Texas; "Texas and the Texans," by H. Stuart Foote; "Our Army on the Rio Grande," and "Our Army at Monterey," by T. B. Thorpe; the Campaign

Sketches of Captain W. S. Henry; "The Conquest of California and New Mexico," by J. Madison Cutts; "Doniphan's Expedition," by J. T. Hughes; and "Adventures in Mexico," by C. Dunnovan.

I have also derived much valuable information from the letters of the regular and occasional correspondents of different public journals, and, particularly, those of the New Orleans press. I have often found these, however, conflicting very materially with the official statements, and, as, from the nature of the case, was to be presumed, more or less tinged with the gossip of the camp. It has, therefore, been sometimes extremely difficult to separate the real from the fanciful; and I can hardly flatter myself with the hope that I have entirely avoided errors, though I trust none may be found, impairing the general fidelity of the work.

It is likewise proper that I should acknowledge my indebtedness to the well-executed maps of Majors Turnbull and Linnard, and the other able and intelligent officers of the Corps of Topographical Engineers, which have accompanied the official reports from the seat of war.

My thanks are further due, to J. S. Meehan, Esquire, the Librarian of Congress, and his assistants, for their kindness and courtesy; and to the Hon. John A. Dix, of the United States Senate, for the receipt of several valuable public documents.

AUBURN, *September* 1, 1848.

CONTENTS

CHAPTER I.

ORIGIN AND CAUSES OF THE WAR.

CHAPTER II.

BATTLES ON THE RIO GRANDE.

CHAPTER III.

CALIFORNIA AND NEW MEXICO.

CHAPTER XI.

REVOLT IN NEW MEXICO.

CHAPTER XII.

CONTRERAS AND CHURUBUSCO.

CHAPTER XIII.

EL MOLINO DEL REY.

CHAPTER XIV.

CAPTURE OF MEXICO

CHAPTER XV.

THE ARMY UNDER TAYLOR.

CHAPTER XVI.

THE GULF SQUADRON.

CHAPTER XVII.

CLOSING SCENES OF THE WAR.

CHAPTER XVIII.

TREATY OF PEACE.

THE WAR WITH MEXICO.

CHAPTER I.

ORIGIN AND CAUSES OF THE WAR.

The Government and People of the United States—Revolutions in Mexico—Claims of American Citizens—Negotiations—Warlike feelings—Settlement of Texas—Revolution—Proposition for Annexation to the United States—Treaty of President Tyler—Joint Resolutions—Admission of Texas—Her Boundaries—March of General Taylor to the Rio Grande—Hostile demonstrations on the part of Mexico—Capture of Thornton and his party.

From the time of the cessation of hostilities with Great Britain, in pursuance of the treaty concluded at Ghent, in December 1814, until 1846, a period of more than thirty years, the government of the United States was not involved in war with any of the nations of the earth. Occasional interruptions of her friendly relations with other countries and governments temporarily disturbed the harmony previously existing between them; but the causes of dispute were soon removed, and every difficulty satisfactorily adjusted, with, perhaps, the single exception—that which terminated in the war with Mexico. The American Confederacy was formed, not for the political aggrandizement of its members, collectively or individually, but solely and entirely for purposes of mutual protection and defence. It has been our uniform policy, since the assertion and successful vindication of our independence, though never sacrificing anything of national dignity, to keep aloof from all entangling alliances with foreign powers, to avoid subjects of contention likely to furnish an excuse for their interference in our domestic affairs, and assiduously to cultivate the arts and the institutions of peace. The elements of greatness and power are ours; yet these have been manifested, not so much in the achievements of our armies, and the splendor of our military establishments, as in the protection afforded to our commerce, and the encouragement given to the agricultural and industrial pursuits to which our people are devoted. The growth of the nation has been rapid, beyond parallel. At the beginning of the present century, she was weak and feeble—she is now great and powerful. But her career of glory, unexampled as it is, has been marked, more than all, by the development of new principles in government, by the energy and industry which have made the wilderness to blossom like the rose, and by the extension of human civilization, from the frozen regions of the north to the land of perpetual flowers—from the rock-bound coast of the Atlantic to the prairies of the West—" the gardens of the desert," whose " very weeds are beautiful," and whose

" waste
More rich than other climes' fertility."

At the close of the Revolution, a new government was established, and we became, emphatically, a new people. It was our aim and object to remain at peace with the world, and to continue forever wholly independent of every other power. Our land was the refuge of the oppressed of every nation and creed; the natural enmity of the Briton and the Gaul was forgot ten; the traits and characteristics which were always found arrayed in hostility upon the Eastern Continent, were here blended harmoniously together; and those prejudices calculated to diminish or impair the strength of the alliance, were softened and subdued by the consciousness that its preservation was essential to our safety. The terms "Anglo-Saxon," and "Anglo-American," are often applied to us; but is not this the language of mere affectation and cant? Surely they are inapplicable to us and to our children. We have sprung from the Saxon, the Norman, and the Celt, with here and there an admixture of nearly all the other races of the earth. We are Americans!—neither more nor less—and why should we claim a different title from that which Washington and his contemporaries were proud to own? This is ours, justly ours; and it has become a passport to respect and confidence throughout the world.

While engrossed in the prosecution of those peaceful pursuits, for the security of which their government was formed, the American people have not been unmindful of the efforts that have been made to establish institutions similar to their own, in other quarters of the globe. Their sympathies were never withheld from the oppressed, nor their assistance denied, when it could be rendered consistently with their duties and obligations as a nation. Neither have they failed to assert, at all proper times, and on all proper occasions, their rights as a separate and independent sovereignty. The martial spirit of a republic, whose independence was secured by force of arms, could not be easily subdued. Every citizen among us shares the privileges and the responsibilities of government; each one can say, like the French monarch, though in a far different spirit, "I am the state!" and hence it is, that the language of menace, or an act of outrage or insult committed in the remotest section of the Union, sends an instantaneous thrill through the breasts of our countrymen. Peace societies and conventions have denounced feuds, and contentions, and wars; they have striven to inculcate mildness and forbearance in the adjustment of all difficulties among governments; they have labored, earnestly and zealously, to make forgiveness the law of the council-room and the audience-chamber; but, however praiseworthy their efforts, or benevolent their intentions, they have produced little change in the feelings and dispositions of the American people. Go where we may, at home or abroad,—on the sea or on the land,—wherever we find one of our citizens, standing beneath the broad folds of our national flag, we shall see his eye kindle and his bosom throb, as he gazes on the proud emblem floating above him; and if, at such a moment, violence be offered, either rightfully or wrongfully, to him or to it, his arm is nerved for the defence with tenfold vigor and strength!

The moralist who can sit calmly down to analyze the sentiment which is thus manifested, may discover something of error mixed up with what is commendable; but so long as it forms the same part of our natures with patriotism and love of country, it cannot well be separated. If it be dangerous to arouse it, without justifiable and sufficient cause, it is far more so, to trifle with, or insult it with impunity. This sentiment, or emotion, or impulse, by whatever name it may be dignified, has become a fixed and abiding principle in the hearts of our fellow-citizens; and it was never more signally exhibited than during the progress of the Mexican war. Differences of opinion existed with regard to the necessity for the commencement of hostilities; but when once determined on, all classes and parties aided in their vigorous prosecution. Our young men, at the plough and in the workshop—in the office and the counting-house—in town and in country—had no sooner heard of battles, than they longed "to follow to the field." The recital of the brilliant deeds performed by men animated by such a spirit, will, no doubt, be welcome to the reader: but before proceeding with the narrative, the origin and causes of the war seem very appropriately to demand attention.

The republic of Mexico, for such she has claimed to be, amid all the phases and changes in her political condition, has never possessed a firm or stable government since 1821, when she ceased to be one of the dependencies of the Spanish crown, except during the first presidency under the federal constitution. Her prolonged struggle for independence was not viewed with indifference in the United States. The government of the latter was the first to recognize her separate existence, and her battle fields were crimsoned with the blood of many an American citizen. In the darkest hour of her fortunes, in the midst of peril and difficulty, she was cheered and encouraged by those who had encountered similar trials and dangers, and who were then basking in the sunshine of freedom, and enjoying the rich reward they had labored to secure. The ties and associations thus formed, it was hoped would become more firm and enduring, as the commercial and social intercourse between the two countries was extended. But the character and habits of the Mexican people unfitted them for the rational enjoyment of free institutions; and they became the easy prey of the military despots, who by turns harassed and oppressed them. The descendants of the Spaniard, while they have retained many of the more noble traits of their ancestors, they have acquired all the baser passions and characteristics of the different races with which they have amalgamated.* They are passionate and vindictive, treacherous and cruel, indolent and selfish; and their bravery is an impulse rather than a sentiment. The *fierté* of the ancient Hidalgo, the pride of the old Castilian, are almost forgotten; and the faith of their forefathers is corrupted by the traditions of Tlascala and Cholula.

In 1822, Iturbide was proclaimed Emperor of Mexico, by the lawless and licentious soldiery whom he had rendered obedient to his wishes. His short reign was characterized by the profligacy, anarchy, and corruption, which reigned everywhere triumphant. The money and property of foreign merchants were seized without warrant or justification, and the laws of nations openly and constantly disregarded. His attempt to unite the descendants of the Spaniards, and the original natives of Mexico, on terms of amity and friendship, in support of a government whose rapacity was only limited by its power of gratification, proved utterly abortive. He was dethroned and put to death by an exasperated people, in 1824, at which time the federal constitution, modelled after that of the United States, was adopted, and Victoria elevated to the presidency. Aside from the revolt of General Bravo, the vice-president, which was soon quelled, his term of office was comparatively tranquil and peaceful; yet, in several instances, the prop-

* The population of Mexico is about 7,000,000. One-fifth of this number are whites, of Spanish origin; two-fifths, Indians; and the remainder, partly negroes, but mainly composed of a mongrel population, descended from whites, Indians, and negroes, who are termed *Mestizoes*, *Mulattoes*, and *Zamboes*.

erty of American citizens was illegally wrested from them by the corrupt agents of the government. Upon the expiration of Victoria's term, a bloody contest ensued between the rival candidates for the succession. General Guerrero was the successful candidate, and his competitor, Pedrazo, was banished. Within a year the former was deprived of his power and his life. Confusion, disorder, and misrule, prevailed throughout the republic. Two great parties, embracing numerous minor factions, were contesting for the supremacy. The Federalistas were in favor of adhering to the constitution of 1824, and the Centralistas desired to establish a central consolidated government. Guerrero was succeeded by the vice-president, Bustamente, a prominent and leading centralist. The war between the two parties was waged more fiercely than ever. Bustamente was finally banished, and General Antonio Lopez de Santa Anna, one of the heroes of the revolution, was raised to power by the joint efforts of the aristocracy and clergy. The constitution of 1824 was nominally preserved during all these dissensions; but in October, 1835, it was set aside by Santa Anna, and the country divided into departments, with governors appointed by the central authorities.* The southern states, or provinces, generally concurred in the change; but those at the north refused to accede, until they were chastised into submission by the presidential dictator, who had broken the league of federation, and established centralism in its stead. Texas alone refused to surrender her state sovereignty, and maintained a successful

* Under the federal constitution, Mexico was divided into 19 states, 4 territories, and a federal district. The provinces of Coahuila and Texas were formed into a state bearing the names of both.

resistance against the armies sent to subdue her.* This consolidated government, formed in 1835, underwent no material change, until the year 1846, although its founder was compelled to share the power secured to the central head, in turn, with Bustamente, Herrera, and Paredes.†

While the republic of Mexico was divided and distracted by these internal tumults and disorders, the government of Spain attempted its re-subjugation. Expeditions and armaments were fitted out, but they only served to exhaust the treasuries of both the mother country and her former colony. The Mexican authorities employed the most illegal measures to replenish their coffers. The position of the United States, in the immediate vicinity, and the extent of their commerce in the Gulf, caused them to feel the effects of the arbitrary proceedings which were resorted to, more seriously than any other nation, and rendered it im-

* Yucatan followed the example of Texas, in 1840, and declared herself independent. In 1843 she was reunited to Mexico; but in 1846, she again revolted, and, assuming a position of neutrality, refused to take part in the war against the United States.

† Paredes is an avowed monarchist in principle, and after his accession to power, the calling of a foreign prince to the throne was advocated in the columns of the "Tiempo," a journal conducted by Lucas Alaman, one of his confidential friends, and the author of his *convocatoria*, or edict, calling together the constituent Congress, promulgated on the 27th of January, 1846. The same idea was suggested by a French author, (M. de Mofras,) in a work on Oregon and California, published with the approbation of the Court of France, in 1844. He advocated the establishment of a European monarchy, and thought a suitable person to occupy the throne might be selected from the infantas of Spain, the French princes, or the archdukes of Austria. From a statement made by Señor Olozoga in the Cortes of Spain, on the 1st of December, 1847, it appears that large sums of money were drawn from the treasury in Havana, in the year 1846, for the purpose of establishing a Spanish prince on the throne of Mexico.

possible to maintain that strict amity which, under other auspices, might have been forever preserved between the two great republics on the Western Continent. Vessels sailing under the American flag were plundered; the goods of our merchants confiscated, and the owners, or their agents, imprisoned with impunity. The advent to power of each new usurper, was attended by renewed violations of public law and private rights. Useless and oppressive blockades were attempted to be enforced by one party against the other, though fighting beneath the same banner, and loudly professing their attachment to the same country. That the adventurous citizens of the American Union, knowing little or nothing of civil strife and commotion in their own country, should be unable at all times to distinguish between the party in power and their opponents, and should sometimes disregard the regulations and enactments which appeared to them to have been unjustly and arbitrarily established, were the natural consequences of the unsettled character of the Mexican government.

For a long time the authorities of the United States contented themselves with remonstrating against these proceedings, and making reclamations in behalf of our citizens. Promises of redress were postponed or evaded, and remonstrances were followed by new acts of depredation, and still more wanton outrages. At length, a treaty of amity, commerce, and navigation, was concluded between the two republics, on the 5th of April, 1831. The condition of things, however, remained unchanged. Although the provisions of the treaty were clear and positive, "the course of seizure and confiscation of the property of our citizens, the violation of their persons, and the insults to our flag, pursued by Mexico previous to that time, were scarcely suspended for even a brief period."* The situation of that country was, indeed, most deplorable; the accumulating burdens beneath which she struggled, threatened to blot out her national existence; and it was thought best to exhibit towards her a spirit of forbearance and magnanimity, in the hope that corresponding feelings would be produced on her part, to be followed by an amicable adjustment of all difficulties and disputes. On the contrary, additional indignities were heaped upon the officers and flag of the United States; applications for the redress of grievances were unavailing; and in 1837, the American government was itself insulted by the Mexican minister at Washington.† These circumstances constituted, in the opinion of the then Executive, a sufficient justification for immediate war; but desirous, as he was, to avoid this alternative, and in view of the embarrassed condition of Mexico, he thought one more opportunity of atoning for the past should be given, before taking redress into our own hands. "To avoid all misconception," he said, "on the part of Mexico, as well as to protect our national character from reproach, this opportunity

* Message of President Polk, December, 1846.

† It is but just to Mexico, to remark, that one ground of complaint on her part, and one excuse for delaying the settlement of the American claims for spoliations and personal injuries, was, the interference of our citizens in the revolutionary struggle in Texas. This, however, was but a pretence which fortunately presented itself, and should have had little weight with a nation disposed herself to be just. The authority of the general government was exerted to prevent any act of interference in contravention of existing laws or treaties; but it was impossible to place any restraint upon the right of expatriation. American citizens have always claimed and exercised this right, and numbers of them fought on the side of the Texans, as they had previously done in behalf of the Mexican people themselves.

should be given with the avowed design and full preparation to take immediate satisfaction, if it should not be obtained on a repetition of the demand for it. To this end, I recommend that an act be passed authorizing reprisals, and the use of the naval force of the United States, by the Executive, against Mexico, to enforce them, in the event of a refusal by the Mexican government to come to an amicable adjustment of the matters in controversy between us, upon another demand thereof, made from on board of one of our vessels of war on the coast of Mexico."*

The two houses of Congress coincided with the President in the opinion, that the government of the United States would be fully justified in taking redress into her own hands; but, in order that "the equity and moderation" with which she had acted "towards a sister republic," might be placed beyond doubt or question, they advised "the experiment of another demand," to be "made in the most solemn form." The recommendation was carried into effect, and a special messenger dispatched to Mexico, by whom a final demand for redress was made, on the 20th of July, 1837. The reply of the Mexican government, made on the 29th of the same month, abounded in expressions of an anxious desire "to terminate the existing difficulties between the two governments" upon fair and honorable terms, in a speedy manner, and in accordance with "the sacred obligations imposed by international law, and the religious faith of treaties." It was also stated, that the decision made by the Mexican government in each case, would be duly communicated to the government of the United States, through her minister at Washington. These promises and assurances answered the object

* Special Message of President Jackson, February, 1837.

which Mexico appears to have had in view—that of securing further delay and postponement.

The annual message of President Van Buren, in December, 1837, informed Congress, that "for not one of our public complaints had satisfaction been given or offered;" that but "one case of personal wrong" had been favorably considered, and but four cases, "out of all those formally presented, and earnestly pressed," had been decided upon by the Mexican government. This tedious mode of proceeding, especially where the claims were so numerous, and had so long been the subjects of discussion and negotiation, was certainly unworthy of any nation. The American Executive recommended the adoption of prompt and decisive measures; but the pecuniary embarrassments of the country, and a desire to avoid hostilities, induced Congress to hesitate. A new negotiation was opened with Mexico, and on the 11th of April, 1839, a joint commission was appointed "for the adjustment of claims of citizens of the United States of America upon the government of the Mexican republic," whose powers were to terminate in February, 1842. The commissioners met, and organized on the 11th of August, 1840. Four months were spent in the discussion and determination of frivolous questions raised by the Mexican commissioners; and it was not until the month of December following, that the board commenced the examination of the claims. The powers of the commission ceased in February, 1842, before one half, in amount, of the claims submitted to them had been disposed of. The amount of claims allowed by the board, and by the umpire authorized to make a final decision in cases of disagreement between the Mexican and American commissioners, exceeded two millions of dollars. The claims pending before the umpire, who considered that his authority expired simultaneously with that of the joint commission, amounted to more than nine hundred thousand dollars; and those left undecided, for want of time, amounted to near three and a half millions.*

The sum acknowledged and awarded to the American claimants by the joint commission and the umpire, was admitted by the Mexican government to be an actual liquidated debt; and at her request, and for her convenience, its payment was postponed by a convention concluded on the 30th of January, 1843, and entered into, as therein expressed, "for the accommodation of Mexico." The interest due on this sum, on the 30th of April, 1839, and three of the twenty instalments provided for by the terms of the convention, were paid; but the remaining instalments, commencing with that payable in April, 1844, were still due by Mexico on the breaking out of hostilities. The convention of January, 1843, also made provision for another convention, for the settlement of the remaining claims; in accordance with which, a third convention was signed at the city of Mexico, on the 20th of November, 1843. This convention was ratified by the Senate of the United States, in January, 1844, with two amendments, which were both just and reasonable. Although the subject was repeatedly urged upon the consideration of the Mexican government, she did not decide whether she would or would not accede to those amendments.

During the pendency of these negotiations for the settlement and payment of the American claims, which were characterized on the part of Mexico, by delay, prevarication, and evasion; and from the time when reclamations were first made by our government, the re-

* The amount of these claims, in the aggregate, was $6,291,604 61.

lations existing between the two countries were far from being of a friendly or pacific character. Had they been otherwise, it is not unlikely that the subjects of dispute which afterwards arose, and which constituted the immediate cause of war, would not have led to any interruption of the harmony demanded by the permanent welfare and happiness of both nations. But this predisposition to hostilities was heightened and strengthened by the negotiations for the acquisition of Texas, and assumed a positive and decided form, upon its incorporation into the American confederacy.

Prior to the year 1690, the territory embraced with in the limits of the present state of Texas, formed a nominal part of the conquest of Cortés. In that year the Spaniards drove out a French colony, who had established themselves at Matagorda, and made their first permanent settlement at San Francisco. The old Spanish town of San Antonio de Bexar, the original capital of the province, was founded in 1698; La Bahia, afterwards called Goliad, in 1716; Nacogdoches in 1732; and Victoria at a still later date. For many years, but little was known in regard to the soil, climate, or position of the country. Its limits were not accurately defined, nor its natural history correctly understood, by the Spanish historians and geographers, while it remained under the dominion of Spain.* Humboldt's great work, "La Nouvelle Espagne," written in 1803, and published in 1807, is the most reliable authority of that day; but the boundaries laid down in his Atlas seem to have been arbitrarily adopted, as they do not follow any of those great natural landmarks which would probably have been selected, had they

* Diccionario Geográfico—Historico de Las Indias Occidentales ó América: Madrid, 1789, Tom. v. p. 109.

been established by any legitimate authority.* The statistical information furnished by Pike, in the narrative of his expedition undertaken in 1807, was deemed very valuable, though it added nothing to the accuracy of the geographical knowledge of the country. The northern portion was inhabited by the Camanches, Apaches, Mescaleros, and other predatory tribes of Indians; and the few white inhabitants at the south were careless and indifferent as to its cultivation, and appeared entirely ignorant of its resources and its capacity for improvement. It was quite natural, therefore, that the most erroneous ideas should have been entertained with regard to its fertility and productiveness, by the people of other countries. The skirt bordering on the coast was supposed to be a barren waste, or desert prairie; and the interior cold, sterile, and mountainous. Later historians and travellers represent the level strip lying along the Gulf, as resembling that in the other southern states, in all its principal features; as being well adapted to the culture of sugar and cotton, and remarkably fertile in the vicinity of the numerous creeks and rivers.† North of the 32nd

* Atlas Géographique et Physique, du Royaume de La Nouvelle Espagne. Paris, 1808.

† The country lying between the Nueces and the Rio Grande has been generally understood to be a desert prairie, and is sometimes called "the stupendous desert." Probably there has been some confusion in relation to the precise locality of the great desert of Muerto, lying west of the Guadalupe mountains. In a speech delivered by Mr. Sevier, of Arkansas, in the Senate of the United States, on the 4th of February 1848, the "desert" between the two rivers is stated to be, in fact, "a large fertile prairie, resembling the famous blue-grass pastures of Kentucky." After traversing 119 miles, near three fourths of the distance from Corpus Christi to Point Isabel, General Taylor, in his letter to the adjutant general, dated at "El Sauce," March 18th, 1846, represents his command to be "in fine condition and spirits." The march was

parallel of latitude, the climate is colder, but the country is rolling and fertile, or, if broken, possessing well-watered valleys, and destined eventually to be occupied for raising stock and grain.*

After the cession of Louisiana to France, and its purchase by the government of the United States, in 1803, it was claimed by the latter, that the Rio Grande del Norte formed the south-western boundary of the acquired territory. This claim was never acknowledged by Spain; and when Pike passed through the country, on his way from the Passo del Norte to Nacogdoches, he saw no evidence that the people deemed themselves connected in any way with the Louisiana purchase; on the contrary, their habits, customs, and feelings, were thoroughly Spanish and Mexican. The title to the disputed territory was repeatedly asserted by the United States; but all the claims of the latter to the country west of the Sabine, were surrendered to Spain in 1819. The acquisition of Louisiana was followed by an influx of population from the northern states. Enterprise and industry soon altered the appearance of the rich lands in the valley of the Mississippi. Their value was enhanced to such an extent, that it attracted attention in Mexico, or New Spain, as it was then called. Texas possessed the same natural advantages; yet, although it had been settled for so many years, the population amounted to but little more than 3000 in 1820; they had made but few improvements, and lived in perpetual dread of the

undoubtedly a tedious one, as is always to be expected in a new country, but the "desert" could hardly have been as cheerless and unpleasant as has been supposed.

* Pike's Narrative—Kennedy's Texas—Farnham's Observations—Folsom's Mexico in 1842.

Indians prowling about their towns. On the 17th of January, 1821, Moses Austin, a citizen of the United States, obtained permission from the supreme government of the eastern internal provinces of New Spain, to settle in Texas with a colony of his countrymen ; and in December of the same year, his son, Stephen F. Austin, arrived on the river Brazos with the first settlers from the United States. These colonists, and those who afterwards joined them, have often been termed "speculators and adventurers;" but the same language might be applied, with nearly, if not quite as much propriety, to nine-tenths of the inhabitants of the valley of the Mississippi and its tributaries. Their energy and activity contrasted most favorably with the indolent habits and snail-like progress of the Spanish inhabitants, and in a few years changed the whole aspect of the country.

The Spanish population of Texas, it must be admitted, were not, at first, well disposed to the American settlers ; but the importance of strengthening themselves against the Indian depredators on their northern frontier, and, subsequently, against the efforts of Spain to reconquer her revolted provinces, led to the adoption of measures designed to encourage and promote immigration from the United States, and from other countries. On the 4th of January, 1823, the Mexican Congress passed a national colonization law, which was approved by the Emperor Iturbide, and on the 18th of February following, a decree was issued authorizing Austin to proceed with his settlement. After the abdication and overthrow of the emperor, this decree was confirmed by the first executive council, in accordance with the special directions of Congress. The federal constitution of Mexico, similar to that of the United States in all its essential features, was adopted on the 2nd of February, 1824, and on the 7th of May, the provinces of Texas and Coahuila were united into one state. This union was always unpopular, and was violently opposed by the Texans, though finally acquiesced in, as provision was made in the decree for giving a separate constitution to Texas, whenever her population should be large enough to warrant it. A second general colonization law was passed by the Mexican Congress, in August, 1824, and in March, 1825, a similar enactment received the assent of the Legislature of Coahuila and Texas. The most flattering inducements were held out to foreigners to make settlements, and a strong current of immigration was soon turned in that direction. Texas rapidly increased in population and influence. The Spanish inhabitants became jealous of the increasing prosperity of its citizens, and the Centralistas were particularly alarmed, lest the federal doctrines of the American Union, upon which the Mexican constitution was professedly based, would acquire a permanent foothold, and put an end to all their hopes of effecting a change in the government. This feeling was increased by the dispute that ensued in relation to the question of slavery, which had been abolished by the constitution of 1824.* Many of the American settlers had brought their slaves with them from the United States, and large numbers were imported from other countries. The general government endeavored to check the increase of slavery; but the

* It is a singular fact, that servitude for debt, one of the most odious forms of slavery, has continued to exist in Mexico. The victims of this system are called *peons*, and rarely, if ever, regain their freedom. From this circumstance it may fairly be inferred, that envy and jealousy prompted, in some degree, the proceedings in relation to slavery in Texas

Texans insisted, as has always been contended by the slave states in the American Union, that it was a subject wholly of municipal regulation. An attempt was made, however, to put an end to the immigration from the United States, by the passage of a law in the Mexican Congress, on the 6th of April, 1830, totally prohibiting the admission of American settlers into Texas. Military posts were established by the central government, and the civil authorities interrupted in the discharge of their duties under the state laws. These proceedings were regarded as being arbitrary and oppressive in the extreme, and calculated to destroy the separate sovereignty guaranteed to Texas by the constitution and laws; and the act of prohibition was openly evaded and disregarded.

Centralism was temporarily established by Bustamente in 1832, and the Texans took up arms in defence of the federal constitution. They captured the garrisons at Velasco, Anahuac, and Nacogdoches; but hostilities were soon after suspended by the defeat of the centralists, and the elevation of Santa Anna to the presidency. In the spring of 1833, the citizens of Texas held a convention at San Felipe de Austin, and adopted a constitution as a separate state, in conformity with the decree of the 7th of May, 1824. The population was now almost exclusively American, and their habits, feelings, associations, and ideas of government, were totally at variance with those of the citizens of other Mexican states; yet they appear to have been willing to continue under the same federal head, provided there was no interference with their internal affairs. Stephen F. Austin was commissioned by the Texan convention to present the constitution to the

Mexican Congress, together with a petition for their admission into the Union.

No attention was paid to the petition, and Austin wrote home to his friends to organize a government, notwithstanding the refusal to ratify the proceedings of the convention. His letter was intercepted, and he himself for a long time detained in confinement. The Texans were indignant; but remonstrated in vain. While matters were in this situation, Santa Anna declared in favor of centralism. The northern provinces of Mexico refused to concur in the establishment of a consolidated government, until, one by one, they were forced to yield to the dictator. Zacatecas and Durango stood out nobly, but they, too, were overcome by superior numbers. Having completed, as he supposed, the work of subjugation in the northern provinces, Santa Anna detached General Cos into Texas, with an armed force, to secure obedience to the central government, to compel the observance of the act of 1830, and to secure the person of one Lorenzo de Zavala who had proposed a law in the Mexican Congress levelled against the monopoly of property by the clergy. He was also directed to deprive the people of their arms, in accordance with a decree of the general Congress made in 1834. The Mexican general dissolved the legislature of Coahuila and Texas at the point of the bayonet, and arrested all the officers of the government.

One of the most sacred rights secured to the citizens of the United States by their constitution, is that of bearing arms; and the act to disarm the population of Texas, in connection with the overthrow of the federal government, very naturally created a desire for producing a revolution. The standard of revolt was at once raised. On the 28th of September they defeated a Mexican force at Gonzales, on the Rio Guadaupe. The fortress at Goliad was taken in October, and a few days later the city of San Antonio de Bexar, the head-quarters of General Cos, was invested. They were also successful at Conception, Sepantillan and San Patricio, and in two battles fought in the vicinity of San Antonio. On the 5th of December the city itself was stormed, by a force of 300 men, under General Milam, and after five days' severe fighting, General Cos surrendered himself and 1,300 Mexicans, who were afterwards set at liberty, on their parole of honor, not to oppose in any way, thereafter, "the federal constitution of 1824."

The delegates of the people of Texas assembled at San Felipe on the 3rd of November, 1835, for a "general consultation," and solemnly declared that they had taken up arms in defence of the federal constitution ot 1824; that Santa Anna and his military chieftains had "dissolved the social compact which existed between Texas and the other members of the Mexican confederacy;" and that they no longer felt themselves bound by the confederation, but would be willing to adhere to it if the provisions of the constitution were sacredly regarded. A temporary government was organized by the delegates, and a convention appointed to be held for the adoption of a constitution, on the 1st of March, 1836. The central government of Mexico was determined effectually to subdue the revolted state, and General Santa Anna took the field in person, with 8,000 troops. The cruelties practised under his directions, and in pursuance of his orders, awakened a most desperate spirit of resistance, and on the 21st of April, 1836, he was defeated and taken prisoner by an inferior force under General Samuel Houston, upon the banks of the San Jacinto.

After his capture, the Mexican commander was permitted to visit the United States, though not yet absolutely released by the Texan authorities; but he was subsequently allowed to return to Mexico, upon his entering into a convention, prescribing, among other things, the boundaries of Texas, and in which it was stated "that the President Santa Anna, in his official character as chief of the Mexican nation, and the Generals Don Vincente Filisola, Don José Urrea, Don Joaquim Ramires y Sesma, and Don Antonio Gaona, as chiefs of armies, do solemnly acknowledge, sanction, and ratify, the full, entire, and perfect independence of the Republic of Texas, with such boundaries as are hereafter set forth and agreed upon for the same: and they do solemnly and respectively pledge themselves, with all their personal and official attributes, to procure, without delay, the final and complete ratification and confirmation of this agreement, and all the parts thereof, by the proper and legitimate government of Mexico, by the incorporation of the same into a solemn and perpetual treaty of amity and commerce, to be negotiated with that government at the city of Mexico, by ministers plenipotentiary to be deputed by the government of Texas for this high purpose." A copy of this document was forwarded to General Filisola, then at the head of 5,000 troops, the remains of the shattered army of invasion. He concurred in its stipulations, and was permitted, in accordance therewith, to retire with his forces west of the Rio Grande. The convention also received the approbation of other Mexican officers, though never ratified by the government of that nation. It was expressly disallowed by the Congress of Mexico, notwithstanding it was concluded by a chief magistrate exercising dictatorial power, and preparations were made, on several future occasions, for the re-invasion and subjugation of Texas. The troops of the Mexican republic entered her territories under Urrea in 1837, and under Woll in 1842, but were soon compelled to retire. The distracted state of the country prevented any further attempts to recover the province. The Texan convention assembled on the 1st of March, 1836, and on the following day made a formal and absolute declaration of independence. A constitution was also adopted, and submitted to the people for their ratification. The government thereby organized went into operation, and continued to exercise its powers until the year 1845. The government of the United States promptly recognized the independence achieved at San Jacinto, and her example was imitated by all the other great powers of the world.*

The citizens of Texas, having acquired that independent position for which they had contended, naturally turned their eyes to the land of their nativity, around whose constitution and laws there clustered a thousand cheering and animating recollections. The sympathies of a common origin, and a common tongue, were not obliterated. Their hearts yearned towards the homes of their brethren, and the burial-places of their fathers. They longed to return again to the fold which they had left, to be sheltered beneath "the flag of the stars," and enjoy the privileges and the institutions in which they claimed an interest, as the legacy of the same ancestry. The question of annexing the young republic to the United States was referred to the peo-

* The reader is referred to Kennedy's Texas for a detailed account of the Revolution in Texas.

ple by the convention of 1836, and there was an almost united vote in favor of the measure. In compliance therewith, a proposition to that effect was made by the Texan minister, on the 4th of August, 1837, which was declined by President Van Buren, upon the following grounds: that the acknowledgment of the independence of Texas admitted her separate existence as a government *de facto*, but not *de jure;* that while a state of war continued between her and Mexico, and the United States remained at peace with the latter, the question of war with her adversary was necessarily involved; and that the conditions of the existing treaty of amity and commerce should be scrupulously observed, so long as Mexico performed her duties, and respected the rights of the United States.*

On the 14th of June, 1838, a resolution declaring that it was desirable to re-annex Texas, whenever it could be done with her consent, and consistent with the treaties, stipulations, and faith of the United States, was laid on the table in the Senate, by a vote of twenty-four to fourteen.† The subject was again agitated in the summer and fall of 1842, and instructions were given to her minister, by the government of Texas, for the renewal of negotiations. No corresponding action was taken by the American Executive, and the instructions were withdrawn in August, 1843. Meanwhile, through the interposition of Great Britain, hostilities had been suspended by an armistice between Mexico and Texas,

* Senate Doc. 341, (pp. 103, et seq.) 1st session, 28th Congress.—Attempts were made to purchase Texas from Mexico, during the administrations of John Quincy Adams, and General Jackson. Spain was then, ostensibly, at war with Mexico; but it is supposed that measures would have been taken to secure her consent, although her rights at that time were merely nominal.

† Senate Journal: 1st session, 25th Congress.

for the purpose of treating on terms of peace. Santa Anna insisted on regarding the latter as "a department of Mexico," which character had been applied to all the Mexican states, on the abrogation of the federal constitution; but the President of Texas refused to surrender, in any manner, her claims to be considered as a sovereign state under the confederacy, and the negotiations terminated in no satisfactory result.

A discussion took place in the British House of Lords, on the 18th day of August, 1843, between Lord Brougham and Lord Aberdeen, (Her Majesty's Principal Secretary of state for Foreign Affairs,) in relation to the subject of Texas and Texan slavery, which occasioned considerable agitation and alarm in the United States. It was insisted that there was a design on foot to abolish that institution in Texas;* and that, if ca ried into effect, the property invested in slaves, in the southern states, would be rendered so insecure, that it must rapidly depreciate in value. Instructions were given to the American Minister in London, to call the attention of Lord Aberdeen to the subject, which was accordingly done. It appeared that the government of Great Britain had recommended to Mexico the acknowledgment of the independence of Texas, connected with the subject of the abolition of slavery; but, as the former had given no encouragement to the suggestion, nothing had been done.† Lord Aberdeen also transmitted a dispatch to the British Minister at Washington, at a later date, but not until after it was known, or understood, in England, that the project of annexation had been again revived, which

* By the provisions of the present Constitution of Texas slavery cannot be abolished.

† Letter of Mr. Everett to Mr. Upshur, November 16th, 1843.

was communicated to the Secretary of State of the United States, and in which it was denied that the British government had sought, in any manner, to establish a dominant influence in Texas, or to disturb the tranquillity of the slave-holding states. The desire of Great Britain to promote the abolition of slavery in Texas, was admitted by her secretary, but he declared that she would not "seek to compel, or unduly control," either her, or Mexico.*

Much of the alarm manifested on this subject may have been unfounded, and the facts do not warrant the conclusion, that the government of Great Britain intended to interfere directly in the matter. Still, it was for her interest to destroy the competition between the slave labor of the southern states, and the free labor of her West Indian colonies; the Oregon question threatened to disturb her peaceful relations with the United States, and several of her leading journals called the public attention to the importance of Texas as a cotton growing state, and predicted her future independence of the American Union, if she could secure the monopoly of that product in another quarter; and besides, the foreign policy of England has not always been of the most frank and open character. The protection of an association of merchants in the East Indies, of a fur company in North America, and of the opium trade in China, furnished excuses for the extension of her power and authority in those quarters of the globe; and the philanthropic motives which she avowed, might have served a similar purpose in regard to Texas. Private individuals could have acquired interests in that country, which England would have

* Senate Doc. 341, (p 48), 1st session, 28th Congress.

felt bound to protect, whenever the disputes and differences which would naturally have been engendered between the citizens of the slave states, and the inhabitants of a free state on their borders, had placed them in jeopardy. These considerations may be wholly inferential; yet they deserve to be regarded as of some weight, and especially so, because the security of the institution of slavery in the southern states, and the prevention of foreign interference with the republics of America, in connection with the advantages of the acquisition, in a commercial point of view, were the controlling reasons for the annexation of Texas.*

In the meantime, a formal proposition for the conclusion of a treaty of annexation was made to the republic of Texas, by Mr. Upshur, the American Secretary of State, under the direction of President Tyler, which was accepted. Commissioners were appointed, and a treaty concluded, at Washington, on the 12th day of April, 1844. The treaty was submitted to the Senate of the United States, but was rejected by that body on the 8th of June, after a long and animated discussion. At the ensuing session of Congress, the subject was again brought forward, and joint resolutions, providing for the annexation, were adopted on the 1st day of March, 1845. The people of Texas, represented in convention, signified their assent to the terms of the resolutions on the 4th of July, and adopted a state con stitution. This was confirmed by the American Congress, and Texas finally admitted into the Union as a state, on the 29th day of December, 1845.

The proceedings of the government of the United States in relation to Texas, did not pass without notice

* See diplomatic correspondence, Senate Doc. 341, 1st session, 28th Congress.

on the part of Mexico. On the 23rd of August, 1843, Mr. de Bocanegra, the Mexican Minister of Foreign Relations, officially informed Mr. Waddy Thompson, the American Minister in Mexico, that "the Mexican government [would] consider equivalent to a declaration of war against the Mexican Republic, the passage of an act for the incorporation of Texas with the territory of the United States; the certainty of the fact being sufficient for the immediate proclamation of war, leaving to the civilized world to determine with regard to the justice of the cause of the Mexican nation, in a struggle which it [had] been so far from provoking." The tone of a portion of the note of Mr. de Bocanegra was harsh and dictatorial, and received a sharp reproof from Mr. Thompson. A second note was written by the former, in September, which was more subdued in its character, and assured the American Envoy, that Mexico did not threaten, still less provoke or excite; but that she would "regard the annexation of Texas to the United States as a hostile act."* The same Mexican official, however, addressed a circular letter to the European ministers resident in Mexico, on the 31st of May, 1844, in which he pronounced the treaty of annexation, absolutely, "a declaration of war between the two nations."

The Mexican Minister at Washington, General Almonte, wrote a note to Mr. Upshur, on the 3rd of November, 1843, protesting, in the name of his government, against the annexation, and declaring that. "on sanction been given by the Executive of the Union to the incorporation of Texas into the United States, he [would] consider his mission ended, seeing that, as the Secretary of State [would] have learned, the Mexican

* Senate Doc. 341, (pp. 89 et seq.), 1st session, 28th Congress.

government [was] resolved to declare war so soon as it [received] information of such an act."* Santa Anna, then President of Mexico, made a similar announcement on the 12th of June, 1844, and expressed the determination of Mexico to re-conquer Texas. This announcement was followed by a requisition for thirty thousand men, and four millions of dollars, to carry on the war. Generals Canalizo and Woll were ordered to the north with an armed force, but accomplished nothing in the way of subjugation. On the 6th of March, 1845, General Almonte protested against the resolutions of annexation, and demanded his passports, which were granted; and on the 2nd of April, the American Minister in Mexico was refused all intercourse with that government, upon the ground, as stated by the Mexican Minister of Foreign Relations, that the government of Mexico could "not continue diplomatic relations with the United States, upon the presumption that such relations [were] reconcilable with the law" of annexation. President Herrera issued a proclamation on the 4th of June, 1845, declaring that the annexation in nowise destroyed the rights of Mexico, and that she would maintain them by force of arms. Two decrees of the Mexican Congress were affixed to this proclamation, providing for calling out all the armed forces of the nation.†

* Senate Doc. 341, (p. 94), 1st session, 28th Congress.

† Apprehensions of a war growing out of the annexation seem to have been early entertained by President Tyler and his cabinet. On the 15th day of April, 1844, three days after the treaty was signed, confidential instructions were issued to Commodore David Conner, then in command of the Home Squadron, to concentrate his force in the Gulf, and show himself occasionally before Vera Cruz. He was also instructed, if any armed force threatened the invasion of Texas, pending the ratification of the treaty, to remonstrate with the commanding officer,

Under these circumstances the diplomatic intercourse between the two republics was interrupted, and a *quasi* state of war existed from the spring of 1845, until the commencement of actual hostilities.

The acknowledgment of the independence of Texas, admitted merely the fact of her separate existence as a nation; but in annexing her territory, the American government went one step further. It was assumed that she was independent *of right*, and, therefore, capable of treating, and being treated with, like all other powers. In October, 1843, Mr. Thompson, the minister in Mexico, was instructed by Mr. Upshur, to inform that government, that the United States regarded Texas as an independent and sovereign power, and that, as she had "shaken off the authority of Mexico, and successfully resisted her power for eight years," they would "not feel themselves under any obligation to respect her former relation with that country."* The hostile demonstrations made by Mexico, for nine years after the battle of San Jacinto, were confined, with two exceptions—when Urrea and Woll crossed the Rio Grande but were forced to retire—to the clandestine forays of rancheros† and Indians. Distracted by her intestine

and assure him, that the execution of such a hostile purpose, in the event of the ratification, would lead to actual hostilities. Similar orders were issued on the 27th of April to Brevet Brigadier General Zachary Taylor, of the 1st Infantry, then in command of the first military department, and stationed at Fort Jesup, Louisiana, to which post he had been transferred but a few days previous. The force under his command was largely increased, and he was instructed to communicate, *confidentially*, with the President of Texas.—Senate Doc. 341, (p. 76), 1st session, 28th Congress.

* Senate Doc. 341, (p. 94), 1st session, 28th Congress.

† The *rancheros* of Mexico were originally herdsmen, like the *guachos* on the pampas of Buenos Ayres. They are small of stature, but wiry and muscular. Their usual costume is quite picturesque; consisting

divisions, Mexico lacked the means to recover the country, though her intention to do so was repeatedly declared. The predatory warfare* waged on her part, only served to demonstrate her utter inability to subdue the province, and an indirect admission to this effect was made by the offer in March, 1845, to acknowledge her independence, upon the condition that she would not annex herself, or become subject to any other country. Texas, on the contrary, had shown that she was able to resist every effort upon the land, and her vessels of war had spread terror and alarm in the Mexican ports on the Gulf.

Adopting the principle, then, that Texas was actually and rightfully independent, a treaty was concluded under the administration of President Tyler, without consulting the feelings or wishes of the Mexican government. But a state of war nominally existed between the two countries, and the relations of one party, in the event of the ratification of the treaty, were to be assumed by the United States. The latter was desirous of negotiating for the settlement of all questions in difference, for the entire cessation of hostilities, and the

of loose trowsers, green jackets slashed with yellow, broad-leafed hats, boots of untanned leather, and heavy spurs with long rowels. Most of their time is spent on horseback, and they throw the lasso with such dexterity as to catch wild horses or cattle, or even to drag a horseman from the saddle. During the war they acted as irregular cavalry, and in addition to their ordinary weapons, the lasso and hunting knife, were armed with long curved sabres and lances. They did not, however, prove a very formidable body. Their cowardice was so great, that they never ventured to attack anything like an equal force, and the wild shout of a "Texan Ranger" would scatter them like the leaves in a whirlwind.

* Mr. Webster, as Secretary of State, in 1842, instructed the American Minister in Mexico to call the attention of that government to the manner in which the war against Texas was prosecuted, as being totally opposed to the usages of civilized nations.

establishment of a boundary line, which was necessarily left undetermined during the existence of the war. Immediately after the conclusion of the treaty, the American Chargé d'Affaires, by the direction of Mr. Calhoun, who had succeeded Mr. Upshur as Secretary of State, assured the Mexican government, that it was the desire of the President of the United States to settle all questions between the two countries, that might grow out of the treaty, "or any other cause, on the most liberal and satisfactory terms, including that of boundary;" and that the boundary of Texas had been purposely left without specification in the treaty, so that it might be "an open question, to be fairly and fully discussed and settled, according to the rights of each, and the mutual interest and security of the two countries."* Shortly after this, an Envoy, (Mr. Shannon,) was sent to Mexico, with full and adequate powers to enter upon the negotiation. He, also, was instructed by Mr. Calhoun, on the 10th of September, 1844, "to renew the declaration made to the Mexican Secretary by our Chargé d'affaires, in announcing the conclusion of the treaty, that the measure was adopted in no spirit of hostility to Mexico, and that, if annexation should be consummated, the United States [would] be prepared to adjust all questions growing out of it, including that of boundary, on the most liberal terms."† Assurances of the same purport were made to General Almonte, after the passage of the joint resolutions, by Mr. Buchanan, on the 10th of May, 1845. But Mexico, unmindful of the leniency which had so long been

* Letter of Mr. Calhoun to Mr. Green—Senate Doc. 341, (p. 53), 1st session, 28th Congress.

† Public Documents accompanying President's Message, 2nd session, 28th Congress.

exhibited towards her, and forgetting what courtesy, in view of this fact, appeared to require at her hands, would listen to no terms—would hear no propositions. All intercourse was suspended, and no other course remained for the government of the United States to pursue, but that of asserting her title to the territory acquired, by an armed occupation. The boundary was left "an open question," as stated by Mr. Calhoun, in the treaty of 1844, and the joint resolutions of annexation asserted no claim to any territory except that "rightfully belonging" to Texas. Mexico chose not to enter into any negotiations on the subject of the boundary, and it was therefore necessary for the United States to decide for themselves, and to act upon that decision, until the matter was settled by negotiation.

The political limits of Texas Proper, previous to the revolution, "were the Nueces river on the west; along the Red River on the north; the Sabine on the east; and the Gulf of Mexico on the south."* The dissolution of the Mexican confederacy, and her separation from the other states composing the federal association, gave her no greater extent of territory than what she already possessed; and her title to all accessions made subsequent to the revolution, must rest upon conquest and occupation, or the assent, express or implied, of the Mexican government.† The advantages of the Rio Grande as a great natural military obstacle,

* Letter of H. M. Morfit, special agent sent by President Jackson to Texas.—House of Rep., Doc. 35, 2nd session, 24th Congress.

† The claim of the government of the United States, uniformly asserted from 1803 to 1819, that Texas extended to the Rio Grande, is sometimes referred to in support of the title to that river. But it seems to deserve little consideration as an argument. The boundaries of Texas were fixed, with her consent and approbation, by the constitution of 1824, and we cannot well go back of that arrangement.

were so apparent to the Texan officers in 1836, that in the convention entered into with Santa Anna,* it was agreed that that river, from its mouth to its source, should constitute the south-western boundary of the country. But this agreement, or convention, was never officially confirmed by the Mexican government. He had, previous to his capture, exercised dictatorial powers, and good faith might have required Mexico to ratify his acts, though she preferred to disavow them. Texas, however, decided to adhere to the Rio Grande as the boundary, and on the 19th of December 1836, an act was passed by her Congress, establishing that river, from its mouth up its principal stream to its source, as such boundary. From the source of the river, the line on the north and east was declared to be "as defined between the United States and Spain." In compliance with a call of the Senate, pending the discussion on the treaty of 1844, President Tyler sent in a map of the country proposed to be ceded, upon which the boundaries, as above described, were marked in red lines.† The act of the Texan Congress was unrepealed, at the time of her final admission in 1845; the new constitution adopted, impaired its validity in no respect, as it expressly provided for continuing all prior enactments in full force; and on the 31st day of December, two days after she was admitted as a state, the Congress of the United States passed a law establishing "a collection district in the State of Texas," and Corpus Christi, west of the Nueces, was made a port of delivery, for which a surveyor was afterwards appointed. At the opening of the session, President Polk had informed Congress that the army had been "ordered to take a position in the country

* See page 36.

† Senate Doc. 341, 1st session, 28th Congress.

between the Nueces and the Del Norte, [Rio Grande], and to repel any invasion of the Texan territory which might be attempted by the Mexican forces." No measures were taken to recall any portion of the troops at this session, and at the following one a law was passed, establishing post-offices upon, and post-roads extending to the Rio Grande. These facts show, therefore, that the claim originally made by Texas to the left bank of the river, was adopted and asserted by the government of the United States, from the inception of the project of annexation, until and after the commencement of the war, with the following qualifications:—A willingness to negotiate upon the question of boundary was evinced by the terms of the joint resolutions, which provided for the annexation, subject to the adjustment, by the United States, "of all questions of boundary that [might] arise with other governments;" and, secondly, the claim to any territory east of the Rio Grande, and north of the ancient limits of Texas, was tacitly, if not expressly waived.

The boundary claimed by Texas embraced a considerable portion of the province of New Mexico, lying east of the Rio Grande, and containing a number of towns and a large population. This province was first visited by the Spaniards, under Vasquez Coronado, in 1540, who occupied the country until 1542, when they voluntarily evacuated it. They revisited it again in 1583, and made some temporary settlements. The final subjugation of the country was effected by them, under their leader Onate, in 1595; twelve years before any permanent settlement had been made in North America, except by the Spaniards themselves, and long previous to Father Hennepin's voyage down the Mississippi. The Indians drove the Spaniards away in 1680, but they returned in 1681, and after a long struggle succeeded in establishing their authority on a firm foundation. The French government did not claim any part of New Mexico, and the royal charter declared that province to be the western boundary of Louisiana. Texas never occupied the country, nor exercised any acts of sovereignty there, and her claim could only have been founded upon the convention made with Santa Anna, which was hardly sufficient to support it. The government of the United States appears to have taken this view of the question. The same Congress that adopted the joint resolutions, passed a law allowing a drawback on foreign merchandise re-exported in the original packages to "Santa Fé, in New Mexico," one of the towns situated east of the Rio Grande, and the capital of the province. The instructions given to General Kearny, and the proceedings of that officer, are conclusive evidence that this portion of New Mexico was not regarded as forming a part of Texas. She was treated as a conquered province, and President Polk in his annual message, in December, 1846, referred to Santa Fé as a captured town.*

The claim of Texas, and subsequently of the United States, to the country lying between the Nueces and the

* There is one fact, which deserves to be noticed in this connection. The joint resolutions of annexation contained a proviso relating to all that portion of the territory lying above the parallel of 36° 30′ north latitude; Texas proper did not extend above that parallel; and hence it is urged, that Congress intended to claim the whole country east of the Rio Grande. Perhaps a majority of those who voted for the proviso had not examined the question with reference to that fact, and the line was intended rather to apply to the territory, if it should be obtained by negotiation, than to confirm a claim which had never been supported by possession or occupation. It may be doubted, whether Texas herself designed to insist upon her title to any part of New Mexico, in a negotiation for peace. It was the lower Rio Grande, from the

.ower Rio Grande, appears to have been much better founded. The intention to insist upon that river as the boundary, was asserted in the convention with Santa Anna, which, if it had no other effect, operated as notice to Mexico of the extent of the claim. After it became known that Mexico would not ratify the convention, and that Urrea was preparing to invade Texas, General Rusk, then at the head of the Texan army, ordered General Felix Huston to take position, with a detachment, at Corpus Christi; and the latter sent his scouting parties to the Rio Grande. At that time there were no permanent settlements on the left bank of the river, with the exception of a few ranchos opposite Mier, Camargo, Reinosa, and Matamoras, the occupants of which had been engaged in herding and smuggling, but took refuge on the west side of the Rio Grande, upon the approach of Huston's troops. The great majority of the inhabitants retired to the rear of Rusk's army, in compliance with his orders. Urrea crossed the river but once, and soon returned. Although he had 10,000 men at Matamoras, General Huston held in subjection the whole country to the Rio Grande, and his advanced corps traversed it at pleasure. In December, 1836, when the law prescribing the boundaries of Texas was passed, she was in possession of the disputed territory, and her civil and political jurisdiction was extended over it. Custom-houses, post-offices and post-roads, and election precincts, were established west of the Nueces. The county of San Patricio was laid out reaching to the Rio Grande. The public lands between

Pass to the Gulf, which she desired to have as a boundary; and Judge Ellis, the President of the Texan Convention of 1836, and a member of the Congress of 1836-7, has said, that the claim covered a large extent of territory, in order that there might be room to yield, if necessary.

the two rivers were surveyed and sold, and all the evidences of grants and transfers of land, subsequent to the revolution of 1834, were entered among the records of Texas. Persons holding colony contracts made by the department of Tamaulipas, which was bounded on the east by the Nueces, prior to the revolution, voted at Corpus Christi under the laws of Texas.* Members of the Texan Congress were elected, who resided on the right bank of the Nueces, several years prévious to the annexation; and that part of Texas was also represented in the Congress and the Convention by which the joint resolutions of 1845 were accepted. The collectoral district of Aransas was established by the first Congress, and extended from the mouth of the San Antonio to the Rio Grande. Boats were repeatedly sent out by the collector to watch the coast, and reconnoitre the Laguna Madre, and the Brazos. In the fall of 1838, when their ports were blockaded by the French fleet, the Mexicans landed a cargo of flour at a place about ten miles west of the present town of Corpus Christi, now called "Flour Bluffs" from this circumstance, for the purpose of secretly conveying it across the country. The flour was destroyed, and the vessel seized under the orders of the collector of the district, for violating the revenue laws of Texas.

In the spring of 1837, the Mexican rancheros again ventured across the Rio Grande to herd their cattle; but they were immediately attacked by the Texan "cow-boys," as they were termed, and compelled to cross over to the right bank. Repeated efforts were made by the rancheros to establish themselves perma-

* The place of voting was near the Nueces, and upwards of 150 miles from the Rio Grande; but a similar state of things has frequently existed in the western part of the United States.

nently, but the "cow-boys," though not acting under any positive orders of the Texan government, resisted every attempt, and during the desultory contests which took place, from 1837 to 1842, drove off nearly 80,000 head of cattle. The Mexican authorities uniformly discountenanced the establishment of any permanent settlements north of the river, and the civil jurisdiction of the department of Tamaulipas was exerted but rarely, if at all, in that part of its ancient dominions. After the defeat of the federalistas, who revolted against the central government of Mexico in 1839, Generals Anaya and Canales, two of their leaders, crossed over the Rio Grande for protection. The latter united his forces with those of Captain Ross, of the Texan rangers, and a number of "cow-boys." They then crossed the river, and drove the Mexican army into Matamoras. Canales took shelter in Texas again, in 1840, when he was joined by Colonel Jordan, with near two hundred "cow-boys." They crossed the Rio Grande a second time, and penetrated as far into the country as Saltillo, where Canales betrayed his allies, who succeeded, however, in fighting their way back to the river. After the invasion and defeat of Woll in 1842, the Texan army drove him across the Rio Grande and took possession of Laredo. At this point there had been a military organization, previous to the revolution in Texas, which was in existence when the army of the United States marched to the Rio Grande. On account of their liability to be attacked by the Indians in their vicinity, the inhabitants of Laredo were excepted from the operation of the act disarming the citizens of Coahuila and Texas; but they claimed to belong to the latter whenever they were visited by Hays and McCulloch's rangers, who frequently crossed over the country from San Antonio, to that and other points on the river; and Canales called them Texans, in one of his proclamations in 1846. They were, no doubt, of Mexican extraction; but, although the authority exercised over them by Texas was somewhat questionable, still it was more decided than that of Mexico. Besides the settlement at Laredo, there were a few straggling huts at Point Isabel, near the Brazos Santiago, occupied by Mexican fishermen and smugglers. During the difficulty with France, and the war with Texas, the goods imported by the merchants at Matamoras were often landed at the Brazos, in order to escape the notice of the enemy's vessels lying off the mouth of the Rio Grande. An agent of the custom-house at Matamoras was sent down to the Point, to collect the duties before the goods were taken over the river; and a revenue officer was continued there until the approach of General Taylor with his army, whose main duty it was to prevent the smuggling constantly kept up, on account of the neglect of Mexico to occupy the country. Had she supposed her title to be good, is it not likely that she would have taken more effectual measures to protect her revenue than she actually did?*

The legal enactments of the Texas Congress in relation to the boundary, could certainly give her no title to the disputed territory, except as they were supported by the military and civil authority which she exercised. She did not fortify the whole left bank of the Rio Grande, nor establish military posts at every prominent point on the Gulf; but her ability to drive the Mexicans from the territory, at pleasure, was demonstrated, and if private individuals returned there and estab-

* The regular custom-house at the mouth of the Rio Grande was on the right bank of the river, near the Gulf.

lished themselves, it would seem to have been done merely by her sufferance. The authority exercised by Texas, in the valley of the Nueces, and upon its western bank, including the settlement at Corpus Christi, was undoubted and undeniable. In the other part of the territory in dispute, there could not have been one hundred persons as late as 1844, and it cannot be said with justice, that the Mexicans then had any "actual possession or fixed habitation east of the Rio del Norte," between the Gulf of Mexico and "the mountainous barriers at the Pass,"* with the exception of what they might claim at Laredo and Brazos Santiago. Mr. Donelson, the American Chargé d'Affaires, called the attention of the government of the United States, and of General Taylor, to the existence of these settlements, or posts, in the spring of 1845.† The latter was expressly instructed, when he entered the territory, not to interfere with the establishments made by Mexico, and to respect the rights and property of private citizens; and it is unnecessary to say, that his orders were faithfully observed.

But, in addition to these facts, Mexico herself, through her agents and officers, tacitly admitted the claim of Texas to the lower Rio Grande, on several occasions; although, as a general thing, she made no distinction in regard to any part of the country between that river and the Sabine. Her claim extended to the whole of Texas, and the comparatively unimportant question of boundary was merged in the greater one of title. Always insisting upon her right to every part and parcel

* Memoir of Lieut. Emory. Senate Doc. 341, (p. 56), 1st session, 28th Congress.

† Letters to Mr. Buchanan, June 30, and July 11;—to General Taylor, June 28th, and July 7.

of Texas, whenever, subsequent to the battle of San Jacinto, she adopted, either voluntarily or by compulsion, a limit to the territory, all of which she regarded as having been forcibly and unjustly wrested from her, that limit was the Rio Grande. The southern and western bank of the river formed the outer limit of her military posts and fortifications. When her armies crossed it in force, the preparations made, the dispositions for the march, and the orders of the officers, showed that the movement was considered one of invasion; and when compelled to retreat, they retired behind it as to a place of refuge. An armistice was entered into in 1843, in which it was stipulated that the Mexicans should confine themselves to the right bank of the river, and that the Texans should remain on the left bank. Tornel, the minister of war, in his letter dated July 7th, instructed General Woll, the commander-in-chief of the army of the north, that hostilities against Texas were "to be immediately suspended at all points of the line under [his] command," and that he must withdraw to it his advanced parties.* The line commanded by General Woll was the Rio Grande; and in his proclamation declaring the armistice at an end, he gave notice that every individual found one league from the river, on the east, would be looked upon as favoring "the usurpers of that territory," and be brought to trial before a court-martial, to be severely punished, if found guilty. Here, it seems, the Mexican general treated the question as one of usurpation, and admitted that the territory usurped extended to the Rio Grande. Canales, also, issued a *pronunciamento* against the government of Paredes, at Camargo, in February 1846, in which he described himself as being

* Senate Doc. 341, (p. 84), 1st session, 28th Congress.

"on the northern frontier."* It is very questionable whether he would have used this expression, if, in his opinion, the actual frontier was the Nueces, from 150 to 200 miles further north. The intention of General Taylor to advance to the Rio Grandè was known long before his army commenced its march; reconnaissances of the different routes by land and water, of Padre Island, the Laguna Madre, and the Brazos, were made early in February, 1846; and the fact that a forward movement was in contemplation, had been communicated by the Mexican officers on the frontier to their government. Notwithstanding this, no preparations were made to resist the approach of the American general, and he was induced, from the entire absence of such preparations, to believe that he would encounter no opposition.† The situation of the country afforded numerous opportunities for harassing the American troops on their march, and the passage of the Arroyo Colorado, if disputed, would have been attended with great loss. "This stream," says General Taylor, "is a salt river, or rather lagoon, nearly one hundred yards broad, and so deep as barely to be fordable. It would have formed a serious obstruction to our march, had the enemy chosen to occupy its right bank, even with a small force."‡

The Mexican Minister, Peña y Peña, in his confidential interview with Mr. Black, and in his note to that gentleman, insisted on the withdrawal of the American naval force off Vera Cruz, previous to the reception of

* House of Rep. Executive Doc. 196, (p. 106), 1st session, 29th Congress.

† Letters to the Adjutant General, October 8th, 1845, and February 4th and 16th, 1846.

‡ Letter to the Adjutant General, March 21, 1846.

a minister, in order that his government might not even appear to act under an implied menace. General Taylor was then known to be at Corpus Christi, and in the actual occupancy of territory lying west of the Nueces; but this was not made the subject of complaint, nor even thought worthy of mention. At no time did the government of Herrera pretend that the occupation of the disputed territory was one of the reasons for refusing to receive Mr. Slidell: neither did Castillo y Lanzas, the minister of Paredes, in his note communicating the final determination of the Mexican government, allege that the occupation, or the contemplated advance to the Rio Grande, was the cause of the refusal.* Paredes once issued orders to attack the American army early in March, when the intentions of General Taylor were unknown; and near the close of the month, when it was understood in Mexico, that he designed to advance, he issued a manifesto, declaring that the Mexican government would itself commit no act of aggression; thus acknowledging that the United States had committed no new act of that character, otherwise it would certainly have been mentioned. Mexico undoubtedly considered every movement for the establishment of the authority of the United States as an act of hostility; and in his proclamation of the 23rd of April 1846, declaring that the war had been commenced, Paredes referred to the occupation of Corpus Christi, the appearance of the naval squadrons in the Pacific and the Gulf of Mexico, the advance to the Rio Grande, and the blockade of the river, each and all, as so many aggravations of the original cause of offence—the annexation of Texas. That

* See Diplomatic Correspondence, House of Rep. Exec. Doc. 196 st session, 29th Congress.

act was the principal grievance, and the others but so many incidents. This idea also appears to have been entertained by the Mexican commissioners, Herrera, Conto, Villamil, and Atristain, who stated expressly, in their letter to Mr. Trist, on the 6th of September, 1847, that the war was "undertaken solely on account of the territory of the State of Texas."*

Opposed to these admissions, direct or implied, of the Mexican authorities, are the proclamations and dispatches issued by Mejia, Ampudia, and Arista, on the approach of General Taylor. All three of these generals declared that the advance of his army was a hostile movement; yet they appeared to differ with respect to the proper point to which the invading forces, as they were called, should be allowed to extend their occupation. Mejia announced, through his representative, that the passage of the Arroyo Colorado would be regarded as an act of war; Ampudia desired General Taylor to retire beyond the Nueces; and Arista insisted, that the law annexing Texas gave no right to occupy the Rio del Norte, without attempting to confine the American army to any precise limits.† The prefect of the northern district of Tamaulipas, Jenes Cardenas, also issued his protest, dated at Santa Rita, on the 23rd of March, against the occupation of any portion of the department; but it must be remembered that the head-quarters of his prefecture were at Matamoras, and it is doubtful whether he ever exercised authority north of the Rio Grande. Besides, General Taylor very properly regarded him as a mere tool of

* Senate Exec. Doc. 20, (p. 9), 1st session, 30th Congress.

† See Mejia's proclamation, dated March 18th, 1846; General Taylor's letter, March 21st; Ampudia's dispatch, April 12th; and Arista's proclamation to the foreigners in the American army, April 20.

the military authorities in Matamoras, and after the capture of that city, he proved himself to be as corrupt as he was pusillanimous.*

The diplomatic relations between the United States and Mexico having been interrupted by the act of the latter, it was thought advisable to prepare for the prompt assertion of the claim of Texas to the left bank of the Rio Grande, as the only remaining alternative. Immediately on the issuing of the proclamation of the President of Texas, in April 1845, calling a convention, and an extra session of Congress, to take into consideration the joint resolutions of annexation, it was officially announced by the government of Mexico that preparations for an invasion would be forthwith made.† Upon the receipt of this information, confidential instructions were issued from the War Office of the United States, to General Taylor, then in command of the forces at Fort Jesup,‡ to put himself in communication, at once, with the authorities of Texas, and the diplomatic agents of the United States in that republic, and, after he should be advised that her convention had acceded to the terms of annexation, to employ his command in defending her territories against foreign invasion, and Indian incursions. He was also instructed to regard the west-

* In his interview with Colonel Twiggs, after the surrender of Matamoras, the prefect entirely lost sight of his fellow citizens, for whom he had previously shown so much solicitude. Instead of looking to their comfort and well-being his first and last request was, that he might be allowed to retain his o fice.

† Herrera was then at the head of affairs, he having overthrown Santa Anna in the fall of 1844.

‡ General Taylor was instructed soon after the passage of the joint resolutions, viz: on the 21st of March, 1845, to hold his troops in readiness to move into Texas. After the orders issued to him in the spring of 1844, and previous to his entering Texas, his command was known as the "army of observation."

ern frontier of Texas, the Rio Grande, as the point of his ultimate destination; to select and occupy, on or near that river, such a position as would best consist with the health of the troops. and be best adapted for the protection and defence of the country; but not to effect a landing on the frontier until the terms of annexation had been actually accepted. Additional orders were issued to him, at different times, before and after his arrival in Texas, to avoid all acts of aggression, unless an actual state of war should exist; to extend his protection to the whole territory east of the Rio Grande, but not to disturb the Mexican forces at the posts in their possession, if any, on the east side of the river; to take position with a portion of his troops, at least, west of the Nueces; to call upon the authorities of Texas for what auxiliary forces he might require, and, in his discretion in case of emergency, upon the respective governors of the states of Louisiana, Alabama, Mississippi, Tennessee, and Kentucky, for such number of volunteers as he deemed necessary; and to regard the assembling of a large Mexican army on the borders of Texas, and the crossing, or attempting to cross, the Rio Grande, with a considerable force, as an invasion of the United States, and the commencement of hostilities. Other acts, such as committing depredations on the commerce of the United States, by the public armed vessels or privateers of Mexico, were to be considered by him in the same light; and he was left to decide for himself as to any act of a similar character, not enumerated, that might be committed. Should hostilities commence, he was instructed to act upon the offensive as far as his means would permit.*

* See the instructions to General Taylor, House of Rep. Exec. Doc. 196, (pp. 68, et seq.), 1st session, 29th Congress.

Simultaneously with the instructions to General Taylor, orders were issued to the naval force in the Gulf of Mexico, commanded by Commodore David Conner, to co-operate with the army; and to the Pacific squadron, to be prepared for a state of war, and act accordingly. Officers of the corps of engineers, topographical engineers, and ordnance corps, were directed to repair forthwith to the army destined for the occupation of Texas; the different bureaus were employed in providing the *matériel* for active operations; and, in addition to the ordinary complement of artillery and other arms, 11,000 muskets and rifles were forwarded to Texas, for the use of the auxiliary forces and volunteers, if called into service, and subject to the orders of General Taylor. Such was the alacrity with which the preparations for war were made, that in a very few weeks one half of the disposable force of the army, and all it was then thought proper to withdraw from the northern frontier and Atlantic coast, on account of the threatening aspect of our relations with Great Britain, was already established in Texas, or *en route* for General Taylor's camp.

With the promptitude which has always constituted a striking feature in his military character, General Taylor* proceeded, without delay, to carry out the instructions and orders which he had received. His command was immediately put in motion. The terms of annexation proposed by the United States were duly accepted by Texas on the 4th day of July, 1845; and

* This officer entered the army as a lieutenant in the 7th Infantry, in the year 1808. He served with great credit in the war of 1812, and the war with the Sacs and Foxes in 1832. Having been promoted to the command of a regiment, he joined the army in Florida, in 1836, and was brevetted a brigadier general for his gallantry and good conduct at the battle of Okee-chobee.

on the 7th, her Congress and Convention requested that the army of the Union, to which she now belonged, might be employed for her protection. On the day after receiving the information, which was to be the guide for his movements, General Taylor left New Orleans with his army, and arrived at the inlet of Aransas bay, on the 28th of July. The troops were temporarily landed on St. Joseph's Island, but afterwards transferred to Corpus Christi, on the bay of that name, and west of the Nueces, where a permanent camp and dépôt were established. The debarkation on this coast, from the shoalness of the water, and the prevalence of unfavorable winds, was not free from difficulties and embarrassments, but they appear to have been overcome without any serious hinderance or obstruction.

Having succeeded in landing his army, and establishing it in a secure position, General Taylor commenced a rigid system of instruction and discipline, which he found to be necessary in order to fit it for the active duties of the field. Many of the companies had been for a long time stationed at remote posts on the frontiers, and were wholly unacquainted with the evolutions of the line; but, in a short time, every thing was changed, and the troops in the camp at Corpus Christi were probably the best disciplined corps which, prior to that time, had ever been collected on the continent. Nothing was neglected on the part of the commanding officer of the "army of occupation," to perfect its discipline, and to increase its efficiency. Every attention was paid to the health and comfort of his command; and the idea at all times uppermost in his mind appears to have been, to prepare it for any emergency, and to enable it, when the time came for action, to strike promptly, and with effect.

Soon after his arrival at Corpus Christi, General Taylor's army was strengthened by the arrival of the reinforcements which had been ordered to join him, and early in the autumn, his force amounted to upwards of 4,000 men, all regular troops. In addition, he mustered into the service of the United States, several companies of Texan rangers, some of which were stationed at San Antonio, and others at Austin.

In the meantime the Mexican government had not been idle. The determination avowed by Herrera to invade Texas was not a mere threat. Efforts were made to increase the army, and provide the means for carrying on the war. The embarrassed condition of the finances prevented the immediate accomplishment of the wishes of the government, although General Arista was ordered from Monterey to Matamoras, in the month of August, with a force of 1,500 men, to reinforce the troops already in that quarter, then about 500 strong. Later in the season, between eight and nine thousand men were assembled at San Luis Potosi, under General Paredes, then in command of the army of the north.

In the month of September, 1845, information was received from Mexico, which rendered it probable that the government of that country would be willing to restore her former diplomatic relations with the United States. Accordingly, Mr. Black, the American Consul at the city of Mexico, was instructed by Mr. Buchanan, the Secretary of State, to ascertain whether the Mexican government would receive an envoy, "intrusted with full power to adjust all the questions in dispute between the two governments;" and if the reply to his inquiry should be in the affirmative, he was informed that "such an envoy" would be "immediately dispatched to Mexico." A confidential interview took place between Mr. Black and Peña y Peña, the Mexican Minister of Foreign Relations, in which the substance of the dispatch received from his government was made known by the American Consul; and on the 13th of October, he addressed an official note to the Mexican Minister, communicating the instructions he had received, in the precise terms of the letter of Mr. Buchanan, as before quoted. On the 15th of October, Peña y Peña informed Mr. Black, in writing, that his government was "disposed to receive the commissioner of the United States," who might come "with full powers" "to settle the present dispute in a peaceful, reasonable, and honorable manner;" but requested, as a preliminary step to negotiation, that the naval force in sight of Vera Cruz should be recalled. Great secrecy was observed by Peña y Peña in his communications with Mr. Black, and the guarded language employed in his note shows that the Mexican government designed, at that time, to lay the foundation for a refusal to comply with the terms of the proposition which they professed to accept, although it positively precluded the idea of any negotiation except in relation to all causes of difference between the two countries. The offer to send a minister was made in a frank and honorable manner, and presumed to have been accepted in a similar spirit; and hence no notice was taken of the apparent discrepancy between the terms of the proposition as made by the American government, and as accepted by the Mexican Minister. Herrera, the President of Mexico, had always been regarded as a firm and decided federalist, and was supposed to be favorable to an amicable settlement of the differences with the United States. Previous to his elevation to the Presidency, he manifested considerable spirit and determination, and succeeded in overthrowing Santa Anna, only after a long and desperate struggle; but the very moment he entered upon the administration of the government, and when prompt and vigorous measures were necessary to maintain his authority, he began to waver and hesitate. Among his supporters, in opposition to Santa Anna, was a small, but influential faction of monarchists, headed by Paredes; and, being desirous of conciliating them, he doubted the expediency of carrying out the federal doctrines which he had previously avowed. His timidity displeased many of his warmest friends, and they became lukewarm in his support; while the monarchists managed silently to secure the control of the army, at all times potential in Mexico, which a single prompt movement on his part would have effectually prevented.

Jealousy, suspicion, and distrust, were manifested by all classes and parties in Mexico, at the time when the proposition to resume her diplomatic relations with the United States was received and accepted. The arrangement, however, was approved by the Mexican Congress in secret session; the American naval force off Vera Cruz was withdrawn; every thing wore a promising aspect; and towards the close of October, the Mexican Minister of Foreign Relations expressed some anxiety to know when the envoy from the United States might be expected. The American Executive, immediately upon the receipt of Mr. Black's dispatches, appointed Mr. John Slidell as Minister Plenipotentiary to the Government of Mexico, and gave him full instructions and powers to settle and adjust all differences between the two countries.* Mr. Slidell arrived at

* In his annual message in December 1845, President Polk stated

Vera Cruz on the 30th of November, and hastened forward, immediately, to the city of Mexico. At Puebla he was met by Mr. Black, who informed him that the Mexican government were alarmed by his arrival at such an inopportune moment, as they had not expected him until the 1st of January, and matters had not been prepared for his reception. The first intimation received by Mr. Black, that the time of the arrival of an envoy was deemed of any importance, was on the 3rd of December, in an interview with Peña y Peña, and he had hastened from Mexico to meet Mr. Slidell, and communicate with him before he reached the capital. It appeared that the administration of Herrera had been constantly growing weaker and weaker. Instead of seizing, into his own hands, the means which might have enabled him to control the turbulent government over which he was placed, he suffered them to be used for his own destruction. Finesse and management were resorted to, when nothing could have so much strengthened his administration, as promptitude, firmness, and decision. Early in November he began to be seriously alarmed; the fidelity of Paredes was suspected; and orders were issued for him to break up his cantonment at San Luis, and to scatter the troops in different parts of the country. Herrera and his ministers were probably well disposed to the United States, but their indecision was followed by its legitimate results; and when Mr. Slidell presented himself, they attempted to bolster up the tottering administration, by a refusal to receive him. The arrival of an envoy from the United States was a matter that it was impossible

that he did not think it advisable to recommend any "ulterior measures of redress," in consequence of the favorable change in our relations with Mexico.—See letter of instructions to Mr. Slidell, November 10, 1845.

to conceal, after he had once landed; the evil which might easily have been prevented, if the Mexican government had but intimated the necessity for delay, was past all remedy; and Mr. Slidell concluded to continue his journey to Mexico.

The fact that the administration of Herrera had consented to receive a minister, was known long previous to the arrival of Mr. Slidell, although the *pronunciamento* of Paredes against the government, issued at San Luis, did not appear until the 15th of December. For several weeks before Mr. Slidell reached Mexico, the monarchists and centralists in the capital were very busily engaged in preparing the *plan* of their anticipated movement. An outbreak was regarded as a matter of certainty, unless the administration took measures to prevent it. On the second day after his arrival in Mexico, Mr. Slidell addressed a letter to the Mexican Minister, dated the 8th of December, informing him of his arrival, and desiring to know when his credentials would be received and himself accredited. No answer was returned to this communication; and in two private interviews between Mr. Black and Peña y Peña, held on the 8th and 13th of December, the latter exhibited so many symptoms of a desire to evade a compliance with the terms of the proposition which the Mexican government had accepted, that Mr. Slidell wrote a second note, on the 15th of the month, requesting to know when he might expect a reply to that previously written. On the following day he was informed by Peña y Peña, that there had been difficulties in regard to his reception, which it had been found necessary to submit to the council of government for their determination. The difficulties alluded to were—that Mr. Slidell's appointment had not received the sanction of Congress, or been confirmed by the Senate; and that the Mexican government had consented to receive a commissioner to settle the question relating to Texas, but not a resident minister. These objections were evidently mere pretences, as the only argument urged against the administration, by Paredes and his supporters, was, that it had consented to receive a minister, and listen to a proposition for opening new negotiations. This was the only question involved, as admitted by Herrera himself, in a letter written to Pacheco, Minister of Foreign Relations, on the 25th of August, 1847.* The bad faith of the Mexican administration in this transaction was subsequently exhibited in a most unenviable light, by the publication of a communication made to the council of government by Peña y Peña, in his official capacity, on the 11th of December, at the very time when he was professing so, much friendship towards Mr. Black and Mr. Slidell, in which the refusal to receive the minister was recommended in positive and express terms.† The deliberations of the council, though nominally secret, were matters of public notoriety. Its members were well known to be decidedly opposed to the reception, and, on the 18th of December, their *dictamen* advising against it was made public. Information of this fact, and of the evident want of frankness and candor on the part of Herrera's administration, in their intercourse with him, was communicated by Mr. Slidell, on the same day, to the government of the United States.‡

The dispatch of Mr. Slidell was received on the 12th day of January, 1846, and on the succeeding day

* Senate Exec. Doc. 1, (p. 41), 1st session, 30th Congress.

† House of Rep. Exec. Doc. 196, (p. 49), 1st session, 29th Congress.

‡ Ibid. (pp. 18, et seq.)

General Taylor was instructed to advance and occupy, with the troops under his command, positions on or near the east bank of the Rio Grande, as soon as it could be conveniently done; and several vessels of war were ordered to reinforce the squadron in the Gulf. He was also directed not to enforce the common right to navigate the river, without further orders, or treat Mexico as an enemy, until she should assume that character; but if any open act of hostility should be committed, he was not to act merely on the defensive, if the means at his disposal enabled him to do otherwise. In every possible event, he was required to protect private property, and respect the personal rights and religion of the Mexican people. Texas having been duly admitted into the Confederacy, he was further authorized to make a requisition on the governor of that state, for such of its militia force as might be necessary.*

The American army encamped at Corpus Christi, during the pendency of negotiations, had been constantly engaged in perfecting its discipline, and preparing for the field. Occasional rumors were heard, of the concentration and movement of he enemy's forces towards the frontier, and now and then a report would reach the camp that an invasion was to be apprehended. The idle stories put in circulation created no uneasiness in the breast of General Taylor; he never distrusted his ability to maintain his position, or to make a forward movement, if required so to do; and so far was he from apprehending any danger, and so confident that he might rely under all circumstances on the brave men under his orders, that he informed the adjutant general on the 26th of August, 1845, that

* House of Rep. Exec. Doc. 196, (pp. 77, et seq.) 1st sess., 29th Cong.

he considered his command "fully adequate to meet any crisis that might arise." Early in that month, a rumor had reached New Orleans in regard to the march of troops from the interior of Mexico, which had been magnified to such an extent, that it produced no little consternation and alarm. General Gaines, who was then in command of that military division, immediately mustered a volunteer battalion of artillery into the service of the United States, and sent them to reinforce General Taylor. Their arrival produced some little surprise in the camp at Corpus Christi, as the general in command had not required their services. In consideration of their alacrity in obeying the call of General Gaines, who was determined not to have the army suffer any reverse if it could be prevented, the Louisiana volunteers were retained until the expiration of the term allowed by law for their enrolment; and General Taylor requested that thereafter no militia force should be sent to him without his requisition.*

The instructions issued to General Taylor to move forward to the Rio Grande, were received on the 4th of February. Reconnoitering parties were at once thrown out, and examinations made of the different routes to the river, by land and water. The fact that he intended to advance to the Rio Grande was communicated to some citizens of Matamoras, who visited his camp in February, to dispose of some mules. He stated to them, that the movement was not intended to be a hostile one; that the Mexicans living on the east side of the river would not be disturbed in any way; that every thing required for the use of the army would

* See correspondence, House of Rep. Exec. Doc. 196, 1st session, 29th Congress.

be purchased at a fair price; and that, in no case would he go beyond the Rio Grande, unless hostilities were commenced by Mexico. Similar sentiments were expressed to the Custom-house officer at Brazos Santiago, by Captain Hardee, the officer who commanded the escort covering the reconnaissance of Padre Island. The American troops were also commanded, in general orders, to refrain from the commission of any act of nostility, and to observe the rights and respect the religion of the Mexican people.* Every thing being in readiness for the march, a dépôt of forage and subsistence was thrown forward to the Santa Gertrudes, about forty miles from Corpus Christi, on the 28th of February, and on the 8th of March, the advance brigade of the main army, consisting of the cavalry and Major Ringgold's light artillery, the whole under the

* The following is a copy of the order issued by General Taylor previous to his march from Corpus Christi, copies of which, translated into Spanish, were sent in advance, and distributed in all the Mexican towns on the right bank of the river. The terseness and vigor of General Taylor's style, as illustrated in his dispatches and orders, elicited universal admiration:

"The army of occupation of Texas being now about to take a position upon the left bank of the Rio Grande, under the orders of the Executive of the United States, the general-in-chief desires to express the hope that the movement will be advantageous to all concerned; and with the object of attaining this laudable end, he has ordered all under his command to observe, with the most scrupulous respect, the rights of all the inhabitants who may be found in peaceful prosecution of their respective occupations, as well on the left as on the right side of the Rio Grande. Under no pretext, nor in any way, will any interference be allowed with the civil rights or religious privileges of the inhabitants; but the utmost respect for them will be maintained.

"Whatsoever may be needed for the use of the army will be bought by the proper purveyor, and paid for at the highest prices. The general-in-chief has the satisfaction to say that he confides in the patriotism and discipline of the army under his command, and that he feels sure that his orders will be obeyed with the utmost exactness."

GENERAL TWIGGS.

command of Colonel Twiggs,* left the encampment. The two brigades of infantry followed in succession, the last leaving Corpus Christi on the 11th. General Taylor and staff accompanied the rear brigade. The steamers and transports, containing the provisions and supplies for a dépôt to be established at Point Isabel,† the siege train and field battery, together with a company of artillery and the engineer and ordnance officers, commanded by Major Munroe, left Corpus Christi at the same time, under convoy of the brigs of war Porpoise and Lawrence, and the revenue cutter Woodbury.

Meanwhile, the anticipated revolution had taken place. Mr. Slidell waited two days after the publication of the dictamen of the council of government, in the expectation of receiving a reply to a note he had addressed to Peña y Peña, on the 16th of December, desiring to be informed what were the difficulties in the way of his reception. Having received no communication from the Mexican Minister, he wrote a second note on the 20th instant, to which a reply was returned on the same day, communicating the positive determination of the Mexican government not to receive him. This decision was made too late to save the administration. Its want of firmness and decision was so manifest, that the military in the capital pronounced in favor of the revolutionists on the 29th of December, and on

* General David E. Twiggs entered the army in 1812, as a captain in the 8th Infantry, and served during the war. He also acted under the orders of Generals Gaines and Jackson during the Seminole war, and rendered efficient services in the difficulties with the Sacs and Foxes, and the Florida Indians. He was appointed Colonel of the 2nd Dragoons on the 8th of July, 1836, and promoted to the rank of brigadier general on the 30th of June, 1846.

† Point Isabel lies north-east of the island of Brazos, on the opposite side of the Laguna Madre. The village at the Point was called by the Mexicans, Frontone.

the following day Herrera resigned the presidency, without making a single effort to quell the outbreak. The tide had been turned for months, and he lacked the courage to stem it for an instant. Paredes entered the city with his troops, in triumph, on the 2nd of January, and on the next day was chosen provisional President. Soon after he was elected to the same office, by the Constituent Congress. He had come into power for the avowed purpose of putting an end to all negotiations with the United States, and of declaring and carrying on an offensive war. The desire to establish himself firmly in his place rendered him loth to remove the army to a distance, and no immediate measures of hostility were adopted. In a short time after his elevation, the establishment of a monarchy in Mexico was suggested by some of his most intimate friends. This movement proved to be unpopular, and prevented his obtaining the necessary loans for the support and increase of the army. The condition of the relations between the United States and Great Britain also boded war, and he was quite willing to wait and see the former engaged with a more powerful antagonist, before venturing to cope with her forces single-handed. Mr. Slidell had retired to Jalapa in February, to await the termination of the revolutionary contest in Mexico. As an entirely different government had been established, after the country became more quiet, he addressed a note, on the 1st of March, to the new Minister of Foreign Relations, Castillo y Lanzas, calling his attention to the subject of his reception, and requesting to know the views of the new administration in regard to the question. He was informed, in reply, by the note of the minister, written on the 12th, that he could not be received as a resident minister, and similar reasons were

GENERAL PAREDES.

given for the refusal to those previously expressed by Peña y Peña. In consequence of this final rejection of the offer to negotiate, Mr. Slidell requested the necessary passports, and, in a few days, set out on his return to the United States.* The Mexican government immediately commenced making preparations for war. Loans were obtained, arms and supplies provided for the army, and its numerical force augmented; and on the 4th of April, positive orders were issued to the officers commanding on the northern frontier, to attack the American troops.

The march of the American army from Corpus Christi, was not obstructed by the Mexicans. Small armed parties were occasionally seen in the distance, who disappeared on the approach of the advancing columns of General Taylor's force. For a few miles from their late encampment, the roads were found to be in good order; but further in the interior, the country presented a more unfavorable appearance. It was for the most part unbroken, but either low and marshy, or dry and sandy, with here and there a stretch of prairie land, covered with thick matted grass, and dotted at intervals with muskeet bushes, and clumps of chaparral. The route was toilsome and fatiguing, yet the soldiers bore every hardship without a murmur or complaint.† On the 19th of March, the advanced corps halted within three miles of the Arroyo Colorado, in order to effect a concentration of the force preparatory to crossing the stream, the passage of which, it was thought, might be

* See Diplomatic Correspondence, House of Rep. Doc. 196, 1st session, 29th Congress.

† The distance from Corpus Christi to Matamoras, according to the route pursued by the American army, was 168 miles—to Point Isabel, 160.

disputed. A reconnaissance was made of the ford, when a party of rancheros were discovered on the right bank, who signified to the officer in command, that an attempt to pass the river would be considered an act of hostility. General Taylor promptly made his dispositions to cross under fire. A road was opened down the bank of the river, and early on the morning of the 20th, the cavalry and first brigade of infantry advanced towards the ford, while the batteries of field artillery were so placed as to sweep the opposite shore; the port-fires were lighted, and every preparation made for action. The rancheros again appeared, and stated to Captain Mansfield, who was sent to communicate with them, that they had positive orders to fire on the Americans if they endeavored to cross the river. A second party now came up, at the head of which was a person who represented himself to be the adjutant general of the Mexican troops, though he was afterwards discovered to be a private citizen of Matamoras.* He, too, said he had peremptory orders to fire upon the Americans, and that the passage of the river would be considered as a declaration of war. A proclamation issued by General Mejia, the Mexican commander at Matamoras, on the 18th instant, was also presented by him, in which a similar announcement was made.

Orders were now given by General Taylor to proceed with the passage; and the enemy notified not to obstruct it in any manner. The second brigade of infantry was formed on the right, and the crossing commenced. Not a gun was fired, and the Mexicans retreated in the direction of Matamoras. The whole

* In reply to a question put to him, this individual admitted that the order of General Taylor announcing the spirit in which he proposed to occupy the country, had been received at Matamoras.

army passed the river, with their wagon trains, entirely unmolested, and pursued their march towards the Rio Grande. A few rancheros were seen on the route, but did not approach within hailing distance. On the morning of the 24th, General Taylor halted at a point on the road from Matamoras to Point Isabel, about eighteen miles from the former and ten from the latter. General Worth* was then ordered to advance with the infantry brigades on the Matamoras road, until he came to a suitable position for an encampment, where he would halt his command, and await the return of General Taylor, who proceeded to Point Isabel with the dragoons, to meet the transports and establish a dépôt. Understanding that a Mexican force had taken possession of the village of Frontone, he determined not to molest them. While on his way to the Point, he was met by a civil deputation from Matamoras, who desired an interview. They presented to him a formal protest against the occupation of the country, signed by the prefect of the northern district of Tamaulipas. He had not time to make his reply, when the buildings at Frontone were discovered to be on fire. Believing that he had been trifled with, and considering the destruction of property on disputed territory as an open act of hostility, he informed the deputation that he would answer them on his arrival opposite Matamoras, which he afterwards did.

* General William J. Worth joined the army as private secretary to General Lewis, in 1812. He afterwards obtained a commission, and acted as aid to General Scott, in the memorable battles of Chippewa and Niagara. He was appointed Colonel of the 8th regiment of infantry, on the 7th of July, 1838. The war with the Seminole Indians in Florida was brought to a close through his instrumentality, and his services were rewarded in 1842, with the brevet of brigadier general. The additional brevet of a major general was conferred on him for his gallant services in Mexico.

Colonel Twiggs hastened forward with the dragoons, to extinguish the flames and capture the incendiaries. On their arrival, they found but two or three inoffensive Mexicans in the village; the remainder having fled at their approach. The fire, which appeared to have been the work of the port captain, under the orders of General Garcia, consumed but three or four houses before it was arrested. On reaching the Point, General Taylor was gratified to find that the steamers and transports had just arrived in the harbor. A dépôt was established, and defences thrown up for its protection, in pursuance of his directions; he then set out to rejoin General Worth, leaving Major Munroe in command, with two companies of artillery.

On coming up with the main body of his army, General Taylor again ordered the march to be resumed, and arrived opposite Matamoras, on the 28th of March, without meeting any resistance. Two of his dragoons, sent forward from the advanced guard, were captured by the Mexicans, but were subsequently released. On his approach to the river, great excitement appeared to be produced in the city of Matamoras; troops were moved to and fro, and batteries prepared to command his position. Being desirous of announcing, in due form, the object of his advance to the river, and of affording an opportunity of establishing friendly intercourse, a white flag was exhibited on the left bank, under his orders A communication was opened with the Mexican officers, and General Worth was dispatched, with his staff, across the river, as the bearer of a communication to General Mejia, informing him of the desire of General Taylor for amicable relations, and his willingness to leave the port of Brazos Santiago open to the citizens of Matamoras, until the question of boundary should be definitely settled. An interview with General Mejia was refused, but General Worth was met on the right bank of the river, by General La Vega, who was attended by the Licenciádo Casares, representing the civil authorities of Matamoras, and several other persons. The dispatch of General Taylor was read to General La Vega, who was also told by General Worth, that he was directed to deliver it to the commanding officer at Matamoras. This was refused; whereupon General Worth, having been informed that the American consul was at liberty, and in the exercise of his official functions, demanded an interview with him, in the name of his government. The demand was not complied with, and the American general returned, and reported the result of his mission to General Taylor.*

* The following extracts from the minutes of the interview between Generals Worth and La Vega, show with what pertinacity the Mexicans persisted in maintaining on this occasion, that there was no war, although, as they alleged, so many acts of hostility had been committed. (House of Rep. Exec. Doc. 196, p. 114, 1st session, 29th Congress:)

"*General Worth.* Is the American consul in arrest, or in prison?—*General La Vega.* No.—*General Worth.* Is he now in the exercise of his proper functions?—*General La Vega.* (after apparently consulting with the Licenciádo Casares for a moment) replied that he was.—*General Worth.* Then, as an American officer, in the name of my government and my commanding general, I *demand* an interview with the consul of my country. (No reply.)—*General Worth.* Has Mexico declared war against the United States?—*General La Vega.* No.—*General Worth.* Are the two countries still at peace?—*General La Vega* Yes.—*General Worth.* Then I again demand an interview with the consul of my government, in Matamoras, in the presence, of course, of these gentlemen, or any other that the commanding general in Matamoras may be pleased to designate.

"General La Vega reiterated that the consul was in the proper exercise of his functions; that he was not in arrest, nor were any other Americans in arrest in Matamoras; that he would submit the *demand* to General Mejia, adding, that he thought there would be great difficulty.

The Mexicans still persisting in keeping up a hostile attitude, a position was selected for a permanent encampment, and the American flag planted for the first time on the left bank of the Rio Grande.

The construction of defensive works was immediately commenced by General Taylor, in imitation of the example of the Mexicans, who had already erected several batteries and redoubts. Fifteen hundred soldiers were constantly employed on fatigue duty, working day and night with commendable patience and perseverance. Intrenchments were thrown up, and a fort erected, with six bastions, large enough to accommodate a force of two thousand men. Batteries were also completed, and mounted with heavy guns bearing directly upon the public square of Matamoras. The defences of Point Isabel were, in like manner, strengthened as rapidly as circumstances would permit.

Notwithstanding these hostile preparations, no actual collision with the enemy's forces took place for several days, and the impression that there would be no war became generally entertained. In this belief, General

"This *demand* was repeatedly made in the most emphatic manner, and a reply requested; General La Vega stating the consul continued in the exercise of his functions, and that Gen. Worth's demand would be submitted to Gen. Mejia. * * * * *

"No reply having been received from Gen. La Vega relative to the demand for an interview with the American consul, the question was again introduced by Gen. Worth, and the demand for the last time reiterated.

"Gen. La Vega then promptly refused to comply with the demand, replying, without waiting for the interpretation, 'No, no.'

"*General Worth.* I have now to state that a refusal of my demand to see the American consul is regarded as a belligerent act; and, in conclusion, I have to add, the commanding general of the American forces on the left bank of the river will regard the passage of any armed party of Mexicans in hostile array across the Rio Grande as an act of war, and pursue it accordingly."

Worth expressed a desire to be separated from his command, on account of some difficulty in relation to his brevet rank. This was done on the 7th of April, and he soon after returned home, with the intention of resigning his commission.*

Aside from the presence of the two armies, the scene presented at this time, on the banks of the Rio Grande, was of a peaceful, yet imposing character. On the opposite shore from the American encampment was the city of Matamoras, with its towering cathedral, its neat houses, and pretty gardens; on the verge of the town were the small reed and thatched habitations of the humbler classes; and in the distance, the cultivated fields of cotton and cane, and smiling haciendas imbosomed amid groves of ebony and lignum-vitæ. At sunset the whole population of the city crowded down to the river's side, to hear the bands belonging to the American regiments discourse "the eloquent music" whose rich notes were borne to their ears mingled with the low murmuring of the Bravo; and, in default of more chivalric enterprises, it is said that many a love-passage took place between our young officers and the gay Mexican senoritas. But this quiet was only the hush that preceded the tempest; and the angry passions smothered for the moment, soon burst forth, like the wrath of Jove, with redoubled vengeance.

On the 11th of April, General Ampudia arrived from Monterey, and assumed the command at Matamoras. He was accompanied by 200 cavalry, and a force of

* General Worth insisted that his brevet entitled him to precedence over Colonel Twiggs, whose commission as colonel was of an older date than his own. In conformity with the rule adopted by the War Department, General Taylor decided that brevet rank gave no command, except where there was a regular assignment to duty according to such brevet rank.

2,200 men followed close in his rear. When passing through Reinosa, he ordered all Americans to leave that place within twenty-four hours, and to retire to Victoria. A similar order was issued on his arrival at Matamoras, where his entrance was hailed by the ringing of bells, the firing of cannon, and other demonstrations of joy. His assumption of the command was understood to be the signal for the commencement of hostilities; a rigid non-intercourse was established with the Americans on the left bank; and the Mexican pickets were extended above and below the city for several miles. Copies of a proclamation issued by him, on the road to Matamoras, addressed to the soldiers of foreign birth in the American army, and artfully appealing to their cupidity to induce them to desert, were secretly introduced into General Taylor's camp. A number of desertions took place, but the prompt measures taken by the American commander soon put an end to them. Some of those who attempted to escape were drowned in the river, and others were fired upon by the guards. Those who reached the Mexican lines were loaded with favors, and every mark of distinction conferred upon them, almost without solicitation.

A dispatch was received by General Taylor from Ampudia, on the morning of the 12th of April, formally requiring him to break up his camp "in the peremptory term of twenty-four hours," and retire to the other bank of the Nueces, pending the negotiations for the settlement of the Texas question;* and advising him, "that arms, and arms alone, must decide" between them, if he insisted on remaining in his position, and that the war to be thus commenced, would be conducted

* The final refusal of the Mexican government to receive Mr. Slidell, though anticipated at Matamoras, was not yet positively known.

on his part, "conformably to the principles established by the most civilized nations." General Taylor replied on the same day, declining to enter upon any discussion in regard to the international question, but reminding General Ampudia that, although Mexico had hitherto refused to hear any proposition for negotiation, he had been instructed, in occupying the country, to abstain from all acts of hostility, which instructions had so far been carefully observed. He added, however, that he should not avoid the alternative presented by the Mexican commander, and would leave the responsibility with those who rashly commenced hostilities.* General Ampudia having thus announced the existence of a state of war, General Taylor prepared himself for

* "I need hardly advise you that, charged as I am, in only a military capacity, with the performance of specific duties, I cannot enter into a discussion of the international question involved in the advance of the American army. You will, however, permit me to say, that the government of the United States has constantly sought a settlement, by negotiation, of the question of boundary; that an envoy was dispatched to Mexico for that purpose, and that up to the most recent dates said envoy had not been received by the actual Mexican government, if, indeed, he has not received his passports and left the republic. In the meantime, I have been ordered to occupy the country up to the left bank of the Rio Grande, until the boundary shall be definitely settled. In carrying out these instructions, I have carefully abstained from all acts of hostility, obeying, in this regard, not only the letter of my instructions, but the plain dictates of justice and humanity.

"The instructions under which I am acting will not permit me to retrograde from the position I now occupy. In view of the relations between our respective governments, and the individual suffering which may result, I regret the alternative which you offer; but, at the same time, wish it understood that I shall by no means avoid such alternative, leaving the responsibility with those who rashly commence hostilities. In conclusion, you will permit me to give the assurance, that on my part, the laws and customs of war among civilized nations shall be carefully observed."—Extract from General Taylor's reply to Ampudia, April 12th, 1846.

the consequences, intending, as he had previously done, to act strictly on the defence. Instructions were given to the naval commander at Brazos Santiago, on the 13th instant, to blockade the mouth of the Rio Grande, in order to stop all supplies intended for Matamoras. The second regiment of infantry was removed out of reach of the shot from the Mexican batteries, and the field-work occupied by the third regiment, and two batteries of light artillery. Strong guards of foot and mounted men were stationed along the margin of the river, and every precaution adopted to prevent surprise. An additional force was ordered to Point Isabel, and the fort well supplied with artillery and ammunition.

The peremptory term specified by Ampudia expired without producing any act of hostility on his part, and every thing continued quiet for several days. While matters were in this condition, the American army was called upon to lament the loss of Colonel Trueman Cross, Deputy Quartermaster-general, and a most estimable officer. He was accustomed to take daily exercise on horseback, and on the morning of the 10th of April rode out as usual. It was supposed for a long time that he had been taken prisoner, and conveyed across the river, but his body was subsequently discovered in a dense chaparral, some miles from the fort, in a horribly mutilated state. He was only recognized by his uniform, and was undoubtedly murdered by the lawless banditti who hung around the Mexican camp, but acted under no orders except those given by their own chosen leaders.

On the 17th instant, and previous to the discovery of the body of Colonel Cross, Lieutenants Porter and Dobbins, each with a party of twelve men, were sent out to obtain intelligence in regard to the missing officer. The two detachments took different directions. On the second day out, Lieutenant Porter met a party of Mexicans, about eighteen miles from General Taylor's camp, and one third of that distance north of the river, numbering near one hundred and fifty, one of whom snapped his piece at him. He instantly discharged both barrels of his gun, and the Mexicans disappeared in the thicket. Their camp, with their horses and equipage, were captured. On their return, the Americans encountered another body of Mexicans, who had probably been joined by those previously seen. It was nearly nightfall, and raining heavily. They were instantly fired upon, but were unable to return it on account of their ammunition being damaged. Lieutenant Porter and one of his men were killed, and the remainder of the party returned to camp.

Two vessels bound to Matamoras with supplies for the army were warned off the mouth of the Rio Grande, on the 17th of April, by the blockading force. On receiving information of the fact, Ampudia remonstrated against the blockade. His letter to General Taylor was dated on the 22nd instant, and on the same day, a reply was made, in the usual sententious and impressive style of the American commander. He briefly reviewed his proceedings since he had left Corpus Christi with the army under his orders; pointing out the numerous evidences of his desire to avoid hostilities, and showing conclusively that the responsibility of producing them did not rest with him. When authoritatively informed by General Ampudia, that war would be the consequence of a refusal to abandon his position, he issued the order to the naval commanders for the enforcement of a blockade, which, he insisted, was not only justifiable under the circumstances, but could not be removed, unless an armistice was desired, in which case he would cheerfully open the river. As for the consequences that might result, and which were intimated in the remonstrance of General Ampudia, he begged to be understood that he was prepared for them, whatever they might be.

General Arista* arrived at Matamoras on the 24th of April, and assumed the chief command, information of which was communicated by himself, in a courteous note to General Taylor, stating, also, that he considered hostilities commenced, and should prosecute them. A second proclamation, prepared by him, was distributed among the American soldiers, inviting them to desert, and promising large bounties of land as a reward for espousing the Mexican cause. A few, a very few, of those to whom the proclamation was addressed, accepted the offer; but, to their honor be it said, the great majority spurned it with the scorn and indignation which it merited.

On the evening of the 23rd of April, General Taylor's spies reported that 2,500 Mexicans had crossed the Rio Grande above the American encampment, and about 1,500 below, with the intention of surrounding his position, and cutting off all communication with the depôt at Point Isabel. Captain Ker was dispatched

* General Arista commanded the army on the northern frontier of Mexico. in the summer of 1845. He returned to the interior in the fall, when the revolutionary movements were in progress. He was opposed to Paredes, and it was at one time supposed that he would *pronounce* against him, as the Mexicans term it, but it seems that he was content to wait for a more favorable opportunity. After his defeat by General Taylor, in May 1846, he endeavored to organize a revolutionary faction, but was unsuccessful, and soon after retired from the army. He is said to have been one of the ablest generals in the Mexican service

on the following day, with a squadron of dragoons, to reconnoitre the crossing near Burrita, and returned in a few hours, with the intelligence that the alarm was unfounded. At the same time another squadron, under Captain Thornton, was sent to scour the country above. They proceeded up the river about twenty-six miles, without discovering any signs of the enemy, although their inquiries on the way tended to show that they had crossed the river in strength. At this point the guide refused to go any further, alleging that the whole country was full of Mexicans. The orders of Captain Thornton were, to discover the position and force of the enemy, if they had passed the river, but to proceed with care and caution. He was entirely ignorant of the country, but perfectly fearless, and somewhat impetuous. Having decided to go on without the guide, his advanced guard was increased, and the party again moved forward. At a distance of about three miles further, they discovered a plantation, inclosed by a chaparral fence, except on the side facing the river, with a farm-house situated about two hundred yards from the entrance, which was narrow, and secured by a pair of bars.

Captain Thornton halted the advanced guard, and went into the field ahead of his men, to speak with some persons who appeared to be at work. Sufficient precautions had not been taken to guard against surprise, and a signal to the guard was mistaken by the remainder of the force all of whom entered the inclosure. In an instant the chaparral swarmed with the Mexicans, who had completely surrounded them, and apparently cut off every chance of escape. A body of cavalry also made their appearance, and charged upon the little band, who met them gallantly, and with success. A destructive fire was now poured upon them, which it was impossible to resist, and orders were given by Captain Thornton to his men, to cut their way through the enemy. With a single bound he cleared the fence, overturning a number of the Mexicans who endeavored to stop him, and darted ahead in the direction of General Taylor's position. In leaping a precipice, his horse fell with him, and he remained for some time insensible. When he recovered, he again started for the camp, but was taken prisoner before he reached it. Meanwhile Captain Hardee, who had succeeded to the command of the squadron, ordered his men to ford the river ; but the banks were found to be so boggy, that this was impossible, and he then surrendered himself and men prisoners of war. In this affair the American loss was ten killed, and about fifty taken prisoners. The Mexican force consisted of cavalry and infantry, over three hundred strong, commanded by General Torrejon. General Taylor forthwith communicated the particulars of the enounter to his government; and, deeming that the time had arrived when additional forces were necessary, he made a requisition on the Governor of Louisiana for four regiments of infantry, and on the Governor of Texas for two regiments of mounted men, and two of foot, all which were to be sent into the field as soon as possible.

CHAPTER II

BATTLES ON THE RIO GRANDE.

The intelligence of Thornton's Capture received in the United States—Fears for the Safety of General Taylor—Proceedings of Congress—Preparations for War—Prompt response to the call for Volunteers—The Army of Occupation—Skirmishing—March to Point Isabel—Bombardment of Fort Brown—Battle of Palo Alto—Resaca de la Palma—Capture of Matamoras, and other Mexican Towns on the Rio Grande.

THE fiery cross, borne by the swift-footed Walise, as the signal for the marshalling of the Scottish clans, did not arouse a deeper or more intense feeling of anxiety than the intelligence of the capture of Thornton and his command on the banks of the Bravo. With the rapidity of the electric fire, it was communicated from one extremity of the country to the other. One rumor followed close upon another. Exaggerated accounts of the forces of the enemy, and the dangers that beset the army of occupation, were circulated far and near; each new repetition affording wider scope to the imagination, and magnifying the causes of alarm, until the public mind was actually prepared for any disaster or reverse. Cut off from all communication with his dépôt of provisions and supplies, hemmed in and surrounded by a force trebling his own in numbers, General Taylor was represented to be in a most perilous position. The information that he was authorized to call on the governors of the neighboring states for volunteers whenever he deemed it necessary, quieted the fears and apprehensions of the community but for a moment, and all were soon prepossessed with the idea that he had waited until it was too late. Even those who were best acquainted with his qualities as a soldier, and knew that he would not rashly thrust himself into danger, trembled for his safety; and, although they were satisfied that he would fight like the stag at bay, whatever might be the strength of his assailants, they feared lest courage and determination would avail him nothing, against the powerful army which threatened to overwhelm him.

In the city of New Orleans, and the adjoining country, the excitement was so great that it could scarcely be controlled. Partaking of the enthusiasm of those who surrounded him, the veteran General Gaines,* then in command of that division, without waiting for orders from Washington, made large requisitions for volunteers, on the Governors of Louisiana, Alabama, Mississippi, and Missouri, in addition to those called for by General Taylor.† There was no lack of applicants to meet all the requisitions, and the only strife was, who should be first and foremost in the rescue. Within a

* Major General Edmund P. Gaines has been in the service almost half a century. He was appointed an ensign in 1799, and received his commission as a brigadier general in 1814. He received the brevet of major general for his brave defence of Fort Erie, against the assault of the British army under General Drummond.

† The calls made by General Gaines were countermanded as soon as they came to the knowledge of the President, though recognized to the extent of the number of troops already furnished. These unexpected additions to his force, not only exhausted General Taylor's supplies, but they also seriously embarrassed his movements.—(Letters to the Adjutant General, May 20th, June 3rd, and July 1st, 1846.) But no one doubted that the motives of General Gaines were eminently praiseworthy. Too much credit, perhaps, was given to the rumors against which he and

very short time a considerable force was mustered into the service of the United States, equipped and provided, and on their way to the seat of war.

Congress was still in session, when the information that hostilities had commenced on the Rio Grande reached Washington. A special message was received from the President, on the 11th of May, communicating the dispatches of General Taylor, and recommending the most energetic measures for the prosecution of the war. Two days were occupied in the deliberation and discussion of the subject, and on the 13th, an act was passed, with great unanimity, declaring that a state of war existed "by the act of the republic of Mexico," and authorizing the President to accept the services of fifty thousand volunteers. The sum of ten millions of dollars also was appropriated to carry on the war.

Energy and activity were at once infused into every department of the public service. Consultations were held between the President, the Secretary of War, and General Scott,* the general-in-chief of the army. Memoranda were furnished to the different staff officers and heads of bureaus. Quartermasters, commissaries, and medical purveyors, were busily engaged in making calculations, preparing estimates, and providing the

the War Department had been warned by General Taylor; but he could not see a brother officer in supposed peril, without volunteering to aid him. When he heard the sound of cannon, he knew it was time to fight, as Napoleon said, "without waiting for orders."

* Major General Winfield Scott is so well known, as the Hero of Chippewa and Niagara, that it is almost superfluous to refer to his military history. He entered the army, with the rank of captain, in 1808, and in March, 1814, at the age of twenty-eight, was made a brigadier general. In the same year he was brevetted a major general, for his distinguished services on the Niagara frontier, and on the 25th of June, 1841, he was appointed General in Chief of the Army, to fill the vacancy occasioned by the death of General Macomb.

necessary supplies for the comfort and health of the troops, their sustenance and equipment, and the requisite facilities for transportation. How well the duties of these officers were discharged, is attested by the fact, that an additional force of near 20,000 men was sent into the field early in the ensuing summer.

The general plan of the campaign, determined on at Washington, was, to make a series of flank invasions, or attacks, on the western, northern, and eastern frontiers of Mexico. A strong naval squadron was already lying in the Gulf, and orders were issued to Commodore Conner, on the 13th of May, to blockade the Mexican ports. Instructions had been previously given to Commodore Sloat, the officer commanding the Pacific squadron, to take possession of the principal ports and towns on that coast, as fast as his means would allow, whenever he was credibly informed that hostilities had commenced. The land forces of the United States were to penetrate the enemy's country in three divisions—one proceeding from Fort Leavenworth on the Missouri river, under Colonel (afterwards General) Kearny,* into New Mexico and California; the second, under General Wool,† to rendezvous at San An-

* Brigadier General Stephen W. Kearny received his first commission, that of a lieutenant, in 1812. He served during the war with credit, and after the peace was mainly employed on the western frontier. He rose by regular promotion to the rank of brigadier general, which appointment was conferred on him on the 30th of June, 1846.

† Brigadier General John E. Wool obtained a captain's commission in 1812. His military début was made at the battle of Queenston, where he highly distinguished himself. He also bore a conspicuous part under General Macomb at Plattsburg. In 1816, he was appointed inspector-general of the army, and continued to act in that capacity for twenty-five years. His acquirements as a disciplinarian, and his skill as a tactician, are conceded to be of a high order. He was promoted to the rank of brigadier general in 1841.

tonio de Bexar, and march due west towards Chihuahua; subject, however, to the orders of the officer in command of the third division, which was to constitute the main body of the army, and assuming the Rio Grande as the base line of its operations, to overrun and occupy the provinces of Coahuila, New Leon, and Tamaulipas. If found to be practicable, a movement in the direction of the city of Mexico was designed to be made from this quarter; but, if otherwise, two projects were in contemplation—a march from Tampico on San Luis Potosi, and the capture of Vera Cruz—to be followed by an advance movement towards the Mexican capital; one or both of which were to be adopted, as circumstances might render expedient. In order to secure the possession of California, without weakening the column under General Kearny, a regiment of volunteers, with a small body of regular soldiers, were to be sent round by sea.

An examination of the map will show the nature and the propriety of these different movements. The idea of making a permanent conquest of any portion of the republic of Mexico, for the sake of territorial aggrandizement alone, was disavowed by the administration, and would have been as foreign to the purposes for which our government was formed, as it was abhorrent to the wishes of the American people. But it was foreseen, at the outset, that the prosecution of the war, if successful, would be followed by the acquisition of some part of the domain of Mexico. She was confessedly bankrupt; her mines, her revenues, her lands, indeed all her most valuable resources, were pledged for the security of other obligations; and she possessed no means of satisfying the claims of the American citizens, and those which would necessarily grow out of a state of hostilities, except by a cession of her territory. It was thought expedient therefore, to take possession of that lying contiguous to the United States, and, pursuing the same policy, to establish temporary civil governments in New Mexico and California, to be continued in another form, if those provinces were annexed, and to be suspended in the event of their restoration. By carrying the war, at the same time, into the interior, into the heart of the country, it was evident that the government of Mexico would be ultimately driven to abandon her position of refusing to negotiate, and to conclude a treaty of peace on fair and honorable terms.

The several projects adopted by the principal executive and military officers of the government, with such modifications and changes as were discovered to be necessary, were carried into effect. General Wool found it impracticable to continue his route over the mountains to Chihuahua, and turned aside to Monclova and Parras, afterwards effecting a junction with General Taylor's army at Saltillo. The demonstration from Tampico, against San Luis Potosi, and the march into the interior of Mexico from the north, were also abandoned.

It was originally designed that the main body of the army should be placed under the immediate command of General Scott, whose official position, to say nothing of his ability, seemed to render the selection a proper and desirable one. An unfortunate misunderstanding, between the President and Secretary of War on the one hand, and himself on the other, was followed by a change in the orders which had been given, and he was directed to confine his services to the city of Washington. It would be out of place in a work of this character, to enter into the details of that controversy. It is sufficient to say of it, that although there was too little deference shown on the one side, towards those whom the law and the constitution had intrusted with superior authority, it was forgotten on the other, that the wounds of a soldier who had fought and bled in the service of his country, were to be held sacred, and that a single hasty word, or an ill-advised act, ought to weigh as nothing against the qualifications which placed their possessor in the front rank of military men in the world. There are few friends of General Scott but will lament this occurrence; and it is equally true, that the efforts made to supersede him will never be regarded with favor. Neither Congress nor the country approved them; and if mentioned at all, they should only be regretted.*

The proclamation of the President of the United States, announcing the existence of the war with Mexico, was issued on the same day with the passage of the act in Congress. So prompt was the country to respond to the call for volunteers, that in a few weeks the services of more than two hundred thousand men were offered to the Executive. But a small portion of these could be accepted, and only twenty-four regiments, whose aggregate strength was 18,000 men, were immediately called into the field. Early in the session of

* A bill was introduced in Congress, in May, 1846, providing for the appointment of two additional major generals, and authorizing the President to assign them their relative command and rank. It failed to become a law in that shape; and provision was afterwards made for the appointment of one major general, and two brigadiers. General Taylor was appointed the major general, and the brigadiers selected were Generals Twiggs and Kearny. At the session of 1846-7, the project of creating the office of lieutenant general was brought forward, but Congress could not be induced to sanction it. The appointment was intended to be conferred on a civilian, who would thus have been elevated above all the more experienced, if not abler, officers of the army.

Congress a bill had been introduced, in pursuance of the suggestion of the general-in-chief, authorizing an increase of the rank and file of the regular army. It was not pressed forward with as much celerity as it should have been, and became a law but a short time prior to the act of the 13th of May. All the disposable recruits enlisted for several months previous had been sent to General Taylor, and this was continued after the passage of the bill. The regular force in Mexico was increased, during the season, to almost 7,000 men.

Though deprived of any active command, General Scott, in connection with the able staff officers under his orders, applied himself vigorously to the task of fitting the volunteers for the scenes that awaited them. The city of New Orleans was to be the grand dépôt of supply, and all the *matériel* for carrying on the war was hurried forward as rapidly as possible to this point. Whatever determination, perseverance, and ability could accomplish, was performed. Delays and embarrassments sometimes occurred, but these were to have been expected in a country without a standing army, and which was called upon in an emergency to raise and equip a large volunteer force. Temporary inconvenience was felt on all hands, yet this was of minor importance, in comparison with the evils which might follow from keeping up a large military establishment.

While all these preparations were being made at Washington, and in other parts of the country; and while so much apprehension and alarm were entertained for the safety of General Taylor and the army on the Rio Grande, he appears to have been entirely unconscious of his and their danger. In a letter written to the adjutant general on the 20th of May, 1846, he said, that he knew, if the Mexicans fought him at all, "it would be before the arrival of the volunteers." He never doubted his ability to maintain himself, with the force already under his command, against the whole Mexican army; and the sequel proved that his confidence in the bravery and discipline of his men was well founded. Nevertheless, it is to be regretted that a much larger army was not sent, in the first instance, to assert, by its presence, the claim of the United States to the disputed territory. The reluctance always exhibited in Congress to increase the regular military force; the jealousy with which any proposition of that character would be regarded by the people; the supposition that it might be looked upon in England as a measure of intimidation, while the Oregon negotiation was in progress, and there was no actual war with Mexico; and the necessity of keeping the Atlantic coast, and the northern frontier, well protected, until that question was settled, were strong reasons for the course adopted by our government. But a single consideration will show that this policy was an unfortunate one, though it may have been necessary. The great body of the Mexican army at Matamoras were ignorant and cowardly, but of an excitable temperament, and, after the capture of Thornton and his dragoons, easily wrought upon to engage in any enterprise which their leaders thought proper to undertake; but had General Taylor's force been double what it was in numbers, those leaders must have seen that it would be madness to think of contending against him, and it is scarcely probable that they would have hastened on the war by crossing the river.

After the capture of the party under Captain Thornton, the Mexican detachment on the left bank of the river, commanded by General Torrejon, was increased by large reinforcements from the opposite shore. A part of this force, by making a détour to the left, gained a position between General Taylor's camp and Point Isabel, and the remainder occupied the country above. The communication between the Point and the main army was now closed, and the teams employed in conveying provisions and supplies from the dépôt, were compelled to return without reaching their destination. Captain Walker had been stationed with his company of Texan Rangers, between the two positions, with instructions to keep the road open; and on being informed by the teamsters that the Mexicans had completely obstructed it, he left his camp with about half his force, on the 28th of April, to reconnoitre. The captain was an experienced frontier soldier, and gave his men special directions to guard against a surprise. During his absence, the camp was suddenly attacked by a large body of ranchero cavalry, supposed to be nearly 1,500 strong. The rangers were mostly new volunteers, and did not obey the injunctions of their leader; they were instantly thrown into confusion, and he returned in time to check, but not to remedy the disaster. A smart engagement was kept up for a few moments, during which the Mexicans lost thirty men, but the captain was forced to make a hurried retreat to the Point. His own loss was nine, in killed and wounded.

The information brought in by Captain Walker occasioned much alarm and anxiety at the Point. The enemy could not be ignorant of the value of the stores collected here, and an attack was hourly expected. Every man connected with the service was provided with arms, and the masters and crews of the vessels and transports lying in the harbor promptly came on shore and tendered their services. The entire force which Major

Munroe was thus enabled to collect for the defence of the post, including the two companies of artillery and the rangers, amounted to about 500 men. His artillery consisted of sixteen brass six pounders, two long eighteens, and two ship's guns. He was amply provided with ammunition, and felt confident that he could withstand a force three times his own in number.

Though the enterprise was a most hazardous one, Captain Walker offered to be the bearer of a communication from Major Munroe to General Taylor, apprizing him of the situation of the dépôt, provided four men would accompany him. Permission was given him to make the attempt, and six men volunteered to go with him. He left the Point with his party, on the morning of the 29th of April; the service was full of peril, as every bush and thicket were supposed to conceal a hidden enemy; but he succeeded, on the evening of the same day, in reaching the camp opposite Matamoras, in safety, after making several hair-breadth escapes; on one occasion cutting his way through a body of Mexican lancers who endeavored to intercept him.

Previous to this time, General Taylor had been informed that the enemy were preparing to cross below his camp, with the view of effecting a junction with the force under General Torrejon. The design of Arista was at once apparent. Ever since the blockade, provisions had been scarce in Matamoras. The prize at Point Isabel had attracted his attention, and he had determined to secure it. This position in his hands, General Taylor would be cut of from his supplies, and from all communication with New Orleans, by water, the only mode by which he could be immediately reinforced, or furnished with military stores and provisions. The unfinished state of his field-work, and the necessity of placing it in a good condition for defence, had hitherto prevented General Taylor from acting on the offensive but as his own ammunition and provisions were becoming reduced, and his principal dépôt was menaced he determined to march to the Point with the main body of the army as soon as possible, and put an end to the land blockade which the enemy appeared disposed to enforce against him. The troops were employed without intermission, on the field-work, until the morning of the 1st of May, when it appeared to be capable of being defended by an inferior force, and orders were then issued to prepare for the march.

The seventh regiment of infantry, with Captain Lowd's and Lieutenant Bragg's companies of artillery, numbering, in all, about 600 men, were detailed to garrison the field-work, and complete its defences. Major Brown, of the 7th, was left in command. At half-past three in the afternoon of the 1st, the main force marched under General Taylor, leaving all their sick behind them at the post; and at eleven o'clock on the same evening bivouacked in the open prairie, about ten miles from Point Isabel. The march was resumed the next morning, and they reached the dépôt early in the day, without discovering any indications of the enemy.

The departure of General Taylor, with the greater part of his army, was hailed in Matamoras with every manifestation of joy. His march was pronounced a hasty retreat, and it was said that he had shut himself up in the fort, and lacked sufficient courage to meet the Mexicans in the field. The newspapers published in Matamoras abounded in declarations to this effect; and *El Monitor Republicano* boastfully announced, that the American general "dared not resist the valor and enthusiasm of the sons of Mexico." Within a week they were taught to know him better, and their loud boasting changed to mournful lamentations.*

General Arista, who now had not far from 8,000 men under his command, left Matamoras with the principal part of the troops remaining on the right bank of the river, several hours before the departure of General Taylor from his position opposite the city. On arriving at the crossing-place below Matamoras, the flat boats were found to be so much injured, that considerable delay was produced before he could concentrate his forces for the contemplated attack on the Point. General Taylor was on his way to its relief, and he did not think it advisable to hazard an engagement, in the then disordered condition of his army. The detachment under General Torrejon occupied the left bank, to cover the crossing, and the Americans were therefore unmolested on their march.

An attack on Fort Texas, as the American field-work opposite Matamoras was called,† next suggested itself to the Mexican commander. The necessary orders were given, and the firing commenced at daylight on Sunday morning, the 3rd instant, from a battery of seven guns, (eight-pounders,) protected by a breastwork of sand-bags. The réveillé was beaten at every point of the Mexican line, and the solemn stillness of

* It was claimed by the Mexican journals that their army made every effort to come up with the Americans, but were unable to do so. This is not at all probable. Arista left Matamoras at eleven o'clock in the forenoon of the 1st, and his troops had preceded him several hours. General Mejia who remained in command in the city, dispatched a messenger with the news of General Taylor's march soon after it commenced. If the Mexicans had desired to overtake General Taylor, they could have found him that night on the prairie.

† The name was subsequently changed to Fort Brown.

the day was soon broken by the thunder of the cannon, the pealing notes of the church bells in Matamoras, and the loud *vivas* of the inhabitants who had assembled to witness the scene, and to cheer and animate their countrymen. The American batteries were quickly manned, and a strong fire kept up from the eighteen and six-pounders, for thirty minutes, when the enemy's fort was silenced. Two of their guns were disabled, and the remainder were removed to another fort lower down. A few shells had been thrown from a mortar in the sand-bag fort, but this was also removed to the lower fort, and a heavy cannonade commenced from that point, which was continued, almost without intermission, until 12 o'clock at night, during which time from twelve to fifteen hundred shot were discharged. But little damage was done by the Mexican guns, though the embrasures were frequently struck. The only real annoyance was produced by the mortar, from which a number of shells were thrown that exploded in the fort. Finding that his six-pounders produced no effect, Major Brown ordered them to be posted in the rear to prevent an assault. A steady and deliberate fire was then continued from the eighteen-pounders by Captain Lowd, and a number of houses and other buildings in the city were considerably injured by the balls. An attempt was made to fire the town by throwing hot balls, but they could not be sufficiently heated to answer the purpose. At ten o'clock in the forenoon Major Brown ordered the fire to cease. It was found to be impossible to silence the mortar, and, as the enemy's guns did no harm, he wished to husband the small supply of ammunition in the fort. During the cannonade and bombardment, the garrison continued their labors on the unfinished works, under the superintendence of the efficient engineer officer, Captain Mansfield. But one man was killed in the fort, and none were wounded.

The cannonade in the direction of Matamoras on the 3rd instant was heard at Point Isabel, and General Taylor dispatched Captain Walker, with ten of his rangers, protected by a squadron of cavalry under Captain May, to communicate with Major Brown. The party set out at two o'clock in the afternoon, and at nine came in sight of the watch fires of the enemy, who were encamped near Palo Alto. Taking a wide circuit, Captain May gained a position in the rear, where he concealed his men in a thicket of chaparral, while Captain Walker proceeded to the fort. The latter accomplished his errand, and communicated the orders of General Taylor, not to hazard the safety of the fort by a sally, under any circumstances, but to defend it to the last. Having obtained fresh horses, he returned to the place where he had parted with the cavalry escort, but found it deserted. He was then compelled to seek safety in the fort during the day. At night he ventured forth again, and reached the Point unharmed, notwithstanding there were numerous parties on the alert to capture him. His bold and daring feats as a partisan were known to the Mexicans, and they were anxious to get him in their power, but he eluded all their efforts.

Meanwhile Captain May had waited until daylight, and finding that Captain Walker did not return, he supposed he had been taken by the enemy, and as his own position would soon be an unsafe one, he decided to return. In order to reconnoitre the enemy's position, he passed within half a mile of their camp at a full gallop. When about twelve miles from Point Isabel he encoun tered a body of one hundred and fifty lancers, whom he charged and pursued nearly three miles; but as their horses were fresh, and his much jaded, he was unable to overtake them. Fears were now entertained for the safety of Captain Walker, but all alarm was banished by his subsequent reappearance. He brought the information that the firing of the batteries at Matamoras had recommenced on the morning of the 4th, but was kept up only at long intervals, and without producing any damage.

The partial cessation of the enemy's fire enabled Major Brown to continue the work on the defences of the fort, without any serious molestation. On the night of the 4th the Mexicans crossed the river and erected a strong battery, provided with cannon and mortars, in the rear of his position. About five o'clock in the afternoon, the field-battery commenced playing, and at the same time a constant discharge of shot and shells was kept up from the batteries in Matamoras. The garrison were not daunted by reason of their being exposed to this cross fire, but returned it with spirit until the enemy's batteries were silenced for the day. Towards evening detachments of Mexican lancers and rancheros were observed hovering about in the vicinity of the fort on the north and east. Lieutenant Hanson, at his request, was sent out with a party to reconnoitre, and returned with the intelligence that the enemy were making preparations to invest the fort. The investment was completed before night, and Major Brown now fired his eighteen-pounders at regular intervals, which was the preconcerted signal to inform General Taylor of his situation.

Having failed in his design of capturing the dépôt at Point Isabel, General Arista had drawn his forces around the fort opposite Matamoras, in the hope of effecting its reduction before it could be relieved. The firing was renewed from his batteries, on the morning of the 6th, with increased vigor. Owing to the scarcity of ammunition in the fort, Major Brown ordered his men to cease firing, but to be prepared for resisting an assault. Soon after giving this order, he was struck by the fragments of a shell which exploded near him. The injury proved to be mortal, and terminated his career on the 9th of May. His loss to the service was a severe one, and, as General Taylor afterwards remarked, to the army under his orders it was "indeed irreparable."

After the fall of Major Brown, Captain Hawkins, of the same regiment, assumed the command. From the fact that the guns of the fort had ceased playing, the Mexicans supposed them completely silenced. About noon they also stopped firing, and every thing remained quiet for two hours, when one of their batteries commenced a slow fire. The light companies near the fort moved within musket range, as if preparing for an assault, but were soon driven away by Captain Lowd's battery, which opened upon them. At five o'clock the Mexicans sounded a parley, and two officers approached the fort, with a written communication from General Arista, summoning the garrison to surrender, to which a reply was to be returned within one hour. A council of his officers was convened by Captain Hawkins, and the summons laid before them. The stern and unanimous response was—to defend the fort to the death! * The reply of the American commander was

* The reply of Captain Hawkins to that part of Arista's note summoning him to surrender, was so brief, and yet so pertinent, that it deserves to be copied: "Your humane communication," said he, "has

followed by a terrible cannonade, much more severe than any which had preceded it. At night the garrison slept on their arms, in readiness for the anticipated attack. During the whole of the following day they were on the alert. A severe cannonading was constantly kept up by the enemy, and assaulting parties were several times formed, though as often dispersed by a few rounds of canister and grape fired from the fort. In the evening Captain Mansfield sallied out with a party, and levelled the traverse and some clumps of chaparral, which had sheltered the sharp-shooters, whose fire had been quite annoying to the Americans. At midnight the garrison was aroused by volleys of musketry and bugle calls, which continued until near daylight. An assault was confidently anticipated, but the brave defenders of the fort were happily disappointed.

At dawn of day on the 8th, the firing was renewed, and continued with very little intermission, until two o'clock in the afternoon. The forces of the enemy did not appear to be as numerous as they had been, and when this was discovered, the hopes of the garrison began to revive. Wearied and worn out with the constant watching, the labor and fatigue of the last six days, they lay down to rest themselves upon the ramparts which had witnessed their long and anxious vigils. Their ammunition was reduced so low, that they had been ordered to refrain from firing, unless the enemy approached within eighty yards of the fort.* This, of itself, would have discouraged men who were not sus-

just been received, and, after the consideration due to its importance, I must respectfully decline to surrender my forces to you."

* The tents of the 7th infantry were cut up, also, during the bombardment of the fort, to make sand-bags for the protection of the garrison.

tained by the indomitable courage that nerved their hands, and strengthened their hearts. They still feared the worst, but they did not wholly despond. For a few moments all was still,—and then the silence was suddenly broken by the thunder of heavy artillery. Each man sprang to his feet, and for an instant held his breath. Boom!—boom!—those low, deep echoes were repeated and prolonged in the distance. The sound could not be mistaken—General Taylor was on the road to rescue them—the bronzed countenances of that band were lit up by a smile of joy, and their glad hurrah rang loud and clear down the valley of the Rio Grande.

On the 6th of May, a body of recruits for General Taylor's army arrived at Point Isabel. The garrison of the fort at the dépôt was strengthened by the addition of this detachment; and having completed his preparations, General Taylor left the Point on the afternoon of the succeeding day, with a force of about 2,300 men, accompanied by a large wagon train containing his ammunition and supplies. Occasional guns were heard in the direction of Matamoras, which assured him that everything was right in that quarter. It was his determination to fight the enemy, if they offered him battle,* and his intentions were communicated to the army. On the night of the 7th, his forces bivouacked about seven miles from Point Isabel. The march was resumed on the following morning, and continued until about noon, when his cavalry advance reported that the Mexican army were drawn up in front, near the water hole of PALO ALTO.

* "If the enemy oppose my march, in whatever force, I shall fight him."—Letter of General Taylor to the adjutant general, May 7th, 1846.

The Mexican position was admirably chosen. Their column was over a mile in length. In front was the open prairie, flanked on either hand by small pools of fresh water, and surrounded by groves of dwarfish trees,* clumps of chaparral, and thickets of prickly pear. Their left, consisting of a heavy force of cavalry, commanded by General Torrejon, occupied the road, resting on the chaparral in the rear, while to the right extended their long lines of infantry, with an occasional party of lancers. The artillery, twelve pieces in number, was posted in the intervals, under the direction of General Requena. General Ampudia acted as second in command to Arista. The array presented by his forces was splendid and striking; the day was bright and clear; and a slight breeze rustled among the leaves, and gently lifted the standards and guidons beneath which they were marshalled for the fight.

On reaching the water, General Taylor ordered a halt to refresh his men, who were thirsty and fatigued, though anxious to be led forward to the attack. Having filled their canteens, the troops were formed in line of battle. The right wing, commanded by Colonel Twiggs, consisted of the 5th infantry, Lieutenant Colonel McIntosh; Major Ringgold's light artillery; 3rd infantry, Captain Morris; two eighteen pounders in command of Lieutenant Churchill; and 4th infantry, Major Allen—the 3rd and 4th regiments, composing the third brigade, were commanded by Lieutenant Colonel Garland. The two squadrons of dragoons, under Captains Ker and May, were also posted on the right. The left was composed of the battalion of artillery, Lieutenant Colonel Childs; Captain Duncan's light artillery; and the 8th infantry, Captain Montgomery—

* This species of tree is called "Palo Alto."

GENERAL TAYLOR AT THE BATTLE OF PALO ALTO
May 8th, 1846.

all forming the first brigade, and commanded by Lieutenant Colonel Belknap. The wagon train was strongly parked near the water in rear of the right wing, under the direction of Captains Crossman and Myers, and protected by Captain Ker's squadron.

At two o'clock the army took up the march by heads of columns, all moving with the utmost regularity and promptitude, and the stillness broken only by their measured tread, the firm tones of command, the heavy tramp of cavalry, the rumbling wheels of the artillery, and the shrill notes of martial music. While they were advancing, Lieutenant Blake, of the topographical engineers, volunteered a reconnaissance, which he executed in the most daring manner, to the admiration of all who beheld it. Approaching to within rifle shot of the enemy's line, he dismounted, and coolly surveyed their position with his spy-glass. He then remounted, and galloped along the whole line, discovering the artillery, which had been previously masked by the tall grass of the prairie, and estimating the number of their cavalry and infantry with singular accuracy.*

General Taylor halted his columns, and deployed them into line, within seven hundred yards of the enemy, whose artillery began to pour forth its warlike music. Their guns were by no means skilfully served; the balls almost invariably bounced over the heads of the Americans, and ricocheted along the plain in the rear, or ploughed deep furrows in the prairie, and filled the air with clouds of dust. On both sides the battle was mainly confined to the artillery. The guns of Ringgold, Churchill, and Duncan, were finely managed.

* The career of this officer was brief indeed. He accidentally shot himself with one of his pistols on the morning of the 9th of May, and died before night.

For two hours the roar was almost deafening. Whole columns of the enemy were swept away, as if by the breath of the tornado. The American infantry exhibited the highest proof of soldiership, in remaining inactive under a severe fire, yet ready at any moment to protect the artillery from a charge of cavalry. The Mexican lancers grew impatient, and demanded that some movement should be made to check the fire committing such dreadful havoc among them, or that they should be allowed to retire. General Torrejon led them to the charge on the right flank, but Colonel Twiggs promptly met it with the 5th infantry, Captain Walker's rangers, and a section of Ringgold's artillery, under Lieutenant Ridgely. They could not withstand the iron torrent poured upon them, and retreated in confusion. Colonel Montero rallied a part of the force, and reformed them; but his advance was soon checked by the 3rd infantry. Meanwhile, the dry grass of the prairie had burst into a blaze, and dark, dense clouds of smoke almost shut out the light of day, and hung in heavy festoons over the combatants. The enemy's fire now slackened, and they fell back on the left nearer to the chaparral in their rear.

The firing of both armies ceased for nearly an hour, and it was then resumed by the Americans, with the same terrible effect before witnessed. General Taylor had been steadily gaining ground, and the eighteen-pounders occupied the position formerly held by the Mexican cavalry. The two lines were nearly parallel, when the battle was renewed by incessant showers of balls thrown from the American batteries. The Mexican fire was concentrated, for a few moments, on the light battery of the right wing, and the eighteen-pound-

MAJOR RINGGOLD.

ers. Major Ringgold* was mortally wounded, while directing his pieces, and Captain Page, of the 4th infantry, which had been ordered to the support of Churchill's guns, also received a severe wound, under which he lingered for several weeks, but finally expired. The artillery companies, under Lieutenant Colonel Childs, were afterwards ordered up to defend the eighteen-pounders, which was bravely done. The battalion was formed in square to receive the charge of cavalry; but the advancing squadrons were scattered by a deadly discharge of canister from the guns. A brisk fire of small arms was then opened on the square, which was silenced by a well-directed volley.

Several attempts were made, in the meantime, to turn the left flank, but foiled by the vigilance of Lieutenant Colonel Belknap, with the 8th infantry, the light battery, and the dragoons. Protected by the smoke, Captain Duncan dashed upon a column, before they were aware of his approach, and delivered a raking fire that drove them from the field with immense loss. About half an hour before sunset, Captain May made an attempt to charge the left flank of the enemy, but was forced to desist on account of the inadequacy of his force.

Darkness at length separated the contending armies. The enemy retired into the adjoining chaparral, and during the night continued their retreat to a more favorable position, still further in the rear. They found it entirely useless to attempt a contest in the open plain.

* Major Ringgold will long be remembered by the army and the country, for his accomplishments as an officer. The light artillery, now acknowledged to be one of the most efficient arms of the service, was introduced, and brought to its high state of perfection, mainly through his instrumentality.

Their artillery was shown to be ineffective against the better-directed fire of the American batteries, and every attempt to outflank General Taylor's little army, although their force consisted of 6,000 men, was met by skilful manœuvering. If a demonstration was made on the American right, that wing half-wheeled to the left by regiments, and marched by its right flank upon a point a little beyond the enemy's left; if on the left, that wing half-wheeled to the right, and marched by its left flank on a point beyond the enemy's right. When the Mexican cavalry, availing themselves of the open spaces produced by these movements, prepared to charge, at the instant the word was given to form by companies, right and left, into line, and barriers of glittering steel were at once presented to check their progress.

The American loss in the battle of the 8th was ten killed, including the two officers, and forty-four wounded. That of the enemy was near one hundred and fifty killed, and three hundred wounded.* Worn out and overcome with fatigue, General Taylor's gallant army lay down upon the field where their courage had been so severely tested, while the dragoons kept watch around them, to think over the events of the day, and what the morrow might bring forth, and, perhaps, to dream of their far-off homes, and of those who were near and dear. The night was serene and beautiful; the early moon shed its mellow light over the scene; but that dark pall of smoke still hung above the battle-field.

Early in the morning of the 9th, General Taylor ordered his command under arms, and called a council of war to decide upon the course it was proper to pur-

* In his official dispatch, Arista set down his total loss at 252.

sue. Differences of opinion prevailed; some being in favor of returning to the Point; others thinking it best to intrench themselves in their position; and others still, recommending the resumption of the march in the direction of Matamoras. General Taylor reconciled all the differences, and closed the council, with the emphatic declaration that he would be opposite Matamoras before night, if he lived!

Arista had not been discouraged by his defeat on the 8th, and was determined to try his fortunes in a second engagement. About midway between the battle-ground at Palo Alto and the Rio Grande, and in the centre of the dense forest of chaparral extending from one point to the other, a distance of full seven miles, the road crosses a semi-circular ravine, with the opening towards Point Isabel, on an elevated ridge. Here it was decided to make another stand. Embankments were thrown up nearly breast high, and the infantry ranged in two lines, one under the front bank of the ravine, and the other behind the wall of chaparral on the opposite side. A strong battery was planted in the road, in the centre of the front line, and two smaller batteries on either side of the ridge, but on the rising ground in the rear. These were supported by veteran infantry regiments, and the Tampico battalion, a brave and well-appointed corps. Another battery was stationed on the right wing of the front line. During the night, and in the morning, Arista had ordered up reinforcements, until his effective strength equalled, if it did not exceed, that of the previous day. The nature of the ground, however, deprived him of the assistance of his cavalry in a great measure; but this was more than counterbalanced by the strength of his position, surrounded, as it was, by almost impervious thickets, and the main road, the only open space, completely covered by his cannon. Such were the dispositions made by the Mexican general at the RESACA DE LA PALMA,* for the reception of the American army on the road to the relief of the garrison opposite Matamoras.

General Taylor commenced his march about midday on the 9th, and on arriving at the edge of the chaparral, learned that the enemy were in force upon the road in his front. The supply train was secured at its former position, and protected by the battalion of artillery, except the light companies, under Lieutenant Colonel Childs, and the two eighteen-pounders of Lieutenant Churchill, with two twelve-pounders which had not been in the action of the 8th. The wounded officers and men were at the same time sent back to Point Isabel. Captain McCall was then detached with the light companies to feel the enemy. While moving along, he was suddenly fired upon by a masked battery, and lost several of his men. Having reconnoitred the enemy's position, he fell back within reach of support, and sent word to General Taylor.

Lieutenant Ridgely, who had succeeded to the command of Major Ringgold's battery, was now ordered to move forward, supported by the light companies. The 5th infantry and one battalion of the 4th were thrown into the forest on the left, and the 3rd regiment and the other battalion of the 4th on the right, with orders to support the battery, and engage the Mexican infantry. Lieutenant Ridgely advanced at full speed, and immediately opened his fire. The Mexican batteries saluted him, in turn, with a constant roar, which continued for nearly an hour. Most of their balls flew over the heads of his men, otherwise they must have been lite-

* The dry river, or ravine, of the Palm.

rally cut to pieces. The Mexican infantry gave way before the severe fire of musketry from the American line, but so long as their batteries continued to play, the advantage gained could not be improved. But one resource was left. Captain May was ordered up with his squadron of dragoons, and directed by General Taylor to charge the battery in the road. Ranging his men in column of fours, the captain gave the word to follow, and away they went with the speed of the wind. Halting a moment, while Lieutenant Ridgely drew the enemy's fire, they dashed on again, clearing the breastwork, and overturning the gunners at their posts, by the resistless impetuosity of their charge. The work was done, but the loss was severe. One officer, (Lieutenant Inge,) and nine men of the squadron, with eighteen horses, were killed, and ten men, and the same number of horses, severely wounded. When Captain May reined in his steed on the opposite side of the ravine, but six of his men were within call, the remainder having been either killed, or unhorsed, or separated in the confusion of the melée; with these he turned and captured the Mexican artillery, taking General La Vega prisoner, who had vainly endeavored to rally his men to the defence of their guns.

At the same time with the charge of the dragoons, the American infantry advanced towards the ravine, and after a series of desperate hand-to-hand encounters, in which Lieutenant Colonels Belknap and McIntosh,*

* Colonel Belknap was at the head of the 8th infantry, and, in the thickest of the fight, seized a Mexican standard with which he waved his men on to the charge. The flag was soon after carried away by a ball, but he continued to press on with the staff still in his hand. Colonel McIntosh was attacked by a large body of Mexican lancers and infantry, in the midst of the chaparral. His horse fell dead beneath him, and he was also thrown to the earth, and pinned down by a bay-

Captains Morris, Montgomery, Buchanan, and Barbour, particularly distinguished themselves, the enemy were completely defeated. The Mexican lancers were brought up, and attempted to stem the victorious Americans, now bearing every thing before them, but it was all in vain. The 5th infantry drove off the artillerists, who had returned to the guns silenced by Captain May, and the 4th captured Arista's camp, with his splendid pavilion, his official correspondence and dispatches, the military chest of the army, and large quantities of plate. The Tampico battalion was the last to quit the field, but they were routed, and their tri-colored standard, which they had so bravely defended, became the prize of the victors. Among the spoils were eight pieces of artillery, several colors and standards, five hundred pack-saddles; stands of small arms, ammunition-boxes and cartridges, without number; and, what was equally welcome to the American soldiers, an ample supper, which the Mexican cooks had provided in anticipation of the victory they expected to achieve.

The defeat was total. The battalion of artillery, Captain Duncan's battery, and the dragoons, pursued the retreating columns of the enemy to the banks of the Rio Grande. Numbers of the fugitives were cut down in their flight, and when they reached the river, it was but to experience the cruelty and ingratitude of their countrymen. The means provided for the crossing were totally inadequate, and when the flats were filled

onet, which entered his mouth and came out behind his ear. Seizing the weapon with one hand, he raised his sword with the other to cut down his antagonists. He was then fastened more securely to the ground by two additional bayonets, one passing through his arm, and the other through his hip. From this position he was fortunately rescued, and survived his wounds, terrrible and severe as they were, but to fall on another glorious field.

N. ORR & RICHARDSON. N. Y.

GENERAL TAYLOR AT THE BATTLE OF RESACA DE LA PALMA

May 9th, 1846.

with the infantry, the lancers charged down upon them, and took the places of the occupants, who were driven over into the river, and drowned. The loss sustained by the Mexican army on this occasion must have been great—probably not less than five hundred in killed and wounded. A number of prisoners were also taken by the Americans, and among them were fourteen officers. General Taylor's loss was thirty-nine killed and eighty-three wounded.

On the evening of the 8th of May, the long and anxious suspense, in which the American garrison opposite Matamoras remained during the battle at Palo Alto, was terminated by the arrival of a Mexican fugitive, from whom they learned the particulars of the conflict. They continued to fire their eighteen-pounders at intervals, to inform General Taylor that all was still well with them. The Mexican batteries again opened on the morning of the 9th, and kept up their fire until the cannonading at Resaca de la Palma was heard, when they suddenly ceased, having continued the bombardment for upwards of one hundred and sixty hours. The garrison listened breathlessly to the roar of the artillery, and when it paused they well knew a charge had been made. In a short time the flying Mexicans came in sight, followed by the victors of the field, whose appearance was hailed with loud and hearty cheers from the garrison. Their heavy guns were now turned upon the Mexicans, and aided to complete the rout and overthrow.

In a single week, the proud array with which Arista had crossed the Rio Grande, boasting of his ability to drive General Taylor from his position, and to capture his military stores and armament, had melted away like snow beneath the rays of a summer's sun. The inhabitants of Matamoras had seen their army go forth to battle, confident that they should witness their return with the trophies of victory. The triumphal festival was in readiness, and wreaths and decorations prepared in honor of the deeds of gallantry and daring which fancy pictured to their view. The tidings from Palo Alto and Resaca de la Palma dissolved all their bright hopes and expectations, and filled their hearts with sadness and sorrow. Confusion and alarm usurped the places of merriment and festivity. Numbers of the citizens retired into the country with their effects, and those who were left behind awaited the capture of the city, which they anticipated with fear and anxiety, but were powerless to prevent.

Had General Taylor been supplied with the requisite means for crossing the river, his army might have bivouacked in the plaza of Matamoras, on the night after the battle at Resaca de la Palma. He had requested the government to furnish him with a ponton train several months previous, but this had been neglected, and he was therefore obliged to remain inactive for several days.

But the victories achieved by General Taylor and his army were not without their good results. Besides effecting the complete expulsion of the Mexican forces from the territory north of the Rio Grande, and convincing the world that American valor and intrepidity did not exist only in name, they served to remove many unfounded, but long-cherished prejudices, which existed at home, and to pave the way for the brilliant campaign that followed. The army had been looked upon by many as an unnecessary organization—the soldiers were said to be inefficient, and the officers better fitted to grace the *salons* of fashion and pleasure, than to meet the stern realities of the battle-field. The military school at West Point had also received its portion of censure, and there were those who termed it a nursery for carpet-knights, instead of warriors. But how soon were these errors dispelled when the day of trial came, and that little band on the Rio Grande were seen fighting their way, inch by inch, and step by step, over coming every obstacle, as if moved by one mind, and animated by one impulse!—how soon did the American people learn to respect and admire the genius and skill of the brave men who were instructed on the banks of the Hudson, and imbued with the revolutionary spirit still lingering around the scenes where they were nurtured!

It was fortunate for General Taylor, fortunate for the country, that the army under his orders was composed of regulars alone, who knew no such word as "fail!" Volunteers might have fought as well—their bravery has been too often tested to be doubted now—but had they faltered, what might have been the result?—and where the spirit of emulation that cheered and encouraged the citizen soldiers, who fought at Monterey and Buena Vista, at Cerro Gordo and Contreras?

On the 10th of May, the Americans buried their dead, and an exchange of prisoners was effected, by means of which Captain Thornton and his command were recovered. In honor of its brave defender, the field-work opposite Matamoras was called Fort Brown; and the name of Fort Polk was given to the defences at Point Isabel. General Taylor, accompanied by a small escort, rode over to the Point in perfect security on the 11th, to meet Commodore Conner, who had left Vera Cruz with his squadron, on receiving the information that the Mexican troops were concentrating at Matamoras, and had now anchored off the Rio Grande, with the intention of rendering such assistance to the army as might be in his power. A combined expedition with the naval and land forces against the Mexican towns on the river was determined on, and five hundred sailors and marines were landed and organized under the command of Captain Gregory. The movements of some of the old "salts" are stated to have been rather awkward at the first, but they soon learned to manœuvre with the accuracy and precision of landsmen.

It was reported, on the 13th instant, that the Mexicans were collecting a large force at Burrita, a small town on the southern shore of the Rio Grande, situate between Matamoras and the Gulf. An expedition was arranged for the capture of the town, but in consequence of the roughness of the bar, occasioned by the unfavorable weather, the boats from the squadron were unable to enter the river until the 15th. On the 14th General Taylor returned to Fort Brown with over six hundred men, mostly volunteers from Louisiana and Alabama, who had just arrived, a train of artillery and mortars, and two hundred and fifty wagons containing army stores. Lieutenant Colonel Wilson crossed the river on the 15th with a battalion of the 1st infantry and three companies of volunteers, and took possession of Burrita without encountering any resistance.

General Taylor was unable to complete his preparations for the capture of Matamoras until the 17th of May. His arrangements having been perfected in the morning of that day, Colonel Twiggs was ordered to cross above the town with the advance, consisting of the light companies and regular and volunteer cavalry, to be followed by the main body of the army, while Lieutenant Colonel Wilson was directed to move up the river from Burrita, and thus make a diversion in their favor. Batteries were also set and mortars planted, for the purpose of bombarding the city, if any attempt should be made to defend it. Before the army had commenced its march up the river, General Taylor was waited upon by General Requena, who had been authorized by General Arista to treat for an armistice until the two governments should finally settle the questions in dispute. This was refused by General Taylor, inasmuch as he had proposed an armistice to General Ampudia, which had not been accepted, and now that hostilities had been provoked by the Mexicans, nothing would content him but the surrender of Matamoras, though the Mexican army would be permitted to retire, but not to take the public property with them. A reply to the answer given to General Requena was promised in the afternoon, but, as it did not come, General Taylor renewed his orders for crossing the river, which were carried into effect. It afterwards appeared that the proposition was only made to gain time. Arista left Matamoras during the night of the 17th, with his forces, and on the following day General Taylor took possession of the town without molestation.

The Mexican citizens remaining in Matamoras were evidently inclined to look upon the Americans with fear and distrust. But a rigid system of police was established by the direction of Colonel Twiggs, who had been appointed governor of the city, and order and regularity took the place of the confusion which had prevailed. The inhabitants did not regard the change with indifference, and became at once more friendly and well disposed. Several hundred wounded Mexicans were found in Matamoras, and a quantity of military stores, which had been secreted by the enemy before leaving the city. Lieutenant Colonel Garland was dispatched with a body of cavalry, upon the road taken by the Mexican army, with orders to harass their rear. He pursued their route for sixty miles, when he returned, on account of the scarcity of water and the unfitness of his horses to proceed further, having had a slight skirmish with a small party which he captured. After establishing his army in comfortable quarters at Matamoras, General Taylor sent out a party of the Texan rangers, under Captain McCulloch, who entered Reinosa, Camargo, Mier, and Reveilla, without opposition.

LIEUT. COLONEL FREMONT.

CHAPTER III.

CALIFORNIA AND NEW MEXICO.

Frémont's Expedition—Jealousy of the Mexican Authorities—Affair at Sonoma—Declaration of Independence—The Pacific Squadron—Capture of all the prominent points in the Californias—March of the Army of the West from Fort Leavenworth to Santa Fé—Conquest of New Mexico—Departure of General Kearny for California—Counter Revolution—Battle of San Pascual—Passage of the San Gabriel—Ciudad de los Angelos—Arrival of Troops, and complete occupation of the Country.

The conquest of New Mexico and the Californias, though bloodless in comparison with the military operations conducted in other quarters of the Mexican republic, and presenting but few incidents likely to be commemorated "in story and in song," is of too much consequence, both with reference to the geographical extent of the territory overrun, and the commercial advantages which it has been supposed would be secured by its acquisition, to be entirely lost sight of amid the more brilliant achievements of the war. There were no powerful armies in the field—there were few victories won—few trophies gained; but our officers, both of the army and the navy, discharged the duties they were required to perform, faithfully and well, and therefore deserve to be commended. But little resistance was offered to their movements, yet whenever encountered, it was promptly met, and as promptly put down. In addition to the other important points on the Pacific coast, the harbor of San Francisco, asserted by many of the ablest and most experienced navigators, to be the best and the safest on the North American continent,* now belongs to the United States. Its value as a dépôt of refreshments and supplies for American whalemen, and its importance in connection with the China and East India trade, can scarcely be over estimated. In the progress of time it must become to our commerce with the Asiatic governments, what the city of New York now is to that with the countries lying along the Mediterranean, and the eastern shore of the Atlantic.

Previous to the war, the trade between Santa Fé and the United States, principally carried on through the city of St. Louis, amounted annually to nearly two millions of dollars. The profits realized by the American citizens, whose active enterprise had established and fostered this inland commerce, early excited the envy of the Mexican government, and on the 23rd of September, 1843, a decree was issued forbidding foreigners, after six months from the date of its promulgation, from selling by retail any goods within the confines of Mexico. One of the objects of this decree was, to cut off the commerce between the United States and the province of New Mexico, and compel the latter to become tributary to the towns on the Gulf, or to secure to the Mexicans themselves the entire monopoly of the retail trade. It also afforded the means of gratifying the cupidity of the officers appointed in New Mexico by the central government, and served as a cloak for imposition and extortion. Evasions of the ordinance were invited and connived at, only to be followed by the most arbitrary exactions. To such an

* See Balbi's Apégé de Géographie.

extent was this carried by Manuel Armijo, the governor of New Mexico, prior to and at the time of the commencement of the war, that, in repeated instances, a duty of five hundred dollars was collected on each wagon load of goods belonging to American traders. The permanent acquisition of this province will put an end to similar violations of international comity, and leave the trade free to seek its natural channel, unchecked and unrestrained.

In the fall of 1845, Captain John C. Frémont,* of the corps of Topographical Engineers, was dispatched by the War Department, with a small party of men, armed and equipped for hunting, and for protecting themselves against the Indians, upon an exploring tour beyond the Rocky Mountains, the object of which was to discover, if possible, a new and shorter route to the mouth of the Columbia River. In order to accomplish his purpose, he found it necessary to enter the territory of California, early in the winter of 1846. On the 29th of January he halted his party about one hundred miles from Monterey, and proceeded alone to that city, to explain the object of his visit, and to secure permission to remain during the winter in the valley of the San Joaquim. General de Castro, the military commandant, complained, at first, of the hostile appearance of the party; but, on being informed by Captain Frémont of his rank, and of the peaceful object of his visit, the desired permission was granted, apparently with great cordiality. The captain immediately returned and brought his men nearer to the city, when he was apprised by Mr. Larkin, the American Consul, that Gen-

* This officer had been previously distinguished for his scientific discoveries, and his successful explorations of the country in the vicinity of the Rocky Mountains.

eral de Castro was raising a large force to attack him He had but sixty-two men, and was ill prepared to encounter a body of troops superior to his own, and especially so for the reason that nothing of the kind had been anticipated.

Surprised and astonished at the treachery of the Mexican officer, and conscious that an attack had not been provoked on his part, either by his acts or his in tentions, Captain Frémont took a position about thirty miles from Monterey, on the summit of a mountain range overlooking the town, where he intrenched himself, and raised the American flag, determined, in self-defence, to resist every attempt to dislodge him. De Castro did not approach within attacking distance, but remained in the vicinity for several days, apparently threatening a movement on the position occupied by the little band. No attack having been made, Captain Frémont marched out with the intention of resuming his journey towards Oregon, on the 10th day of March. Supposing that there was no more cause for alarm, he discharged a number of his party, who wished to remain in the country, and refused to receive others in their stead, on account of his desire carefully to avoid arousing the prejudices or apprehensions of the Mexican authorities. Continuing his march by slow degrees, with de Castro following in his rear, accompanied by a force of near five hundred men; and the hostile Indians, excited by the latter, constantly hovering in his neighborhood, and harassing his command; he reached the Great Tlamath Lake, in the territory of Oregon, on the 15th of May. The deep snow still lin gering on the summits of the Sierra Nevada, obstructed his further progress, and the Tlamath Indians continued to annoy him. While here a courier arrived, who had been sent forward to say that Mr. Gillespie and five men were endeavoring to overtake him. Knowing the treacherous character of the savages in the vicinity, he accompanied the courier on his return, with ten men. The distance to be travelled was sixty miles, and he was unable to come up with the party in one day. His men were fatigued and wearied with the ride, and failed to keep guard during the night. This neglect well nigh proved destructive to the whole band. A number of Tlamath warriors, whom they had supplied but a few days before with tobacco and provisions, stole suddenly upon their encampment, and killed three of the men, and wounded a friendly Delaware. The savages were finally repulsed, and Captain Frémont soon after returned to the Bay of San Francisco, with his whole party. While on his way, he had several encounters with the Indians, in which both he and his men behaved with great gallantry.

While yet hesitating what course to adopt, Captain Frémont was informed that General de Castro was rapidly approaching, with the design of cutting off his party, and destroying or driving from the country the American settlers in the valley of the Sacramento.* The security of his men, and of the inhabitants who had once been his countrymen, was now placed in extreme jeopardy, and it became necessary that prompt and decided measures should be instantly adopted. The permanent safety of the settlers appeared to depend, not merely on the defeat of de Castro, but on the

* Captain Frémont was charged by the Mexican authorities with instigating the American settlers to revolt. When he occupied his intrenched position overlooking Monterey, the settlers manifested a disposition to take part with him against de Castro, and probably would have done so had he been attacked. This appears to have been the only foundation for the charge.

total overthrow of the Mexican authority, and the establishment of an independent government in California. On the 6th of June, 1846, Captain (now Lieutenant Colonel) Frémont* determined to accomplish these objects. Boldly turning on his pursuers, by a series of rapid movements, conceived and executed with equal daring and skill, he soon drove the Mexican general from that portion of the territory north of the Bay of San Francisco. On the 11th of June, a party of de Castro's men, consisting of one officer and fourteen privates, with two hundred horses, were surprised and captured by twelve of Lieutenant Colonel Frémont's command. At daybreak on the 15th instant, the military post at Sonoma was taken, with nine brass cannon, two hundred and fifty stand of arms, a quantity of ammunition, and a number of prisoners, among whom were Colonel Vallejo and several other officers. Leaving a garrison of twelve men to defend the post, Lieutenant Colonel Frémont proceeded to the Rio de los Americanos, a branch of the Sacramento, to procure assistance from the American settlers. Soon after he reached there, an express arrived with the information that de Castro was preparing to cross the bay and attack the post. This intelligence was received in the afternoon of the 23rd of June, and he immediately returned with ninety mounted riflemen, whom he had collected in the valley. By riding night and day, they traversed the intervening distance of eighty miles before two o'clock on the morning of the 25th. The enemy had not yet made their appearance. A party of twenty men were sent out to reconnoitre, and fell in with the vanguard of de Castro's force, consisting

* He was appointed a Lieutenant Colonel in the regiment of mounted riflemen, on the 27th of May, 1846.

of seventy dragoons, who had just crossed the bay. A smart skirmish ensued, which resulted in the defeat of the Mexicans, with the loss of five men in killed and wounded. Frémont's party were uninjured. The Mexican commander, De la Torre, escaped with his men, losing his transport boats and his artillery, the latter being spiked.

Having succeeded in driving the Mexicans from the northern shore of the bay, Lieutenant Colonel Frémont returned to Sonoma on the 4th of July. On the following day he collected the Americans together, and, after explaining the condition of things in the territory, advised an immediate declaration of their independence. This was accordingly made, and he was selected to assume the chief direction of affairs. In the meantime de Castro had established himself at Santa Clara, an intrenched post on the south side of the bay, with four hundred men and two pieces of field artillery. An attack on his position was decided on. In order to reach Santa Clara, it was necessary to make a circuit of upwards of one hundred miles. Lieutenant Colonel Frémont commenced his march on the 6th of July, with one hundred and sixty mounted riflemen, and in three days reached the American settlements on the fork of the Sacramento. Here he learned that de Castro had abandoned Santa Clara, and was retiring to Ciudad de los Angelos,* the place of residence of the governor-general of the Californias, and about four hundred miles south of San Francisco. Every thing was prepared for continuing the pursuit, when the information was received that the war had been commenced, and that Commodore Sloat had taken the ports on the Pacific. The American flag was now

* City of the Angels.

substituted for the flag of independence, and the party started to overtake de Castro. They captured St. Johns on the 18th of July, a few hours previous to the arrival of Purser Fauntleroy, who had been sent by Commodore John D. Sloat to hoist the flag of the United States at the mission, and to recover some cannon and munitions of war which had been buried by the enemy. In company with the naval forces, Lieutenant Colonel Frémont returned to Monterey on the 19th instant.

While lying off Mazatlan, on the 7th of June, Commodore Sloat, then in command of the Pacific squadron, was informed that the Mexican troops had crossed the Rio Grande and attacked General Taylor's army, and that the squadron under Commodore Conner was then blockading the Mexican ports in the Gulf. In accordance with instructions previously issued,* he sailed for the coast of California, to commence offensive operations, on the 8th instant, in the frigate Savannah. He arrived off Monterey on the 2nd of July, and on the 7th summoned the town to surrender. A definite answer was not returned to his summons; whereupon a body of marines and sailors were landed, in order to capture the place. No resistance was offered; and the American flag was raised in the town without opposition. On the 8th, Commander Montgomery, of the sloop of war Portsmouth, took possession of San Francisco and the adjoining country, in the name of the government of the United States. Commodore Robert F. Stockton arrived at Monterey, in the frigate Congress, on the 15th of July, and on the 23rd was ordered to duty on shore.

* The instructions to Commodore Sloat were issued on the 24th of June, 1845, but did not reach him until several months afterwards.

On his arrival at Monterey, Lieutenant Colonel Frémont informed Commodore Sloat of his proceedings, and of his desire to capture the force under de Castro. The commodore declined to aid him in the enterprise, as he was about to return to the United States, in consequence of his enfeebled health; but when the authority on shore was intrusted to Commodore Stockton, he entered into the project at once, and gave it a most hearty and efficient support. A battalion of mounted riflemen, consisting mainly of the American settlers in California, was immediately formed, and the command given to Lieutenant Colonel Frémont, with the rank of major—the fact of his promotion being still unknown in California. This force was organized for the purpose of co-operating with the marines and sailors employed on the land under the orders of Commodore Stockton.

It was understood, at this time, that Pio Pico, the Governor of California, and General de Castro, the military commandant, were near Ciudad de los Angelos, at the head of seven hundred cavalry, well mounted, and brave and expert horsemen.* A threatening proclamation had been issued by the governor, denouncing

* The force under Pico and de Castro was chiefly composed of armed Californians, under Mexican leaders. The former are celebrated for their skilful horsemanship, and their dexterity in the use of the lance. Their horses are small, but remarkably fleet, easily trained, and capable of great endurance. In March, 1847, Lieutenant Colonel Frémont, with two companions, travelled on horseback, from Ciudad de los Angelos, to Monterey, and returned again immediately, at the rate of one hundred and twenty-five miles in a day. Each of the party had three horses, which were in turn, under the saddle. The six loose horses ran ahead, without bridle or halter, and were caught with the lasso when required. At the end of the journey the horses were apparently as fresh as ever. The riders, also, it may be added, showed themselves capable of enduring extraordinary hardship and fatigue without difficulty.

the foreigners in the territory, and expressing his deter mination to drive them forthwith from the soil of Cali fornia. On the 25th of July, the sloop of war Cyane, Captain Mervine, sailed from Monterey, with Lieutenant Colonel Frémont and his battalion, for San Diego, to intercept the retreat of General de Castro, while Commodore Stockton was to land at San Pedro, and attack him in front. Commodore Sloat gave up the entire command of the squadron to Commodore Stockton, on the 29th, and returned home. The latter soon completed his arrangements for the contemplated attack on de Castro. He left Monterey on the 1st of August, in the Congress, and arrived at San Pedro, about twenty-eight miles from Ciudad de los Angelos, on the 6th; having stopped at Santa Barbara on the way, and taken possession of the place. In the meantime Lieutenant Colonel Frémont had reached San Diego, and landed with his battalion, but experienced great difficulty in procuring horses. He succeeded, at length, in mounting his men, and pushed forward in the direction of the enemy, who were encamped on the Misa, with seven pieces of artillery.

Commodore Stockton landed at San Pedro, with a force of three hundred and sixty sailors and marines, established a camp, and commenced drilling and instructing his men. Not being provided with field artillery, he procured two or three pieces of small ordnance from a merchant ship, and mounted them on cart-wheels, together with an eighteen-pounder carronade taken from his own ship. While engaged in making these preparations, two commissioners came from the camp of de Castro, with a flag of truce, to enter into negotiations. The gallant commodore cheerfully listened to their propositions; but when informed that, as a preliminary step to negotiation, he must pledge himself to remain where he was with his forces, he instantly closed the conference, and informed the commissioners that this was out of the question, and that he "would either take the country, or be whipped out of it!" One of the commissioners returned, in a few days, with a letter from General de Castro, written in the most extravagant language, and proclaiming his determination to defend the territory to the last. The commodore declined making any reply to the communication, but sent orders to Lieutenant Colonel Frémont to join him on the route, and commenced his march. Notwithstanding his boastful declarations, the Mexican general wisely concluded not to risk an engagement with the force advancing against him; his cannon were buried; his men dispersed; and Governor Pio Pico and himself fled to Sonora for safety.

The commodore was joined on his march by Lieutenant Colonel Frémont, with his battalion of volunteer riflemen, numbering one hundred and twenty men. The retreat of the enemy was so precipitate that they could not overtake them, and they entered Ciudad de los Angelos, and took possession of the government house, without opposition. Parties of the riflemen were sent out to capture the Mexican officers who had headed the Californians.* A number of them were taken, but were allowed to go at large on their parole. Commodore Stockton soon after issued his proclamation, declaring the territory of California to be a part of the United States, by right of conquest, and announcing himself as the governor thereof. Lieutenant

* The inhabitants of California are principally of Indian, or mixed descent, and military officers were sent from Mexico to take command of them.

Colonel Frémont was appointed military commandant of the territory; laws and regulations were established, and officers selected to enforce them. In the brief period of sixty days possession had been taken of every important town in the territory, and it was supposed that the conquest was permanently secured.*

From the necessity of the case, the government of the United States relied upon the naval squadron in the Pacific to commence offensive movements in California, on the breaking out of the war. It was foreseen, however, that the presence of a military force would be necessary to secure the possession of the country. Accordingly, a company of artillery was embarked from New York, in August, 1846, and followed, in September, by a regiment of volunteer infantry, under Colonel Stevenson.† On the arrival of these troops, and of General Kearny with such part of his force as could be spared from New Mexico, it was expected that the command on shore would be assumed

* The instructions issued to the officers commanding the Pacific squadron contemplated the establishment of a temporary civil government in California, but did not authorize any political rights to be conferred on the inhabitants; leaving it for the event of the war to determine, whether the jurisdiction thus assumed, as an incident to the conquest, should be permanent.—Letter of the Secretary of the Navy, June 14, 1847.—Special message of President Polk, 2nd session, 29th Congress.

† The regiment of volunteers commanded by Colonel Stevenson, was raised upon the condition that they should be discharged, wherever they might be, at the termination of the war, provided it was in a territory of the United States. Men were selected to compose it, under the instructions of the Secretary of War, who would be likely to remain in Oregon, or in that quarter of the country, in order that the authority of the United States, if the territory of California should be permanently acquired by the terms of a treaty of peace, might be more readily maintained, through the instrumentality, if necessary, of the American settlers.

by the officers of the army, and that the naval squadron would enforce the blockade. Instructions to this effect were issued from the Navy Department, but did not reach the commanding officer of the Pacific squadron until February, 1847.* The company of artillery arrived in California in the same month, and the regiment under Colonel Stevenson in March following.

On the 30th day of June, 1846, General Kearny, who had been assigned to the command of "the Army of the West," left Fort Leavenworth with a force of about 1,000 men, on his march towards New Mexico. Before entering the enemy's territory, he was reinforced by a battalion of Mormon emigrants, on their way to Oregon or California, who were mustered into the service of the United States, and placed under the command of Major Cooke, of the 2nd dragoons. With this and other additions, his army was subsequently increased to near 1,900. The regular dragoons, commanded by Major Sumner, were but two hundred strong; the remainder of the force was composed of volunteers. A large part of the latter, however, were mounted men, and many of them, in addition to their ordinary arms, were provided with knives and revolving pistols. Their artillery consisted of eight long brass six-pounders, and two twelve-pounder howitzers.

Pursuing the military road, the Army of the West crossed the grassy prairies lying between the Missouri and Kansas rivers, and clothed at this season of the year in the richest verdure, and gemmed with countless flowers, of every shape and hue. On the 4th of July they struck the main road leading from Independence to Santa Fé, at Elm Grove, and were soon upon

* See the Proceedings of the Court Martial for the trial of Lieutenant Colonel Frémont.

the Great Prairie, extending to the north and to the south, to the east and to the west, miles on miles, the same monotonous plain, for ages the pasture-ground of the elk and the buffalo, and its solitary echoes woken but rarely by the sound of human voices. Occasionally their path was crossed by a small stream murmuring softly along on its way to mingle its waters with those of the mighty river of the West; and the fresh green foliage of the timber skirting its banks would form a most agreeable contrast to the short dry grass of the intervening waste, broken only here and there by small tufts of bushes, or giving place to sandy barrens, still more cheerless and uninviting. The parties of Indians whom they discovered on the prairie avoided their track, and the buffalo fled at their approach. Their appearance, however, enlivened the scene, and it was a relief even to encounter the habitations of the prairie-dogs, whose burrows teemed with an unnumbered progeny. At sunset they were cheered by the breeze which swept over the plain, refreshing them with its cool breath, after a day of weary travel; but very often when they lay down to rest, the mournful howl of the gray wolf, who roamed about the encampment, was the only lullaby to which they listened.

The army reached the Arkansas on the 19th of July, and continued their march along its northern bank to Bent's fort,* a small post established for trading with the Indians, where they arrived near the close of the month. This was the rendezvous of the different detachments, and large quantities of stores had been sent here to await their arrival. Having refreshed his men

* This post is 574 miles from Fort Leavenworth. It was established by George and Charles Bent, the latter of whom was appointed Governor of New Mexico by General Kearny.

BRIGADIER GENERAL KEARNEY.

by a short halt, and supplied himself with mules to draw the artillery, instead of the horses which were completely worn down in the march, General Kearny proceeded on his route. After leaving the valley of the Arkansas the country became more mountainous. The road lay over the spurs of the Cordilleras, between the head waters of the Cimmaron and Canadian rivers, and those of the Rio Grande. The first range which they crossed was the Raton. The scene presented from its summit is described as being of great sublimity.* To the northwest was Pike's Peak, the highest point of the Rocky Mountains north of the city of Chihuahua; while to the south and west were tall mountain ridges, some covered with evergreens, but most of them mere masses of rock, entirely destitute of wood, here glistening like silver in the sunlight, and there "grim, old, and gray," as the ruins of antiquity. To those who gazed upon them, it was easy to fancy they often saw in the distance the turrets and donjon keep of a feudal castle, with the banners of its lord streaming proudly in the wind from the time-worn battlements; and further on, the tottering spire, the crumbling arch, and broken nave, of some old cathedral fallen to decay.

General Kearny arrived at the Lower Moro, the first Mexican town upon the road to Santa Fé, on the 13th of August, and at the Upper Moro, on the following day. At the latter point there was a fort which had been occupied by a small party of soldiers, who had retired on the approach of the American army. At each village through which he passed, General Kearny directed the alcalde to take the oath of allegiance to

* Journal of Lieut. Emory.

the United States, and assured him and the citizens generally, that their persons, property and religion, would be sacredly respected.

While at the Upper Moro, the scouts sent out by General Kearny reported that the enemy were in force at the Moro Pass, a defile among the mountains about a mile distant from the village. On arriving there his men were drawn up in battle array, and preparations made to dislodge the Mexican forces. Just as the army were advancing, the general was informed that the enemy had retreated to the Pecos Pass, a remarkably strong position still further in the rear. At this place the cañon, or valley, is contracted to a narrow gorge not more than twenty yards wide, through which the road passes on a shelf of rock jutting out from the cliffs, which rise almost perpendicular, several hundred feet high, on each side of the pass. Governor Armijo had collected here between three and four thousand men, with an apparent determination to dispute the passage with the American army. At the top of the ascent he planted his artillery, which raked the road, and were protected by a breastwork of felled trees. The mountain barriers securely guarded his flanks, and the position could only have been taken by a *coup de main.* With resolute defenders it might have been the Thermopylæ of New Mexico; but Armijo and his officers concluded to abandon it without firing a single gun in its defence, and retired in hot haste to Chihuahua. General Kearny passed through the defile, and entered the city of Santa Fé, the capital of New Mexico, on the 18th of August, without encountering the least resistance. Proceeding to the governor's house he took formal possession of the city and province. The American flag was hoisted in the plaza, and a salute of thirteen guns fired in honor of the bloodless conquest which had been achieved.*

On the 23rd of August General Kearny issued his proclamation, declaring the department of New Mexico to be a part of the United States, absolving the inhabitants from their allegiance to the Mexican republic, and claiming them as American citizens. A civil government was organized, and the proper officers appointed.†

The citizens of Santa Fé appeared quite downhearted and dispirited for several days after the arrival of the American army; but General Kearny took every opportunity to pacify them, and adopted the most rigorous measures to prevent the commission of any injury to their persons or property by his troops. Their apprehensions gradually disappeared, and it was not long before it seemed to be a matter of indifference what rulers exercised authority over them, provided they could dispose of their choice Muscatel grapes, their melons and peaches, their corn and red peppers, to good advantage, and be allowed to drink their wine or coffee, and smoke their cigaritos, undisturbed. In order that no excesses or outrages should be committed, and that the efficiency of the army might remain un-

* The whole distance from Fort Leavenworth to Santa Fé, travelled by the American army in six weeks, was 883 miles.

† General Kearny was authorized to establish a temporary civil government in New Mexico, and all his measures designed to promote this object were approved by the government of the United States; but so far as he attempted to confer any political rights of a permanent character, his course was disapproved. His absolving the inhabitants of New Mexico from their allegiance, if it had any effect, simply amounted to a declaration that while the authority of his government was exerted in the province, and they refrained from taking up arms, they would not be treated as enemies.—Letter of the Secretary of War to General Kearny, January 11, 1847.—Special Message of President Polk, 2nd session, 29th Congress.

impaired, the coffee-house keepers were forbidden to sell liquor to the American soldiers, and gaming of every kind was prohibited.* Order and quiet were established, and every thing wore a peaceful and contented aspect.

Early in September General Kearny made a recon naissance down the valley of the Rio Grande, accompanied by 750 men. He passed through San Domingo, Albuquerque and Valencia, as far as Tomac, about one hundred miles below Santa Fé, from whence he returned, without discovering any evidences of a desire to resist his authority. A party of fifty men were soon after sent to the north to bring in some Apache chiefs, with whom a treaty was formed on favorable terms. The conquest of the province having been effected, and tranquillity perfectly restored, General Kearny appointed Charles Bent governor of the territory, and departed for California on the 25th of September, attended by Major Sumner with 300 of the 1st dragoons. Proceeding down the river to Albuquerque he crossed over to the right bank, and continued his way south until the 5th of October, when he met an express sent by Commodore Stockton and Lieutenant Colonel Frémont, who reported that they were already in possession of the Californias, and that the war was ended in that quarter. On receiving this welcome intelligence he directed Major Sumner to return with 200 of the dragoons, reserving the remainder as an escort for him-

* The inhabitants of New Mexico are inveterate gamesters, and passionately devoted to their favorite "monte." As in California, the great majority are the descendants of the ancient Aztec tribes. Those of Spanish descent are comparatively few, yet they treat the Indian population, though more numerous than themselves, rather like serfs than fellow-citizens.

self. Following the valley of the Rio Grande for the distance of two hundred and thirty miles below Santa Fé, he there left the river, and marched westward, by the way of the Copper Mines, to the Rio Gila, where he arrived on the 20th instant. He then proceeded down this stream to its junction with the Colorado of the West, a distance of five hundred miles; halting but two days on the road, at the village of the Peños Indians, to obtain provisions and recruit his horses. His course now lay down the Colorado for forty miles, and thence sixty miles across the southern extremity of the great desert of California.* His long and toilsome march terminated on the 2nd of December, when he entered one of the frontier settlements of the territory. Hearing that a counter-revolution had taken place in the Californias, he dispatched a messenger to Commodore Stockton, with a letter requesting that a party might be sent out to open a communication with him. Without waiting for a reply, he moved forward cautiously, and was met on the 5th instant, about forty

* "This immense plain, the existence of which was until very recently wholly unknown, is situated in the central part of Upper or New California. It is limited on the north by a mass of rocks, which separate it from the head waters of the Lewis river, on the west by an irregular chain of mountains, extending in parallel ridges along the shores of the Pacific ocean, on the east by the western branches of the Colorado, and on the south by the valley of the Colorado. Its area is equal to that of Virginia, and consists of an elevated plateau or table land, flanked on all sides by descents more or less inclined, according to their geological structure. * * * It presents little less than an arid surface, broken at intervals by a few detached mountains, of limited extent, but rising in some instances above the region of perpetual snow. From these mountains small streams flow during the rainy seasons. On reaching the plains, these torrents instantly disappear in the sand, leaving no other trace of their existence than the fragments of rocks and other débris, which are borne down by the currents, and deposited at the bases of the hills."—Re-issue, American Family Magazine, Part 14.

miles from San Diego, by a detachment of California volunteers, and carbineers from the Congress, with a field-piece, under Captain Gillespie, from whom he learned the particulars of the attempted revolution.

Commodore Stockton left Ciudad de los Angelos, with his sailors and marines, on the 2nd of September, and proceeded to San Francisco, at which place he designed to make arrangements for an attack on Mazatlan and Acapulco, in conjunction with Lieutenant Colonel Frémont. The latter joined him on the 12th of October, with 170 men of his battalion, having left Captain Gillespie with a small party in command at the capital. The expedition immediately started; the Commodore sailing with his force for San Pedro, in the Congress; and Lieutenant Colonel Frémont in a vessel chartered for the purpose, intending to land at Santa Barbara.

No sooner had the greater part of the American forces been withdrawn from the vicinity of the capital, than symptoms of a revolt began to be manifested. The inhabitants did not appear willing to acquiesce at once in this sudden change of their government, and the disaffected were encouraged to make resistance by the Mexican officers still in the territory. An appeal to arms was determined on, and a body of the enemy, numbering five or six hundred, took the field under the command of General Flores. Captain Gillespie was besieged in the government house and forced to capitulate, having obtained permission, however, to retire with his men on board the Savannah, then lying off San Pedro. Captain Mervine, in command of the frigate, promptly landed a portion of his crew, and marched towards the capital. He met a party of the enemy with one piece of artillery, a short distance from San Pedro, whom he attacked. Being without artillery, and finding it impossible to capture that of the enemy, on account of the speed of their horses which they attached to the piece whenever a charge was attempted, he returned to the vessel, having lost several men in killed and wounded.

About the time that these insurrectionary movements commenced, an armed Mexican schooner, the Malek Adhel, appeared on the coast, and was captured by the sloop of war Warren. A rising also took place at Santa Barbara, which was put down without difficulty; the enemy appearing to concentrate their forces between San Diego and the capital, with the design of making their principal effort in that quarter.

Lieutenant Colonel Frémont found that he would be unable to mount his command at Santa Barbara, and therefore landed at Monterey. After considerable delay he succeeded in providing horses for his men, and set out towards the capital. In the meantime, Commodore Stockton had left San Pedro, and sailed for San Diego, which he found to be threatened by the enemy. The body of sailors and marines whom he had before employed on shore, and who cheerfully performed the duties of cavalry, infantry and artillery, as occasion required, were landed forthwith, and preparations commenced for re-subjugating the country in an effectual manner. Matters were in this position when General Kearny arrived in the territory.

On his way to join General Kearny, Captain Gillespie learned that there was an armed party of Californians, with a number of extra horses, at San Pascual, about three leagues distant on another road leading to San Diego. Lieutenant Hammond was sent forward with a party in the evening to make a reconnaissance.

He returned at two o'clock in the morning of the 6th of December, and reported that he had discovered the enemy, who had seen but did not pursue him. At break of day the whole force was in motion. Captain Johnston led the advance guard of twelve dragoons mounted on the best horses; then followed fifty dragoons under Captain Moore, most of whom were mounted on the mules which they had ridden from Santa Fe,* Captain Gillespie's volunteers, two mountain howitzers managed by dragoons, and commanded by Lieutenant Davidson; the rest of the troops, including the men from the squadron under Lieutenant Beall and Passed Midshipman Duncan, remained in the rear with the baggage, under the direction of Major Swords.

At the dawn of day they approached the enemy, who were already in the saddle. They proved to be a body of men, about 160 strong, under André Pico, brother of the late governor. Captain Johnston charged furiously upon them with the advance, followed by the remainder of the dragoons. They could not meet the shock, and gave way in a few moments; General Kearny, with Captain Moore and the mounted men, were soon in hot pursuit. The Californians were well mounted, and discovering that a part of the Americans had become separated from their companions, turned like lightning upon them. For five minutes the ground was fiercely contested, the enemy inflicting terrible wounds with their long lances, and displaying no little dexterity and promptness in their manœuvres. On the approach of the remainder of General Kearny's force, they abandoned the field, carrying away most of their dead and wounded,—only six being left behind them.

* The distance travelled from Santa Fé was 1,050 miles.

General Kearny was unable to bring his howitzers into action, in consequence of the mules before them becoming frightened and unmanageable.

The affair at San Pascual was of brief duration, but spirited, and attended with the loss of several valuable officers. Captain Johnston fell at the commencement of the action, and Captain Moore and Lieutenant Hammond were lanced when the enemy turned upon them. General Kearny himself received two severe lance wounds. The total loss was three officers killed, and four wounded; sixteen privates killed, and eleven wounded.

On the following morning General Kearny buried his dead and provided ambulances for the wounded, when the march was resumed. The enemy appeared on the hills in their front, but retired on their approach, to San Bernardo, where they took possession of a hill and seemed inclined to make a stand. The advance drove them from this position, killing and wounding five of their number, without loss to themselves. The situation of his command General Kearny now found to be hazardous in the extreme. A number of them were wounded; they were but ill provided, and surrounded by enemies, evidently watching an opportunity to cut off the whole party. Orders were therefore given to encamp, and an express dispatched to Commodore Stockton for assistance. Lieutenant Gray was sent forward by the Commodore from San Diego, with 215 men, and joined General Kearny on the 11th instant. Thus reinforced the General arrived at San Diego on the next day without again encountering the enemy.

Every thing being in readiness for the movement on Ciudad de los Angelos, which Commodore Stockton had projected, at his request General Kearny asssumed the command of the expedition; the Commodore himself accompanying the troops on their march. The total strength of the force was 500 men, consisting of 60 mounted dragoons under Captain Turner, 50 California volunteers, and the remainder marines and sailors, with a strong battery of artillery. The march was commenced on the 29th of December, and continued without interruption until the 8th of January, 1847, when the enemy appeared in force on the heights which commanded the crossing of the San Gabriel. They numbered 600 mounted men, with four pieces of artillery, under the command of General Flores. A strong party of skirmishers were thrown forward in front of the American line, and the whole force crossed the river, pressing on firmly and steadily under a severe fire, stormed the heights, and drove the enemy from their position, after an action of about an hour and a half. The heavy artillery was pushed in the advance when they began to waver, and completed the rout. A charge upon the American left flank was once attempted, but the enemy were quickly repulsed.

The American forces proceeded towards the capital on the 9th instant, and again met the enemy on the plains of Misa near the city. Their artillery opened, but did not check the advance of the Americans. The fire was returned with spirit. A constant skirmishing was continued for two hours, at the end of which time the enemy made an unsuccessful effort to charge, and finally moved off, carrying with them their killed and wounded. In these two actions the Americans lost but one man killed, and thirteen wounded. The brave tars from the national vessels proved as efficient, during the whole march of one hundred and fifty miles, as their companions who belonged to the army, and vied with them in the display of courage and endurance.

The Americans entered the capital of the Californias on the 10th of January, and on the 13th the leaders of the revolt capitulated at Couenga to Lieutenant Colonel Frémont, who was on his way from Santa Barbara with 400 men and four pieces of artillery, after having suppressed the attempted rising in that quarter of the territory. The enemy surrendered their artillery, and with the exception of an occasional *émeute*, quite limited in extent, submitted peaceably to the authority of the American officers.*

A serious disagreement between Commodore Stockton and General Kearny in relation to their respective powers, interrupted the harmony which had characterized their previous intercourse, soon after they entered Ciudad de los Angelos. The dispute originated in the indefinite character of their instructions; the conquest of California having been achieved before those of a more positive nature had reached them. This was not contemplated, it would seem, by either the Navy or the War Department, and produced a great deal of ill-feeling and animosity. Both officers claimed the right to exercise the chief command. On the 16th of January Commodore Stockton appointed Lieutenant Colonel Frémont governor of the territory, who accepted the office, and continued to exercise its functions until the month of March, although General Kearny insisted that the power in fact belonged to himself exclusively. Commodore Stockton was relieved by Commodore W. Branford Shubrick in the month of February, and

* On the arrival of the Mormon battalion under Major Cooke, in January, 1847, the Californians manifested a disposition to attack them, but were finally quieted.

returned over land to the United States. Commodore Shubrick was succeeded in a few days by Commodore James Biddle, who arrived on the 2nd of March, and assumed the chief command. More definite instructions had now been received, and the presence of a larger military force enabled General Kearny to maintain his rights as the commanding officer on shore. The naval commanders thereafter voluntarily confined themselves, under their orders, to the enforcement of the blockade, and Lieutenant Colonel Frémont was superseded in his authority as governor.*

On the arrival of the New York regiment under Colonel Stevenson, it was distributed among the different posts, and the territory constituted into a military department. General Kearny remained in command until the 31st of May, when he returned home; being succeeded by Colonel Mason, of the 1st dragoons, as the commanding officer of the department.

* For the particulars of this controversy, see the Proceedings of the Court Martial for the trial of Lieutenant Colonel Frémont, held at Washington in the winter of 1847–48. The finding of the Court fully sustained the position assumed by General Kearny, that Lieutenant Colonel Frémont had been guilty of mutiny and disobedience of orders. A majority of the Court, however, deemed the case one not requiring a severe punishment, especially in view of the meritorious services of the accused, and the sentence was remitted by the President. Believing that he had acted in entire good faith, the Lieutenant Colonel resigned his commission, which terminated his connection with the army.

CHAPTER IV.

MONTEREY.

Censure of General Arista—Arrival of Volunteers on the Rio Grande—Proclamation—Difficulty in procuring Transportation and Supplies—Advance of the Army—Encounter at Ramos—Defences of Monterey—Skirmish at San Jeromino—Storming of Federacion Hill and the Soldada—Diversion in the lower part of the Town—The Enemy's line of defence penetrated—Terrible slaughter among the Assailants—Capture of the Bishop's Palace—The Americans in the City—Street-fighting—Capitulation.

In addition to the mortification of defeat, General Arista was fated to experience the bitterness of the truth, that the unsuccessful warrior rarely finds sympathy among those whom he has vainly endeavored to serve. Heroes are but too often the creatures of chance, and "a breath unmakes them, as a breath has made." The government of Paredes had not entertained the idea that the army under General Taylor would dare to cope with the well-appointed legions which had been sent into the field; they were ignorant of the spirit that animated the American soldiers; they did not know, that ere the flag of their country should have trailed in defeat, not one would have been left to witness its humiliation.

After leaving Matamoras, Arista retired with the remnant of his army to the vicinity of Linares, and subsequently to the city of Monterey. Pickets were thrown out on the road to Matamoras, in anticipation of a general pursuit. This was not attempted by the American commander, and the enemy were allowed to collect their scattered forces at Monterey entirely unmolested. Arista was severely censured by his superiors, and relieved from his command. Galling under the rebuke, and never being particularly friendly to the elevation of Paredes, he attempted to produce another revolution in public affairs. His reverses had alienated the army, in a great measure, and he was unable to secure their co-operation. The design, therefore, could not be carried into effect, and he retired to his hacienda near Monterey, refusing to obey the summons directing him to repair to the capital. On the 16th of June, 1846, Paredes was regularly chosen to the Presidency, and a change was made in the officers commanding the forces on the northern frontier. General Arevalo was ordered to Monterey, and General Ampudia to San Luis Potosi, to collect reinforcements, and be in readiness to relieve any point that might be menaced by the American army. Proclamations were at the same time issued by Paredes, exhorting the Mexican people to make greater exertions, and promising them certain success for the future.

Congratulations were liberally showered, from every quarter of the Union, upon the army of occupation, for their gallant achievements on the banks of the Rio Grande. The captured standards and colors brought to Washington by Lieutenant Colonel Payne, of the 4th artillery, acting Inspector-general of the army, who had been disabled at Resaca de la Palma, were deposited among the national archives. The thanks of Congress, and of the people in their public meetings, were freely tendered. General Taylor was rewarded with the brevet of Major General, and soon after re-

GENERAL ARISTA.

ceived a full commission of the same rank, in pursuance of a law authorizing the appointment of an additional officer of that grade. The volunteers enlisted under the act of Congress were sent forward to the Rio Grande as expeditiously as possible, and early in the month of June the army under General Taylor numbered not far from 9,000 men.*

In anticipation of a movement towards the interior of the enemy's country, General Taylor caused a proclamation prepared at the War Department, and translated into the Spanish language, to be circulated among the Mexican people, in order to apprize them of the objects for which the war was prosecuted, and the manner in which it would be conducted.† The first and most

* The general officers appointed to the command of the volunteers were William O. Butler of Kentucky, and Robert Patterson of Pennsylvania, Major Generals; and Gideon J. Pillow of Tennessee, Thomas L. Hamer of Ohio, John A. Quitman of Mississippi, Thomas Marshall of Kentucky, Joseph Lane of Indiana, and James Shields of Illinois, Brigadier Generals. Generals Butler and Patterson were officers in the army during the last war with Great Britain, and the former, then a member of General Jackson's staff, was highly commended for his gallantry at the battle of New Orleans. Governor J. Pinckney Henderson of Texas, acted as Major General of the volunteers from that state.

† "We come to obtain reparation for repeated wrongs and injuries; we come to obtain indemnity for the past, and security for the future; we come to overthrow the tyrants who have destroyed your liberties; but we come to make no war upon the people of Mexico, nor upon any form of free government they may choose to select for themselves. It is our wish to see you liberated from despots, to drive back the savage Camanches, to prevent the renewal of their assaults, and to compel them to restore to you from captivity your long lost wives and children. Your religion, your altars, your churches, the property of your churches and citizens, the emblems of your faith and its ministers, shall be protected, and remain inviolable. Hundreds of our army, and hundreds of thousands of our citizens, are members of the Catholic Church. In every state, and in nearly every city and village of our Union, Catholic churches exist, and the priests perform their holy functions in peace and

important point to be secured, after the capture of Matamoras, was the city of MONTEREY,* situated at the base of the Sierra Madre, at a point where all the principal approaches from the Rio Grande concentrated, and commanding the main pass through the wall of mountains, the only road practicable for artillery leading to the heart of Mexico. Two routes lay open for the choice of General Taylor; the one to leave the river at Matamoras, and follow the track of the retreating Mexicans through the interior; and the other to proceed up the Rio Grande as far as Mier, and then take the road through Seralvo and Marin. The first was almost entirely destitute of subsistence; on the second there was but a limited supply; and an army moving in either direction would be compelled to depend on its principal dépôts upon or near the Rio Grande. But by pushing his supplies up the river, General Taylor found he could establish a dépôt much nearer to Monterey than the position at Matamoras, besides being more convenient to the route by way of

security under the sacred guaranty of our Constitution. We come among the people of Mexico as friends and republican brethren, and all who receive us as such, shall be protected, whilst all who are seduced into the army of your dictators shall be treated as enemies. We shall want from you nothing but food for our army, and for this you shall always be paid in cash the full value. It is the settled policy of your tyrants to deceive you in regard to the character and policy of our government and people. Those tyrants fear the example of our free institutions, and constantly endeavor to misrepresent our purposes, and inspire you with hatred for your republican brethren of the American Union. Give us but the opportunity to undeceive you, and you will soon learn that all the representations of Paredes were false, and were only made to induce you to consent to the establishment of a despotic government."—Extract from the Proclamation addressed to the Mexican nation.—House of Rep. Exec. Doc. 119, (p. 15.) 2nd session, 29th Congress.

* The King of the Mountain.

Seralvo and Marin. He therefore decided to pursue that route, as it would require less transportation by land, and to establish his main dépôt at Camargo.*

The Rio Grande has been very properly termed, "the muddiest, crookedest, and swiftest river in North America." The channel is constantly shifting, and the navigation obstructed by so many sand-bars, that it is difficult for the smallest steamboats to proceed further up than Reinosa, except in high water. Notwithstanding the efforts made by the Quartermaster's Department to forward supplies for the army, and procure suitable boats to navigate the river, most of which had to be obtained in the United States, and at remote distances from the seaboard, it was not until the month of August that General Taylor was able to move forward with his troops. The causes of this delay were various, and, in most cases, could not well have been avoided. In some instances requisitions were not made in due season; in others the contractors failed to fulfil their obligations; and in others still, the officers of the bureau may have been at fault, although the official correspondence of General Jesup, the Quartermaster-general, and his subordinates, shows that they labored most assiduously in the performance of their duties.†

* Camargo is situated at the mouth of the San Juan, on its southern shore, and on the right bank of the Rio Grande. It is 48 miles above Reinosa, and 98 from Matamoras.

† In September, 1846, General Jesup asked, and obtained leave to join the army on the Rio Grande, and remained there and at New Orleans for several months, constantly employed in the duties of his office. After this time, there was less complaint in regard to the want of transportation and supplies.—See Correspondence of Quartermaster's Department, House of Rep. Exec. Doc. 119, (pp. 250, et. seq.) 2nd session, 29th Congress.

Had General Taylor been in a situation to advance with a large army, immediately after the capture of Matamoras, there can be no doubt that Monterey might have been taken without the least difficulty, and, perhaps, without striking a single blow. At first blush this would seem to have been a most desirable result; but a moment's reflection will suggest an important consideration decidedly opposed to such a conclusion. The history of the war, as conducted in the provinces of California and New Mexico, presents one truth in bold and strong relief,—which is, that something more than the occupation of an enemy's territory by an armed force apparently sufficient to overawe the inhabitants, is necessary to constitute an effectual conquest. General Taylor might have overrun the whole country between the Rio Grande and the Sierra Madre, and yet there have been no safety for his army, if separated into detachments, until the enemy had concentrated their forces, and there had been a fair trial of strength in the field. To conquer a people at home, on their own soil, their moral energies must be prostrated, and that can only be done by a defeat. The loss before Monterey was severe, but was it not better thus, than that the valley of the San Juan should have been deluged with the blood of American soldiers lulled into a false security, and unprepared for the sudden onslaught of Mexican guerilleros and rancheros?

After the arrival of the volunteers, and while waiting for boats to navigate the river, General Taylor wisely directed that the troops should be thoroughly drilled and disciplined. The sickly season came on before he proceeded up the Rio Grande, and large numbers of the volunteer corps were swept away by the noxious vapors of the *tierra caliente*, aggravated, no doubt, in their influence, by the irregular habits formed in the camp by those who were unaccustomed to this new mode of life. Notwithstanding the interference of General Taylor, and the adoption of more stringent regulations, the causes of this mortality were never wholly removed, though they were ultimately checked to a great extent.

The army commenced moving towards Monterey early in August. General Taylor arrived at Camargo on the 8th instant, and on the 17th, General Worth* marched for Seralvo, with the first brigade of his division, followed by the second brigade on the 25th. The spy companies had previously been thrown forward, but had not found the enemy posted in force on either side of the San Juan. On the 11th of August, a party of sixty Mexicans, armed with carbines, and well supplied with ammunition, were captured and brought into Camargo. Captain McCulloch, with his company of fifty men, discovered a body of irregular cavalry, over one hundred strong, at China, and made his dispositions to attack them, but they prudently avoided an engagement.

On the 4th of September, General Taylor received a dispatch from General Worth, informing him that Ampudia had arrived at Monterey with reinforcements; that the Mexican cavalry were supposed to be at Caiderita; and that General Canales was at Marin with 600 men, and had his advance at Papayallos on the road to Seralvo. On the following day, the remaining divisions of the army commenced the march;

* General Worth was in Washington when the intelligence was received that hostilities had commenced on the Rio Grande, and had already handed in his resignation. He promptly withdrew it and returned to the seat of war, resuming the command of his division on the 28th of May.

the Texas cavalry, under General Henderson, being sent round by China and Caiderita, with orders to join the main army at Marin; and General Taylor, with the rest of his forces, crossing the San Juan at Camargo, and moving forward by the other road to Seralvo.

The entire strength of the army destined for the reduction of Monterey, was about 6,600, nearly one-half of whom were regulars, whose coolness and constancy in battle were not to be questioned. But few of the volunteers had ever been in an engagement; but they were all brave and ambitious, well disciplined, and determined to accomplish something that would reflect honor on the country to which they belonged, and to follow, in all things, the bidding of the leader under whose banner they marched, to fight and to conquer. General Patterson was left in command on the Rio Grande, with near 3,000 men. A portion of these troops might have been added to the main column under General Taylor, but he was convinced that it would be impracticable to sustain a larger body of men, in consequence of the deficiency in transportation. He was forced to depend upon the resources of the country, and it was with great difficulty that he procured a sufficient number of pack mules to carry the necessary supplies for his men on the march.*

* The main army was organized by General Taylor into three divisions:—the first, under General Twiggs, consisting of four companies of the 2nd dragoons, Lieutenant Colonel May, and Captain Ridgely's battery; Captain Bragg's battery, 3rd infantry, Major Lear, and 4th infantry, Major Allen, forming the third brigade of regulars, and commanded by Lieutenant Colonel Garland; and the 1st infantry, Major Abercrombie, and the Baltimore and Washington battalion, Lieutenant Colonel Watson, forming the fourth brigade, commanded by Lieutenant Colonel Wilson; the second division, under General Worth, consisting of Lieutenant Colonel Duncan's battery, the artillery battalion, Lieu-

The army halted for a few days at Seralvo, where a dépôt was established. The first division resumed the march on the 13th of September, and was followed, on successive days, by the other divisions; the troops being provided with eight days' rations, and forty rounds of ammunition. The advance, consisting of McCulloch's rangers, Captain Graham's dragoons, and a small body of pioneers and engineers, marched early on the 12th. The roads were generally hard and level, but occasionally crossed by a deep gully, which required some preparation to fit it for the passage of artillery. From Papayallos the advance were always in sight of the Mexican pickets, who retired slowly before them. On the 14th, the rangers encountered a body of two hundred cavalry at Ramos. Dashing furiously upon the enemy, they routed them in an instant, and drove them rapidly through the town. They entered Marin, near the San Juan, on the next day, and there found General Torrejon, with 1,000 cavalry, who were drawn up in the principal street, their bright and new escopetas and

tenant Colonel Childs, and 8th infantry, Captain Scrivner, forming the first brigade, commanded by Lieutenant Colonel Staniford; and Lieutenant Mackall's battery, 5th infantry, Major M. Scott, 7th infantry, Captain Miles, and Captain Blanchard's company of Louisiana volunteers, forming the second brigade, commanded by Colonel P. F. Smith, of the mounted riflemen; and the third, or volunteer division, under General Butler, consisting of the 1st Kentucky regiment, Colonel Ormsby, and 1st Ohio regiment, Colonel Mitchell, forming the first brigade, commanded by General Hamer; and the 1st Tennessee regiment, Colonel Campbell, and Mississippi regiment, Colonel Davis, forming the second brigade, commanded by General Quitman. The Texas division, consisting of the 1st and 2nd regiments of mounted volunteers, under Colonels Hays and Wood, was commanded by General Henderson, and detached, as occasion required, to co-operate with the other divisions. The artillery consisted of one ten-inch mortar, two twenty-four pounder howitzers, in charge of Captain Webster, with a company of artillery detached, and four light field batteries of four guns each.

lances glowing with sunbeams, and their gay scarlet uniforms presenting a most brilliant appearance. The Mexicans were soon in great commotion, and fancying that General Taylor's army was about pouncing down upon them from the neighboring hills, retreated in haste towards Monterey, without firing a single gun.

It was not unusual, on the march from the Rio Grande, to behold the most decided evidences of terror and apprehension among the Mexican inhabitants, and more particularly whenever they caught sight of the Texan rangers, with their wide-brimmed sombreros shading the swarthy countenances whose ferocity was enhanced by their long beards and mustachios,—each man's belt garnished with revolvers, the deadly rifle slung over his shoulder, and, still fresh in his heart, the recollections of Salado and the Alamo.* The husbandman would shrink behind the covert of muskeet bushes lining the roadside, while his wife and daughters, with their dark eyes half-veiled beneath the drooping lashes, and swimming with tears, and their clear olive complexions blanched in affright, would press their trembling lips to the glittering crosses suspended from their necks, and hurriedly murmur forth a fervent prayer to

* Besides performing other important services, the Texan volunteers, or rangers, were found by General Taylor to be of great assistance as scouts and vedettes. They were skilful horsemen, and had learned many of the arts of the Indian warriors. It was said of the regiment of Colonel Hays, that there were few of its members who could not pick a silver dollar from the ground, when at full speed, or shelter themselves from the fire of an enemy, without dismounting, by wheeling their horses to either flank, and throwing their bodies behind them. They were armed with short rifles, revolving pistols, and sabres; and in making a charge, were instructed to fire first with the rifle, then to discharge their pistols while advancing on a gallop, and to complete the work with the sabre. A body of men, thus equipped and drilled, would be formidable enough on an open plain.

"our Lady of Gaudalupe," to protect and shield them from the invader. But when the army under General Taylor came upon the track of the Mexican cavalry, they found that the poor and inoffensive inhabitants had been stripped of their property, or compelled to witness its destruction, in order, as they were assured, that no supplies might be left on the route for the enemy; and *los buenos Americanos* were repeatedly entreated to save them from the cruelty of Torrejon and the rancheros.

The different corps of the American army were concentrated at Marin, 107 miles from Camargo, and within 24 miles of Monterey, on the 17th of September. Early in the morning of the 18th, they were again in motion. In case the enemy were met in force on the march, the line of battle was ordered to be formed, with the first division on the right, the second division on the left, and the volunteer division in the centre. After leaving Marin, the country appeared much more fertile than between that town and the Rio Grande. The valleys, irrigated by the mountain streams, abounded in the most luxuriant vegetation; there were large fields of corn and sugar cane, tempting patches of melons, gay parterres of tropical flowers, groves of figs and olives, with an occasional thicket of chaparral, whose dark foliage added a great deal to the beauty of the landscape; and the soft breeze that sighed among the jagged cliffs of the Sierra Madre, or rippled the waters of the San Juan, was laden with the fragrance of the wild rose and the jasmine, the orange and the pomegranate.

Numerous copies of proclamations issued by General Ampudia, repeating the inducements to desert offered to the American soldiers opposite Matamoras, were found scattered along the road to Monterey. This was, indeed, a most singular mode of warfare, but it appears to have been the one brilliant idea conceived by the Mexican generals, in their own estimation, if we may judge by the pertinacity with which they adhered to it during the continuance of the war.

The American army lay at San Francisco during the night of the 18th, and arrived before Monterey on the 19th. The Mexicans had destroyed a bridge on the road, but its place was soon supplied with corn-stalks from a neighboring field, and the troops crossed over with their baggage and artillery without difficulty. General Taylor selected a position for his encampment, at Walnut Springs, in a grove of walnut trees, about three miles from the city, and then rode forward with the general and staff officers to reconnoitre. They were accompanied by a detachment of dragoons and Texan rangers, and on approaching within a few hundred yards, were fired upon by the enemy's batteries. A number of shot were thrown, but without doing any injury. A body of Mexican cavalry also made their appearance on the plain, but after firing a volley from their escopetas they retired into the town. The American soldiers manifested considerable impatience, because they could not advance against the enemy at once. The information which General Taylor had been able to obtain in regard to the defences of the city, and the strength of the garrison, was quite limited, and the confidential messengers whom he employed, appear either to have deceived him, or to have been themselves deceived.* He was not strong enough to invest the city, and was not provided with a siege train, hav-

* See Correspondence, House of Rep. Exec. Doc. 119, (pp. 130, 139 2nd session, 29th Congress.

ing only the ten-inch mortar that could be of any especial service. He was aware, therefore, that the place must be carried by assault, but determined not to advance hastily, or without proper precautions. The engineer officers were directed to make the necessary examinations, and in order that the army might be prepared for any sudden attack, the men were directed to sleep on their arms.

The city of Monterey was originally founded more than two centuries ago. It is the capital of the State of New Leon, and is situated on the left bank of the Arroyo* San Juan, a small branch of the main river of the same name, which winds down the pass leading to Saltillo, and after encircling the town on the south, and partially on the east, continues its way to the stream of which it is a tributary. Upon the north, the plain rises gradually from the river, its well-tilled fields, and beautiful gardens and groves, exhibiting indications of a high state of cultivation. South and west are the mountain ridges of the Sierra Madre, with the gorge opening on the south-west. It is approached on the north-east from Caiderita and Marin, and on the north-west from Monclova and Presquina Grande. The main road to Saltillo leaves the city at its south-western extremity, and passes along the left bank of the Arroyo San Juan, with a branch crossing the stream, and penetrating the mountains through a smaller defile a short distance east of the principal pass. There are three large squares or plazas: the Plaza de la Capella,† in the western part of the town, the Plazuela de Carne,

* This term is of frequent occurrence in the geography of Mexico. It is the Mexican word used to designate a small stream from a larger one of the same name.

† This is the cemetery referred to in some of the dispatches.

nearer the centre, and the great Plaza upon which stands the Cathedral, in the south-east corner. The houses are built of stone, in the old Spanish style, with flat roofs, and battlements, or parapets, between two and three feet high; and, with the exception of the public edifices around the main plaza, they are generally but one story in height. To almost every house there is attached a small garden inclosed by stone walls. The streets are laid out with great regularity, running parallel to each other, with the intersecting streets crossing at right angles.

The natural position of the city rendered it easy of defence, and every advantage had been improved to the utmost. On the north side of the town, between the road to Monclova and that to Marin, there was a large rectangular fortress, known as the citadel, covering nearly three acres of ground, with four bastion fronts, surrounded by a work of solid masonry, and supplied with heavy guns. At the north-eastern angle, in the suburbs, there was a strong redoubt of masonry of four faces, with an open gorge of ten feet, prepared for four guns, overlooked and commanded by a large stone house in the rear, also fortified. South of this was a second redoubt of four faces, with three guns, and defended by an open gorge of twenty feet, commanded by another redoubt with three guns, overlooking the Caiderita road crossing the Arroyo San Juan by the bridge Purissima, which was also defended by a tête du pont of masonry. And still further south, there were two other redoubts, only one of which, with three guns, was occupied, having in its rear a stone house prepared for infantry, with loop-holes and sand-bags. All these redoubts were connected by fleches of masonry, or breastworks of earth and brush. Along the southern edge of the city, overlooking the river, ran a stone wall four feet thick, with embrasures for guns, and banquettes for infantry. Upon the west was an isolated hill, called Loma de Independencia, towering up to a height of seven hundred feet, and sloping towards the town on the east, but presenting a steep and almost perpendicular acclivity on the west. On the summit of this hill was a gun-battery, with a breastwork of sand-bags, and about midway of the slope a strongly fortified structure, called the Bishop's palace, with outworks of masonry, containing two or three guns mounted in barbette. About six hundred yards south of the hill of Independence, and on the opposite side of the Arroyo San Juan, between the two gorges of the Saltillo road, was Federacion hill, with strong batteries on its crest, and the Soldada fort on the same height, but retired about six hundred yards from the batteries. This hill not only commanded the hill of Independence, but guarded all the approaches to the town in that quarter. The city itself was one continued fortification. The plazas and streets were barricaded and defended by artillery. Breastworks were thrown up in every direction. The walls of the cemetery on the west side of the town, the sides of the houses, the parapets on the house-tops, and even the garden walls, were pierced with crénelés and loop-holes for musketry; and wherever the firm mason-work was deemed insufficient, sand-bags were provided for the protection of those behind them. The cathedral in the main plaza was the principal magazine for the ammunition. Months had been spent in completing these defences; forty-two pieces of artillery were planted in different quarters of the town; and General Ampudia had with him about 7,000 regular troops, and two or three thousand volunteers and citizens,—yet strongly fortified as was his position, by nature and art, it was doomed to fall before the resistless energy of the American soldiers.

Reconnaissances of the city and its defences were made, on the eastern side, by Captain Williams of the topographical engineers, and on the west by Major Mansfield, of the corps of engineers. The latter reported that the enemy's position could be turned by throwing forward a column to the Saltillo road, and carrying the detached works in its vicinity. General Worth was selected, with his division and Colonel Hays' Texan regiment, to execute the important enterprise. He commenced his march from General Taylor's camp, at two o'clock in the afternoon of the 20th; his men being supplied with two days' rations, but taking no tents. Making a wide circuit to the right he reached the Presquina Grande road at six o'clock, having traversed only six miles, on account of the delay in making the route practicable for artillery. Halting his division out of range of the battery on the hill of Independence, a reconnaissance was made to the intersection of the Presquina Grande road with the Saltillo road, and the troops bivouacked at their position during the night. The movement had not escaped the notice of the enemy, and reinforcements were thrown towards the Bishop's palace and the height above it. In order to divert their attention, General Taylor directed the divisions under Generals Butler and Twiggs to be displayed in front of the town until dark. In the night the mortar and twenty-four-pounder howitzers were placed in battery, with a view of opening a fire upon the citadel on the succeeding day.

Early in the morning of the 21st, General Worth put his division again in motion, having written a note to

BATTLE OF MONTEREY.

The Americans forcing their way to he Main Plaza. Sept. 23d, 1846

General Taylor, suggesting a diversion in his favor, on the north and east of the town. The road wound in and out around the ridges projecting from the mountains on the west, and sometimes brought the column within range of the batteries on the hill of Independence. On turning one of these angles, at the hacienda of San Jeromino, a strong force of Mexican cavalry and infantry came suddenly upon the advance, which consisted of Hays' Texans, supported by the light companies of the first brigade under Captain C. F. Smith, and Duncan's battery. The rangers met the charge with a deadly fire from their unerring rifles, and the light companies also opened upon the attacking party. Duncan's battery was in action in a moment, together with a section of Lieutenant Mackall's battery. The conflict lasted about fifteen minutes, when, as the whole first brigade had now formed to the front, the enemy retired in disorder along the Saltillo road, closely followed by the Americans, who took possession of the gorge, and thus prevented their return to the city, and excluded all reinforcements and supplies from entering in that direction. The enemy left one hundred of their men, either killed or wounded, on the ground, and among them a colonel of lancers.

General Worth halted his division at the opening of the gorge, but on discovering that his men were still within reach of the enemy's fire, he advanced about half a mile further on the Saltillo road. At twelve o'clock, Captain C. F. Smith was detached with four companies of the artillery battalion, and six companies of Texan rangers, on foot, under Major Chevalier, about three hundred men in all, to storm the batteries on Federacion hill.* The movement could not be masked,

* "General Worth rode up as the command moved off, and pointing

and the party was almost regarded as a forlorn hope, when the enemy's guns opened a plunging fire upon them, and their light troops were seen descending the slopes, and preparing for the onset. Captain Miles was instantly ordered, with the 7th infantry, to support the assaulting party. Instead of taking the more circuitous route pursued by the former detachment, the regiment moved directly to the foot of the height, pressing forward with alacrity, though the waters of the river, as they forded it, hissed and foamed with the shot which fell thick and fast around them. Without wavering or faltering in the least, both detachments advanced up the hill, clinging to the pointed rocks and bushes of thorn for support, as the loose stones and earth crumbled away beneath their feet, with the balls whistling over their heads, and fragments of rock and gravel falling constantly upon them. They halted only to deliver their fire, and the enemy were driven steadily before them. Heavy reinforcements now appeared on the height, and again there was danger. Colonel P. F. Smith† hastened with the 5th infantry under Major Scott, the Louisiana volunteers, and fifty of the rangers under Colonel Hays, to the assistance of his comrades. On arriving at the foot of the ascent, he saw that he could take advantage of the ground, and, by moving a part of his force obliquely up the hill to the right, carry both batteries at once. The move-

to the height, said, 'Men, you are to take that hill, and I know you will do it.' With one response they replied, 'We will.'"—Reid's Scouting Expeditions of the Texas Rangers.

* Colonel Smith held the rank of Brigadier General of the Louisiana Volunteers first mustered into service, but who were discharged before the army marched to Monterey. He was appointed colonel of the regiment of mounted riflemen of the regular army, in May, 1846, and afterwards brevetted a brigadier general.

ment was ordered. Up they all went, animating each other by the loud cheers that rang down the hill side, and echoed among the gorges. Captain Smith drove the enemy from the breastwork, like chaff before a whirlwind, and then came a contest between the victors, as to who should first reach the Soldada. The assault terminated in a race. Each man strained every nerve. The 5th was foremost, though hard pressed by the other detachments, and entered the fort at one end, as the Mexicans retired at the other. The works of the enemy on the southern bank of the river were carried, and their guns turned upon Independence hill and the Bishop's palace.

Previous to the reception of General Worth's note, General Taylor had determined to make a diversion against the lower part of the town. The first division of regulars, and the division of volunteers, moved towards the city in the morning, having left one company of each regiment as a camp guard. The dragoons under Lieutenant Colonel May, and Colonel Wood's regiment of Texan mounted volunteers, under the immediate command of General Henderson, were directed to the right to support General Worth. Lieutenant Colonel Garland advanced with Bragg's battery, the 1st and 3rd infantry, and the Baltimore and Washington battalion, piloted by Major Mansfield, against the defences at the north-eastern angle of the city, while the mortar served by Captain Ramsay, and the howitzer battery under Captain Webster, opened their fire. General Butler remained with his division in rear of the battery. The remaining regiment of General Twiggs' division, the 4th infantry, was also held in reserve; the general himself, though suffering severely from sickness, being present, and directing the movements of his command.

The column under Lieutenant Colonel Garland was soon exposed to the converging fire of the citadel and the redoubts, and annoyed by the galling discharges of musketry from the adjacent houses and stone walls. Moving rapidly to the right of the fort at the north-eastern angle, an attempt was made to carry it by gaining a position in the rear. Shower upon shower of balls fell upon and around them; yet they pressed nobly on. Again and again that "iron sleet" poured down,

> "In deadly drifts of fiery spray."

The stoutest hearted of them all began to quail. The best and bravest, of both officers and men, had fallen, and the whole column seemed devoted to immediate destruction. Still those men were ready for the advance; their bosoms throbbed with anxiety, but they sheltered no coward hearts. It was madness, however, for the officers further to expose their commands, while the enemy were protected by their breastworks and barricades; and most of them were temporarily withdrawn to places of comparative security. The battery under Captain Bragg was terribly cut up, and compelled to retire out of range. Captain Backus, of the 1st infantry, with portions of the different companies, gained the roof of a tannery looking directly into the gorge of the fort; and had just commenced pouring his destructive volleys into the work, when General Quitman arrived upon the ground with his brigade of volunteers, and three companies of the 4th infantry under Major Allen. They, too, encountered a most withering fire. The Tennessee regiment sustained a severe loss, and the companies of the regular infantry, in the advance, were deprived of one third of their officers and men, who were struck down in an instant. For a moment they staggered and fell back ; but the officers, both of the regulars and volunteers, as if animated by one sentiment, sprang into the front line, and encouraged the men by their words and their example. Being joined by the remaining companies of the 4th infantry, they again moved forward, no longer to be repulsed. The breastworks were surmounted, and the battery won.

Meanwhile General Butler had entered the edge of the town with the 1st Ohio regiment, the remaining regiment of General Hamer's brigade, the 1st Kentucky, being left to support the mortar and howitzer battery. Discovering that nothing could be gained in his front, and being advised by Major Mansfield to withdraw his command, he was about retiring, when he learned that the first fort had been taken. The direction of his column was promptly changed, and he advanced under a severe fire to within one hundred yards of the second fort, called El Diablo. He here found that the intervening space was completely swept by the fire of three distinct batteries, but being anxious to capture the work, if within his power, he was preparing to storm it, when he received a severe wound which compelled him to halt. He afterwards surrendered the command to General Hamer, who moved the regiment to a new position, and within sustaining distance of the batteries under Captains Ridgely and Webster, which had already occupied the first fort, and were vigorously playing upon the second. General Taylor now came up, and ordered Lieutenant Colonel Garland, with such men as could be collected of the

1st, 3rd, and 4th infantry, and Baltimore and Washington battalion, with a section of Ridgely's battery, to enter the town, penetrate to the right, and carry the second battery, if possible. The command advanced beyond the bridge, Purissima, exposed to an incessant fire from the forts and the citadel, where they sustained themselves for some time, but finding it impracticable to gain the rear of the battery, they withdrew to the captured fort.

While these efforts were being made to carry the advanced works, several demonstrations were made by the enemy's cavalry; one of which, on the opposite side of the river, was dispersed by Captain Ridgely's battery; another was repulsed, with considerable loss, by the Ohio regiment and a part of the Mississippi regiment; and a third, by Captain Bragg's battery, supported by Captain Miller of the 1st infantry, with a mixed command. On the approach of evening, the troops were ordered back to camp, with the exception of Captain Ridgely's company, and the regular infantry of the 1st division, reinforced by one battalion of the Kentucky regiment, who remained on guard during the night in the captured fort. Intrenching tools were procured, and the works materially strengthened before morning.

For six long hours had this contest continued in the lower part of the town. The streets were slippery with the blood of the assailants. They had lost three hundred and ninety-four men, in killed and wounded, during the operations of the day, among whom were some of the ablest and most accomplished officers in the service. The line of the enemy's defences had been penetrated, and a foothold gained, but at a great sacrifice It was truly a scene of havoc and slaughter. In the midst of the horrors of that terrible conflict, a Mexican woman was seen going about among the dead, regardless of her own danger, and making no distinction between friend and foe, as she proceeded on her errand of love, binding up the broken limbs, moistening the parched lips of the dying, and ministering to the comforts of the wounded. While thus engaged, while thus displaying the gentle virtues, the tenderness, and the unwavering fortitude of her sex, she was struck by a chance ball, and fell to the earth among the armed men who lay in heaps around her. The American soldiers knew how to appreciate such nobleness of heart,—the magnanimity of such a sacrifice. They nursed her tenderly until she died, and on the following day they buried her, amid the constant fire from the Mexican batteries. It was all they could do to testify their sympathy, but it will be long ere they forget the kind and tender-hearted being,

> " who found a martyr's grave,
> On that red field of Monterey."

The capture of Federacion hill and the Soldada, only rendered it more necessary that the possession of the hill of Independence and the Bishop's palace should also be secured. The party who stormed the former, had been nearly thirty-six hours without food, and to add to their hardships, a violent storm came up towards evening on the 21st. Without any covering to protect them from the pelting rain, they lay down with their arms upon the ground, to snatch a few hours sleep. At three o'clock in the morning of the 22nd, they were aroused to storm the hill Independencia. The execution of this enterprise was intrusted to Lieutenant

Colonel Childs, with three companies of his artillery battalion, three companies of the 8th infantry under Captain Scriven, and two hundred Texan riflemen, under Colonel Hays and Lieutenant Colonel Walker.* There were faint gleams of morning light dancing on the summits of the hills, but the sky was curtained by a thick veil of clouds, and the valley still in deep shade. Proceeding cautiously along, the party picked their way up the steep hill, among the rocks and thorny bushes of chaparral, and at daybreak were within one hundred yards of the breastwork on the summit. Here they encountered a body of Mexicans who had been stationed in a cleft of rocks on the night previous, in anticipation of an attack. Three men of the artillery battalion, having advanced with too much haste, came unexpectedly upon the enemy. They instantly yielded, but were shot down with the very pieces which they had surrendered. It did not require this act of cruelty and outrage to kindle the zeal and fire the ambition of their comrades. With a loud fierce shout for vengeance they sprang up the height. A deadly volley from their guns, and a charge with the bayonet, placed them in possession of the work; the enemy delivering an ineffectual fire as they retreated. The next object of attack was the Bishop's palace, about four hundred yards distant. The Mexicans had withdrawn their guns from the battery, and the detachment were obliged to wait for their own cannon. Lieutenant Rowland, of Duncan's battery, was ordered from the main rank with a twelve-pounder howitzer, and in two hours his men had dragged and

* The rank of this officer in the Texan Volunteers was that of Lieutenant Colonel; but he is better known as "Captain Walker." He received a captain's commission in General Smith's regiment of mounted riflemen.

lifted their piece up the hill, by main strength, and were showering their missiles upon the enemy.

The detachment on the height was also reinforced by the 5th infantry and the Louisiana volunteers. The enemy saw the advantage which had been gained, and manifested a determination to recover the heights. Several feints were made, and then a heavy sortie supported by a strong body of cavalry. The Americans were prepared for the movement. Captain Vinton advanced under cover of the rocks, with two companies of light troops, to draw the enemy forward, followed by the main column under Lieutenant Colonel Childs, with the Texans on either flank. The Mexicans advanced boldly, but were scattered in confusion by one general discharge from all arms. Before they could regain their works, the American soldiers rushed down upon them, shouting as they ran. Entering the palace by a door which had been barricaded, but opened by the fire of the howitzer, they completed the victory. Lieutenant Ayres was the first to reach the halyards and haul down the flag, which was soon replaced by the American standard, waving proudly in the breeze. The captured guns, together with Duncan's and Mackall's batteries, which came up at a full gallop, were effectively served upon the Mexican soldiers, who fled towards the city, pouring in confused masses down the street leading to the Plaza de la Capella, the prolongation of which was now held by the Americans. With the loss of but seventy men in killed and wounded, General Worth had accomplished the purpose for which his division was detached. The enterprise was executed promptly and skilfully, and with entire success. His whole force was soon after concentrated in the vicinity of the palace, in readiness to co-operate with General Taylor in an assault upon the town.

The main body of the army spent the 22nd in burying their dead, and caring for the wounded; although the enemy did not remit their fire from the citadel and the works on the east side of the town. Many an anxious eye was turned from General Taylor's camp towards the scene of General Worth's operations, and when the American flag was unfurled on the Bishop's palace, the welkin rang with glad hurrahs. General Quitman's brigade relieved Lieutenant Colonel Garland's command, with the exception of Ridgely's battery, in the occupation of the captured fort, and an assault on the remaining works was now contemplated to be made on the following day: but at early dawn on the 23rd, it was discovered that the enemy had abandoned their defences in the lower part of the town, and were concentrating their forces near the main plaza, for a last desperate struggle. The brigade of General Quitman, the 2nd regiment of Texan volunteers under General Henderson, who had returned from General Worth's position, and Captain Bragg's battery, supported by the 3rd infantry, immediately entered the city. Detachments of the troops proceeded gradually, breaking through the stone walls, springing from one house to another, mounting to the flat roofs, and driving the enemy before them, until they had advanced within two squares of the main plaza. About noon a communication was received from the governor of the State of New Leon, requesting permission for the inhabitants who were non-combatants, to leave the city. This application was made too late, and General Taylor refused to grant the request. At three in the afternoon he directed the troops on the east side of the town to retire from their advanced position. They had been constantly engaged for eight hours, and needed both rest and food to enable them to continue the attack.

Meanwhile General Worth had not been idle. In the morning of the 23rd, he sent a detachment to take possession of the gorge near Santa Catarina, and had designed to move forward into the city under favor of the ensuing night; but on hearing the heavy firing upon the opposite side of the town, he organized two columns of attack, who were ordered to press on to the first plaza, keeping under cover as much as possible, to get hold of the ends of the streets beyond it, and then, entering the houses, to break through the longitudinal sections of the walls with picks and bars, and work their way from house to house. The light artillery followed the columns in sections and pieces to support the movement.

All day long the work proceeded. Step by step, slowly, but surely, the Americans won their way into the city. The solid masonry yielded before their ponderous blows. The inhabitants were stricken as with a panic. For years Monterey had defied the arms of Spain; but here were soldiers who mocked at every obstacle, and overcame every difficulty. Begrimed with dust and smoke, imagination pictured them as beings from another world. As they sprang, like magic, through the firm walls of the apartments where pale-faced women had retired for shelter, shriek upon shriek rent the air, and only ceased when those who uttered them were assured, in friendly tones, that there were wives and daughters by the firesides of those dark warriors, who waited for their coming, and whose purity and innocence were not forgotten even in the wild excitement of that hour, by those who esteemed and loved them. Galleries and corridors, chambers and balconies, which had oft resounded with the notes of merriment and joy, or listened to the endearments of affection and the soft accents of love, now echoed with the rattle of musketry, the sharp crack of the rifle, the clash of steel against steel, the exulting shout and the dying groan; and, high above all the din, rose the unceasing thunder of artillery.

At sunset General Worth's division had reached a street but one square in rear of the great plaza, leaving a covered way behind them, and had carried a large building overlooking the principal defences of the enemy. The mortar had been sent round by General Taylor, and this was placed in position in the Plaza de la Capella, masked by the church wall, and opened on the main plaza and the cathedral, where the enemy were principally collected, and whither the aged and helpless had retired as to their only remaining place of refuge. Two howitzers and a six-pounder were also mounted on the captured building, and every preparation made during the night to renew the assault at dawn of day. But this was rendered unnecessary. Monterey was already lost and won!

Early in the morning of the 24th a flag was sent out by General Ampudia, accompanied by Colonel Moreno as the bearer of a communication to General Taylor, proposing to evacuate the city with the *personnel* and *matériel* of war. This was positively refused, and a surrender of the town demanded. Soon after a conference took place between General Taylor and General Ampudia, at the quarters of General Worth, which resulted in the appointment of commissioners and the capitulation of the city.*

* Considerable parleying took place at the conference, and at the

sittings of the commissioners, and hostilities were several times upon the point of being renewed. At the request of General Ampudia, the word "surrender" in the articles was changed to "capitulation," and he afterwards desired to have this softened down into "stipulation." Several hours were spent in disputes upon immaterial points, until General Taylor peremptorily announced that he would be trifled with no longer. On one occasion, he is reported to have said to General Ampudia—"Sir, I hold you and your army in the hollow of my hand; the conference is closed,—in thirty minutes you shall hear from my batteries!" The Mexican general hesitated no longer, the terms were agreed upon, and the capitulation signed.

CHAPTER V

WOOL'S COLUMN

Terms of the Capitulation at Monterey—Armistice—Revolution in Mexico—Return of Santa Anna—Proposition to negotiate—Evacuation of Monterey—Concentration of troops at San Antonio de Bexar—March of General Wool—Change of Route—Monclova—Termination of the Armistice—Occupation of Saltillo, Parras, and Tampico—The Mexican Army at San Luis Potosi—Threatened Attack on Saltillo—March to Victoria.

In whatever light it may be viewed, the capture of Monterey must be regarded as one of the most brilliant achievements recorded in the annals of modern warfare. Though most advantageously situated and well defended, the city was compelled to capitulate, after three days' fighting, to an inferior force, without heavy artillery, and destitute of the means usually employed for the reduction of fortified towns. A simple statement of the difficulties to be overcome by General Taylor and his army, and of the success which crowned their efforts, is all that is required to establish their claims to the gratitude and admiration of their countrymen. The terms of the capitulation, however, were not entirely satisfactory to the army, or rather, to the Texan volunteers, who, it cannot be denied, were but too anxious to redress the wrongs which they had received during their revolution; neither were they approved by the Executive authorities of the United

GENERAL WOOL.

States.* It was thought by the President, that an unconditional surrender of the Mexican forces in Monterey, and of their arms and munitions of war, should have been insisted upon by General Taylor; and that the article providing for an armistice was both unnecessary and unadvisable.†

General Taylor might have taken the city without a surrender. There was no misgiving on the part of his soldiers. However obstinate the defence, it would certainly have been overcome in the end, even though every street and plaza had been drenched in blood. On the evening of the 24th of September, the exact distance to the cathedral and the main plaza was ascertained by the officer having charge of the mortar, and he was prepared to throw his shells accordingly. Had no offer to capitulate been received, the fire would have

* See Correspondence between the Secretary of War and General Taylor, House of Rep. Exec. Doc. 119, (pp. 77, et seq.) 2nd Session, 29th Congress.

† The following were the terms of the capitulation:

"Terms of capitulation of the city of Monterey, the capital of Nuevo Leon, agreed upon by the undersigned Commissioners, to wit: General Worth, of the United States Army, General Henderson of the Texan Volunteers, and Colonel Davis, of the Mississippi Riflemen, on the part of Major General Taylor, commanding-in-chief the United States forces, and General Requena and General Ortéga, of the Army of Mexico, and Señor Manuel M. Llano, Governor of Nuevo Leon, on the part of Señor General Don Pedro Ampudia, commanding-in-chief the Army of the North of Mexico:

"ART. I. As the legitimate result of the operations before this place, and the present position of the contending armies, it is agreed that the city, the fortifications, cannon, the munitions of war, and all other public property, with the undermentioned exceptions, be surrendered to the commanding general of the United States forces now at Monterey.

"ART. II. That the Mexican forces be allowed to retain the following arms, to wit: the commissioned officers their side-arms, the infantry their arms and accoutrements, the cavalry their arms and accoutrements, the artillery one field battery, not to exceed six pieces, with twenty-one rounds of ammunition.

been kept up for a few hours, and this would have been followed by an assault, probably on the night of the 24th. The powder of the enemy was stored in the cathedral, and the women and children were collected in and near the main plaza. The loss of life which must inevitably have attended the assault, and the consequent explosion of the magazine, would have been frightful. Every principle of humanity demanded that this should be avoided, if possible, and General Taylor and the American commissioners were very willing to be governed by such a consideration, when they found it was impossible to prevent the escape of the Mexican soldiers, with all their light arms and baggage, through the numerous narrow passes in the rear of the city, which they were unable to guard. In his dispatch to the Mexican minister at war announcing the surrender, dated on the 25th of September, Ampudia intima-

"ART. III. That the Mexican armed forces retire, within seven days from this date, beyond the line formed by the pass of Rinconada, the city of Linares, and San Fernando de Parras.

"ART. IV. That the citadel of Monterey be evacuated by the Mexican and occupied by the American forces to-morrow morning at ten o'clock.

"ART. V. To avoid collisions, and for mutual convenience, that the troops of the United States will not occupy the city until the Mexican forces have withdrawn, except for hospital and storage purposes.

"ART. VI. That the forces of the United States will not advance beyond the line specified in the 3rd article, before the expiration of eight weeks, or until orders or instructions of the respective governments can be received.

"ART. VII. That the public property to be delivered, shall be turned over and received by officers appointed by the commanding generals of the two armies.

"ART. VIII. That all doubts as to the meaning of any of the preceding articles, shall be solved by an equitable construction, or on principles of liberality to the retiring army.

"ART. IX. That the Mexican flag, when struck at the citadel, may be saluted by its own battery.

"Done at Monterey, Sept. 24, 1846."

ted that he would have been compelled to open his way with the bayonet. His assertion, however, is not entitled to much weight, because he undoubtedly anticipated censure, and was anxious to avoid it by representing his situation to have been desperate as possible. Military men who have examined the ground, and all the abler and more experienced officers in the army of General Taylor, concur in the opinion that the terms of the capitulation were as rigorous as ought to have been required; and he must be a bold man who would undertake to question the judgment of those who are so competent to decide.

The armistice was another feature of the capitulation to which objections were made. General Taylor was not in a situation to advance from Monterey, or to prosecute the war, on account of the severe loss he had sustained, and the want of necessary supplies, until a very few days before the expiration of the term prescribed in the article. So far, therefore, as the force under his immediate command was concerned, the delay would have been necessary under any circumstances, and could have produced no injurious results. The enemy desired the armistice; it might have had the tendency to restore friendly relations at once; and good policy required the concession to be made. But while the army was on its march to Monterey, and employed in its reduction, an expedition was planned by the President and his cabinet against Tampico and the southern part of the department of Tamaulipas, below the line which neither party was to cross while the armistice was in force. In the month of June previous, General Taylor had been placed in the full command of all the land forces of the United States operating against the republic of Mexico, south of the prov ince of New Mexico;* this order had not been coun termanded; the contemplated movement against Tampico was not known to him or to the American commissioners; and they did all that was required of them, in leaving the armistice subject to the ratification of their government. But beside all this, General Taylor was instructed by the Secretary of War, that hostilities were to be prosecuted for the conquest of a speedy and honorable peace;† Ampudia expressly stated in the conference that propositions for peace had been made; it was notorious, too, that negotiations had been, or were, in progress; the object of the war seemed about to be gained; and the commissioners of both countries were influenced in their deliberations by these considerations.

The propositions for peace alluded to by Ampudia, were made by the authorities of the United States, in the month of July, in consequence of a change in the Mexican government. Paredes was never firmly seated in power. As early as the 8th of March, 1846, Santa Anna, then in exile at Havana, addressed a confidential letter to a friend in Mexico, accompanied with his *plan* for a revolution. He declared that his sentiments were changed in relation to the proper form of government for his countrymen, and that he was willing one should be established by a Congress to be chosen in accordance with the electoral laws under which the members of the Congress of 1824 were elected. These views were satisfactory to the leading federalists, and it was designed to make a movement on the 1st of April.‡ The

* House of Rep. Exec. Doc. 119, (p. 50,) 2nd Session, 29th Congress.

† Ibid., loc. cit.

‡ House of Rep. Exec. Doc. 4, (pp. 34, et seq.) 2nd Session, 29th Congress.

main reliance of Paredes was upon the army, and this could not be withdrawn from him, or secured by the friends of Santa Anna and the federalists, until after the battles on the Rio Grande. The cry was then raised, that the war had not been conducted with sufficient vigor or skill. Paredes was deposed and thrown into prison, but afterwards made his escape to Havana. General Salas, the firm friend of Santa Anna, was chosen provisional President, and immediately issued a decree requiring a Congress to be elected and to assemble on the 6th of December following, under the laws in force in 1824. In the meantime it was declared that the constitution of 1824 should be the supreme law of the land. Santa Anna arrived at Vera Cruz on the 16th of August, having been allowed to pass the blockading squadron without opposition, in pursuance of instructions from the Navy Department.

The order received by Commodore Conner to allow Santa Anna to enter the Mexican ports freely, if he endeavored to do so, although he could unquestionably have returned had it not been in existence, was issued on the 13th of May 1846. It was then supposed that his presence in Mexico might lead to the overthrow of Paredes, and to the establishment of a government more favorable to peace; but this proved to be a mistake.* Paredes originally came into power as the friend of war; yet the very men who were the most active in deposing him were compelled to make similar professions. The popular feeling was warlike, and the army were dissatisfied in consequence of their reverses. Whatever may have been the private sentiments of Santa Anna, however much he was inclined to peace,

* Annual Message of President Polk, December, 1846: Special Message and accompanying documents, January 12, 1848.

he could never have regained any part of his former influence, except as the decided supporter of war measures. He was too wise not to understand that the true policy of his country should have been the restoration of peace, but he was also too ambitious not to yield to the current bearing every thing before it. He was not ignorant of the prevailing fondness of the Mexican people for military heroes, and he well knew that his own fame must be rejuvenated, and the laurels which had been withered at San Jacinto, restored to their original freshness, before he could succeed in guiding or controlling them. Had he been able to have achieved one victory,—had he forced his way through the wall of living men who blocked up the narrow pass of Angostura, or maintained his position on the heights of Cerro Gordo, he would have been hailed with loud acclaim as the saviour of his country. At such an hour, and under such circumstances, he might have recommended peace, and his advice would have been followed without hesitation.

As soon as it became known that a new government had been established in Mexico, the olive branch was again tendered to her. Mr. Buchanan addressed a letter to the Mexican minister of foreign relations, on the 27th of July 1846, proposing that negotiations should be opened for the conclusion of a peace. The minister, Mr. Rejon, replied on the 31st of August, declining any action in the premises, except that of simply laying the proposition before the Congress to assemble in December.* The result of this attempt to open negotiations between the two countries for the adjustment of their difficulties, was not known at

* House of Rep. Exec. Doc. 4, (pp. 40, et seq.) 2nd Session, 29th Congress.

the time of the capitulation at Monterey. A government supposed to be more favorable to peace was in existence, and friendly overtures had been made. For this reason the request of Ampudia for an armistice was granted by General Taylor and the American commissioners.

On the 25th of September the citadel in front of Monterey was occupied by a detachment of the American army under Colonel P. F. Smith, and the Mexican troops soon after evacuated the town. Ampudia retired with his forces to Saltillo. He endeavored to prevail upon the inhabitants to fortify the place and prepare for resistance. Being unsuccessful, he proceeded with the main body of his army to San Luis Potosi, where he was placed in arrest, and ordered to be tried by a court martial, for neglecting to maintain his position at Monterey.

Thirty-five pieces of artillery, and a large amount of ammunition, were surrendered to General Taylor in pursuance of the terms of the capitulation. The loss sustained by his army before Monterey was 488; eighteen officers were killed, or subsequently died of their wounds,* and twenty-six were wounded; there were one hundred and eight men killed, and three hundred and thirty-seven wounded. The loss of the enemy was not ascertained, but was supposed to exceed five hundred.

* The names of the officers killed were, Captain Williams, topographical engineers; Lieutenant Terrett, 1st infantry; Major Barbour, Captains Morris and Field, Lieutenants Irwin and Hazlitt, 3rd infantry; Lieutenants Hoskins and Woods, 4th infantry; Captain M'Kavett, 8th infantry; Lieutenant Colonel Watson, Baltimore and Washington battalion; Captain Battlem and Lieutenant Putnam, 1st Tennessee; Lieutenant Hett, Ohio regiment; and Captain Gillespie, Texan volunteers. Lieutenant Dilworth, 1st infantry, Major Lear, 3rd infantry, and Lieut. Graham, 4th infantry, died of their wounds after the occupation of the city.

Immediately after the passage of the act of May 13, 1846, General Wool was ordered to muster into service the volunteers from Ohio, Illinois, Indiana, Kentucky, Tennessee and Mississippi. In the brief period of six weeks fourteen and a half regiments were organized, and on their way to the seat of war. Ten thousand men were sent to reinforce General Taylor, and the remainder, about twenty-five hundred in number, were ordered to San Antonio de Bexar. General Wool landed at La Vaca on Matagorda Bay, on the 2nd of August, with the 1st and 2nd Illinois regiments, and from thence marched to the appointed rendezvous of his division. Colonel Harney, of the 2nd dragoons, had been previously stationed at San Antonio with a small force of regular cavalry, and several companies of Texan volunteers, for the protection of the frontier from Indian incursions. The other regiments and detachments ordered to join General Wool arrived during the month of August. Several weeks were spent in hauling the supplies for the army from La Vaca, the nearest point to San Antonio on the Gulf; but the time was profitably employed in organizing and drilling the command preparatory to taking the field.

All things being made ready, the advance of the army of the centre, under Colonel Harney, marched from San Antonio on the 26th of September. General Wool left on the 29th; the 1st Illinois regiment under Colonel Hardin marched on the 2nd of October; and the rear under Colonel Churchill, Inspector-general, followed in a few days, consisting of the 2nd Illinois and various detachments belonging to the different corps.* From San Antonio the route lay westward to

* The central division, under General Wool, consisted of four companies of the 2nd dragoons, Colonel Harney; one company of the 4th

the Rio Grande opposite Presidio, a distance of one hundred and fifty-seven miles, through a tract of country about equally divided into fertile prairies, sandy barrens, and marshy chaparrals. Boats had been constructed at San Antonio for crossing the Rio Grande, and transported over land. The passage of the river, therefore, was effected without difficulty, on the 10th of October.

General Wool anticipated resistance on entering the enemy's country, but was amply prepared to meet it. His men were well provided, and in a fine state of discipline. The rules and regulations which he laid down and enforced were often regarded as being too harsh and severe, but they contributed materially to preserve the health and efficiency of his command. Every halt or delay was improved in drilling and manœuvring the troops; complaints were loud and frequent among the volunteers; yet their commander would permit no relaxation. Himself a soldier in every sense of the word, he knew what constituted the real strength of an army. He would not suffer the discipline of his command to be neglected upon any consideration, and those who complained the most bitterly learned to bless the cautious foresight that saved them from utter destruction on the bloody field of Buena Vista.*

Leaving the Rio Grande at Presidio, General Wool marched through Nava and San Fernando to Santa

artillery, Captain Washington, with eight pieces, two twelve pounders, and the remainder six pounders; battalion of 6th infantry, Major Bonneville; Colonel Yell's regiment Arkansas mounted volunteers; 1st Illinois infantry, Colonel Hardin; 2nd Illinois, Colonel Bissell; and one company of Kentucky Cavalry, and one of Texan volunteers. Total strength, 2,829.

* See the Correspondence between General Wool and the Illinois volunteers, June, 1847.

Rosa, taking peaceable possession of the different towns on his route; the Mexican population neither possessing the means, nor the inclination, to oppose his movements. At Santa Rosa he unexpectedly found an impassable barrier to his further advance in the direction of Chihuahua. The tall peaks of the Sierra Gorda, fringed with cedars, and concealing countless stores of wealth within their bosoms, towered to the very clouds before him, and looked down frowningly upon the sterile plains, the fertile valleys, the beautiful haciendas and olive groves, of Coahuila. There was no pathway through the mountains, and to storm that mighty breastwork which nature had reared, was beyond the power and skill of his soldiers. He therefore turned aside to Monclova, the ancient capital of the province, where he arrived on the 29th of October. The Spanish inhabitants of this town are wealthy, intelligent and refined, hospitable and courteous. The American army were received and treated with marked kindness and condescension; and on informing General Taylor, then at Monterey, of his arrival at Monclova, General Wool was directed to remain there until further orders.

Immediately upon his landing at Vera Cruz, Santa Anna issued a proclamation containing similar sentiments with those communicated to his friends, while he was at Havana, and retired temporarily to his hacienda of Mango de Clavo, where he remained until the month of September. He then set out for the city of Mexico, and arrived at Ayotla, on the 14th of September. At this place he received a communication offering him the supreme executive power, or dictatorship, of the republic, in the name of the provisional government. This was accepted on the same day, and he thus became, as he styled himself, "the Commander in Chief of the Liberating Army of Mexico." On the 15th of September he entered the capital amid the congratulations of his fellow-citizens, thousands of whom assembled to celebrate the re-establishment of the federal constitution, to join in "the glorious cry of Dolores," and to welcome the soldier and hero whom they already fancied as their deliverer. Decrees had been previously issued providing for the increase of the forces, their supply and equipment; and Santa Anna hastened directly to the head-quarters of the northern army at San Luis Potosi, to receive the new levies, and conduct the future operations of the war in that quarter. The spirit of the nation was aroused. San Luis was soon filled to overflowing with troops, and even the women came down in crowds, from San Diego and Tlascala, to cheer the soldiers by their presence, and encourage them by their approving words and smiles.

On the second of September a dispatch was forwarded to General Taylor from the War Department, directing him to make preparations for an expedition against Tampico, to be commanded by General Patterson, in which allusions were made to an advance upon San Luis Potosi if found practicable. This dispatch was intercepted by the enemy, and preparations were forthwith made by the Mexican forces at San Luis to check the advance of the American army, which was supposed to be in contemplation. Deeming it impossible to hold Tampico, the garrison was withdrawn on the 27th of October. Early in November Santa Anna was officially notified by General Taylor that the armistice would terminate on the 13th instant, and that hostilities would thereupon be recommenced. The work on the fortifications erected at San Luis was now prosecuted as rapidly as possible; the water-tanks on the road leading from Saltillo were destroyed; and General Miñon was ordered with a body of cavalry to hold that route in observation, while General Urrea was sent to Tula with a similar force, to keep watch over the passes in the vicinity of Tampico and Victoria.*

General Taylor remained quietly at Monterey for several weeks after the capitulation. Occasional excesses were committed by some of the lawless volunteers under his command; but this evil was promptly checked by an order forbidding their free ingress into the town. The main body of the troops were encamped at Walnut Springs, and the city occupied by a garrison detailed for that purpose. On the 5th of November he notified Santa Anna that the armistice would terminate previous to the expiration of the time specified in the articles of capitulation, in accordance with instructions received from the War Department; and on the 13th he advanced towards Saltillo, the capital of Coahuila, about seventy miles beyond Monterey, accompanied by General Worth with about 1200 men under his command. General Taylor regarded the occupation of this town as being of the highest importance. It appeared to be a necessary outpost to Monterey, and covered both the defile leading from the lower country to the table land in the interior, and the

* It is stated in a letter written from Mexico, that Santa Anna collected his army at San Luis Potosi, with the intention of advancing against General Taylor, (Frost's Life of General Taylor, p. 214.) The movements of the Mexican commander do not appear to justify any such conclusion. He expected to be attacked, and made preparations to defend his position. Indeed, after the dispatch of the 2nd of September was intercepted, he could have formed no other opinion. General Taylor did not advance, and when a portion of his troops were withdrawn, and the Mexican people began to complain on account of the delay, Santa Anna moved forward with his army, but not until that time.

road to Parras, situated in one of the richest sections of northern Mexico, and from which large supplies of cattle and breadstuffs could be drawn if required. No opposition was made to the occupation of Saltillo, the governor of the State contenting himself with a mere protest. General Worth was left in command, and General Taylor returned to Monterey.

Tampico was taken without opposition, by a portion of the Gulf squadron, on the 14th of November, and soon after garrisoned by eight companies of artillery, under Lieutenant Colonel Belton, and a regiment of Alabama volunteers, well supplied with heavy ordnance and provisions, the whole commanded by General Shields. Towards the close of the month General Wool was ordered with his force to Parras, where he experienced the same kind treatment from the inhabitants which he had met at Monclova. He lay encamped for a number of weeks in the Alameda; every attention was paid to his wants; and whenever his men were sick, he was invited by the citizens to bring them into their houses. Saltillo and Santa Fé being in possession of the American troops, it was not thought advisable for him to proceed to Chihuahua, as that town could be occupied at any moment if it should be found necessary.

The distance from Saltillo to San Luis Potosi is not far from three hundred miles, and for a greater part of the way very poorly supplied with water. General Taylor early formed the opinion that a march to San Luis would not be expedient, but that if the war was to be prosecuted, an expedition against Vera Cruz, and an advance movement from thence in the direction of the capital, would be preferable. These views were communicated at different times to his government.* In anticipation of receiving the necessary orders to prepare a part of the troops under his command for the expedition, he left Monterey for Victoria, the capital of Tamaulipas, with all his disposable forces, under the command of Generals Twiggs and Quitman, on the 15th of December, having already directed General Patterson to join him at that place with the regiment of Tennessee cavalry, and two regiments of volunteer infantry. General Butler remained in command of the reserve at Monterey. At Montemorelos General Taylor effected a junction with the 2nd infantry under Colonel Riley, and the 2nd Tennessee foot. While here he received a dispatch from General Worth, informing him that Saltillo was threatened by Santa Anna, who was within three days' march, and that he could hold the position for that time against any force that might be brought against him, but would require assistance on the fourth day. General Quitman was ordered to continue his march to Victoria with the volunteers, reinforced by a field battery, and General Taylor returned to Monterey with the regulars under General Twiggs.

Generals Butler and Wool had also been advised of the threatened attack on Saltillo, and had moved rapidly

* "I am decidedly opposed to carrying the war beyond Saltillo in this direction, which place has been entirely abandoned by the Mexican forces, all of whom have been concentrated at San Luis Potosi. * * * * If we are, (in the language of Mr. Polk and General Scott,) under the necessity of 'conquering a peace,'—and that by taking the Capital of the country,—we must go to Vera Cruz, take that place, and then march on the city of Mexico."—Letter of General Taylor to General Gaines, November 5, 1847. See also, General Taylor's letters to the Adjutant General, dated July 2nd, October 15th, November 8th, 9th, and 12th, and December 8th, and to President Polk dated August 1st, in House of Rep. Exec. Doc. 119, 2nd session, 29th Congress.

COMMODORE CONNER.

to join General Worth with all their available forces. General Wool received the intelligence on the evening of the 17th, and in two hours his whole army was in motion. He was three nights upon the road, and his men were aroused at one o'clock in the morning to resume the march. When they arrived near Saltillo, his soldiers, who had confidently anticipated a battle, were much chagrined to find that the alarm proved to be unfounded. On the 21st of December General Wool took position with his command at Agua Nueva, a small rancho seventeen miles south of Saltillo and near the great pass through the mountains, in order to hold the approaches from San Luis in observation.

On his way to Saltillo General Taylor was informed that the position was no longer in danger. He therefore retraced his steps to the camp near Monterey, and in a few days again started for Victoria. At Montemorelos, an officer of the topographical engineers, with a squadron of cavalry, under Lieutenant Colonel May, was dispatched to reconnoitre a pass through the mountains to Labradores, and thence to Linares. The reconnaissance was effected, but on the return of the party to Linares, the baggage and ten men of the rear guard were cut off in a narrow pass beyond San Pedro. Lieutenant Colonel May dismounted a portion of the squadron and repassed the defile, in the hope of rescuing his men. Occasional shots were fired upon him from the cliffs overhead, but he did not encounter the enemy.

General Quitman occupied Victoria without resistance on the 29th of December. A body of the enemy's cavalry, numbering about 1,500, and belonging to a strong division of observation stationed at Tula under General Valencia, were in the town when he approached, but retired before he came up, to Jamauve. General Taylor arrived on the 4th of January with the regulars under General Twiggs, and was joined on the same day by General Patterson with the regiments ordered from Matamoras. The united force amounted to more than 5,000 men. With the possession of Victoria, every prominent town on the line of the Sierra Madre, between Saltillo and Tampico, was occupied by General Taylor with the forces under his command.

CHAPTER VI

NAVAL OPERATIONS IN THE GULF.

The American Navy—The Home Squadron—Blockade of the Mexican Ports—Loss of the Truxton—Laws passed by the Government of Mexico to encourage Privateering—Attempt against Álvarado—Attack on Tabasco—Occupation of Tampico—Burning of the Creole—Wreck of the Somers—Capture of Laguna.

When the American people shall forget how freely the generous blood of Lawrence and Decatur was shed in maintaining their rights, and defending their flag,—when the valor and intrepidity of Porter and Hull, of Perry and Macdonough, and the brave associates who shared their dangers, and contributed to their renown, are no longer remembered,—then, but not until then, will the navy upon which they have never yet relied in vain, cease to occupy the prominent place in their estimation and regard, which it has so long maintained. If the country had derived no other benefit from its organization, the security rendered to her commerce would be an ample repayment for every outlay; but, in addition to this, we are indebted to it, in no unimportant degree, for the deference and respect manifested by the nations of the world in their intercourse with us. The officers and seamen of our navy have shown themselves, on repeated occasions, and under the most trying circumstances, to be prompt and zealous in the performance of their duty. We have learned to look upon them as the appointed guardians of the national honor, on other shores, and in foreign lands; and it is something of which they may well be proud, that they have never proved faithless to their trust.

On the day of the passage of the act declaring that war existed with Mexico, Commodore Conner was officially notified of the event, and instructed to blockade the Mexican ports on the Gulf; his attention being more particularly directed to that part of the coast between the Goatzacoalcos and the Rio Grande.* Several vessels of war were also dispatched, as soon as they could be got in readiness, to reinforce the squadron under his command.† Anterior to this he had rendered important services to the army of occupation, commanded by General Taylor, in their operations on the Rio Grande; and upon the reception of his instructions, he prepared at once to carry them into effect. Most of the time, during the summer months, was spent in discharging the inactive, and sometimes irksome duties of the blockade, varied but rarely by any incident of more than ordinary moment. Commodore Conner made an unsuccessful attempt to capture the port of Alvarado, on the 7th of August, 1846; none of his vessels being of sufficiently light draught to cross the bar.‡ Commander Carpenter,

* This direction was given, in order to exempt Yucatan from the blockade.

† After the arrival of the vessels ordered to the Gulf, the Home Squadron consisted of the frigates Cumberland and Raritan, 44 guns each; sloops of war, Falmouth, John Adams, and St. Mary's, 20 guns each; steamer Mississippi, 10 guns, (Paixhan); steamer Princeton, 9 guns; brigs Porpoise, Somers, Lawrence, Perry, and Truxton, 10 guns each; and the schooner Flirt. Total number of guns, 217.

‡ One effect produced by the Gulf stream is, to cause the accumulation of numerous sand-bars along the eastern coast of Mexico, and especially across the mouths of the rivers. But very few of the ports can be

of the brig Truxton, was still more unfortunate, in a similar enterprise against Tuspan, on the 15th of the same month. His vessel grounded on the bar at the mouth of the river; every effort was made to get her off, but all proved of no avail. It was found impossible to save her, and she was abandoned. Lieutenant Hunter made his escape with a boat's crew, to another vessel of the squadron, and the remaining officers and men surrendered to the enemy, but were afterwards exchanged, at the instance of the Mexican government, for General La Vega, and other prisoners taken by General Taylor.

Though it may not have been often expressed in words, it is certain that a very general feeling of regret was entertained throughout the country, when it became known, after the commencement of hostilities with Mexico, that no opportunity would be afforded to the navy for the performance of distinguished services upon their own appropriate theatre. Mexico was almost without a naval establishment; her marine consisting only of a few brigs, small steamers, and gunboats, intended rather for coast and harbor defence, than for offensive operations on the ocean. Soon after the return of Santa Anna, however, a plan was devised for annoying American commerce, which it was thought, at one time, would afford an opportunity for our navy to display its unquestioned gallantry and heroism. On the 11th of September, a special decree was enacted by the Mexican Congress, for the naturalization of foreigners, and on the 24th instant, regulations were established for privateering, under which prize letters

entered at all, except by vessels of light draught, unless with the assistance of camels; and the principal harbor, the bay of Vera Cruz, has been justly called "nothing more than a bad roadstead."

were issued by General Salas, then charged with the supreme executive power. Officers in the Mexican service were sent to Havana, and other ports, with blank commissions for privateers, letters of citizenship, and naturalization papers for crews, which were offered for sale. The prompt measures taken by the Captain General, in conformity with the stipulations of the treaty between Spain and the United States, to prevent the fitting out of privateers in the harbors on the island of Cuba, and the absence of sufficient pecuniary inducements to risk a capture by the American men-of-war, rendered the attempt of the Mexican government entirely abortive.*

Small steamers and schooners adapted for entering the harbors in the Gulf, were purchased for the use of the Home Squadron, in the fall of 1846; and on the 15th of October, Commodore Conner made a second effort to capture Alvarado. The entrance of the river was defended by several batteries that opened a brisk fire on the American vessels, which attempted to cross the bar in two divisions. The first, consisting of the schooners Reefer and Bonita, towed by the steamer Vixen, crossed in safety, and engaged with the batteries; the steamer Mississippi, commanded by Commodore Matthew C. Perry, having also gained a favorable position, brought her heavy guns to bear, and nearly destroyed one of the enemy's breastworks; but unfortunately, the steamer McLane, with the schooners Nonata and Petrel, and the revenue cutter Forward, in tow, comprising the second division, grounded on the bar, and the enterprise was again defeated. Commodore Conner thought it would be imprudent to go for-

* House of Rep. Exec. Doc. 4, (pp. 40, et seq.) 2nd session, 29th Congress.

ward with the first division alone, and reluctantly ordered it to retire.

On the following day Commodore Perry sailed for Tabasco with the steamer Mississippi and the small vessels. This town is the capital of the State of the same name, one of the richest and most fertile in Mexico, and is especially celebrated for its exportation of spice, produced in the extensive forests near the river Baraderas. It is situated on the river Goatzacoalcos, about eighty miles in the interior, and has formerly possessed considerable trade, mainly carried on by foreign merchants. The small town of Fronteira lies near the mouth of the river seventy-four miles below Tabasco, and, in the early part of the war, was a famous place of rendezvous for the vessels and steamers of the enemy engaged in bringing munitions of war from Yucatan into Mexico.

Commodore Perry arrived off the débouchure of the Goatzacoalcos on the 23rd of October. The Mississippi remained at anchor outside, in charge of Commander Adams, while the Commodore crossed the bar in the Vixen, Captain Sands, having in tow the Bonita, Lieutenant Benham, and Forward, Captain Nones, and several barges containing a detachment of sailors and marines organized for service on shore, if required, under Captain Forrest. The Nonata, Lieutenant Hazard, followed under sail. Notwithstanding her heavy drag, the Vixen steadily ascended the stream against a four-knot current. On arriving near Fronteira, they found that the alarm had been given, though the enemy were unprepared for resistance. Two steamers were discovered firing up, in order to make their escape by ascending the river; but it was too late. The Vixen cast off her tow in an instant, and darted in advance, with the other vessels and barges following quickly in her wake. No attempt was made to defend the town, or the Mexican vessels in the port, all which were captured by the Americans. The schooner Amada endeavored to get up the river; but she was pursued by the Bonita, and easily overtaken.

Being anxious to reach Tabasco before the enemy had time to strengthen their defences, Commodore Perry ordered the detachment under Captain Forrest to be transferred to the Petrita, the largest of the captured steamers, which also took in tow the Nonata and Forward, with the barges. The Bonita was attached to the Vixen as before. The flotilla being in readiness, they proceeded up the river on the morning of the 24th, Lieutenant Walsh having been left with a party in command at Fronteira. At nine o'clock in the forenoon of the ensuing day they came in sight of Fort Accachappa, erected to command a difficult pass in the river, where the high and steep banks approached nearer to each other, and the graceful branches of the cotton-wood, the fan-like leaves of the palmetto, the velvet foliage of the magnolia, and the long trailing moss, growing upon the opposite shores, mingled their rich hues together in the watery mirror beneath them. Anticipating resistance at this point, arrangements were made to land Captain Forrest with his detachment, when it was found that the men had fled who were employed in preparing the guns in the fort for service. After spiking the artillery the fleet passed on its way unmolested. At noon the whole flotilla anchored in front of Tabasco, within musket range of the town, and formed in line of battle. Captain Forrest was immediately sent on shore with a flag to summon the city to surrender; and in the meantime five merchant vessels found at anchor in the river were secured.

The governor of Tabasco was inclined to be exceedingly valiant of speech, though very careful that history should chronicle no exhibition of his daring and prowess in defending the State from invasion; and in reply to Commodore Perry, he not only refused to capitulate, but invited him to open his fire as soon as he pleased. The town was completely at the mercy of the American vessels; but the Commodore was unwilling to destroy it, and therefore ordered the guns of the Vixen to be fired at the flag-staff and over the houses. At the third discharge the flag-staff was seen to fall, whereupon Captain Forrest again went ashore to inquire whether it had been shot away or struck by the enemy. He was informed that it had been cut down by the shot, and that the city would not be surrendered. The firing was now renewed, and the detachment of sailors and marines landed under cover of the guns. Captain Forrest took a position in the town with his command, notwithstanding a scattering fire of musketry from the enemy, and remained there until the approach of evening, when Commodore Perry directed the party to return to the vessels, fearing that they might be cut off in the narrow streets after dark, as they were unused to this kind of warfare, and would naturally be too indifferent to their personal safety and security.

During the night the American sailors lay at their quarters, ready to return the fire of the enemy's artillery, which it was supposed would be planted in the streets opening towards the river. Nothing of the kind was attempted, although the straggling fire from their small arms was kept up, but without producing any alarm, or causing serious injury. Soon after the attack was renewed on the following morning, Commodore Perry learned that the foreign merchants, who had been the greatest sufferers from his fire, and the citizens generally, were in favor of an immediate capitulation, but were overruled by the governor, who appeared entirely unconcerned for the safety of them or their property. An earnest appeal was made to the American commander, by the merchants, not to destroy the town. It was not designed to occupy the place, in any event, on account of its insalubrity, and as the main object of the expedition, the capture of the Mexican vessels, had been accomplished, the commodore decided to drop down the river with his prizes. The latter were soon got under way, in advance of the flotilla, and a white flag was hoisted, as a notice to the citizens of the town, that they would not be again molested. At this moment it was discovered that one of the prizes in command of Lieutenant Parker, had drifted ashore, and that a large body of the enemy had collected behind the houses in the vicinity, and were pouring volley after volley of musketry into her. The movement down the river was forthwith suspended, and a general fire from the flotilla opened upon the town. A number of houses were demolished, and the smoking ruins attested the severity of the chastisement which had been so cowardly provoked. The enemy's fire was speedily silenced. Lieutenant Parker bravely defended his vessel, and succeeded in getting her afloat, with the loss of one man killed, and two wounded. Lieutenant Morris was also killed while bearing an order from the commodore to Lieutenant Parker.

No further attempt was made to molest the American vessels or their prizes, and they continued down the river. On his return to Fronteira, Commodore Perry dispatched his prizes that were of sufficient value to be manned, to Vera Cruz, and destroyed all the smaller craft. The McLane and Forward were left to blockade the river; and on the 31st, the remainder of the fleet proceeded to rejoin Commodore Conner.

Orders were issued from the Navy Department, in October, to capture and occupy Tampico, with a view of masking an attack on Vera Cruz and the Castle of San Juan de Ulua, then in contemplation. In accordance therewith, Commodore Conner sailed for that port on the 13th of November, with a considerable portion of his squadron, and on the 14th took possession of the city, without opposition,—the armed forces of the enemy having been previously withdrawn.*

During the absence of the squadron, the brig Somers, Lieutenant Semmes, remained off Vera Cruz, to continue the blockade. On the evening of the 20th of November, a most daring exploit was performed by Lieutenant Parker, and Passed Midshipmen Rodgers and Hynson, belonging to the vessel, in a small boat manned by six men. Protected by the darkness of the night, they surprised the bark Creole, which had been engaged in conveying munitions of war into the country, in defiance of the blockade, as she lay at anchor, beneath the walls of the castle. The men left to guard

* A number of small vessels were also captured in the harbor of Tampico; the prize money for those taken at this place and at Tobasco amounting to about $220,000. Previous to the capture of Tampico, Commodore Conner received full information in regard to its defences, with a plan of the town, the forts, and the harbor, from Mrs. Ann Chase, the wife of the American Consul. She manifested an extraordinary degree of intrepidity and determination on the approach of the squadron. In spite of the opposition of the ayuntamiento, (city counc), she persisted in hoisting the flag of her country, and was neither mo ed by solicitations, nor intimidated by menace.

the vessel were put on shore, and the craft set on fire. On the 5th of December, Midshipman Rodgers, in company with Assistant Surgeon Wright, and one of the crew, went ashore to reconnoitre the enemy's magazines. They had proceeded but a short distance from the beach when they were surrounded by a party of Mexicans. Dr. Wright fortunately made his escape, but his two companions were taken prisoners.* This event was followed by a still more serious disaster, on the 8th instant. Indications of a northerly gale were observed in the evening of the 7th, and the Somers took shelter under Green Island. A sail was reported from aloft the next morning, and she stood out for several miles, when the approaching vessel was ascertained to be the John Adams, on her way back from Tampico, to relieve the Somers in the blockade. As the latter was returning to her anchorage, a suspicious-looking craft was discovered standing in for Vera Cruz. The canvas was crowded upon the Somers, her officers being determined not to be found remiss in their duty, and all haste was made to intercept the strange vessel. In the effort to avoid the reef de Pajordas, on her lee, she was overtaken by the norther. At the first gust she was thrown upon her beam-ends. She careened over rapidly, and in half an hour was ingulfed beneath the angry billows, now howling and hissing with the fury of a Phlegethon. Acting Mas-

* After being transferred from one place of confinement to another, and encountering the severest hardships, Midshipman Rodgers succeeded in making his escape in the fall of 1847, from the city of Mexico, where he was then detained, and took part with the beleaguering army under General Scott in its capture, serving as a volunteer in the staff of General Pillow. While a prisoner he obtained much important information, which was communicated, at different times, to the American officers.

ter Clemson and Passed Midshipman Hynson, with nearly one half of the crew, which consisted of eighty persons, were carried down with the vessel, and found a watery grave on that stranger shore, "uncoffined and unaneled." The remaining officers and men were picked up by the John Adams, and the small boats gallantly sent out from the British, French, and Spanish ships of war anchored in view of the wreck, or succeeded in reaching the shore, where they were taken prisoners by the Mexicans.

On the 20th of December, Commodore Perry, with the Mississippi, Vixen, Bonita, and Petrel, took possession of Laguna, in Yucatan, and destroyed the guns and munitions of war found in the fort and town. Commander Sands was left in charge with the Vixen and Petrel. Soon after this occurrence, the vessels belonging to the squadron, which could be spared from enforcing the blockade, were ordered to rendezvous at Vera Cruz, to assist the army in its reduction.

CHAPTER VII.

BUENA VISTA.

General Scott ordered to Mexico—Expedition to Vera Cruz—Withdrawal of Troops from the Army under General Taylor—Surprise of Arkansas and Kentucky Cavalry at Encarnacion—Advance of Santa Anna from San Luis Potosi—The Pass of Angostura—Buena Vista—Position of the American Troops—Approach of the Enemy—The Battle—Bravery of the Volunteers—Skirmish near Saltillo—Disastrous retreat of the Mexican Army—Attack on the Wagon Trains—Pursuit of Urrea.

On the 1st day of January, 1847, and within the short space of eight months from the commencement of hostilities, the provinces of New Mexico, California, Chihuahua, Durango, Coahuila, New Leon, and Tamaulipas, embracing more than one half of the geographical area of the Mexican Republic, were either virtually conquered, or in the actual possession of the American forces. The different military operations thus far conducted, had been executed with unexampled skill and ability, and attended with the most satisfactory results. The territory occupied by the army under General Taylor, could not, indeed, have been regarded of much value as a permanent acquisition, if conquest had been the object of the war; but in a military point of view, the campaign on the Rio Grande was as important as it was successful. Every thing had been achieved which was to be desired. On three separate occasions the armies of Mexico had been de-

American Army 4,500 men.
Mexican Army 20,000 men.

BATTLE OF BUENA VISTA,

Fought February 23d, 1847.

The American Army under Gen. Taylor Completely Victorious.

American Loss, 264 Killed.
450 Wounded.
26 Missing.
Mexican Loss, estimated in Killed and Wounded 2000 men.

feated. No superiority of numbers, or advantages of position, could stay the advance of the American soldiers. The power, the military strength and resources of the enemy, were essentially weakened ; and it mattered little upon what theatre this had been effected, whether upon a barren shore or a sandy desert, so long as her capacity for resistance was diminished. A large army, it is true, was soon collected at San Luis Potosi, but the disheartening influences of defeat were felt even there. Rumor asserted that the victorious Americans were moving towards the interior ; parties of observation were thrown forward, and preparations for defence were made ; yet many doubted their ability to maintain the position.*

A descent upon the Gulf coast of Mexico had long been in contemplation at the War Department of the United States ; but the prevalence of the *vōmito* during the summer months forbade any such enterprise. Had the climate and season been more favorable, it is not likely that this would have been undertaken at the commencement of the war, notwithstanding the importance of the movement in order to the conquest of a speedy and honorable peace ; because hopes were entertained, that the northern and frontier departments of Mexico would declare themselves independent of the central government, and establish pacific relations with the American Union. General Taylor was led to believe that such would be the case, from the information

* "You may imagine how we are situated here with respect to the approach of the invaders. * * * * Who can tell what will be our fate ?—yet we have 25,000 men more or less, 52 pieces of artillery, 24-pounders, and below, in excellent condition, an incredible quantity of powder, and ball of every calibre."—Letter of correspondent of El Locomotor, (Vera Cruz,) dated at San Luis, 14th November, 1846.

derived through his agents.* It was certainly no chimerical supposition. The northern provinces were known to be ardently attached to the federal constitution; and when Paredes came into power, there were strong symptoms manifested of a desire to resist his authority. They would naturally have turned to the American army for support, and it is reasonable to suppose, that the fear of losing a large portion of territory south and west of the Rio Grande, might have constrained the Mexican Government to listen to overtures of peace. But before the war had fairly commenced, the project for the re-establishment of the federal constitution, and the return of Santa Anna, was started by the opponents of Paredes, and his subsequent overthrow put an end to the expectations which had been formed in regard to the secession of the northern provinces.

The suggestions of General Taylor in favor of maintaining a defensive position on the line of the Sierra Madre, and the information communicated by him, showing that a march on San Luis Potosi from Saltillo would be attended with serious difficulty and embarrassment, and that the Santa Barbara pass, opening towards Tampico, and that in the direction of Tula, were both impracticable for artillery, led to an abandonment of the movement designed to be made upon San Luis Potosi, from the north; and in November 1846, General Scott was ordered to repair to the Rio Grande, for the purpose of setting on foot and conducting an expedition against Vera Cruz and the castle of San Juan de Ulua. Previous to this time much valuable information had been procured in re-

* Letter of General Taylor to the Adjutant General, September 6, 1845.

lation to the defences of the city and castle, and General Scott had been actively and constantly employed for several weeks in making the necessary preparations. Heavy ordnance, large quantities of missiles and ammunition, transport vessels, bomb-ketches, and surf-boats to land the troops, were ordered to be prepared, and dispatched to the Gulf without delay. A corps of sappers and miners, and mountain howitzer and rocket batteries, were also organized to take part in the expedition, and accompany the army on its march to the Mexican capital.

It was originally intended that the attack on Vera Cruz should be made in co-operation with the navy, by a detachment from General Taylor's army of four or five thousand men, under the command of General Patterson.* After the dispatch of the 2nd of September, intimating an intention to make a descent on the Gulf coast, at Tampico, was intercepted by the enemy, it became evident that a much larger force would be necessary. Tampico was occupied, however, as has been stated, in order to mask the more important enterprise in contemplation.

General Scott had made an unsuccessful application to the President of the United States, to be ordered to the seat of war, in the month of September; but, in consequence of the prior misunderstanding, his request was denied.† At a later day this determination was

* House of Rep. Exec. Doc. 119, (pp. 84, 88), 2nd Session, 29th Congress.

† Allusion has been heretofore made to this controversy (ante, p. 94). It appears to have been mainly of a personal character, and one reflecting little credit or honor on those concerned, though proving, very conclusively, that our military and civil officers, no matter how high their station, are not exempt from the passions and prejudices which sometimes afflict those who move in a humbler sphere. For the particulars

wisely reconsidered, and in accordance with the general expectation of the country, he was directed to take the field. To him, more than to any other man, was the army indebted for its high state of discipline, its usefulness and efficiency; and it was due to his past services, and his talents, that he should be allowed to participate in the active operations of the war. If the laurels won at Chippewa and Niagara could be refreshed and reinvigorated by the cool breezes that swept over the *terra templada* of Mexico,—if there were new victories to be gained that could give additional lustre to the undying fame which formed one of the richest jewels of the nation,—it was but just that the opportunity should be given. Large reinforcements were about to be sent to Mexico, and the occasion seemed most favorable for directing the general-in-chief of the army to assume the command, since it could be done at such a time without prejudice to the officer who had hitherto so skillfully directed its movements.* There was a peculiar fitness, too, in assigning General Scott to conduct the expedition against Vera Cruz, because the merit of planning the move-

of the difference, see Appendix to the Congressional Globe, 1845-6, pp. 650, et seq.; House of Rep. Exec. Doc. 119, 2nd session, 29th Congress; Senate Document, No. 1, 1st session, 30th Congress; and the correspondence between General Scott and the War Department communicated to the House of Representatives, March 20th and April 26th, 1848.

* General Taylor expected that General Scott would be ordered to Mexico, and did not appear in the least disappointed when informed that this had been done. Indeed, it does not seem strange that this should be the case. At the commencement of the war there were a number of officers in the army superior in rank to General Taylor; but within a very few weeks after that time he stood second only to General Scott.

ment was his own, and his experience, sagacity, and skill, were requisite to insure its success.*

The order directing General Scott to repair to Mexico, and clothing him with discretionary power in regard to the future conduct of hostilities, was issued on the 23rd of November, and on the 24th he left Washington for New York, where he embarked for New Orleans.† Before leaving the capital, the necessary preliminary arrangements had been made for the expedition. Nine additional volunteer regiments, including one of Texan horse, were called for; and at the ensuing session of Congress, bills were introduced, and passed, authorizing ten new regiments of regular troops to be raised, and the increase of the artillery regiments and marine corps,—and providing for the appointment of two major generals, and three brigadier generals, and the encouragement of enlistment, by large bounties. The general officers, the ten regiments, and the addition to the marine corps, were to be continued in service only during the existence of the war.‡

* Projects of General Scott laid before the Secretary of War, October 27th, 1846, and November 12th, 16th, and 21st, of the same year.

† "The President, several days since, communicated in person to you his orders to repair to Mexico, to take the command of the forces there assembled, and particularly to organize and set on foot an expedition to operate on the Gulf coast, if, on arriving at the theatre of action, you shall deem it to be practicable. It is not proposed to control your operations by definite and positive instructions, but you are left to prosecute them as your judgment, under a full view of all the circumstances, shall dictate."—Extract from the letter of the Secretary of War to General Scott, dated November 21st, 1846.

‡ The ten regiment bill did not become a law until the 11th of February, 1847, partly in consequence of the attempt made to create the office of lieutenant general heretofore alluded to. (Ante, p. 95, note.) By the terms of the act, the President was authorized to equip one of the infantry regiments as voltigeurs, which was done. Under the law authorizing the selection of additional general officers, Gideon

While in New York, General Scott addressed a letter to General Taylor, informing him that he was about to embark for the seat of war; that he designed to undertake an expedition in a different quarter of the enemy's country; and that he should be compelled, though reluctantly, to take from him the greater part of the troops under his command.* He reached New Orleans near the close of December, and early in January following he was upon the Rio Grande. Instructions with reference to his plans, and the number, and character of the men whom he wished to be prepared for the expedition, were sent to General Taylor, by different messengers. Lieutenant Ritchie, one of

J. Pillow and John A. Quitman, brigadier generals of volunteers, were appointed major generals; and Franklin Pierce of New Hampshire, George Cadwalader of Pennsylvania, and Enos D. Hopping of New York, were appointed brigadier generals. Thomas H. Benton of Missouri, and William Cumming of Georgia, were originally appointed the major generals, but did not accept. The vacancies occasioned in the volunteer service, by the promotion of Generals Pillow and Quitman, were filled by the appointment of Caleb Cushing of Massachusetts, and Sterling Price of Missouri.

* "I am not coming, my dear general, to supersede you in the immediate command on the line of operations rendered illustrious by you and your gallant army. My proposed theatre is different. You may imagine it; and I wish very much that it were prudent, at this distance, to tell you all that I expect to attempt and hope to execute. * * * But, my dear general, I shall be obliged to take from you most of the gallant officers and men, (regulars and volunteers,) whom you have so long and so nobly commanded. I am afraid that I shall, by imperious necessity--the approach of yellow fever on the Gulf coast--reduce you, for a time, to stand on the defensive. This will be infinitely painful to you, and for that reason, distressing to me. But I rely upon your patriotism to submit to the temporary sacrifice with cheerfulness. No man can better afford to do so. Recent victories place you on the high eminence; and I even flatter myself that any benefit that may result to me, personally, from the unequal division of troops alluded to, will lessen the pain of your consequent inactivity."—Letter of General Scott to General Taylor, November 25th, 1846.

the bearers of dispatches, was on his way to seek the latter, when he was attacked, between Linares and Victoria, by a party of rancheros, and cruelly murdered. The papers in his possession fell into the hands of the enemy, and the fact that an expedition against Vera Cruz was projected could no longer be concealed.

When the arrangements for the expedition against Vera Cruz were made at Washington, preparatory to the departure of General Scott, it was not supposed that General Taylor would deem it advisable to advance beyond Monterey, or occupy the lower part of the State of Tamaulipas.* It was intended that he should remain upon the defensive until additional troops could be sent out from the United States. The importance of the position at Saltillo was not correctly understood at the War Department, and hence it was not taken into account in the calculations which had been made. General Taylor might have occupied and held the city of Monterey with a much smaller force than was left under his control; but he wisely decided to keep possession of Saltillo, as being a still more commanding position, and completely covering the single road practicable for artillery, which was the only formidable arm of the Mexican service, to the valley of the Rio Grande. Monterey was well situated for defence; but if the enemy could advance to that point, the communication with his principal dépôts would be more likely to be cut off, and their protection attended with more danger and difficulty.

The whole number of troops upon the Rio Grande, and *en route* for the Gulf, including the new volunteer regiments, was not far from 20,000. General Scott

* House of Rep. Exec. Doc. 119, (pp. 84, 89, 108) 2nd Session, 29th Congress.

required 12,000 of these for the expedition against Vera Cruz. Besides the volunteers embarked from the United States for the island of Lobos, the appointed place of rendezvous, nearly all the regular troops under Generals Twiggs and Worth, and the greater part of the volunteer division of General Patterson, were ordered to the same point. It was with great reluctance that General Taylor parted with the veteran troops whom he had so long commanded ;* but the enterprise which General Scott was about to attempt, was of primary importance. It was necessary that Vera Cruz and the castle of San Juan de Ulua should be reduced, if at all, before the return of the sickly season ; and if that could only be done by an assault, the regular regiments would be especially needed. Moreover, it was to be apprehended that Santa Anna might move his army from San Luis Potosi, in the direction of Vera Cruz, after receiving the information contained in the dispatches borne by Lieutenant Ritchie. Had he done this, the column under General Scott would probably have been decimated ere they could have effected a landing on the Mexican shore. Undoubtedly it would have been a wiser policy to have called out a larger number of volunteers in the summer or fall of 1846 ; but the error was one very likely to be committed in a country like ours. It was too late to correct it when General Scott arrived upon the Rio Grande ; he had no dragon's teeth, from which armed soldiers might be raised at his bidding ; and a

* Letters of General Taylor to the Adjutant General, January 15th and 27th, 1847. General Taylor did not anticipate that he would be required to part with more than four or five thousand of the troops under his command (Doc. 119, p. 94) ; but very magnanimously made the sacrifice when the exigencies of the service required it.

delay, even of a few weeks, could not be permitted. About six hundred regulars, including two squadrons of dragoons, and four of the finest artillery companies in the army, with the best disciplined regiments of volunteers, which had been drilled by General Wool, or under the eye of General Taylor himself, were left upon the line of the Sierra Madre.* In view of the loss of life which afterwards occurred, it may be regretted that the army under General Taylor was necessarily so much reduced; but he knew of what materials it was composed, and did not rashly expose himself to peril. His force was small, but it proved sufficient; and had it not been for the defection of one of his regiments, the repulse at Buena Vista would have been the complete rout of the Mexican army.

After giving the necessary instructions to the troops ordered to join General Scott, General Taylor returned to Monterey. During his absence General Wool had remained encamped with his division at Agua Nueva, until General Worth left Saltillo, when he took position on the heights above and to the south of the city, with a portion of his command, and distributed the remainder through the valley. General Miñon was known to be in the vicinity with his lancers, and scouting parties were constantly kept out to obtain information. On the 22nd of January a party of over seventy men, consisting of Arkansas and Kentucky cavalry, commanded by Majors Borland and Gaines, were surprised at the hacienda of Encarnacion, forty-eight miles beyond Saltillo, by General Miñon. Resistance against so formidable a force would have been

* Generals Patterson, Twiggs, Worth, Pillow, Quitman and Shields, accompanied General Scott, and Generals Butler, Wool, Marshall and Lane remained with General Taylor.

idle, and they surrendered themselves prisoners of war Captain Henrie of the Texan Rangers was with the detachment, but gallantly made his escape on the second day after their capture. On the 27th of January, a picket guard of seventeen men of the Kentucky volunteers, under Captain Heady, were also captured by the enemy. The advanced pickets were repeatedly driven in, and it was confidently rumored, that the main body of the Mexican forces under Santa Anna were marching to attack the American army.

Leaving a force of fifteen hundred men to garrison the city of Monterey, General Taylor proceeded to Saltillo, early in February. While General Worth was in command at this point, a strong redoubt commanding the town and the plain in which it is situated, had been constructed by General Lane's Indiana brigade, under the direction of Lieutenant Kingsbury of the ordnance corps. Captain Webster occupied the redoubt with two twenty-four pounder howitzers, and several pieces of smaller calibre; and Major Warren, of the 1st Illinois foot, was directed to guard the town with four companies of the Illinois volunteers, two of each regiment. On the 8th of February the remainder of the army, about 5,000 strong, moved forward under General Taylor to Agua Nueva, where he could have the advantage of a large plain to drill his troops, and hold in observation the road from San Luis Potosi, and the different passes leading to Parras, Monclova, and Saltillo.

The road from Saltillo to Agua Nueva pursues a south-westerly course, through an irregular and broken valley, varying from two to three miles in width, and bounded on either side by the tall mountain ridges of the Sierra Madre. About five miles south of Saltillo is the hacienda of Buena Vista,* and a short distance beyond this the flanking mountains incline nearer to each other, and form the pass of Angostura. The attention of General Taylor was called to this position by General Wool, as being one which a small army could easily maintain against a larger force. Notwithstanding its advantages, the former decided to proceed to Agua Nueva, as he had at first intended, and if Santa Anna approached with his army, to fall back to the ground which he saw at a glance was well adapted to the limited numbers of his command. By this means he would be enabled to practise a ruse upon the enemy, and lead them to attack him in a position of his own selection, and which he felt fully competent to hold. This determination was strengthened on his arrival at Agua Nueva, which he found to be a more exposed position, and one that could be readily turned on either flank. Information having been received that the Mexican forces were concentrating in his front, General Taylor ordered Major McCulloch, with a party of Texan spies, to reconnoitre the San Luis road. The detachment left Agua Nueva on the 16th of February, and about midnight encountered a small body of the enemy's cavalry, whom they drove towards Encarnacion, and then returned to camp. On the 20th instant a strong reconnaissance was dispatched to the hacienda of Heclionda, under Lieutenant Colonel May, and Major McCulloch made another examination of Encarnacion. The reports of these officers rendered it certain that Santa Anna, instead of marching with the forces which he had concentrated at San Luis Potosi, to meet General Scott at Vera Cruz, had con-

* Beautiful view.

cluded to take advantage of the withdrawal of such a large number of troops from the line commanded by General Taylor, and by one decisive blow endeavor to wipe out the ignominy of past reverses, and retrieve the waning fortunes of the Mexican Republic.

At noon on the 21st, General Taylor broke up his camp at Agua Nueva, and retired leisurely towards the position in front of the hacienda of Buena Vista, which had previously been selected. Colonel Yell remained at Agua Nueva with his regiment of Arkansas cavalry, to look out for the enemy, and cover the removal of the public stores. The 2nd Kentucky foot under Colonel McKee, and a section of Captain Washington's battery, halted at Encantada to support Colonel Yell. The 1st Illinois foot under Colonel Hardin were stationed at the pass of Angostura, where it had been determined to give battle to the enemy. General Taylor proceeded to Saltillo, accompanied by Lieutenant Colonel May, with his squadron of the 2nd dragoons, two batteries of the 3rd artillery, under Captains Sherman and Bragg, and the Mississippi rifle regiment, under Colonel Davis. On the evening of the 21st, the regiment of Kentucky cavalry under Colonel Marshall, and the squadron of the 1st dragoons, Captain Steen, were ordered to Agua Nueva, to reinforce Colonel Yell. General Wool encamped near Buena Vista with the remaining section of Washington's battery, the 2nd Illinois foot, Colonel Bissell, and the 2nd and 3rd Indiana regiments, commanded by Colonels Bowles and J. H. Lane.* Before the removal

* In addition to the forces above enumerated, General Taylor had under his command one company of Texan volunteers, and a spy company commanded by Major McCulloch. The two Indiana regiments formed a brigade under the command of General Lane.

of the stores could be effected, Colonel Yell's pickets were driven in by the enemy, and, in obedience to his instructions, he retired with the reinforcements under Colonel Marshall, after destroying a small quantity of grain remaining at the hacienda, and leaving a few wagons which had been abandoned by the teamsters. At Encantada he was joined by the force under Colonel McKee, and they fell back together to Buena Vista, before daylight on the morning of the 22nd.

From the time of his arrival at San Luis Potosi, in October 1846, Santa Anna labored unceasingly in strengthening his fortifications at that point, and in equipping and instructing the men under his command. Political dissensions and differences, however, were not entirely healed. His approach to the city of Mexico, and his journey to take command of the army of the north, had been attended with all the pomp and parade, the glitter and show, the shouting and rejoicing, of a triumphal procession; but much of this enthusiasm was transient and unreal. The elements of discontent still existed. The Mexican Congress, which assembled in December, elected Santa Anna to the presidency, and made choice of Gomez Farias as vice president, upon whom the executive authority devolved during the absence of the former. The monarchists and centralists were opposed to this arrangement, and did not repress their complaints. Weeks and months rolled by; no enemy appeared; and the army remained inactive. The people became dissatisfied; they expected every thing from Santa Anna, and could not be disappointed. Murmurs were repeatedly heard; and it was at length asserted that motives of personal ambition detained him at San Luis Potosi.* He could hesitate no longer. His private credit was pledged for a loan of one hundred and eighty thousand dollars, and the necessary supplies for twelve days procured for his army. On the 28th of January he commenced moving forward with twenty pieces of artillery, and a force of about 20,000 men, exclusive of the cavalry detachments under Generals Miñon and Urrea already thrown in the advance.† The march was long and tedious. The army was scantily supplied with food, water and clothing; the weather was harsh and inclement; and sickness and desertion fast thinned their numbers. Encouraged by the promise of their leader, that they would soon be supplied from the well-filled storehouses of the American army at Saltillo and Monterey, they

* It is questionable whether the withdrawal of so large a number of troops from the line of the Sierra Madre, formed the controlling reason for the advance of Santa Anna against General Taylor. Political considerations probably had far more influence. The army could have made the march to Vera Cruz, though a longer distance, with far less inconvenience; but he dared not lead them in the direction of the capital. It was said that the presence of so large a force at San Luis, under his orders, was dangerous to the liberties of the country, and the march towards the Gulf, to meet General Scott, would have been the signal for a bloody revolution.

† The accounts are very conflicting in relation to the strength of the Mexican army. In his official report of the battle at Buena Vista Santa Anna states that the force with which he left San Luis Potosi including garrisons and detachments, amounted to 18,133, and that his artillery train consisted of seventeen pieces. Another statement makes the army amount to over 21,000, with twenty-two pieces. The general orders issued on the 28th of January, at San Luis, (Senate Exec. Doc. No. 1, 1st session, 29th Congress, p. 154,) and found on the battle ground at Buena Vista, show that there were twenty pieces of artillery. In his summons to General Taylor, the Mexican commander said the forces under his orders numbered 20,000, including, doubtless, the detachment under General Miñon, and perhaps that under Urrea; but he was more likely to exaggerate his strength than the contrary. Gen-

COLONEL MAY.

continued to advance in spite of the obstacles which were calculated to discourage them.

The various detachments of the Mexican army were concentrated at San Fernando, and on the night of the 20th of February they encamped at Encenada. On the morning of the 21st mass was said in front of the different divisions, and at noon the whole column were again on the march; the brigade of light infantry under General Ampudia, accompanied by a body of lancers, leading the van; the divisions of infantry, under General Lombardini, in the centre; and the division of cavalry and infantry, under General Ortéga, bringing up the rear. General Miñon was ordered with his cavalry brigade to make a diversion in the rear of the American army, and occupy the hacienda of Buena Vista. The detachment under General Urrea at Tula had received instructions to advance from their position, and attack the American posts, and cut off their communications between Monterey and the Rio Grande.

It had been the intention of Santa Anna, on learning the position of General Taylor, to place his forces between the American army and Saltillo, and compel them to fight him at this disadvantage. The retrograde movement to Buena Vista defeated his project. His

eral Miñon's cavalry brigade was 1,200 strong; General Urrea had an indefinite number of men, varying from two to three thousand; General Vasquez remained at Matehuala with a brigade of infantry as a *corps de reserve;* and the main body under Santa Anna probably did not much exceed 17,000 men. The following general officers accompanied the army; Alvarez, general-in-chief of cavalry; Lombardini, commander-in-chief of the infantry; Requena, general-in-chief of artillery; Mora y Villamil, chief of the engineers; Micheltorena, chief of the general staff; and Generals R. Vasquez, Torrejon, Ampudia, Andradé, Juvera, Quintamar, Miñon, (detached,) Jaurequi, Conde, Pacheco, Garcia, Ortéga, Mejia, Flores, Guzman, Mora, and Romero.

troops were elated, however, with the idea that the Americans were retreating before them, and he determined to advance by the direct road to Saltillo. There were other passes through the mountains, by way of Heclionda on his right, and La Punta de Santa Elena on his left, by which he could have gained the Saltillo road in rear of Buena Vista; but either of these routes would have required three or four days' march, and the state of his supplies forbade any further delay. He passed the night of the 21st with his main body, in the vicinity of Agua Nueva, and at early dawn on the following morning took up his line of march towards the pass of Angostura.

The position selected by General Taylor for the reception of the enemy is nearly one mile in advance of the hacienda of Buena Vista. At this point the bases of the mountainous ridges are about two miles apart. The main road to Agua Nueva passes through a narrow defile inclining to the west before it enters the gorge, and then turning to the east. Upon its right is a valley, or alluvial bottom, formed from the débris of the neighboring hills, with a small branch of the San Juan winding through it, and everywhere cut up by deep gullies, and yawning pits and chasms, washed out by the torrents plunging from the mountain sides during the rainy seasons, which render it impracticable for cavalry or artillery; and further beyond, there is an intermediate range of hills, with a narrow pass intervening between them and the mountains. Upon the left the ground descends gradually from the heights towards the road, forming an elevated plain of table land, free from timber, with the exception of a few shrubs and bushes, but intersected by a succession of ravines also worn by the mountain torrents. The ravines are of irregular formation, some extending to the very foot of the mountains, and others terminating midway in the plain. On the extreme left their banks are sloping, and can be passed without difficulty, but nearer the road they are more precipitous, and form a series of steep and rocky bluffs. In the rear of the principal plain, upon which the line of battle was formed, are similar plateaus, separated in like manner by ravines.

On the night of the 21st, the 1st Illinois regiment threw up a parapet on a hill east of the gorge, and dug a small ditch, and made a parapet extending from the road around the brink of a deep gully on the right. In the morning a ditch and parapet were thrown across the road for the protection of a battery of artillery, leaving a narrow passage next the bluff, which was closed by running in two wagons loaded with stone. At nine o'clock the enemy were discovered advancing over the distant hills,

"Winding from cliff to cliff, in loose array."

As they approached the American lines, their columns closed up together. Dense squadrons of horse, with glittering lances and gay pennons, formed the advance, and then came the long serried files of infantry, with artillery and cavalry intermingled; column upon column deploying in the valley, as if there were no end to the stream of warriors which threatened to overwhelm the feeble band before them. But though weak in numbers, the American soldiers were strong in their position, strong in the memory of past victories, strong in the prestige of their leader's name, and stronger yet in the recollection that they were the countrymen —and this was the birthday—of Washington!

In the absence of General Taylor, the line of battle was formed by General Wool. Captain Washington was posted in the road with his battery, with two companies of the 1st Illinois behind the breastwork on his right, and the 2nd Kentucky infantry, Colonel McKee, occupying a spur of the elevated ground in the rear. Colonel Hardin remained in position on the height, with six companies of his regiment, having the 2nd Illinois, Colonel Bissell, and the company of Texan volunteers, Captain Connor, on his left. The Indiana brigade under General Lane, took position on a ridge in rear of the front line, and Captain Steen's squadron of 1st dragoons was held in reserve. The Kentucky and Arkansas regiments of cavalry, under Colonels Marshall and Yell, were stationed on the left of the second line. Soon afterwards the rifle companies of the volunteer cavalry were dismounted, and, with a battalion of riflemen from the Indiana brigade, under Major Gorman, sustained by the remaining companies of the Kentucky regiment, the whole commanded by Colonel Marshall, were ordered to take ground to the front and extreme left. When the commanding general arrived from Saltillo with the remainder of the troops, the squadron of 2nd dragoons, Lieutenant Colonel May, the light batteries of Captains Sherman and Bragg, and the Mississippi regiment, Colonel Davis, were held in reserve with the squadron under Captain Steen. At eleven o'clock General Taylor received a note from Santa Anna, informing him that he was surrounded by twenty thousand men, and requiring him to surrender if he wished to avoid being cut to pieces.

The reply was what might have been expected—a prompt and decided refusal.*

At two o'clock the battalions of Mexican light infantry, under General Ampudia, commenced deploying to the right, evidently intending to outflank the Americans and secure the heights overlooking the broad plateau east of the battery in the road, while a large howitzer opened its fire upon the left of the line. General Lane moved forward with a section of Washington's battery under Lieutenant O'Brien, and the 2nd Indiana regiment, on the left of the 2nd Illinois, to check the movement. A demonstration was also ob-

* The correspondence between Santa Anna and General Taylor was remarkable for its boastful tone on the one hand, and its emphatic brevity on the other. It was as follows:—

SUMMONS OF SANTA ANNA.

"You are surrounded by twenty thousand men, and cannot in any human probability avoid suffering a rout, and being cut to pieces with your troops; but as you deserve consideration and particular esteem, I wish to save you from a catastrophe, and for that purpose give you this notice in order that you may surrender at discretion, under the assurance that you will be treated with the consideration belonging to the Mexican character, to which end you will be granted an hour's time to make up your mind, to commence from the moment when my flag of truce arrives in your camp.

"With this view, I assure you of my particular consideration.

"God and Liberty. Camp at Encantada, February 22, 1847.

"ANTO. LOPEZ DE SANTA ANNA.

"To General Z. TAYLOR,
Commanding the forces of the U. S."

REPLY OF GENERAL TAYLOR.

"Head-quarters, Army of Occupation,
Near Buena Vista, Feb. 22, 1847.

"SIR:—In reply to your note of this date, summoning me to surrender my force at discretion, I beg leave to say that I decline acceding to your request. With high respect, I am, sir,

"Your obedient servant, Z. TAYLOR,
"*Major General, U. S. A. Comm'g.*

"Señor Gen. D. ANTO. LOPEZ DE SANTA ANNA,
Commanding in chief, Encantada."

served on the other flank, and the 2nd Kentucky regiment, with a section of Bragg's battery and a detachment of mounted men, were ordered to take post on the right of the gullies, and some distance in advance of the centre.

Colonel Marshall had anticipated the effort to outflank, and was prepared to meet the enemy. He had secured possession of one of the spurs running out from the mountains, and was preparing to occupy a still more commanding one in his front, when he was induced to fall back through some mistake in the delivery of an order from General Wool. When the enemy's light troops approached, a spirited conflict ensued, which was kept up for several hours. The American loss was trifling, but the fatal fire of their rifles filled the ravines and gorges with the dead and dying of their opponents. Numbers, however, prevailed against courage and determination. Before dark the Mexicans had occupied the sides, and scaled the summits of the Sierra Madre, and had thus outflanked the American position. The recall was sounded, and Colonel Marshall returned with his command to the plain.

During the night of the 22nd, the American troops bivouacked at their respective positions without fires, and lay on their arms. Long before daybreak on the following morning, they were aroused from their slumbers to prepare for the coming contest. The day dawned beautifully. The sky was clear and cloudless. The sunlight streamed over the distant mountain tops, bathing hill and rock, ravine and plain, forest and chaparral, in a rich flood of golden radiance. The cool breeze that swept through the valley was welcomed by many a feverish brow; and it rested softly on many a manly cheek, glowing with hope and enthusiasm, that was cold in death ere the shadows of evening stole along the western hills. There were throbbing bosoms and anxious hearts in that little army; but few among them all were faint in spirit, or dreaded the encounter.

Apprehending that an attempt might be made on Saltillo by the detachment under General Miñon, which had been visible all day in rear of the town, and that the force stationed there would be unable to resist it, General Taylor had returned in the evening of the 22nd, with the Mississippi regiment, and the squadron of the 2nd dragoons, to make further preparations for its defence. Two companies of the Mississippi rifles under Captain Rogers, and one piece from Bragg's battery under Captain Shover, were left to protect the train and head-quarter camp. In the morning of the 23rd the general returned to the field with the remainder of the Mississippi regiment and the dragoons. Before he arrived upon the ground the battle had commenced.

The action was opened on the extreme left of the American line, by the Mexican light troops, and the riflemen who had again moved up the mountains. Major Trail was soon after detached with three companies of the 2nd Illinois to the assistance of Colonel Marshall. The united command bravely maintained their ground against the superior force under General Ampudia, which attempted to drive them from their position. About eight o'clock Santa Anna put in motion his main columns of attack; the divisions of Lombardini and Pacheco, with a portion of the cavalry under Juvera, and a twelve-pounder battery, advancing on the left of the American line, in order to gain the elevated ground; and a strong column of attack under Mora y Villamil, with three pieces of artillery, moving along the road towards the centre. A battery of eight-pounders, consisting of eight pieces, was planted on the crest of a hill near the road where the different columns were formed for the attack, and General Ortéga remained in command of a strong reserve.

The column advancing against the centre was checked in a few moments by a rapid fire from Washington's battery, which opened wide gaps in the opposing ranks. The enemy broke and retired. The lancers were interposed to prevent the retreat, and drive the infantry forward. But they could better meet the spear-points of their countrymen, than the scathing torrent that poured down that roadway. Retreating in confusion they joined the column moving towards the American left. In this quarter the attack was more successful. The heavy Mexican battery was pushed to the foot of the heights which the light troops had ascended, and their cavalry and infantry, advancing up the bed of a ravine in front of the American line, soon gained a position on the plateau.

The battle now commenced in earnest. The 2nd Indiana sustained themselves for a short time without faltering, and Lieutenant O'Brien opened a vigorous fire which mowed down the enemy in scores. His guns were advanced. Once more the Mexican line began to waver, and the infantry were again driven forward by the lancers. A single bold and vigorous onset would have secured the victory. General Lane urged his men to stand firm—to push upon the enemy. But the fire was too terrible. The Indiana regiment reeled to and fro like a drunken man. They staggered back and retired from the field in confusion, at the moment when General Taylor arrived from Saltillo.

Captain Lincoln, assistant adjutant-general in the staff of General Wool, lost his life in attempting to rally the fugitives. Major Dix, of the Pay Department, also dashed forward, and snatching the colors of the regiment, he called upon the men to stand by them to the last. General Lane, though severely wounded, exhorted and entreated them to follow him to victory or to death.* All efforts were in vain. A portion of them were rallied and joined the Mississippi regiment, doing good service throughout the day; of the remainder, some retired to the hacienda of Buena Vista, and others to Saltillo.

The riflemen and cavalry under Colonel Marshall, being thus cut off from the centre, retreated in good order in the direction of Buena Vista. Lieutenant O'Brien maintained the ground with his guns, until all his cannoneers were killed or wounded; but being deprived of his support, he was forced to retire, leaving one of his pieces, the horses attached to which were

* General Lane was completely carried away with enthusiasm, and closed his eloquent and impassioned appeal to the retreating soldiers, by reminding them what a glorious thing it would be to have it said in history, that "*the whole Indiana regiment were cut to pieces!*" Posthumous fame seemed of little value at such a time, and his entreaties were lost upon them. He was too brave a soldier to offer an apology for their retreat; but in his official report there is one fact stated, which should never be forgotten when their conduct is called in question. He says: "The 2nd regiment of my command which opened the battle on the plain, in such gallant style, deserves a passing remark. I shall attempt to make no apology for their retreat; for it was their duty to stand or die to the last man until they received orders to retire; but I desire to call your attention to one fact connected with this affair. They remained in their position, in line, receiving the fire of 3,000 or 4,000 infantry in front, exposed at the same time on the left flank to a most desperate raking fire from the enemy's battery, posted within point-blank shot, until they had deliberately discharged *twenty rounds* of cartridges at the enemy."

either killed or disabled, in the hands of the enemy. The 2nd Illinois at once became exposed to the enfilading fire of the heavy battery. Eight regiments of Mexican infantry came down upon them, and they were forced temporarily to take shelter behind the ravines. Sections of Sherman's battery, under Lieutenants Thomas and French, advanced to their assistance. The 2nd Kentucky regiment, and Captain Bragg's battery, had already been ordered from the right, and, in connection with the 1st and 2nd Illinois, and the sections of Sherman's battery, they drove back the enemy in handsome style, and regained possession of a portion of the plateau. The Mexican columns were compelled to hug the mountain more closely, and their immense hosts began to pour along its base to the rear of the American line. Here they were met by the Mississippi rifles, who came into action in double-quick time. As a column of the enemy's infantry, flanked by their cavalry, moved down the slopes towards the road, Colonel Davis hastened to meet them. His men were halted only when within range of their rifles, and were then ordered to "fire advancing." The front lines of the enemy fell before them. They too suffered severely, but they pressed boldly forward, crossing a deep ravine under a galling fire, until a body of cavalry attempted to gain their rear, when they retired slowly, and after dispersing the lancers, formed again behind the ravine which they had first crossed.

The enemy's battery had been constantly playing upon the front and centre, but its fire was now turned upon the position occupied by the Mississippi regiment. Lieutenant Kilburn, with one piece from Bragg's battery, was ordered to this point, where a new line of battle, forming a crotchet perpendicular to the first line, was taken up. The 3rd Indiana regiment, under Colonel J. H. Lane, accompanied by General Lane, also advanced to redeem the character of the state to which they belonged. This was bravely done. Daring and repeated efforts were made by the enemy against this portion of the line, but they were as often repulsed. At length a large body of cavalry debouched from their cover on the left of the position. The Mississippi regiment immediately filed to the right and fronted across the plain, while the 3rd Indiana formed on the bank of a ravine, and in advance of the right flank of the Mississippians, by which a re-entering angle was presented to the enemy. The Mexican lancers came dashing onward, in close and beautiful order. Captain Sherman now arrived with two pieces from his battery. The American soldiers were firm and steady as experienced veterans, and when the enemy came within thirty yards, a broad sheet of flame flashed from the entire line. Whole masses of men and horses were seen to fall upon the plain. The enemy were instantly checked and thrown into confusion. The Americans advanced, still pouring forth their withering volleys. Captain Bragg also brought his battery round to this position, and commenced raining deadly showers of grape upon the Mexicans, as they retreated for shelter to the gorges and ravines near the mountains. Lieutenant Rucker, at the head of the squadron of 1st dragoons, Captain Steen having been wounded when the left flank was turned, was ordered to move up a ravine and charge them. Before this was done, the order was countermanded, and he was directed to join Lieutenant Colonel May, who was advancing with his squadron of the 2nd dragoons, a squadron of Arkansas horse under Captain Pike, and Lieutenant Reynolds with a section of Sherman's battery, to check the enemy's cavalry, from the head of their column on the left, who were threatening a descent on the hacienda of Buena Vista, near which the train of supplies and baggage had been parked.

Before Lieutenant Colonel May had reached the ground, Colonels Marshall and Yell had encountered the enemy with the Kentucky and Arkansas cavalry. The order to charge was given on both sides at the same instant. Like knights at the tourney they sprang forward to do their devoir. The squadrons met in the centre of the plain. They were interlocked; lances and sabres were shivered; and they grappled each other in the death-embrace. The shock was dreadful; Colonel Yell fell among the foremost; but his fall was fearfully avenged.* The fight was of short duration. The rifle battalions under Majors Trail and Gorman, and a portion of the Indiana infantry which had retreated, were formed under the direction of Major Munroe, chief of artillery, and Major Morrison of the volunteer staff. The enemy did not wait to meet this additional force. Their column divided; one part retreating to the mountains, and the other dashing through the hacienda, where they received a galling fire from the riflemen and infantry. Lieutenant Colonel May had at this moment come up, and aided with his command in completing the rout of this portion of the lancers.

The whole Mexican column which had turned the

* The wounds inflicted by the Mexican lancers were severe. Some of them seemed to take great delight in torturing the wounded and the dying. The body of Adjutant Vaughn, of the Kentucky cavalry, who fell in this charge, contained no less than fourteen wounds, more than one half of which were mortal.

American left were now in a critical position. On one flank the regular dragoons, the Kentucky and Arkansas cavalry, Lieutenant Reynolds' section of artillery, and the rallied men under Majors Trail and Gorman, and on the other the batteries of Sherman and Bragg, and the 3rd Indiana and Mississippi regiments, were advancing to complete their destruction. Behind them was the wall of mountains, and before them a band of determined men, firm as the hills which looked down upon their valor, whose messengers of death were sending so many of their number to their last account. They faced about to retrace their steps, exposing their right flank to the American fire, but caring only to reach some place of safety. Just as they commenced their retreat, a white flag was seen approaching from the Mexican head-quarters. Its bearer delivered a message from Santa Anna to General Taylor, requesting to know what the latter wanted. General Wool was ordered to the enemy's lines, to demand the immediate surrender of the column cut off from the main body, and the American soldiers slackened their fire.

General Wool soon learned that the Mexican commander had practised a ruse. He was unable to induce the enemy to stop the fire of their battery, and returned without having an interview with Santa Anna. The retreating column had in the meantime taken advantage of the pause in the fire, and the configuration of the ground, and were no longer in immediate danger. As they came opposite the American centre, the 1st and 2nd Illinois, the 2nd Kentucky, and Lieutenant O'Brien with two guns from Washington's battery, moved forward to terminate the contest by a vigorous charge. The movement was unfortunate, and again the tide of battle turned. Resolved to make one more final and desperate struggle for the mastery, Santa Anna had already ordered up his reserves, and his batteries redoubled their fire. The reinforcements marched up the ravine in front of the original line of battle, as the Americans were advancing, and formed at the base of the mountains, in connection with the column which had retreated. Against so powerful an host that little phalanx could not have been expected to prevail. Borne down before this overwhelming array which came so unexpectedly upon them, the infantry retired down the smaller ravines to the road. The lancers followed close upon them, slaughtering indiscriminately those who lay helpless beneath their horses' hoofs, those who were willing to surrender, and those who died with a note of defiance on their lips. Colonels Hardin and McKee, and Lieutenant Colonel Clay, were among the slain. Lieutenant Colonel Clay was not mortally wounded, and his men endeavored to carry him from the ground. Seeing so many falling around him, he begged to be laid down upon the field, where he died fighting bravely to the last. A prompt fire from Washington's battery upon the lancers, as they attempted to follow the American infantry into the road, put an end to the pursuit.

Meanwhile Lieutenant O'Brien had never ceased his fire. Two horses were shot under him, and a second time were all his cannoneers cut down. The enemy seemed goaded to desperation, and continued to press forward. Still he remained firmly by his guns, and never left them until the Mexicans were at their muzzles. Both pieces were captured and taken from the field. The crisis of the action had arrived. The centre of the American line was almost forced. But

DEATH OF LIEUT. COLONEL CLAY.

relief was nigh. Captain Bragg hurried forward with his battery at a gallop, and reached the plateau before all was lost. Without any infantry to support him he opened his fire within a few yards of the Mexican line.* General Taylor had also arrived upon this part of the field, which he saw must be maintained at any cost, and his presence served to animate the men. The enemy wavered, but recovered; additional quantities of grape were forced into the American guns; again the Mexicans staggered back, but they rallied once more, like some giant in the last agony struggling with the destroyer death. At this time Sherman had brought his battery to bear upon them, and the 3rd Indiana and Mississippi regiments advanced upon their right flank. Neither man nor horse could stand before that iron torrent, which swept the plain as with the besom of destruction. Repulsed, routed, and in disorder, they abandoned the contest.

As soon as the action commenced at Buena Vista, in the morning of the 23rd, a demonstration was made on the redoubt and encampment at Saltillo, by the lancers under General Miñon. Major Warren had directed the streets to be barricaded, and three of his companies were thrown into the cathedral. Captain Webster opened upon the enemy with his twenty-four pounder howitzers, as soon as they came within range, and drove them beyond the reach of his shells, with the loss of several men and horses. They succeeded,

* In reply to Captain Bragg's request to be furnished with a supporting party, General Taylor, turning to the chief of his staff, said—"Major Bliss and I will support you!" and immediately galloped forward. When the enemy appeared inclined to persist in their advance, the general gave his celebrated order—"A little more grape, Captain Bragg!"—words which will long be remembered in connection with the events of that day.

however, in occupying the road south of the town, and picked up a number of fugitives from the principal field. Between two and three o'clock they began to move towards their former position, when Captain Shover advanced upon them at a gallop, with a six-pounder, in the open plain, and poured his shot into the flank of the column. A number of teamsters and fugitives from the battle-ground now joined him, and he pressed forward. The enemy retired behind a hill, and prepared to charge down upon him as he ascended it; but by moving his piece to the right he gained a favorable position, and a single shot dispersed them. Meanwhile Captain Webster had ordered Lieutenant Donaldson with one gun from the redoubt to the assistance of Captain Shover. Both pieces were brought to bear upon the retiring column, when they broke, and fled up the base of the mountain to their encampment. In the morning they were seen retiring through the Palames pass, and did not make their appearance again on the Saltillo plain.

The battle of Buena Vista does not require words of commendation. The facts are of themselves eloquent. The pass of Angostura, the plain upon which the bravery of those volunteers, many of whom had never before been in action, was tested, and the hills which flank it, will be a perpetual monument. Less than five thousand men, not five hundred of whom were regulars, with fourteen pieces of artillery, maintained their position, though the ravines around them streamed with their blood, from early dawn until set of sun.* Sometimes the day seemed almost lost, and General

* General Taylor's total strength, exclusive of the force at Saltillo, was 4,759. The regulars engaged, deducting the general staff, numbered only 476. Most of his guns were of small calibre.

Taylor was advised by several of his officers to retire to a new position. This could never have been done with volunteers. There was but one alternative: they must fight where they stood, or surrender. Had they been regulars, there would have been more unanimity in their efforts; but it may have been fortunate that they were otherwise. Many of them looked upon the contest as a personal matter, and being unable to appreciate the disadvantages which an experienced soldier would have instantly remarked, so long as they were whole and unharmed, there was no immediate danger. The Mexican troops were wearied and hungry, and in some degree dispirited; yet they literally fought for their bread, and this, too, with the ferocity of wolves, and an energy bordering upon despair.

The loss sustained by the American army on this occasion was dreadfully severe. Seven hundred and twenty-three, nearly one-sixth of the whole number engaged, were either killed or wounded, and there were twenty-three missing. The Mexican loss was between fifteen hundred and two thousand.* The American officers were not behind their men in the exhibition of zeal and bravery. There were three hundred and thirty-four in the battle, sixty-nine of whom, more than one-fifth, were killed or wounded.†

* Santa Anna, in his official report, represents his loss to have been 1,500. The number of prisoners taken by the Americans was 294. General Lombardini was severely wounded.

† There were twenty-eight officers killed in the battle, viz.; Captain Lincoln, assistant adjutant-general; Lieutenants Moore and McNulty, Mississippi rifles; Colonel Hardin, Captain Zabriskie, and Lieutenant Houghton, 1st Illinois; Captain Woodward, Lieutenants Rountree, Fletcher, Ferguson, Robbins, Kelley, Steele, Bartleson, Atherton, and Price, 2nd Illinois; Lieutenants Campbell and Leonhard, Texas volunteers; Captains Kinder and Walker, and Lieutenant Parr, 2nd Indi-

Generals Taylor and Wool were often exposed during the day to the severest fire. Colonel Whiting, assistant quartermaster-general, Colonels Churchill and Belknap, inspectors-general, Major Mansfield of the engineers, Major Munroe, chief of artillery, Major Bliss, assistant adjutant-general, and Captain Eaton, and Lieutenants Garnett and McDowell, aids-de-camp, were conspicuous for their gallantry.

It was late in the afternoon of the 23rd, when Santa Anna finally withdrew his men from the field. The American line had been turned in the morning, but the ground then lost was now entirely recovered. Night once more fell upon that valley; wood could not be procured, and again the soldiers bivouacked at their posts without fires, though the mercury stood below the freezing point. They expected that the contest would be renewed in the morning, but they were ready for the attack. The wounded were removed to Saltillo. Seven fresh companies were drawn from the town, and General Marshall was rapidly coming up with a reinforcement of Kentucky cavalry, and four heavy guns under Captain Prentiss, of the 1st artillery, having made a forced march from the pass of Rinconada, on the road to Monterey. When the morning light broke in upon the American soldiers, their eyes were turned towards the Mexican encampment. The enemy were no longer to be seen; they had vanished in the darkness. It was soon ascertained that Santa Anna had fallen back to Agua Nueva. No pursuit was ordered by General Taylor, as his men had not

ana; Captain Taggart, 3rd Indiana; Colonel McKee, Lieutenant Colonel Clay, and Captain Willis, 2nd Kentucky; Colonel Yell and Captain Porter, Arkansas cavalry; and Adjutant Vaughn, 1st Kentucky cavalry.

yet recovered from their weariness and exhaustion. An exchange of prisoners was negotiated on the 24th, and completed on the following day. On the 26th the Mexican army commenced a disastrous retreat, leaving large numbers of their wounded to be cared for by General Taylor's army. The Americans resumed their position at Agua Nueva on the 27th of February. Colonel Belknap was dispatched with a command to Encarnacion, on the 1st of March, and found the roadside strewed with the dead and dying of the discomfited host hurrying onward to San Luis Potosi, with a dark cloud of vultures hovering constantly on their track.*

While the American and Mexican armies were contending on the field of Buena Vista, General Urrea and his cavalry made their appearance in the valley of the San Juan. They arrived before Marin at noon on the 23rd of February, and threatened an attack upon the force at that place, which consisted of three companies of the 2nd Ohio infantry under Lieutenant Colonel Irvin. Information was immediately sent to Monterey that the post was in danger, and Colonel Ormsby, of the Louisville Legion, then in command in that

* The capture of three pieces of artillery, and a few company marking-flags, were the only trophies borne from the field by Santa Anna; but these were pointed to as affording conclusive evidence that the victory had been won by the Mexican army. General Taylor was not moved from his original position; yet the Mexican commander declared that he would have done this if his army had not been almost destitute of food and water. A few more such victories might have caused General Taylor to repeat the lamentation of Pyrrhus, but Santa Anna never could have entered Saltillo except as a prisoner of war. There was food in plenty behind the American lines, and why did he not take it? He knew he lacked the power, and hence his retreat, to which he applied the milder term of "countermarch," was ordered.

town,* promptly dispatched Major Shepherd with three companies and two pieces of artillery, to the relief of Lieutenant Colonel Irvin. The advance guard of Major Shepherd encountered the enemy on the road, and a slight skirmish took place. The pieces were discharged upon the right and left, and a volley of musketry fired into the chaparral, when the detachment moved forward without interruption, and reached Marin in the morning of the 25th. Several skirmishes had already taken place, but the enemy retired on the arrival of the reinforcement.

Meanwhile Colonel Morgan, of the 2nd Ohio volunteers, was advancing with eight companies of his regiment, about two hundred men, from Seralvo. He had received instructions from General Taylor on the 23rd, to concentrate his regiment at that point, and march to Monterey forthwith. He left Seralvo in the morning of the 24th, and in the evening was met by a courier, who informed him that a most atrocious act of barbarity had just been committed by a portion of the force commanded by General Urrea; that a wagon-train under the escort of Lieutenant Barbour, with forty men, had been surrounded near Ramos; and that the soldiers had been killed or taken prisoners, and the wagoners butchered. He proceeded on his march during the night, and at two o'clock in the afternoon of the 25th reached the scene of the disaster, where he found the bodies of between forty and fifty of the wagoners horribly mutilated, some of them hav-

* General Butler had returned to the United States, under the advice of his physicians, on account of his wound received at the storm-i[illegible]terey, from which he did not recover for a long time. Most of the balls used by the Mexicans were of copper, and very poisonous in their effect, especially in that warm climate

ing been staked to the ground and cut to pieces, the wagons burning, and several of the dead bodies consuming in the flames. The march was continued to Marin, which was found nearly deserted, Lieutenant Colonel Irvin having proceeded towards Monterey upon the arrival of Major Shepherd. At eleven o'clock at night on the 25th the camp-fires of the enemy were seen in the distance, and in an hour Colonel Morgan was again upon the road. On the morning of the 26th, when within a mile and a half of Agua Frio, his flankers reported the enemy to be in force in the chaparral on either side of the road. Forming his men in a square he resumed his march, after driving back a small body of Mexicans who made their appearance on his flanks. A short distance beyond Agua Frio the enemy again appeared, full eight hundred strong; and a constant firing was kept up until the detachment approached San Francisco. Clouds of lancers hovered around, threatening to sweep down upon the small force and overthrow them in an instant. Lieutenant Stevens was now dispatched to overtake Lieutenant Colonel Irvin. Dashing through the enemy who occupied the chaparral flanking both sides of the road, he came up with him at Walnut Springs. The latter at once returned, with one hundred and fifty men and two field-pieces, and joined his regiment in a few hours, dislodging a body of the enemy from their ambush as he advanced in front. In the meantime Colonel Morgan had repulsed a vigorous charge made upon his front and flanks, and on being joined by the reinforcement he ordered an attack. An animated action took place, which continued for a few minutes, when the enemy retreated in confusion, having lost upwards of fifty men in killed and wounded. The American loss was five killed, among whom was Captain Graham, assistant quartermaster, and one wounded. The detachment was not molested again on the route to Monterey.

On the 5th of March, Major Giddings, of the 1st Ohio regiment, with a mixed command of two hundred and sixty men, and two pieces of artillery, escorting a large wagon-train, and Major Coffee and Lieutenant Crittenden, bearers of dispatches, left Monterey for Camargo. On the 7th, he was attacked by the Mexican lancers and rancheros under Generals Urrea and Romero, who completely surrounded his command. The wagon-train was ordered to be parked in the centre, as well as it could be done considering its extent. One company was posted in the rear with a single piece of artillery, and the remainder of the force, with the other gun, were in front. The enemy succeeded in breaking through the train; a number of the drivers deserted their teams; and the frightened mules sprang from the road into the chaparral. Forty wagons were captured by the Mexicans and burned.* A warm fire was kept up from the front; but the rear-guard was in extreme danger. A parley was sounded, and a surrender demanded. This was not to be entertained a single moment. Captain Bradley cut his way through to the rear with eighty men, and the whole train was soon re-united. The enemy could make no further impression, and withdrew towards Seralvo. Early on the 8th, Major Giddings entered the town, and found that the Mexicans had

* One of the wagons burned contained a large quantity of ammunition which exploded, and killed or wounded ten of the enemy. After that time they were more careful how they attempted to make a bonfire of such combustible materials.

evacuated it in the night. Here he awaited the arrival of Colonel Curtis, who had left Camargo several days previous with 1,200 men, in order to obtain a new supply of ammunition. Colonel Curtis reached Seralvo on the 12th, and Major Giddings resumed his march, arriving at Camargo on the 15th.

Colonel Curtis continued on his way to Monterey, attempting in vain to come up with the enemy, until the 18th instant, when he was met near Marin by General Taylor, with Lieutenant Colonel May's dragoons and Bragg's artillery, also in pursuit of Urrea. The general had left Agua Nueva, General Wool remaining in command of the forces in that quarter, as soon as he heard of the outrages which had been committed. The pursuit was continued by the united force, but Urrea eluded them by retiring beyond the mountains. General Taylor returned to Monterey, and on the 31st of March issued a proclamation to the inhabitants of Tamaulipas, New Leon and Coahuila, reminding them of the manner in which the war had so far been conducted on his part, and of the respect paid to their persons and property so long as they remained neutral; but, inasmuch as many of them had been concerned in the destruction of the wagon-trains, and the pillage of their contents, he demanded an indemnification to be forthwith made—each district, or juzgado, being required to pay its due proportion. The assessments were made, and payment enforced. No further outrages of this character were committed, and General Taylor again established his head-quarters at Walnut Springs, leaving General Wool still in command at Saltillo and its vicinity.

CHAPTER VIII.

SAN JUAN DE ULUA.

The Island of Lobos—Rendezvous of American Forces—Offer to negotiate—Vera Cruz—Castle of San Juan de Ulua—Landing of the Troops under General Scott—Skirmishing—Line of Investment—Bombardment—Effect of the Fire—Affair at the Puente del Midois—Dragoon fight at Madellin—Capitulation of the City and Castle—Capture of Alvarado—Advance of the Army into the Interior—Opening of the Mexican Ports.

The island of Lobos is one of the gems of the "Blue Gulf." It is a sweet little spot, barely two miles in circumference, and formed entirely of coral. The Mexican coast is about twelve miles from its western shore; Tampico sixty-five miles to the north-west, and Vera Cruz twice that distance in the opposite direction. It is covered with choice tropical fruits and plants, with trees and shrubs of every variety. There are lemons and figs, banyan and palm-trees—the latter rarely exceeding twenty-five feet in height. Many of the banyans are completely thatched over with evergreen vines, and form most agreeable arbors, through which the sunlight falls, softly and silently, like flakes of snow, and the cool sea breeze finds its way, bearing health, and life, and strength upon its wings.

During the month of February, 1847, the various detachments of troops arrived, which had been ordered to rendezvous at Lobos, preparatory to making the descent upon the main land; General Patterson having marched with his division from Victoria to Tampico, at which point he embarked; Generals Scott and Worth sailing from the Brazos; and the remainder of the forces proceeding directly from the United States to the island. One of the steamers, the Ondiaka, employed in transporting the troops, and having on board a regiment of Louisiana volunteers, under the command of Colonel De Russey, was driven ashore in a gale and wrecked, between Lobos and Tampico. Soon after reaching the land, they encountered a large body of Mexicans commanded by General Cos. The regiment were without arms; yet Colonel De Russey instantly formed them in battle array, as if to receive the enemy. They were summoned to surrender immediately; but an answer was delayed until evening, when camp-fires were lighted, and preparations apparently made to pass the night. The Mexicans were deceived by these appearances, and the American troops took advantage of the darkness and drew off in silence. By making a rapid march they reached Tampico without again meeting the enemy.

Many of the supplies necessary for the army had not arrived at the close of the month; but the soldiers were now in fine spirits, and, as it was already getting late in the season, General Scott decided not to postpone the expedition. Fishing and turtle-hunting were at once suspended, the troops were embarked, and the transports got under way. In the afternoon of the 5th of March the whole fleet came bearing down towards Anton Lizardo before a violent norther, darkening the horizon with their clouds of canvas, and soon filling the bay with a dense forest of masts and spars. It was designed that the attack on Vera Cruz and the castle should be made by the army and navy in co-operation with each other; and on the 7th instant, a reconnaissance of the coast above and below the city, was made by General Scott and Commodore Conner, in the steamer Petrita. From the information obtained on this occasion, and that acquired from time to time by the naval officers employed in that station, it was thought best to effect a landing on the beach south of Vera Cruz, and due west of the island of Sacrificios.

While General Scott was on his way to the seat of war, and preparations were being made for the expedition against Vera Cruz, a third, and more specific proposition, was made to the Mexican government for the conclusion of a peace. On the 18th of January, 1847, Mr. Buchanan forwarded a dispatch to the minister of foreign relations, by the hands of one Mr. Atocha, whose diplomatic abilities do not appear to have been of the very highest order, in which it was proposed that a commissioner, or commissioners, should be appointed, to meet at Havana or Jalapa, clothed with full powers to conclude a treaty of peace. In the absence of Santa Anna, then advancing to meet General Taylor, the vice-president, Gomez Farias, signified his readiness to concur in the appointment of commissioners, but required as a preliminary condition, that the blockade should be raised, and that the American invading forces should evacuate the territory of Mexico or, in other words, that all the advantages which had been gained should be sacrificed, and the American government once more trust solely to that faith which the experience of more than twenty years had shown to be as brittle as a rope of sand. It is almost unnecessary to say, that the President of the United States regarded these conditions as being wholly inadmissible. The Mexican government was informed of his decision, in a dispatch from the Department of State, on the 15th of April. It was also stated, that the offer to negotiate would not again be renewed, until a more pacificatory spirit was manifested by the Mexican authorities; yet, in order that an opportunity to make peace might at all times be afforded, the chief clerk in the State Department, Mr. Nicholas P. Trist, would be sent to the head-quarters of the army forthwith, as a commissioner invested with full powers to conclude a treaty.*

Before this diplomatic correspondence was finally closed, the army under General Scott had carried the victorious standard of the American Union far into the interior of Mexico.

VERA CRUZ† has long been celebrated, both for its commercial importance, and its commanding position at the terminus, on the Gulf, of the great national road leading from the city of Mexico to the sea-coast. It is situated on the exact spot where Hernando Cortés and his brave Spaniards landed, on the 21st of April, 1519. The name of Chalchiuheuecan was then given to it; but no permanent colony was established there at that time. The city was founded near the close of the sixteenth century, while the Marquis of Monterey was governor of Mexico, and received a charter of incorporation in 1615. The location has always been an unhealthy one, as is the case with most of the towns situated in the *tierra caliente*, or low ground bordering upon the Gulf. The climate is moist, and its natural warmth is increased by the reflection from the sandy

* Senate Exec. Doc. No. 1 (pp. 36, et. seq.), 1st Session, 30th Congress.

† The True Cross.

plains in the vicinity. The quality of the water is bad; the atmosphere poisoned by noxious exhalations from numerous ponds and marshes; and the air full of insects, the most annoying and conspicuous of which is the tancudo, a species of mosquito. From October to April, during which time the north winds prevail, the situation is comparatively healthy. The city is small, its population scarcely exceeding seven thousand in 1844; but it is laid out neatly and regularly. The streets are wide, straight, and well paved. The houses are built of the Muscara stone, taken from the sea-beach; they are mostly two stories high, and very neat in their appearance. The churches and public buildings are large and fine structures. On the east the walls of the town are laved by the waters of the Gulf, and on the opposite side there is a dry sandy plain, bounded, beyond cannon range, by innumerable hills of loose sand, from twenty to two hundred and fifty feet in height, which are separated by almost impassable forests of chaparral.

The city is surrounded by a wall of stone and mortar which is not very thick, but has strong towers or forts at irregular intervals. The two most important towers are the Santiago and the Conception, which flank that portion of the wall looking towards the Gulf, and are twelve hundred and seventy Castilian varas, or yards, distant from each other. But the chief feature of the defences of Vera Cruz is the famous Castle of SAN JUAN DE ULUA,* the reduction of which was the

* Juan de Grijalva landed on the small island upon which the castle is built, in 1518. There was then a small temple erected on it, in which human victims were sacrificed to the Aztec deities. The Spaniards understood these sacrifices to be made in accordance with the commands of the kings of Acolhua, one of the provinces of the empire; and the term Ulua is an abbreviation, or corruption, of the former name.

GENERAL WINFIELD SCOTT,
Commander in Chief United States Army.

great object of the expedition under General Scott. Its construction was commenced as far back as the year 1582, upon a bar or small island in front of the town, at the distance of one thousand and sixty-two yards from the main land. Near forty millions of dollars have been expended upon the work. It is entirely surrounded by water. The exterior polygon, facing Vera Cruz, is three hundred yards in length, and that commanding the north channel is not far from two hundred yards. There are several strong bastions, and the castle is supported by water-batteries at the angles of the city, which double the fire on both the north and south channels. The walls of the fortress are from twelve to fifteen feet thick, and constructed of *Madrepora Astrea*, a species of soft coral procured in the neighboring islands, but faced with hard stone. The casemates are impervious to shot, and the magazines are all bomb-proof. There are also seven large cisterns, containing over ninety-three thousand cubic feet of water. Three hundred and seventy pieces of artillery would be a full equipment for the castle, and it would then require a garrison of twenty-five hundred men; but that number of guns have never yet been mounted. In the year 1844, there were one hundred and five cannon, of various calibre, in the castle, twenty-one mortars, and eight obuses; and, in the city, ninety-nine cannon and seven mortars.* When

* Part of the guns in the castle were of very heavy calibre. Among them were ten 84-pounders, ten 64's, and ten 15, 8 and 12-pounders, (all Paixhan guns); thirty-seven brass, and twenty-five iron 24-pounders; and six 18-inch, and eight 14-inch mortars. Besides being sacked by the pirates under Lorencillo in 1683, the city of Vera Cruz has experienced many of the reverses of war. It was besieged and carried by the revolutionists in 1821; and in the following year was besieged by the Spanish troops. From September 1823 to November 1825, it

General Scott landed with his army, there were between two hundred and fifty and three hundred cannon in the city and castle. The latter was garrisoned by near two thousand men, and in the former there was from three to five thousand. As at Monterey, many of the streets in the city were barricaded, and the houses and walls pierced for musketry. The officer in command of the town and castle was Juan Morales, governor and commanding-general of the state of Vera Cruz.

The debarkation of the troops was fixed for the 9th of March The surf-boats were launched, and carefully numbered; and early in the morning of the appointed day, most of the troops were transferred from the transports to the vessels of war, to avoid crowding the contracted anchorage between Sacrificios and the main land with too many sail. At eleven o'clock the

was three times bombarded by the Spanish, then occupying the castle of San Juan. In the latter year the castle itself was captured by the Mexicans, and the city enjoyed a season of repose. It was again besieged by the ministerial troops in 1832. In 1838 both the castle and town were blockaded and taken by the French; whose vessels, however, were allowed to take their position undisturbed. After this last attack, extensive improvements were made in the fortifications of the city, and in the castle itself. During the summer of 1846, it was generally supposed that the squadron under Commodore Conner would attempt the capture of San Juan de Ulua; but it appears, from the letter of instructions of the Secretary of the Navy, dated May 13th, that the naval force in the Gulf was not thought to be strong enough to make the effort. It is stated in a letter written by an officer in the American army, that the Mexican commander of the castle sent word to Commodore Conner, that he might bring his fleet up and fire "until there was not a shot in the locker, and he would promise him not to return a gun until he was done." The castle was very strong, without doubt, and the Mexicans were confident of their ability to hold it; but they would have found it a difficult task to resist the skill and bravery of the army and navy of the United States, although its reduction was effected without putting them to the test.

squadron was in motion, and at three in the afternoon it was abreast of Sacrificios. Every thing appeared to favor the movement. There was nothing like confusion or disorder. The soldiers knew they were about to land in an enemy's country, but it was a moment for which many of them had long panted. The scene was full of interest and animation. The inspiring strains of martial music broke cheerily on the ear. The bay was crowded with vessels, filled with armed men, whose bright muskets and bayonets flashed in the sunlight. The stars and stripes fluttered everywhere in the breeze. In the distance were the officers and crews of the foreign vessels attentively watching the proceedings. Every fore-top and spar was crowded with anxious spectators. It was a bright, clear day, and the air was soft and balmy; the sea was scarcely ruffled by the mild breeze that came in gentle puffs from the south-east,—and the yellow haze of the approaching evening rested, like the mantle of a spirit, upon its broad bosom, rising and falling with the long majestic swells which rolled towards the shore; or it lingered around the tall spires and ancient battlements of Vera Cruz, and the gloomy fortress of San Juan, with its guns piled tier upon tier, frowning defiance to the invaders.

The landing commenced instantly after the arrival of the squadron. The surf-boats, sixty-five in number, which had been towed astern of the larger vessels, were brought alongside to receive the troops, and the steamers Spitfire and Vixen, with five gun-boats, formed a line parallel with the beach, and within good grape range, to cover the descent. The small boats were manned by sailors from the squadron, and each one placed in charge of a naval officer. The first line ordered to disembark, was commanded by General Worth, and consisted of 4,500 men, fully armed and accoutred, and ready to encounter the enemy if the landing was opposed. As soon as the boats had received their respective complements, they formed in a line, abreast, between the gun-boats and the large vessels. A gun was then fired from the Massachusetts, as the signal to "give way." The hardy seamen bent to their task; every muscle was strained; the tough oars quivered; the waters parted; and, like so many frightened gulls, they darted towards the land. As the keels grated on the beach, the men sprang overboard, shouting and cheering as they rushed through the water, in their haste to reach the shore. In a moment the American flag was unfurled, and greeted with long and loud hurrahs. Their comrades remaining on board the vessels,—soldiers and sailors, men and officers,—echoed back the shout, and the bands of music completed the salute with the glorious notes of "the Star Spangled Banner."

On the approach of the American squadron and transports, Governor Morales issued a proclamation abounding in expressions of patriotism; but no attempt was made to oppose the landing of the troops. The beach upon which the disembarkation took place was overlooked by high hills, and a few pieces of artillery, advantageously posted, would have done fearful execution among the invading forces. No attempt was made to oppose them, however,—the Mexican commander, like the ostrich, which fancies itself secure when its head is hid in the sand, deeming himself perfectly safe while he was surrounded and protected by stone walls, garnished with cannon, and bristling with bayonets. Before sunset General Worth had formed his men on the shore in line of battle, as a precautionary measure in case they should be molested. The remainder of the troops were landed by the surf-boats, in successive trips, and at ten o'clock in the evening, the whole army, with the exception of a few straggling companies, consisting of between ten and eleven thousand men, had reached the shore in safety, without the slightest accident—a result unsurpassed and unparalleled in the history of war.*

Great credit is due to Commodore Conner, who was in his small boat personally superintending the movement, and to the officers and seamen under his command, for the skilful and successful manner in which the disembarkation was effected; and to General Scott and his officers belongs the merit of ably seconding the efforts to put them and their soldiers upon the shore, and of making every preparation to gain a foothold, and maintain it, in spite of opposition.

At daylight in the morning of the 10th, a rapid fire of shot and shells was opened from the city and castle upon the position occupied by the American army. A small detachment, under Captain Gordon, was sent out to reconnoitre, and encountered a body of the enemy, whom they compelled to retire towards the town. At sunrise, the steamer Spitfire, Commander Tatnall, moved up, and continued to fire into the city and castle for nearly an hour. General Scott

* The French expedition against Algiers, in 1830, is said to have been "the most complete armament in every respect that ever left Europe." Ample provision was made in means and facilities for landing the troops, and the disembarkation took place in a wide bay. General Scott landed with his army upon an open beach directly on the ocean. No resistance was offered in either case; but the French succeeded in landing only nine thousand men on the first day, and that with the loss of between thirty and forty lives.

landed early in the morning, and at his request the marines of the squadron, organized into a detachment under Captain Edson, were sent ashore, and temporarily attached to the 3rd artillery. During the day another transport arrived, and the total strength of the army was thus augmented to more than 11,000 men. The regulars were divided into two brigades, commanded by Generals Worth and Twiggs, and the volunteer division of General Patterson into three brigades, under the command of Generals Pillow, Quitman and Shields.

Before landing, General Scott had rendered himself familiar with the topography of the country in the neighborhood of Vera Cruz, and the necessary orders had been issued for taking up the line of investment. General Worth's brigade advanced up the beach on the morning of the 10th instant, and occupied the ground designated for his command, on the right of the line, and within range of the heavy guns of the castle. Parties of Mexican infantry and cavalry appeared in the distance, but were dispersed by the mountain howitzers and light batteries. General Patterson then moved forward with his division, for the purpose of forming on the left of General Worth. The movement required considerable labor, and was attended with numerous difficulties. Roads were cut through the thick chaparral, and the men were obliged to drag the cannon over the hills, half blinded by the whirling sand, and exposed to the shot from the enemy's fortifications, which occasionally came whistling over their heads. The brigade of General Pillow, in the advance, had several skirmishes with bodies of Mexicans found posted in the chaparral, who were driven off with loss. A party of the enemy were also discovered in the magazine, a large and strong stone building in rear of the city. Captain Taylor was ordered up with one piece of his battery, and opened his fire, when the Mexicans immediately deserted the building. General Pillow pushed through the chaparral with the 1st Tennessee regiment, and took possession. At night the brigade reached its position, and on the following day Generals Quitman and Shields formed their brigades on the left. In the morning of the 11th, a smart skirmish took place with a body of Mexican infantry and lancers, who were supported by a brisk cannonade from the city. Captain Davis, of the Georgia regiment, was thrown forward with a party of riflemen to bring on an engagement, and sustained himself handsomely until reinforced by two companies of his regiment under Colonel Jackson, and a portion of the South Carolina regiment, under Lieutenant Colonel Dickinson, when the enemy were repulsed and forced to take shelter beneath the guns of the town.

General Twiggs was ordered to take post on the extreme left with his brigade, and commenced his march in the morning of the 11th; the progress of his column was interrupted by impediments similar to those which had disturbed the march of the volunteer division; but the difficulties in his way were no sooner met than they were overcome. His advance guard, consisting of a squadron of the mounted riflemen under Major Sumner, 2nd dragoons, repeatedly came up with parties of the enemy, who were routed in an instant. The head of the column arrived at the hamlet of Vergara, on the beach north of Vera Cruz, about noon on the 13th instant, and the work of investment was then fully completed. On the same day safeguards were sent by General Scott to the foreign consuls in the city, for the protection of themselves, their families, and their property. The toils were now set. A cordon of soldiers, whose encampment extended in a magnificent semicircle, from shore to shore, girt the city upon the one side, and upon the other was the broad ocean occupied by a numerous fleet, well manned, and sufficient to prevent all ingress in that quarter. To break the chain was impossible; and to avoid being crushed by its contracting folds was shown in the sequel to be equally vain.

The line of investment occupied a distance of about seven miles, with an interval of from two and a half to three miles between it and the city, and throughout its whole extent was within range of the enemy's heavy artillery, which kept up an unremitting fire by day and night, though with little or no effect. But very few of the carts and draught horses ordered for the expedition had at this time arrived on the coast, and an incalculable amount of labor was necessarily performed by the troops, in hauling their cannon and supplies by hand, over the sand-hills and through the thickets of chaparral. As soon as they were well established in their positions on the line of investment, detachments were sent out from each brigade to clear its front, including the sub-bourgs, of the enemy's parties. This was quickly accomplished. The Mexican outposts and skirmishers were all driven in, and reconnaissances made of the intervening ground. At midnight on the 18th instant, the trenches were opened by the sappers and miners, within eight hundred yards of the city, and batteries were constructed for the reception of the heavy guns and mortars, under the supervision and direction of Colonel Totten, Major Smith, Captains Lee and Sanders, and the other able and efficient officers of the corps of engineers.

A succession of severe northers* delayed the landing of the mortars and guns for several days, and it was not until the afternoon of the 22nd that three batteries were completed, and seven mortars placed in position. General Scott then summoned the city to surrender; offering to stipulate—for the reason that the heavy guns, and more than one half of the mortars intended for the expedition had not then arrived, and he was in no situation to threaten the castle—that he would not fire from the town upon the latter, unless he should be first attacked by the garrison. Governor Morales chose to consider both the city and castle embraced in the summons, and peremptorily refused to surrender.

Orders were now given to open the fire upon the city, and the commanders of the foreign vessels in the harbor were officially notified by Commodore Perry,† that all intercourse with the shore must for the present cease. The intelligence of the glorious victory at Buena Vista had just been received, and the American soldiers and sailors were full of zeal and enthusiasm. The plans and arrangements of General Scott had been adopted with caution, but they were settled with mathematical precision, and he was ready to carry

* These mimic Siroccos often interrupted the progress of the workmen in the trenches. Their eyes were nearly blinded with the sand, and the ditches filled up as fast as they could be opened.

† Commodore Perry relieved Commodore Conner in the command of the home squadron on the 21st of March. Several vessels of war, in addition to those already in the Gulf, had been ordered to reinforce the squadron, and arrived before and during the siege. Among them were the Ohio, 74 guns; Potomac, 44 guns; Saratoga, Albany and Germantown, 20 guns each; and the Decatur, 16 guns.

them into effect with that rapidity of execution which has ever characterized his military operations. There were engineer, ordnance, and artillery officers, unexcelled in the world for skill and ability, to execute his orders, and to dictate was to perform. The command of the trenches was assigned to Colonel Bankhead, chief of artillery, and, at a few minutes past four o'clock in the afternoon of the 22nd, the bombardment was commenced by batteries numbers 1, 2, and 3, under the charge, respectively, of Captain Brooks and Lieutenant Shackelford, 2nd artillery, and Major Vinton, 3rd artillery. The flotilla of small steamers and gun-boats, led by Commander Tatnall in the Spitfire, were also directed to take a position between Sacrificios and the main land, and commence a simultaneous fire upon the town. In the meantime the enemy's guns were not silent. A vigorous cannonade was opened upon the trenches and the flotilla, from the city and castle, which was as warmly, and far more effectively returned. The toppling walls and blazing roofs marked where

"The booming shot and flaming shell"

had fallen; and when the night came on, it was illuminated by the red glare which flashed up unceasingly from trench and battery. Burning meteors darted hither and thither athwart the sky, and when they disappeared, the surrounding darkness was thrown into yet deeper gloom. Late in the evening the flotilla suspended its fire, but during the live-long night the missiles hurled from the American lines described their fiery circles through the air, and sped away on their errand of death, into that doomed city.

In the morning of the 23rd the land batteries were

placed in charge of Captain McKenzie, 2nd artillery, and Captains Anderson and Taylor, 3rd artillery. Three additional mortars were placed in battery, and the bombardment was kept up without cessation during the day. The flotilla again opened its fire, and Commander Tatnall ventured still nearer to the town and castle; but about nine o'clock all the vessels were recalled by signal, from a position which, as General Scott remarked in his dispatch, had been "too daringly assumed." But the officers and men of the navy were determined to participate in the conflict. At the earnest request of Commodore Perry, General Scott assigned a position in the trenches, to be mounted with guns from the squadron, and worked by seamen. A strong battery, number 5, was constructed by the engineers in the rear of a thick mass of chaparral, and three eight-inch Paixhan guns, and three long thirty-two pounders, were landed, and dragged four miles through the sand by the sailors, assisted by fatigue parties from the brigades of Generals Worth and Pillow. At ten o'clock in the morning of the 24th the pieces were in position; the chaparral was cut away; and torrents of shot and shell were hurled into the town, tearing and crushing every thing in their range.*

Within the city the effect of the American fire was terrible and destructive in the extreme. The earth shook at every discharge. Broad sheets of flame appeared to leap forth from the batteries of the assailants. Smoking ruins, crashing roofs and buildings, attested the severity of the bombardment. The firm pavements were thrown up in masses, and deep ridges ploughed in the streets. The iron gratings of the bal-

* The naval battery was commanded, in succession, by Captains Aulick, Mayo, and Breese.

conies were torn from their fastenings, and casements and lattices shivered in pieces. Stone walls and barricades afforded no shelter. Wailing and lamentation were heard in every quarter of the town. Fathers were stricken down upon their own thresholds, and mothers smitten at the fireside, as they leaned over the helpless offspring who clung to them, in vain, for protection. Stout manhood and decrepit age, the weak and the strong, fell dead together. Late on the night of the 24th the consuls of Great Britain, France, Spain, and Prussia, united in a memorial to General Scott, praying him to grant a truce to enable the neutrals, and the Mexican women and children, to escape from the scene of havoc around them. All this suffering had been foreseen by the American commander; the inhabitants had been forewarned; and the blockade had been left open up to the latest hour, to allow the neutrals to withdraw. The opportunity offered had not been improved, and he informed the memorialists, in reply, that no terms could now be listened to, unless they were to be accompanied by an unconditional surrender.

The Americans suspended their fire but for brief periods. The guns in the city and castle were also in constant activity, though they did little execution. A few shot entered the embrasures of the batteries, and threw clouds of sand into the trenches and over the men serving the pieces; but the casualties were very few in number. On the morning of the 25th, battery number 4 was in readiness, with four twenty-four pounders and two eight-inch howitzers, and its deep-toned thunder was soon added to the din.

During the siege, parties of Mexican rancheros and light troops were frequently seen lurking in the rear of the American lines, to entrap the incautious and unwary. In the afternoon of the 24th, Colonel P. F. Smith, of the mounted rifles, was sent out with a detachment of about two hundred men, to support a reconnoitering party under Lieutenant Roberts, who reported that a body of the enemy were on the heights near the Puente del Midois, a handsome stone structure thrown across a small stream of fresh water running into the river Antigua. On approaching the bridge it was discovered to be barricaded with abattis, and that intrenchments had been thrown up on the heights. An attack was instantly ordered. Lieutenant Roberts displayed in the chaparral on the right with his company, crossed the stream below the bridge, and having reached the enemy's left, drove them with great spirit from their position. Captain Pope seconded the movement with two companies on the other flank, and the whole detachment were almost immediately engaged in the pursuit, which was continued for nearly a mile. At sunset they returned to the camp, having killed and wounded a large number of the enemy, with the loss of but four men wounded.

On the 25th instant, Colonel Harney proceeded with a squadron of dragoons commanded by Major Sumner, and fifty dismounted men under Captain Ker, towards the Madellin river, in consequence of a report that a mounted force was collected in that direction. On arriving near the Puente de Marino, he found it to be regularly fortified, and guarded by near two thousand men, with two pieces of artillery. Small parties of lancers were also seen in the chaparral which skirted the bridge. When the detachment came within sixty yards, the enemy opened a heavy fire, and killed and wounded several of the command. Colonel Harney now fell back, and sent to the lines for two pieces of artillery. In a short time he was joined by Lieutenant Judd of the 3rd artillery, with two guns, one company of the 1st Tennessee regiment, Captain Cheatham, parts of four companies of the 2nd Tennessee, Colonel Haskell, and about forty dismounted dragoons under Captain Hardee. General Patterson also arrived near the scene of action, but declined interfering with the dispositions made by Colonel Harney for the attack. Captain Ker, with the dismounted men, was placed on the left of the road leading to the bridge; the volunteers under Colonel Haskell, on the right; and the artillery moved along the road, supported by Captain Hardee. Major Sumner remained with his command in reserve. In a few seconds they were warmly engaged along the whole line. After six or eight rounds were fired from the guns, the heads of the enemy were no longer seen above the parapet, and a charge was ordered. Colonel Haskell, Captains Cheatham and Hardee, rushed forward at the head of the volunteers and dragoons with fearless intrepidity, and leaped over the fortification, bayoneting the gunners at their posts or driving them from the bridge. The enemy fell back, but re-formed beyond the bridge. This was cleared in a moment, and Major Sumner dashed over it with his dragoons. The Mexican lancers could not stand the shock. Their weapons were broken like reeds by the American sabres. The enemy turned and fled in all directions, leaving more than fifty killed and wounded, in the attack and pursuit. The American loss was two killed and twelve wounded.

The fire was continued during the 25th upon the city of Vera Cruz from the five batteries in operation. In the town, that night was full of horrors. There

BOMBARDMENT OF VERA CRUZ AND CASTLE

was no place of safety to be found. The governor was besought and entreated to spare the further effusion of blood by a surrender. Proud and punctilious to the end he refused to do any thing that would derogate from his honor, but was finally persuaded to yield up the command to General Landero, by whom negotiations were opened with General Scott. At eight o'clock in the morning of the 26th the batteries ceased playing, and articles of capitulation were signed on the following day.* The surrender of the city took place in the morning of the 29th, when the Mexican forces marched out to a plain about one mile outside the

* "Terms of capitulation agreed upon by the commissioners, viz:—

"Generals W. J. Worth and G. J. Pillow, and Colonel J. G. Totten, chief engineer, on the part of Major General Scott, general-in-chief of the armies of the United States; and Colonel José Gutierrez de Villanueva, lieutenant colonel of engineers, Manuel Robles, and Colonel Pedro de Herrera, commissioners appointed by General of Brigade, Don José Juan Landero, commanding in chief, Vera Cruz, the castle of San Juan de Ulua, and their dependencies, for the surrender to the arms of the United States of the said forts, with their armaments, munitions of war, garrisons, and arms.

"1. The whole garrison, or garrisons to be surrendered to the arms of the United States, as prisoners of war, the 29th instant, at 10 o'clock, A. M.; the garrisons to be permitted to march out with all the honors of war, and to lay down their arms to such officers as may be appointed by the general-in-chief of the United States armies, and at a point to be agreed upon by the commissioners.

"2. Mexican officers shall preserve their arms and private effects, including horses and horse furniture, and to be allowed, regular and irregular officers, as also the rank and file, five days to retire to their respective homes, on parole, as hereinafter prescribed.

"3. Coincident with the surrender, as stipulated in article 1, the Mexican flags of the various forts and stations shall be struck, saluted by their own batteries; and, immediately thereafter, Forts Santiago and Conception, and the castle of San Juan de Ulua, occupied by the forces of the United States.

"4. The rank and file of the regular portion of the prisoners to be town, where the American soldiers were drawn up to receive them. After passing between the lines they laid down their arms and colors, and departed for the interior. General Worth was appointed military governor of the town and castle, and immediately entered the city with a portion of his division. Shortly after a grand national salute was fired from the squadron, as the American flag rose above the Plaza of Vera Cruz, and floated in triumph over the ramparts of San Juan de Ulua, the Gibraltar of Mexico.

The reduction of the city and castle was effected by General Scott, with what may be regarded as a trifling loss, in comparison with the importance of the achievement. Including the losses sustained by the navy,

disposed of after surrender and parole, as their general-in-chief may desire, and the irregular to be permitted to return to their homes. The officers, in respect to all arms and descriptions of force, giving the usual parole, that the said rank and file, as well as themselves, shall not serve again until duly exchanged.

"5. All the *matériel* of war, and all public property of every description found in the city, the castle of San Juan de Ulua and their dependencies, to belong to the United States; but the armament of the same (not injured or destroyed in the further prosecution of the actual war) may be considered as liable to be restored to Mexico by a definite treaty of peace.

"6. The sick and wounded Mexicans to be allowed to remain in the city with such medical officers and attendants, and officers o fthe army, as may be necessary to their care and treatment.

"7. Absolute protection is solemnly guaranteed to persons in the city, and property, and it is clearly understood that no private building or property is to be taken or used by the forces of the United States, without previous arrangement with the owners, and for a fair equivalent.

"8. Absolute freedom of religious worship and ceremonies is solemnly guaranteed."

[On account of the roughness of the sea, all communication with the navy was suspended until after commissions had been exchanged, but Captain Aulick was afterwards appointed a commissioner by Commodore Perry, and was present at the signing of the articles of capitulation, which received his approbation.]

there were three officers killed and three wounded, in the debarkation, investment and bombardment, and ten men killed and sixty wounded.* Upon occupying the city it was found to be in a most disgusting state of uncleanliness. General Worth ordered the filth to be removed, and took prompt measures to insure good order, and guard against disease. The poorer inhabitants of Vera Cruz were also ascertained to be in a suffering condition, and ten thousand rations were directed to be issued for their relief; thus presenting a singular feature in warfare—the victors feeding the vanquished, with the stores brought hundreds of miles for their own sustenance and support.

On the 30th instant a detachment of troops under General Quitman left Vera Cruz to co-operate with the squadron under Commodore Perry, in a joint attack upon Alvarado. Lieutenant Hunter was dispatched in advance, with the steamer Scourge, to blockade the port. He arrived off the bar in the afternoon of the 30th, and at once opened a fire upon the forts at the mouth of the river, which were garrisoned by four hundred men. During the night he stood off, but renewed the attack in the morning, when the enemy evacuated their defences. Several government vessels in the harbor were burned, and the guns spiked or buried in the sand before they retired. Leaving a garrison in the fort, Lieutenant Hunter proceeded up the river and succeeded in capturing four schooners. Early in the morning of the 1st of April, he anchored off Thlacotalpan, a city containing near seven thousand in-

* Major Vinton, 3rd artillery, Captain Alburtis, 2nd infantry, and Midshipman Shubrick, of the navy, were the officers killed. The casualties at the Puente del Midois and the Madellin river, are not included in the statement in the text.

habitants, which surrendered to him without offering any resistance. Commodore Perry arrived on the 2nd with the squadron, but the towns on the river were already captured.*

The dreaded vómito would soon be on the coast, and General Scott could not linger at Vera Cruz. Owing to unavoidable delays and accidents, but one fourth of the necessary road-train had arrived, yet he determined to escape the pestilence, as he expressed it, "by pursuing the enemy." Lieutenant Colonel Belton was left with a detachment in command of Vera Cruz and the castle. On the 8th of April, General Twiggs took up the march with his division, and was followed in a few days by the remaining columns of the army. General Scott and his soldiers were now upon the high road to the Mexican capital, confidently trusting —and they were not disappointed—to find it strewn with the laurels and paved with the trophies of victory. After a period of more than three hundred

* Lieutenant Hunter was tried by a court-martial, and sentenced to be dismissed from the squadron for transcending his orders in the attack on Alvarado. His bravery and zeal, ill-timed though they were, cannot be questioned; but the consequences of a disobedience of orders were never more signally illustrated. It was thought by the quarter-master's department, and that not without reason, that about two-thirds of the draught animals required for the use of the army under General Scott could be procured in Mexico. The country extending from Orizaba to Huasiqualco, which was covered by Alvarado and Thlacotalpan. abounded in horses, mules, and cattle; which it was the object of the joint expedition under Commodore Perry and General Quitman to secure. Lieutenant Hunter was sent in advance merely to blockade the river. Ignorant of the intentions of his superiors, he ventured upon an attack. It was successful; but before General Quitman arrived in the rear of the enemy's towns, they had fled into the interior with their horses and cattle, and the very resources which were needed for the American army, were seized by Santa Anna and his officers.—Annual Report of the Quarter-Master General, Nov. 24, 1847.

years, they found themselves upon the pathway made famous by the exploits of Hernando Cortés and his followers. Like the Spaniard, perhaps, they came, for the time, at least, to conquer; but, unlike him, they came to make no war upon inoffensive inhabitants—they violated no altars—they profaned no sanctuaries. They came not to establish a new faith, nor yet in quest of some fabled Pactolus, "rich with golden sands;" but they came as the representatives of their country, to defend her honor and maintain her rights.

After the capture of Vera Cruz, and the other principal ports on the Mexican Gulf, they were opened to our own commerce and that of neutral vessels, by direction of the President of the United States; and a tariff of duties was established for the admission of all articles not contraband of war. The duties were collected by officers of the army or navy appointed for that purpose, and applied to the expenses of conducting the war. The attention of General Taylor had before that time been called to the subject of collecting military contributions of the enemy, if he thought it expedient. When his wagon-trains were destroyed, he required an indemnification to be made, although no systematized plan of enforcing contributions was adopted. General Scott received similar instructions, when on his way to the city of Mexico; but in pursuance of the discretion vested in him, he decided not to exasperate the people, or drive them into open hostility, where they were disposed to be neutral, by the exercise of a belligerent right which might seriously embarrass his operations.

CHAPTER IX.

SCOTT AT CERRO GORDO.

Return of Santa Anna to the city of Mexico—Fortifications at Cerro Gordo—Arrival of the American Army at the Rio del Plan—Storming the Heights—The Enemy routed—Capture of Jalapa and Perote—The Guerilleros—Proclamation of General Scott—Entrance of the Americans into Puebla—Warlike proceedings of the Mexican government—Skirmishing on the road from Vera Cruz—The Army reinforced—March towards the Mexican Capital.

WITH sickness and famine stalking, like giant spectres, in his rear, Santa Anna returned to San Luis Potosi, followed by the remnant of the proud army so signally routed and repulsed, by an inferior force, on the field of Buena Vista. During his absence the city of Mexico had been the scene of continued tumult and confusion, and he now hurried to the capital, with a portion of his soldiers, to put an end to these disorders. The election of Gomez Farias to the Vice Presidency, as has been mentioned, was extremely unpopular. He appears to have been zealous and patriotic ; but these were qualities which many of his countrymen could not, or did not appreciate. He attempted to enforce contributions from the church, for the support of the army and the prosecution of the war, which at once called down upon his head the denunciations of the clergy. The embers of discord were soon fanned into a flame ; for several days the rival factions, unmindful of the prostrate condition of their country, fought like infuriated madmen, in the streets of Mexico ; and the

GENERAL SANTA ANNA.

émeute was only suppressed upon the arrival of Santa Anna, and his assumption of the reins of power.*

This question also occasioned considerable altercation and debate in Congress. Various measures were proposed, some of them of a most violent character, for the removal of Farias; but Santa Anna would not allow any thing to be done except in a constitutional manner. Finally, on the 1st of April, the decree by which the office of vice president had been created, was suppressed; permission was given to the Provisional President to take command of the forces in the field; and a President substitute was ordered to be chosen, to exercise the authority of chief magistrate in the absence of Santa Anna. On the same day General Anaya was elected to fill the office; the appointment appeared to give satisfaction to all parties; and on the 2nd instant he entered upon the discharge of his duties as the acting executive.

The capture of Vera Cruz and the fall of San Juan de Ulua, awakened the Mexican people to the necessity of foregoing the indulgence of their constitutional predilection for party strifes and contentions, if they would resist the march of the American soldiers then advancing upon their capital, under the successful chieftain who led them on to battle and to glory. Governor Morales and General Landero received the reward usually meted out by Santa Anna to his unfortunate officers: for their failure to achieve impossibilities they were arrested, and confined in the castle of Perote. Earnest appeals were made by Santa Anna and Anaya to their fellow-citizens, to forget their feuds and animosities, and to listen only to the suggestions of pa-

* Santa Anna did not assume the supreme power until requested to do so by a majority of the members of the Mexican Congress.

triotism, and unite in making preparations to meet the invaders.

A more warlike spirit was soon manifested. The clergy of the archbishopric of Mexico bound themselves to furnish the government with the sum of one and a half million of dollars, payable in monthly instalments; plans for fortifying the city were adopted; and the public journals devoted their columns to articles designed to encourage the timid, and arouse the faint-hearted.* At the head of 8,000 troops, 5,000 of whom had constituted the flower of the army, at San Luis Potosi,† Santa Anna again ventured forth to try his fortunes on another field. While on the road to check the advance of General Scott, he was joined by a large body of national guards from the State of Puebla; at Jalapa he was reinforced by 2,000 men; and numbers of the jarochada, or lower class of peasantry and laborers, of the State of Vera Cruz, were also pressed into his service. With these additions his army numbered little short of 15,000. After leaving Jalapa, he advanced to the pass of Vaechi, or CERRO GORDO, near the Rio del Plan, which had been the scene of one of his most brilliant efforts during the revolution, and was regarded as being almost impregnable.

About sixty miles from Vera Cruz, and over thirty from Jalapa, the national road crosses the Rio del Plan and the wide rocky plain on its northern bank,

* "In the front of an enemy conquering and menacing, we conjure all Mexicans who love the honor, and even the existence of their country, that henceforth they have but one party,—that of Independence; and but one device,—that of Vengeance and War!"—Extract from an article in the *Republicano*.

† These were the infantry regiments and regular artillerists, who highly distinguished themselves at the battle of Buena Vista.

and then commences the ascent to the elevated plateau of Mexico. Here terminates the low level,—the land of the vanilla and cacao, of the banana, the orange and the sugar-cane,—glowing with the rich vegetation of the tropics, and its shady bowers and sequestered recesses vocal with the melodies of the mocking bird, and the thousand other songsters whose notes are trilled, softly and sweetly, from early morn till eventide. The traveller, as he climbs the steep sides of the Cordilleras, pauses on each terrace, and turns upon his steps, to gaze upon the broad expanse spread out beneath him, like a carpet of rare embroidery;—the tall coronals of the aloe,—the dahlia, the cactus, and the convulvulus, —flowers blushing with every hue of the rainbow,—unfold their beauties at his feet; here a small streamlet, and there an ample river, shimmers through the leafy interstices of the luxuriant woodland; and there are groves, too, of palms, and cocoas, and sycamores, matted together with the waving festoons of unnumbered parasites, whose brilliant dyes fairly dazzle the vision of the beholder. With ravished senses he pursues his way to the interior, and as he lifts his eyes to the snow-crowned summit of Orizaba, it were not strange if he should fancy the mountain peak some hoary warder, whose locks were silvered with the frosts of age, keeping watch over the enchanted realm behind him.

After crossing the stream, the road continues its course to the north until it reaches the foot of the hills, when it turns abruptly to the east. A few hundred yards further on it changes its direction to the north-west, and after pursuing a circuitous course for nearly two miles, now ascending some difficult acclivity or thridding some narrow dell, and now surmounting a steep ridge, and then dipping down between the overhanging banks on the opposite side, it inclines again towards the river, and enters the Pass of Cerro Gordo. As it approaches the defile it is flanked, on the left, by three hills, nearly parallel to each other and to the road, jutting out in the shape of a fan from the same terrace in the rear, and separated by deep ravines, from one to two hundred yards in width. The southernmost ridge is situated just above the deep and impassable gorge through which the river flows. These hills, which command the road, and the defiles leading to the high ground in their rear, formed the right and front of the Mexican position. Intrenchments were thrown up on their eastern extremities, and seventeen pieces of cannon distributed among the different works. In addition to the advanced breastwork on the crest of the central bluff, which was partially masked by brush and a stone wall, there was a redoubt in the rear, with three or four guns, and still further to the rear and left, on a retired line, was an intrenched battery of two guns. The intervals and slopes on the east of this line of intrenchments were for the most part thickly wooded, or covered with underbrush.

Something more than half a mile higher up, on the right of the road, and at a point where it approaches to within eighty or a hundred yards of the river, was a strong battery of six large brass guns, which completely enfiladed the defile. Just beyond this, and a little further to the north, rose the key of the whole position, the main height of Cerro Gordo, towering far above the surrounding hills, and commanding the advanced batteries, and the road, "on a single declination, like a glacis, for nearly a mile." Around the hill, about sixty yards from its foot, was a breastwork of stone for the protection of infantry, and on the summit there was a fortified citadel, or tower, called the *Telegrafo*, also surrounded by a strong work, with six guns mounted on carriages. Immediately in front of Cerro Gordo, were several smaller hills occupied by advanced parties of Mexican infantry and lancers. Nearly one half of the enemy were posted within the intrenchments, or in their vicinity, and the main body, under Santa Anna in person, were encamped on the road, about half a mile west of the tower, with a battery of five guns.

General Twiggs arrived at the Plan del Rio, on the 11th of April, with his division of regulars. The advanced guard of dragoons under Colonel Harney, drove a body of Mexican lancers from the ground, and the division encamped for the night. On the following day, General Twiggs again moved forward, to cover a reconnaissance of the enemy's works, and, if practicable, to make an effective attack. Deeming it unwise to advance further at that time, he returned to his old camp, leaving a strong picket to retain the ground passed over, with the intention of attacking the enemy at daybreak on the 13th. The first and third brigades of General Patterson's volunteer division, commanded by Generals Pillow and Shields, came up on the 12th instant, and the contemplated attack was postponed for one day, in order to allow the volunteers, who were anxious to participate in the engagement, to recover from the fatigue of the march over the long and deep sandy road from Vera Cruz; and on the night of the 13th, all offensive operations were further suspended, by direction of General Patterson, until the arrival of the General-in-chief, who was daily expected.

When General Scott reached the scene of the anticipated conflict, and examined the position occupied by the Mexican forces, he decided to turn their left, and attack them in the rear, while menacing or engaging them in front. The reconnaissance previously commenced by Lieutenant Beauregard, was continued by Captain Lee, of the corps of engineers, for the purpose of discovering a route by which the Jalapa road could be gained, and the retreat of the enemy intercepted. Under the supervision of the engineer officers a road was constructed, leaving the main route a short distance below where it commences inclining towards the river, and extending over rocky slopes and deep chasms, through thickets of chaparral, and beneath frowning precipices, to the left of Cerro Gordo, for a distance of between two and three miles, and within range of the Mexican batteries. When the working parties were discovered, they were fired upon with grape and musketry. Further reconnaissance, therefore, was impossible without an action, and General Scott immediately made his dispositions for storming the whole line of intrenchments and batteries.

General Worth joined the main body on the night of the 16th of April, with the first division of regulars, and on the same evening General Twiggs was directed to advance with his division, early in the morning of the next day, on the line of operations upon the right of the national road. On the 17th instant General Scott issued his celebrated order of battle,—remark able alike for the prescience which seems to have dictated it, and for the undoubting confidence manifested by its author in the officers and men whom he commanded.* To the brave and intrepid Twiggs, whose

* "The enemy's whole line of intrenchments and batteries will be attacked in front, and at the same time turned, early in the day to-morrow,—probably before ten o'clock, A. M.

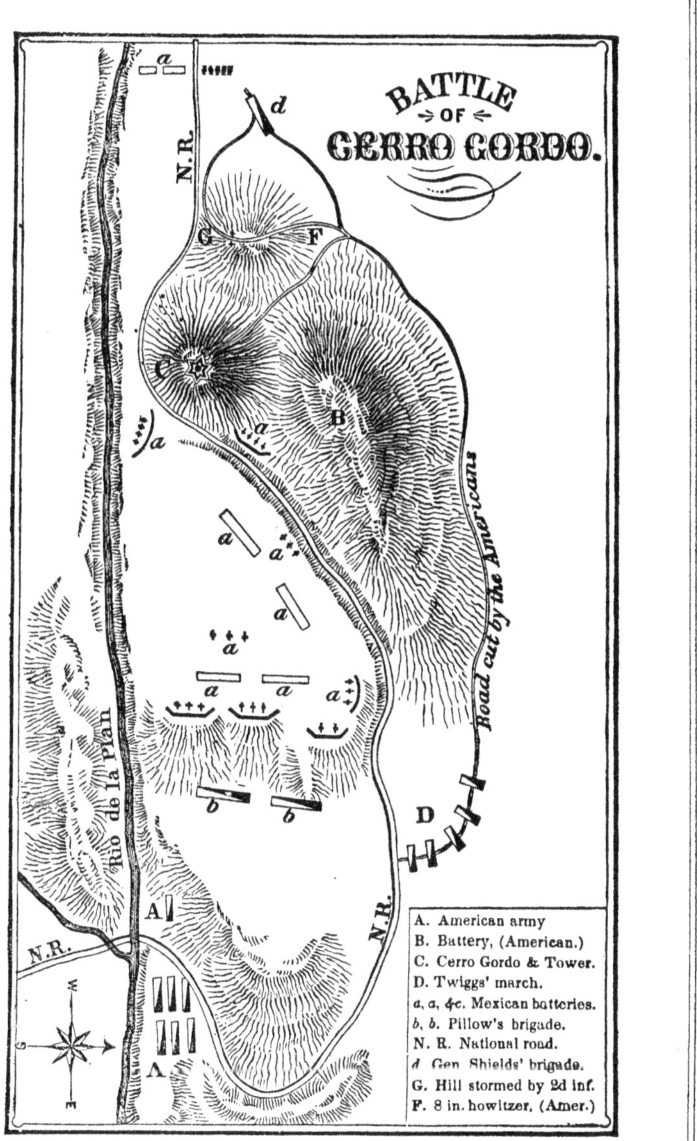
BATTLE
OF
CERRO GORDO.
N.R.
d
G
F
C
B
a
b
D
A
Rio de la Plan
Road cut by the Americans
A. American army
B. Battery, (American.)
C. Cerro Gordo & Tower.
D. Twiggs' march.
a, a, &c. Mexican batteries.
b, b. Pillow's brigade.
N. R. National road.
d Gen. Shields' brigade.
G. Hill stormed by 2d inf.
F. 8 in. howitzer, (Amer.)

division, cavalry excepted, were then well advanced on the principal line of attack, was assigned the task of driving the enemy from the hill of Cerro Gordo, and cutting off their retreat by the Jalapa road; General Shields was directed to reinforce General Twiggs with one or more of the regiments of his brigade, as circumstances might render necessary; and General Worth

"The second (Twiggs') division of regulars is already advanced within easy turning distance towards the enemy's left. That division has instructions to move forward before daylight to-morrow, and take up position across the national road in the enemy's rear, so as to cut off a retreat towards Jalapa. It may be reinforced to-day, if unexpectedly attacked in force, by regiments,—one or two,—taken from Shields' brigade of volunteers. If not, the two volunteer regiments will march for the purpose at daylight to-morrow morning, under Brigadier General Shields, who will report to Brigadier General Twiggs, on getting up with him, or to the General-in-chief, if he be in the advance.

"The remaining regiment of the volunteer brigade will receive instructions in the course of the day.

"The first division of regulars (Worth's) will follow the movement against the enemy's left at sunrise to-morrow morning.

"As already arranged, Brigadier General Pillow's brigade will march at six o'clock to-morrow morning along the route he has carefully reconnoitered, and stand ready, as soon as he hears the report of arms on our right, or sooner, if circumstances should favor him, to pierce the enemy's line of batteries at such point,—the nearer to the river the better, as he may select. Once in the rear of that line, he will turn to the right or left, or both, and attack the batteries in reverse, or, if abandoned, he will pursue the enemy with vigor until farther orders.

"Wall's field-battery and the cavalry will be held in reserve on the national road, a little out of view and range of the enemy's batteries. They will take up that position at nine o'clock in the morning.

"The enemy's batteries being carried or abandoned, all our divisions and corps will pursue with vigor.

"This pursuit may be continued many miles, until stopped by darkness, or fortified positions, towards Jalapa. Consequently, the body of the army will not return to this encampment; but be followed to-morrow afternoon, or early the next morning, by the baggage-trains of the several corps."—Extract from the order of General Scott, dated at the Plan del Rio, April 17, 1847.

was ordered to follow the movement on the enemy's left, and support it, with his division, at sunrise on the 18th. General Pillow had reconnoitered, in person, the works on the right of the Mexican position, and he was instructed to hold himself in readiness to attack them with his brigade, as soon as he heard the report of arms in the morning of the 18th from the other flank. Wall's field battery and the cavalry were to be held in reserve.

The division of General Twiggs arrived at its position before eleven o'clock in the morning of the 17th,—the right of the column being within seven hundred yards of the hill of Cerro Gordo. The first brigade, commanded by Colonel Harney on this occasion, in consequence of the illness of General P. F. Smith, and consisting of the rifle regiment, Major Sumner temporarily in command; the 1st artillery, Colonel Childs; and the 7th infantry, Lieutenant Colonel Plympton, were ordered to seize and maintain all the heights in the neighborhood of the enemy's main work. Accordingly, Lieutenant Gardner, of the 7th infantry, was directed with his company to move to the crest of a hill on the left, and watch the movements of the enemy. While executing the order, he became engaged with a strong skirmishing party sent out to meet him, and followed by a large reserve, in all numbering about two thousand. He gallantly maintained his position under a heavy fire, and held them at bay, until he was succored by the rifles and the 1st artillery, who hurried to his assistance. After a short conflict the Mexicans were driven from the position, and closely pursued. They made a second stand on a hill near the Cerro Gordo, under cover of their guns, which rained showers of grape and canister upon the assailants, who pressed on undaunted, though suffering severely. The hill was stormed and carried. Three times the enemy charged to recover the position, and three times were they repulsed with loss. The American soldiers refused to yield a single inch of ground which they had gained. One section of Major Talcott's mountain howitzer battery, belonging to the voltigeurs, with a number of rockets, under the command of Lieutenant Reno, were ordered up the height, and aided them in maintaining it. In the ardor of the moment, a portion of the troops, headed by Colonel Childs, rushed down the opposite side of the hill, and commenced the ascent of Cerro Gordo. The recall was sounded again and again, but they had approached within one hundred and fifty yards of the enemy's batteries before they discovered that they were not followed bv the remainder of the force. They then halted, and retired down the height.

The 1st artillery rejoined General Twiggs, and the rifles and the 7th infantry bivouacked on the hill for the night. Fires were built underneath the cliffs upon the line occupied by General Twiggs' division, and the work of transporting the heavy artillery to the captured hill was soon after commenced. This duty was performed by the 4th artillery and the volunteer brigade of General Shields, and occupied nearly the entire night. With the aid of picket ropes, one twenty-four pounder gun, and two twenty-four pounder howitzers, were drawn up to the crest of the height, and placed in battery, under the superintendence of Captain Lee. On the same night, under the direction of Lieu tenant Tower, of the engineers, and Lieutenant Laidley, of the ordnance, an eight-inch howitzer was put in position across the river, and opposite to the enemy's right battery, by a detachment of the New York volunteers, commanded by Major Burnham.

Lighted only by the flickering rays of their watch-fires, save when the rising moon appeared above the horizon, the soldiers detailed to perform this arduous task, toiled on without cessation until the work was completed. They complained not of fatigue or exhaustion. No danger appalled,—no labor wearied them. Zealous and enthusiastic, they panted for the coming struggle; and they were strengthened, too, by the confidence of anticipated success,—the feeling of assurance that their efforts would not be in vain.

When the first waves of the morning light surged up over the mountain tops from the distant Gulf, the whole American army, from the right to the extreme left, were in motion. The storming of Cerro Gordo was the first object to be achieved. At seven o'clock on the 18th, the heavy guns planted on the hill opened their fire upon the height above it, and were served with effect by Captain Steptoe and Lieutenant Brown, of the 3rd artillery, Lieutenant Hagner, of the ordnance, and Lieutenant Seymour, of the 1st artillery. The assaulting party consisted of the first brigade of General Twiggs' division, commanded by Colonel Harney, to whom the execution of the enterprise was intrusted, reinforced by the 3rd infantry, Captain Alexander, from the second brigade, and a company of sappers and miners under Lieutenant G. W. Smith, of the engineers. Before the attack upon the main work of the enemy was ordered, a large succoring force were discovered advancing on the national road, in a direction which would have enabled them to turn the assaulting column. The rifle regiment, now commanded by Major Loring, Major Sumner having been wounded on the previous day, were immediately ordered to the left, to hold the approaching force in check until the assault commenced, when they were directed to join in it on that flank. The order was faithfully obeyed, in the midst of a withering fire upon the front and flanks of the regiment, from the enemy's batteries and intrenchments. In the meantime Colonel Harney formed the remainder of his troops for the attack,—the 7th infantry on the right, the 3rd infantry on the left, and the 1st artillery in the rear, with orders to support the infantry. A few moments passed in silence, and then the charge was sounded. The welcome note was echoed and repeated along the entire line. As one man, they sprang over the crest of the hill, dashed down the declivity, and ascended the opposite height.

The 2nd infantry, Captain Morris, and 4th artillery, Major Gardner, forming the remainder of the second brigade, commanded by Colonel Riley, moved forward at an early hour in the direction of the national road, in order to cut off the retreat of the enemy, under the guidance of Captain Lee, who was supported by a company of the 4th artillery, in command of Lieutenant Benjamin. Their course lay directly across a ravine swept by the Mexican batteries, and they soon became also exposed to an annoying fire of musketry from the hill of Cerro Gordo on their left, upon the western slopes of which the enemy appeared in force. A detachment, consisting of two companies of the 2nd infantry, under Captain Penrose, were promptly deployed as skirmishers, with directions to drive the enemy from the hill at every hazard. Observing that Santa Anna was now rapidly extending his line to the left, to keep open his communications with the rear, General Twiggs ordered General Shields to cross a deep ravine on the right, and advance up its left bank with his brigade, against the Mexicans in the road. The skirmishing party sent up the hill in rear of the main work, were warmly engaged with the enemy in a short time, and two additional companies of the same regiment were detached in like manner. Captain Lee continued his course towards the national road with his escort, but the remaining companies of the 4th artillery, accompanied by General Twiggs, followed the movement up the reverse of Cerro Gordo, preceded by the skirmishers, who gallantly charged upon the enemy, and drove them from their positions. Colonel Riley also commenced ascending the hill with the remainder of the 2nd infantry.

A plunging and destructive fire of round shot, grape, canister, and musketry, was poured upon the party of stormers moving to the assault of Cerro Gordo in front. The section and rockets of Talcott's battery, under Lieutenant Reno, returned the fire with spirit and effect. The hill was steep and difficult of ascent. Loose craggy rocks, and tangled chaparral, impeded the progress of the assaulting column. The tops of the smaller trees had also been cut off by the enemy, from four to five feet above the ground, and pointed down the hill, as an obstacle to the advance of an assailing force. A brief delay took place at the breastwork near the foot of the height, but the bayonet did its work truly and well. The barrier was surmounted, and the stormers pushed on with redoubled zeal. The steepness of the acclivity rendered the fire of the enemy less sure and certain than it might otherwise have been; but it was sufficiently severe to make the stoutest hearted stand in awe, had they not been impelled and sustained by a courage that could not falter. Animated by the words and heroic bearing of the undaunted Harney, whose tall and manly form was conspicuous to friend and foe, as he cheered his men on to the conflict, the Americans pressed forward with accelerated speed. The fate of the day never for a moment remained in suspense. Within musket range of the breastwork around the tower, they halted to deliver their unerring fire. Again the charge was ordered. Wreaths of mingled smoke and flame encircled the combatants. Anxious eyes were turned in that direction from every quarter. The colors of the 1st artillery, and of the 3rd and 7th infantry, were planted upon the breastwork, but the Mexican standard was still flying. A few rapid volleys were fired—then the crushing steel bore down every thing before it—and the flag which had waved over so many beating hearts in the hour of victory, floated alone upon the height of Cerro Gordo!

Portions of the rifle regiment joined the storming column, and the foremost companies of the 2nd infantry, who had ascended the opposite side of the hill, also reached its summit, in time to participate in the final assault. General Vasquez, the officer in command, was killed in the tower which he had so bravely defended. The hill was thickly covered with the dead and wounded of the enemy; a number were taken prisoners; and the remainder retreated in haste on the Jalapa road. The guns captured in the fort were turned upon its late occupants, and effectively served by Captain Magruder, of the 1st artillery, and Lieutenant Richardson, of the 3rd infantry, while General Twiggs pushed forward in the pursuit with the 4th artillery and 2nd infantry. The second division, under General Worth, reached the position occupied by General Twiggs on the night of the 17th, before the height was carried, and Lieutenant Colonel C. F. Smith was instantly detached, with his light battalion, to support the assault, but did not arrive in time. General Worth soon after reached the tower, and observing a white flag displayed from the battery on the national road, just beneath the hill of Cerro Gordo, sent out Colonels Harney and Childs to hold a parley. The work proved to be in command of General Pinson, a mulatto officer of considerable distinction, and was surrendered in compliance with the summons of General Worth.

The first brigade of volunteers, commanded by General Pillow, was under arms at sunrise, but did not reach the position assigned to it in front of the enemy's works on the right, until after General Twiggs had opened the action on the other flank. General Pillow immediately divided his command into two storming parties, each supported by a strong reserve. It was his intention to assail the adjacent angles of the two batteries nearest the river, simultaneously; but his position being discovered by the enemy, a galling fire was opened on his ranks, and rather than dishearten the troops by a retreat, Colonel Haskell, who commanded the assaulting force intended for the attack of the central battery, consisting of his regiment, (the 2nd Tennessee foot,) a company of Kentucky volunteers under Captain Williams, and one company of the 2nd Pennsylvania, Captain Naylor, was directed to assault the work, and carry it at the point of the bayonet. An enfilading fire upon the Mexican batteries was obtained from the eight-inch howitzer, in command of Lieutenant Ripley, of the 2nd artillery, on the right bank of the river, and it was kept actively engaged. Colonel Wynkoop, of the 1st Pennsylvania, in command of the storming party designed to attack the battery on the extreme right, moved towards the position where he was ordered to make the assault. The 1st Tennessee, Colonel Campbell, was directed to support the column under Colonel Wynkoop, and the 2nd Pennsylvania, Colonel Roberts, the party commanded by Colonel Haskell.

As the column headed by Colonel Haskell advanced to the attack, they encountered a resistance which they had not anticipated. The fire of seven pieces of heavy artillery was turned upon them, and effected terrible execution. They pressed on undismayed, through dense thickets of underbrush, until they came within range of the enemy's musketry. With an energy and steadiness worthy of experienced soldiers, they still continued on their course, regardless of the havoc made among their number. At length the fire became too terrible, and the party were compelled to retire. General Pillow being severely wounded, Colonel Campbell assumed the command of the brigade, and commenced making his dispositions for a second attack. Colonel Wynkoop, in the meantime, had arrived in front of the battery on the bank of the river, when all further operations were suspended by the capture of the hill of Cerro Gordo. The advanced works of the enemy were now exposed to a fire from the rear which would soon have demolished them; a white flag was therefore displayed over the intrenchments, and this portion of the enemy, now cut off from the main body, surrendered themselves prisoners of war.

Upon the extreme right the brigade under General Shields, consisting of the 3rd and 4th Illinois, Colonels Foreman and Baker, and the New York regiment, Colonel Burnett, were more successful. Crossing a ravine which the Mexicans deemed impassable, and which, up to that time, had never been crossed,* "under a canopy of cannon-balls," they gained its left bank, and advanced against the rear battery, with a celerity which filled the enemy with astonishment. Santa Anna had evidently given up the contest in front, and was hurrying with the greater part of his forces to the rear. General Shields was upon them in a moment. While forming his men for the attack, under a heavy fire from the enemy's guns, a grape shot passed through his lungs, and he fell to the earth completely paralyzed.—Happily for the general himself, and for the service, the wound did not prove to be mortal.—Colonel Baker assumed the command—Major Harris taking charge of the 4th Illinois—and the column was again ordered to advance. General Shields at this time was supposed to have been mortally wounded, and the brave volunteers were determined to avenge his loss. They charged upon the enemy's line with spirit and enthusiasm, and drove them from their loaded guns. Captain Lee, with the company commanded by Lieutenant Benjamin, followed by Colonel Riley at the head of the second brigade, approached on the other flank, and completed the capture of the battery. At this point the rout was complete. Santa Anna, and General Ampudia, the second in command, together with Generals Canalizo and Almonte, had barely time to make their escape. The private carriage of the Mexican President, his baggage,†

* Vindication of Santa Anna, by Manuel Maria Jimen, published in *El Diario del Gobierno*, May, 1847.

† At the siege and capture of San Juan de Ulua, by the French, the Mexican commander lost one of his limbs; and among the trophies captured by the volunteers, in his carriage, was his wooden leg, which afforded them and their comrades no little merriment. The personal property was, of course, returned; but it is extremely doubtful whether this appendage ever found its way back to his excellency.

and the military chest of the army, were captured by the volunteers, who now hurried forward with Riley's brigade, all under the command of General Twiggs, in pursuit of the flying enemy. The cavalry, and the field-batteries of Taylor and Wall, were also pushed on towards Jalapa, as soon as the road was opened, and General Patterson was sent to take command of the advanced columns.

General Scott had not been an inattentive observer of the events of the day, and the result was peculiarly gratifying to his feelings. He arrived on the height of Cerro Gordo shortly after General Worth, and publicly thanked Colonel Harney and his command for the courage and skill displayed in their gallant achievement. Before the sun had reached its meridian, the defile was passed, and the way opened to the table land of Mexico. The network of obstacles which Santa Anna had raised to impede the advance of the American army, proved to be frail as the meshes of the spider's web.* The battle was won, too, by a force barely exceeding 8,000 men, and under circumstances which justly entitle it to a prominent place among the other actions of the war.†

The pursuit was continued until late in the afternoon of the 18th, and many of the enemy were captured or cut down, before the American soldiers were obliged to halt, having become nearly exhausted from the heat and the distance. Captain Taylor brought up his bat-

* In his proclamation to his countrymen announcing the fall of Vera Cruz, Santa Anna said: "If the enemy advance one step more, the national independence will be buried in the abyss of the past." Alluding to this in a postcript to his official dispatch, General Scott pithily remarked, "We have taken that step."

† General Quitman did not arrive with the second brigade of volunteers in time to take part in the action.

tery, and opened his fire upon their rear columns as they ascended the hill of Encerro, when the troops in the advance were halted, and encamped within sight of the white towers of Jalapa. On the morning of the 19th, General Patterson entered the city, escorted by the dragoons, and followed by General Twiggs, with the infantry and artillery, in company with a deputation from its authorities, who came out to implore protection for their fellow-citizens.

Upwards of 3,000 prisoners, more than 4,000 stands of arms, 43 pieces of artillery, many of them manufactured in the royal foundry at Seville, and a large quantity of fixed ammunition, were captured in the battle of Cerro Gordo. The Americans lost 431 officers and men, in killed and wounded;* and the Mexican loss was computed to be from 1,000 to 1,200. Among the prisoners taken were Generals Pinson, Jarrero, La Vega, Noriega, and Obando. General Scott found himself so much embarrassed with the spoils of the victory, in consequence of the feebleness of his own army in point of numbers, that he was compelled to release the prisoners upon their paroles; and the small arms and accoutrements were collected together, and broken in pieces, or burned.

General Worth continued the pursuit beyond Jalapa with his division. The pass of La Hoya, a strong position west of that city, which had been fortified, and defended by a battery of heavy guns, was found entirely deserted. At noon on the 22nd of April, he en-

* Seven officers were killed or mortally wounded in the battle, viz: Lieutenants Ewell and Davis of the rifles; Lieutenant Yearwood, 1st Tennessee; Lieutenants Nelson and Gill, 2nd Tennessee; and Lieutenants Cowardin and Murphy, 4th Illinois. Captain Mason, of the rifle regiment, also died, some months later, from the effects of a wound received at Cerro Gordo.

tered the town, and occupied the castle of Perote, next in importance to San Juan de Ulua, and capable of accommodating over 2,000 troops. No resistance was offered,—the enemy's forces having been previously withdrawn,—and the fortress, with its armament, was surrendered by Colonel Velasquez, who had remained as a commissioner to perform that duty on behalf of his government. Sixty-one bronze guns and mortars, five howitzers, eleven thousand cannon balls, fourteen thousand bombs and hand-grenades, and five hundred muskets, were turned over to the Americans with the castle. General Worth also obtained considerable quantities of corn and flour in Perote and the neighboring haciendas, all which were paid for at fair prices, with the assistance of the alcaldes and padres, who manifested a laudable zeal in aiding him.

The excellent discipline and subordination maintained by General Scott in the army under his command, deserves a passing notice. Strict orders were issued directly after they landed at Vera Cruz, prohibiting the commission of any acts of violence upon the persons or property of non-combatants. No deviation from the regulations which he established was suffered to go unrebuked,—no outrage went unpunished. During the period of temporary inaction after the battle of Cerro Gordo, excesses were occasionally committed, which induced him to issue more positive orders at Jalapa, on the 30th of April, and from that time there were fewer causes of complaint.

A large number of the volunteers attached to his column were enlisted in the months of May and June, 1846: consequently, their terms of service had nearly expired when the army arrived at Jalapa. They were exceedingly anxious to reach the coast, and embark for home, before the sickly season came on, and the commanding general very properly acceded to their request, in the belief that the new levies raised under the ten regiment bill would soon reach his camp. On the 4th of May seven regiments, and two independent companies, in all numbering more than 3,000 men, were ordered to be discharged.* The design of advancing promptly into the heart of the country, however, was by no means abandoned. The elements of the strength and weakness of the Mexican government were concentrated in her capital, and it was of the highest im‸ortance that the army should move as far in that direction as was compatible with its safety and security. Reinforcements were expected in a few weeks, and early in the month General Worth was ordered to proceed to Puebla, seventy-eight miles beyond Perote, and about ninety miles from Mexico, with his division, followed by the brigade under General Quitman.

The Mexican army which General Scott had encountered on the heights of Cerro Gordo, was almost totally dispersed. Santa Anna escaped to the vicinity of Puebla, with a few followers, and Ampudia, at the head of 3,000 cavalry, in a most disastrous plight, passed through Perote, on his way to the interior. The nfantry were utterly disorganized, and fled before their pursuers in small bodies,—some throwing away their arms, and others selling them in the towns through which they passed, for two or three reals. Finding that the American army did not advance immediately

* A portion of the volunteer regiments called out in the fall of 1846, and winter of 1847, were enlisted to serve twelve months, or during the continuance of the war. This will account for their remaining in service after the expiration of the year, as, it will be seen, was the case.

SCOTT COMPLIMENTING COLONEL HARNEY

beyond Perote, the Mexican general-in-chief employed himself for several days, towards the latter part of April and the beginning of May, in the neighborhood of Orizaba, in collecting and organizing a new force, whose assistance had been invoked by his countrymen. As early as the 8th of April, it was proposed to adopt the guerilla system, at a meeting of the principal citizens of Mexico, and orders were issued, and measures taken by the government to carry the suggestion into effect. Among the most efficient of their agents and coadjutors was a padre, by the name of Jarauta, originally an Aragonese curate, who had been compelled to fly from Spain, on account of his participation in the cruelties and barbarities perpetrated by the guerilleros who fought under Cabrera.*

There is something noble in the aspect presented by a people flying to their arms, unitedly and spontaneously, in defence of their altars and their hearthstones,—to save themselves from wrong and injury, and their wives and daughters from outrage and violence. The movements of an excited populace are irresistible as the rush of the mountain torrent. Of what avail were an armed soldiery of 30,000 men, when the citizens of Paris had determined that the Bastile should be razed to the ground? The moors and glens of Scotland, the wild fastnesses of the Emerald Isle, and the dense savannas of Georgia and the Carolinas, tell us what may be done by men, who, seizing the sword, and casting away the scabbard, resist

* Father Jarauta was engaged in his peaceful avocations as a curate, when the war with the United States first commenced; but he appears very soon to have preferred

"The holy text of pike and gun,"

to the ministrations of his priestly calling.

oppression even unto death. For a long series of years La Vendeé bade defiance to the armies of the French republic. The Swiss peasant, as he quaffs the choice vintage of his native land,* never fails to bless the brave men who rescued her from the grasp of the Austrian despot, and the brave descendants who maintained the freedom so nobly won, against the efforts of France and Burgundy. The guerilla mode of warfare adopted by Mina, Empecinado, and their compatriots, had its origin in the same impulses, and their deeds of cruelty and vengeance,—sometimes just, yet always fearful,—are well remembered in the Spanish Peninsula. But the Mexican guerilleros were influenced by no such feelings,—by no such emotions. The principle which animated them was love of plunder, rather than love of country,—and the standard under which they rallied, was the emblem of the bandit,†—not the flag of the patriot!

The line of the national road has always been infested with banditti, and the guerilla bands organized to annoy the American army, were principally composed of that class of the population, their associates and companions, and a few deserters from the Spanish vessels of war lying in the Gulf. With very rare exceptions—and those mainly confined to the civil and military officers of the government,—the better classes

* At the battle of St. Jacob, fought August 26th, 1444, sixteen hundred Swiss withstood as many thousand French, led by the Dauphin, and maintained their ground until all but ten of their number were cut down. The wine produced on the field is called *Schweitzer Blut.*

† The flag of the guerilleros was about two feet long, and from twelve to fifteen inches wide. The centre was composed of a broad stripe of crimson, with the motto, *No Quarter*, wrought upon it with silk; on either side there was a black stripe, of about half the width, ornamented with a death's head and cross-bones. The border was of pale green, with crimson tassels at the points.

stood entirely aloof from the guerilleros, who soon commenced an indiscriminate plunder of friends and enemies, and refused to give them their countenance and support. The announcement that this system of fighting was about to be adopted, would have excited serious apprehensions in the minds of any other soldiers in the world; but a large proportion of the American troops were familiar with the legendary tales of border warfare in their own country, and many had been accustomed, from childhood, to the dangers and incidents of a life upon the frontiers, in the midst of hostile Indians. It was impossible, indeed, at all times to guard against surprise,—yet they knew how to retaliate. On the 11th of May, General Scott issued an eloquent proclamation, addressed to the Mexican people, forcibly depicting their deplorable condition as a nation, and advising them to terminate their dissensions and feuds, and to cultivate harmony among themselves, and friendship and amity with other nations. He assured them that the war would be prosecuted until an honorable peace was obtained, and admonished them to be cautious how they put in force the order to form guerilla parties, and to beware how they provoked him to retaliation. The guerilleros were far from being intimidated by the language of the proclamation, but it induced many to withhold their sympathy, whose assistance had been counted on with confidence.*

* "The hardest heart would be moved to grief in contemplating the battle-fields of Mexico a moment after the last struggle [Cerro Gordo.] Those generals whom the nation has, without service rendered, paid for so many years, with some honorable exceptions, have, in the day of need, betrayed it by their example or unskilfulness. On that field, among the dead and dying, are seen no proofs of military honor, for they are reduced to the sad fate of the soldier,—the same on every occasion, from Palo Alto to Cerro Gordo,—the dead to remain unburied, and the

After leaving Perote, the column under General Worth entered on an open reach of country, at an altitude of nearly seven thousand feet above the level of the ocean, gently undulating, and abounding in the productions of more temperate climes. There were many large plantations of maguey, with its dark leaves and clustering flowers; but there were also waving

wounded abandoned to the charity and clemency of the conqueror. Soldiers who go to fight expecting such a recompense, deserve to be classed among the best in the world, since they are stimulated by no hope of ephemeral glory, of regret, of remembrance, or even of a grave.

* * * * * * * *

"I will not believe that the Mexicans of the present day are wanting in courage to confess errors which do not dishonor them, and to adopt a system of true liberty, of peace, and union with their brethren and neighbors of the north; neither will I believe that they are ignorant of the falsity of the calumnies of the press, intended to excite hostility. No!—public sentiment is not to be created or animated by falsehood. We have not profaned your temples, nor abused your women, nor seized your property, as they would have you believe. We say this with pride, and we confirm it by your own bishops, and by the clergy of Tampico, Tuspan, Matamoras, Monterey, Vera Cruz, and Jalapa, and by all the authorities, civil and religious, and the inhabitants of every town we have occupied. * * * *

"Abandon then, rancorous prejudices, cease to be the sport of individual ambition, and conduct yourselves like a great American nation; leave off at once colonial habits, and learn to be truly free, truly republican, and you will become prosperous and happy, for you possess all the elements to be so * * * *

"The order to form guerilla parties to attack us, I assure you can procure nothing but evil to your country, and no evil to our army, which will know how to proceed against them; and if, so far from conciliating, you succeed in irritating, you will impose upon us the hard necessity of retaliation, and then you cannot blame us for the consequences which will fall upon yourselves.

"I am marching with my army upon Puebla and Mexico; I do not conceal it; from those capitals I shall again address you. I desire peace, friendship, and union;—it is for you to select whether you prefer war. Under any circumstances, be assured I shall not fail my word.—Extracts from the Proclamation of General Scott.

fields of corn, and wheat, and barley. Scattered about over the luxuriant plains were tall mountain peaks, fringed with the funereal pine; or piles of blackened scoriæ, marking the places once lighted by the fires of the now slumbering volcano. At El Pinal they crossed another ridge, and then descended into the valley, in the midst of which lies Puebla—"The city of the Angels."* To the stranger, as he approaches, it seems like some rich gem lying in the bosom of the Cordilleras; but within, vice, degradation, and depravity, the most hideous and loathsome, meet him at every turn. The church, and the few citizens—comparatively the very few—who may be seen at sunset rolling in their antique coaches, around the Alameda, enjoying the fragrance of its flowers, and inhaling the atmosphere cooled by its gushing fountains,—have amassed all the property, and the great multitude are miserably poor and wretched.

General Worth halted at Amasoque, twelve miles from Puebla, with his division, cn the 14th of May, to await the arrival of General Quitman. About eight o'clock in the forenoon he found his position suddenly menaced by about 3,000 Mexican cavalry, commanded by Santa Anna. When first discovered they appeared to be moving along on the right flank of the Americans, towards their rear, and it was soon reported that a heavy column were also approaching on the main road. Colonel Garland, with the 2nd artillery and a section of Duncan's battery, and Major Bonneville, with the 6th infantry and Steptoe's battery, were ordered to attack the cavalry force, and the remainder of the troops prepared to meet the enemy said to be advancing in front. No other party was discovered,

* The Mexican name of the city, in full, is, *La Puebla de los Angelos.*

however, and after twenty-five rounds were fired from the batteries, the Mexican cavalry were routed, and disappeared among the hills. Some prisoners were taken, and ninety-eight of the enemy were killed or wounded. Late at night Santa Anna reached Puebla with his discomfited troops, and evacuated it early on the following day. Having been joined by General Quitman's brigade, General Worth entered the town in the morning of the 15th, without meeting any further resistance, and on the ensuing day took possession of the adjacent heights of Loretto and Guadaloupe, and planted a battery on the hill of San Juan.

History presents few instances of the display of daring and boldness which deserve to be compared with the entrance of the American soldiers into the city of Puebla. But little more than four thousand men, weather-beaten, jaded, and wayworn, with the dust of many a weary day's journey "on their sandal shoon," in the gray fatigue-dress of the service, and unaccompanied by the gay paraphernalia of war, marched through the midst of a hostile population of sixty thousand souls, stacked their arms in the public square, posted their guards, and, when the night-watches came, lay down to sleep without one emotion of fear or alarm. The citizens were evidently chagrined and disappointed; for they had prepared themselves for the approach of warriors of swelling port and proud bearing, all glittering in purple and gold. Fierce and lowering looks were cast upon the soldiers defiling through the streets, from the crowded pavé and balcony, and from behind the vine-covered lattices along their route; but those who marked them well, saw in the kindling eye, the rigid muscle, and the stern lip, that dauntless courage and unconquerable self-reliance, of far more worth than

GENERAL WORTH.

numbers, in the time of danger and of peril. Visits of ceremony were interchanged between General Worth and the civil and ecclesiastical dignitaries of Puebla; the American troops were careful to do nothing that might provoke acts of hostility; yet, after all, their reception was "respectfully and coldly courteous, but without the slightest cordiality."*

Mr. Trist, the American Commissioner, and the bearer of the dispatch addressed, as we have seen, by the Secretary of State, on the 15th of April, to the Mexican Minister of Foreign Relations, joined General Scott at Jalapa, on the 14th of May. Colonel Childs was left in command of the city, with the 1st artillery and the 2nd Pennsylvania; Colonel Wynkoop was ordered to garrison the castle of Perote, where a general hospital was established, with a battalion of the 1st Pennsylvania; and on the 22nd instant General Twiggs marched for Puebla with his division, followed by General Scott, on the 23rd.† The dispatch brought by Mr. Trist was forwarded to the city of Mexico on the 12th day of June.

Foiled in his attempt to prevent the entrance of General Worth into Puebla, Santa Anna advanced towards Mexico, with the feeble force which he still continued to dignify with the appellation of "the army of the east." His approach was the signal for another disturbance in the capital. On the 20th of April, Con-

* Official dispatch of General Worth, May 15th, 1847.—While General Scott lay at Puebla with the main body of his army, a plan was concocted for poisoning his men. After the project was discovered, the principal part of the troops were ordered to encamp without the city.

† After leaving Jalapa, the American army became, in the language of General Scott, "a self-sustaining machine;" and drew its subsistence mainly from the country. The supplies were paid for, however, as had previously been done.

gress had passed a decree declaring it to be treason for any public functionary to entertain a proposition of peace. The tone of the government and of the people was bold and warlike. The star of Santa Anna was still in the ascendant; his enemies were silenced for the time; but when the particulars of the battle of Cerro Gordo were made public, they were loud in his condemnation. The new constitution adopted by Congress was *inaugurated,* and on the 15th of May the regular election for President took place. The result was supposed to be in favor of Herrera, then generally regarded as the peace candidate, but his opponents were strong enough to cause the canvass of the vote to be postponed till the 15th of January, 1848,—thus continuing the office of provisional president. In the midst of the excitement, Santa Anna approached the capital. From Ayotla he addressed a letter to the President substitute, General Anaya, expressing his views in relation to the further conduct of the war and the defence of the city, and intimating his intention to resign unless they were adopted.

The citizens of Mexico were exceedingly averse to bringing the war any nearer to their vicinity, and on the appearance of the General-in-chief of their armies, they heaped upon him every epithet of scorn and opprobrium. The "Bulletin of Democracy" charged him with cowardice and incapacity as an officer, and for a few days it was very uncertain whether he would be able to maintain himself in authority. A vindication of his conduct, prepared by Manuel Maria Jimen, was published in the "Diario del Gobierno," and both that journal and the "Republicano" engaged warmly in his defence. Again he triumphed over his opponents, and assumed the supreme authority. Collecting together a large military force, he commenced fortifying the Pass of Rio Frio, and the approaches to the capital; and General Alvarez was sent with a body of irregular cavalry and Indians from Sonora and Sinaloa, about 5,000 strong, to hover on the road between Perote and Puebla, and cut off the trains coming up to join General Scott, then at the latter place, waiting for the arrival of his reinforcements.

When the dispatch forwarded from Puebla on the 12th of June, reached Mexico, it was laid before Congress. At this time Santa Anna manifested something like a disposition to favor the conclusion of a peace, although he did not openly attempt to infuse a spirit of conciliation into the breasts of his countrymen. Various messages passed between him and the representatives of the nation, in relation to the dispatch. He evidently desired to have the decree of the 20th of April repealed, but no request was made to that effect. The invariable reply returned by Congress to the communications of the Executive, inquiring as to the disposition which should be made of the matter, was, that the incipient steps of a negotiation belonged to the latter, and that they could not interfere. They feared for their own popularity too much to repeal the decree, and Santa Anna was probably influenced by a similar feeling. Nothing was done towards procuring an interview with Mr. Trist; but, on the contrary, the general cry was for the continuance of hostilities. In July General Valencia came up from San Luis Potosi, with over 4,000 men, all eager for war, and ten pieces of artillery. The publication of the different journals issued in Mexico, with the exception of the "Diario del Gobierno,"—the recognized organ of the government,—was suppressed, and when that paper announced the determination of those whose views it represented, not to tender the olive branch of peace until a victory had been achieved over the enemy, the power and influence of Santa Anna were placed on a firmer foundation than ever.

The enlistment of troops under the ten regiment bill did not progress as rapidly as was anticipated by General Scott, and the War department of the United States, considering the large bounties; but the regiments were soon filled up. The first body of troops dispatched to the seat of war, were ordered to the Rio Grande, in command of General Cadwalader, to aid General Taylor in maintaining his line of communications, then supposed to be seriously endangered; but, more recent advices having been received, the order was countermanded, and they were sent to strengthen the column commanded by General Scott. They were followed in a short time by detachments under Generals Pillow and Pierce, which were also ordered to Vera Cruz.

Without the reinforcements which he expected to ioin him, it would have been extremely unwise in General Scott, had he advanced beyond Puebla. Taking advantage of the consternation that prevailed about the time of his arrival in that city, he might have entered the capital, perhaps, without an action. His whole effective force barely exceeded 6,000 men; Santa Anna was known to be in or near Mexico, with a large body of troops; General Alvarez was within striking distance in his rear; and if he moved forward, the detachments coming up would be more exposed to attack; and should they be cut off, his own position must be very insecure. Under such circumstances he decided to remain at Puebla until the reinforcements arrived. He therefore remained inactive for several weeks; but the time was profitably spent in drilling the troops on the plains near the town. The divisions of Generals Worth and Twiggs were rendered almost perfect in discipline, and the volunteers wanted but little of being equal to the regulars, in point of efficiency.

The guerilleros began to show themselves on the road to Vera Cruz towards the latter part of May, and the first of June. Captain Walker was ordered to join Colonel Wynkoop at Perote, with his company of mounted rifles, and he soon commenced the work of retaliation. Following their trails, and tracking them to their lairs, he rendered most efficient service in defeating their plans and counteracting their projects.* On the 4th of June Colonel McIntosh left Vera Cruz for the head-quarters of the army, with three companies of the 3rd dragoons, under Lieutenant Colonel Moore, and six companies of infantry, belonging to different regiments, under Major Lee of the 4th, and Captain Whipple of the 5th, in all numbering about 700 men. The command escorted a large wagon-train containing specie and ammunition. The guerilleros had been made acquainted with the valuable character of the train, and collected in force on the road to reap the rich harvest which they fancied to be within their grasp. Great care was taken by the Americans to prevent a surprise, and flankers were thrown out from one to two hundred yards to the right and left of the advance guard.

Soon after they entered the broken country, the detachment under Colonel McIntosh encountered the

* General Scott also employed a company of Mexican spies, who rendered important services in discovering the haunts of the guerilleros, and in conveying dispatches.

enemy in a narrow pass among the hills. An attemp was made to capture the wagons in the centre, but this was defeated, and the train closed up. Again advancing, they were attacked about half a mile further on, in the midst of a dense growth of cactus and wild thorn. The banditti were in a few moments discovered occupying the hills which flanked the road, and the Americans dashed into the thickets to drive them from their position. This was gallantly effected, and the command occupied the ground during the night. Believing it unwise to proceed, Colonel McIntosh dispatched an express to General Cadwalader, then at Vera Cruz, apprizing him of the attack made on his command, and that his train had been considerably crippled, and requesting that he might be reinforced as soon as possible. In the morning of the 7th he advanced to Paso de Ovejas, a more favorable point for an encampment, beating off with little difficulty a second attack made during the march. In this affair Colonel McIntosh lost twenty-four men in killed and wounded; that of the enemy was not ascertained.

General Cadwalader received the dispatch of Colonel McIntosh on the 7th of June, and on the morning of the 8th was *en route* to reinforce him with about 500 men, consisting of one company of the 3rd dragoor one section of the howitzer battery from the voltigeur regiment, and a detachment of infantry. He arrived at the camp of Colonel McIntosh on the 10th instant, and on the following afternoon the column resumed its march. Upon approaching the Puente Nacional, towards evening, they found the enemy in possession of the road. The bridge was barricaded, and they also occupied the fort on the left, commanding the road in its circuitous descent to the river, and the heights on the opposite bank, from which they had a raking fire upon the advancing columns, and which could only be reached by crossing the bridge. The Mexicans were first driven from the fort by the infantry; the barricade was then breached by the howitzers, and a passage opened by one company of cavalry and two of infantry. The heights beyond were now carried, and the enemy scattered in confusion. The position was a formidable one, but the Mexicans were driven from it, with the loss of only thirty-two men. The assailants, however, were protected to some extent by the darkness; otherwise their loss must have been more severe. The march was resumed on the 13th, and on the 15th they reached Jalapa, with no other annoyance than an occasional discharge of escopetas from the chaparral along the road.

At Jalapa General Cadwalader was joined by Colonel Childs,* with four companies of the 2nd dragoons, the 1st artillery, and the 2nd Pennsylvania. The command left that city on the 18th instant, and on the 20th found the Mexicans posted in considerable force on the heights commanding the Pass of La Hoya, prepared to intercept their progress. Captain Winder, with four companies of the 1st artillery, supported by Major Dimmick, with two additional companies of the same regiment, advanced against the enemy, and drove them precipitately from the hills. Here the routed guerilleros were unexpectedly attacked in the rear by Captain Walker, with his company of mounted rifles, and the battalion of the 1st Pennsylvania, under Colonel Wyn-

* Jalapa was abandoned by order of General Scott, who found himself unable to maintain any garrisons on his line of communications other than those at Vera Cruz, Perote, and Puebla, where his hospitals were established.

koop.—The latter, on hearing of the approach of General Cadwalader, had left Perote, with the companies of his regiment and Captain Walker's men, to aid in driving the guerilleros from the road. Early in the morning of the 20th, Captain Walker, in the advance, encountered nearly five hundred of the enemy at Las Vegas, whom he bravely attacked with his small command of thirty men. Colonel Wynkoop coming up, the guerilleros were soon put to flight.—The two parties under General Cadwalader and Colonel Wynkoop, ioining in the pursuit of the flying banditti, they were driven from hill to hill, nearly three miles, leaving behind them fifty of their number either dead or wounded.

This was one of the severest blows received by the guerilleros during the war. The party which attacked General Cadwalader at La Hoya, was supposed to be about 700 strong, and was commanded by Father Jarauta, and two other priests, formerly Spanish Carlists, like himself. On reaching Las Vegas, General Cadwalader learned that it was the nursery and dépôt of the marauding parties infesting the road. Under his orders the town was laid in ashes,—the neat Catholic church in its centre alone being spared.

While making preparations at Perote for the march to Puebla, General Cadwalader received an order by express from General Pillow, then coming up from the coast with 1,800 men, to await his arrival. The latter reached Perote on the 1st of July, and the united command, now over 3,000 in number, moved on towards Puebla, where they arrived on the 8th instant, without further interruption.

General Pierce left Vera Cruz on the 16th of July, with 2,500 men, of all arms, including a battalion of marines, under Lieutenant Colonel Watson. His column, with the wagon-train, was nearly two miles in length. On arriving near the National Bridge, he found it obstructed and defended, in the same manner as on the passage of the river by General Cadwalader; but he was unable to place his artillery in a commanding position, and orders were therefore given to charge upon the enemy. Lieutenant Colonel Bonham, of the 12th infantry, at the head of his battalion, rushed forward under a heavy fire from the enemy's escopetas, followed by Captain Duperu, with his company of the 3rd dragoons, sword in hand. The men leaped over the barricade upon the bridge, and in the space of ten minutes the guerilleros were flying in every direction. The command proceeded to the Rio del Plan, where they discovered that the main arch of the bridge had been blown up. Having crossed the river, General Pierce continued on his way to join General Scott. He was five times attacked by the guerilleros, including the rencontre at the Puente Nacional, but repulsed them on every occasion.

On the approach of General Pierce with his reinforcement, General P. F. Smith was sent out from Puebla to clear the road in front of the former, said to be obstructed by the enemy, with a considerable detachment. He succeeded in breaking up a large guerilla establishment at San Juan de los Llaños. General Pierce found the way opened before him, and arrived at Puebla on the 6th of August. General Scott had already issued his orders for the advance to the Mexican capital; and on the 7th instant General Twiggs' division, preceded by the brigade of cavalry under Colonel Harney, took up the line of march for the far-famed halls of the Montezumas. The divisions of Generals Quitman, Worth, and Pillow, followed, at intervals of one day.* Colonel Childs remained at Puebla, as civil and military governor, with a garrison of about 1,400 men, consisting of detachments from different regiments.

* The total rank and file of the army which marched to the capital under General Scott, was 10,738. The cavalry brigade under Colonel Harney, consisted of detachments of the 1st, 2nd, and 3rd dragoons, commanded respectively by Captain Kearny, Major Sumner, and Lieutenant Colonel Moore, and a volunteer company in command of Captain McKinstry of the quartermaster's department. The *first division* was commanded by General Worth; the first brigade, under Colonel Garland, consisting of Lieutenant Colonel Duncan's light battery, the 2nd artillery, Major Galt, 3rd artillery, Lieutenant Colonel Belton, and 4th infantry, Major Lee; and the second brigade, under Colonel Clarke, consisting of the 5th infantry, Colonel McIntosh, 6th infantry, Major Bonneville, and 8th infantry, Major Waite. The siege train, under Captain Huger of the ordnance, was attached to Worth's division. The *second division* was commanded by General Twiggs; the first brigade, under General P. F. Smith, consisting of the rifle regiment, Major Loring, the 1st artillery, Major Dimmick, 3rd infantry, Captain Alexander, and Captain Taylor's light battery; and the second brigade, under Colonel Riley, consisting of the 4th artillery, Major Gardner, 2nd infantry, Captain Morris, and 7th infantry, Lieutenant Colonel Plympton. The company of sappers and miners, under Lieutenant G. W. Smith, was attached to Twiggs' division. The *third division* was commanded by General Pillow; the first brigade, under General Pierce, consisting of the 9th infantry, Colonel Ransom, 12th infantry, Lieutenant Colonel Bonham, and 15th infantry, Colonel Morgan; and the second brigade, under General Cadwalader, consisting of the voltigeuers, with the mountain howitzer and rocket battery, Colonel Andrews, 11th infantry, Lieutenant Colonel Graham, and 14th infantry, Colonel Trousdale. Capain Magruder's light battery was also attached to this division. The *fourth division* was commanded by General Quitman, and consisted of the South Carolina regiment, Colonel Butler, and the New York volunteers, Colonel Burnett, forming the brigade of General Shields, with the 2nd Pennsylvania, Colonel Roberts, the battalion of marines, Lieutenant Colonel Watson, and Captain Steptoe's battery.

CHAPTER X.

DONIPHAN'S MARCH.

The Missouri Volunteers—Expedition against the Navajos—Orders to join General Wool—La Jornada del Muerto—Skirmish at Bracito—El Paso del Norte—Fortifications of the Enemy at the Pass of Sacramento—The Battle—Flight of the Mexicans—Entrance into the City of Chihuahua—March to Monterey—Return Home.

WHILE the more important military operations which have been narrated, were being carried on in other quarters of the country, there occurred, in northern Mexico, one of those extraordinary achievements which are rarely undertaken, and which, when accomplished, always challenge admiration. A mere handful of men, —a volunteer force less than one thousand strong—commanded by a bold, fearless, and energetic officer, performed an arduous and fatiguing march of many thousand miles, through a hostile country, chastising or awing the savage tribes which infested their route into submission; encountering the enemy, in superior numbers, on two several occasions, and routing them with the utmost ease and facility. All this was done with comparatively little loss; and when the term of their enlistments expired, these soldiers returned to their distant homes, leaving behind them but very few of their comrades who had been overtaken by sickness, or fallen in battle, or

> "tired on the marches
> Of the war-path, long and drear!"

Among the pledges and assurances given by General Kearny to the inhabitants of New Mexico, in order to render them better satisfied with the new form of government which he established, prior to his departure for California in the fall of 1846, was a guarantee of protection against the Indians in their vicinity. The Apaches, as we have seen, were temporarily quieted; and while on his way to the Pacific coast, the general issued an order at La Joya, in October, requiring Colonel Doniphan, of the first Missouri mounted volunteers, then at Santa Fé, but previously instructed to report to General Wool at Chihuahua, to make a campaign with his regiment into the country inhabited by the Navajo Indians. This was one of the fiercest and most implacable tribes west of the Mississippi, occupying the greater part of the territory between the waters of the Rio Grande and those of the Rio Colorado of the West, and its warriors had long been "the terror and scourge" of the northern provinces of Mexico.

Colonel Doniphan left Santa Fé on the 26th of October, and having divided his command into separate detachments, invaded the Navajo country by three routes. This expedition was attempted late in the season, and was not brought to a close until the troops had suffered severely from the intense cold of winter. Their daily march was through drifts of snow which blocked up the valleys, and across mountains covered with ice Every portion of the Indian territory was visited, and near three-fourths of the tribe, though almost entire strangers to the American name, were collected at the Ojo Oso, where a permanent treaty was made with them. The object of the expedition being attained, Colonel Doniphan returned to the Rio Grande, near Socorro, on the 12th of December. He then crossed over to Valvervede, and on the 14th instant, in obedience to the order directing him to report to General Wool, then supposed to be at Chihuahua, the advance, under Major Gilpin, took up the line of march down the left bank of the river. Lieutenant Colonel Jackson followed on the 16th, with another detachment. While Colonel Doniphan was engaged in bringing the Navajos to terms, Colonel Price, of the 2nd Missouri regiment, the commanding officer at Santa Fé, dispatched Lieutenant Colonel Mitchell, with an escort of 95 men, selected from his regiment, and from the battalion of Missouri volunteer artillery, under Major Clark, to open a communication with General Wool. The detachment left Santa Fé on the 1st of December, and came up with Colonel Doniphan at Valvervede, on the 17th instant. On the following day they proceeded in company with him, and the remainder of the 1st Missouri, upon the route previously taken by the other portions of his command. Before leaving Valvervede, Colonel Doniphan was informed that the Mexicans were collecting a force at El Paso del Norte, to intercept his march, and an order was therefore sent to Major Clark, of the artillery battalion at Santa Fé, to join him at the earliest moment with 100 men, and a battery of four six-pounders, and two twelve-pounder howitzers.*

A few miles south of Fra Christóbal, the road to Chihuahua, instead of following the windings of the river, pursues a direct course from one bend to another, over a dry plain between seventy and eighty miles in length, completely destitute of water, except immediately after

* Colonel Doniphan's force numbered 856 effective men, all armed with rifles; but, at this time, he had no artillery. The twelve-pounder howitzers ordered from Santa Fé were constructed expressly for field prairie service.

a shower of rain, and frequently intersected by broad gulfy ravines. Few zephyrs love to sport among the tussocks of grass which cover this arid stretch of country ; the dark close-set leaves of the grease-wood hang droopingly from their stems ; the tufts of the wild sage seem parched with heat ; occasionally a pile of stones surmounted by a cross, the rude memorial reared above the grave of the wayfarer who perished on his journey, meets the eye of the traveller ; but all is still, solemn, voiceless as the tomb. Most appropriately has the Mexican termed the passage over this dreary waste, *La Jornada del Muerto.** In their progress to the south, the Americans often crossed similar tracts, though less extensive—they were poorly provided with sustenance and raiment, but their hardships and privations were submitted to without murmuring or complaint.

The different detachments of Colonel Doniphan's command were concentrated at Doña Ana, sixty miles from El Paso, and they were now also joined by a number of traders with over 300 wagons, who had left Santa Fé in September, but had become too much alarmed to proceed on their route. Here intelligence was received that seven hundred Mexican troops and

* "This dry stretch of road is called *La Jornada del Muerto*, or, The (days') Journey of Death. Although the word *Jornada* only means a days' journey, yet, from this day forward, our men called every long dry extent of road, a Jornada. In passing through the country, if you ask a peasant how far it is from one place to another, he will tell you so many jornadas (pronounced hornarthars), meaning, that to encamp at water each night, it will take so many days to travel it. But, as they always estimate road by the time it takes a pack-mule to go over it, you must allow accordingly. This long piece of road, La Jornada del Muerto, obtained its name from the circumstance of a Mexican having attempted to cross it in a day, and from his not being provided with water or food, having perished on the road."—Edwards' Campaign in New Mexico.

six pieces of artillery had arrived at El Paso. The column moved forward on the 23rd of December, presenting quite a picturesque appearance as they wound their way across valley and plain; the soldiers all mounted and well armed, and the white cotton tilts of the Conestogas, as the traders' wagons were styled, gleaming brightly in the sunlight.

About three o'clock in the afternoon of Christmas day, Colonel Doniphan had halted, with the advance of 500 men, at Temascalitos, on an arm of the river called Bracito, for the purpose of camping; the horses were unsaddled and sent some distance from the camp to graze, and the men were soon busily engaged in carrying wood and water. While thus employed, a heavy cloud of dust was suddenly discovered rolling up from the south, and in a moment after the advance guard descried the enemy approaching in force. Lieutenant Colonel Jackson was still several miles in the rear with the remainder of the troops. The rally was instantly sounded, and Colonel Doniphan formed his men in open order on foot as skirmishers, throwing the extreme points of the two wings towards the river, to protect his flanks and baggage. The Americans were somewhat taken by surprise, but a few moments sufficed to complete their dispositions. The enemy halted within half a mile, and formed in line of battle—the Vera Cruz lancers on the right, the Chihuahua battalion on the left, and the infantry and militia, with a two-pounder howitzer, in the centre. The Mexican cavalry were gayly decorated with bright scarlet coats and white belts, with shining brass helmets and dark waving plumes, and their polished sabres and escopetas, and their long lances, ornamented with pennons of red and green, glistened in the rays of the evening sun.

Just as the Americans were forming, a Mexican officer, bearing a black flag, rode up to their line, and demanded that their commander should accompany him to confer with the officer in command of the enemy Notwithstanding his declaration, that the penalty of a non-compliance with the demand would be a charge, *without quarter*, he received a peremptory refusal, and returned to those who sent him.* Upon his return the enemy advanced to the charge, opening a simultaneous fire from their whole line. When within rifle-shot the Mexicans attempted to file to the right and left, and pass the flanks of the opposing force : Colonel Doniphan's men had so far reserved their fire, but they now opened upon the enemy from right to left, with such spirit and effect, that they were immediately thrown into confusion. Captain Reid had succeeded in mounting about twenty men, and as the lancers were rallied to the charge on the American left, he fell furiously upon them with his small force, and after a desperate contest, which continued about twenty minutes, succeeded in putting them to flight. As the enemy's infantry gave way, Lieutenant Wright charged upon them with his company, and captured the howitzer. This completed the overthrow of the enemy, and they fled on all sides to the contiguous mountains.

The Mexican force in the affair at the Bracito, numbered 1,220. Of this number 537 were cavalry, and the remainder infantry. A portion of the latter consisted

* "Before we had fully formed, they sent a lieutenant near our lines with a *black* flag, with a demand that the commander of our forces should go to their lines and confer with their commander; declaring, at the same time, unless it was complied with, they would charge *and take him, and neither ask nor give quarters.* The reply was more abrupt than decorous—to charge and be d—d."—Official report of Colonel Doniphan, dated March 4th, 1847.

of militia from El Paso. The advance only of Colonel Doniphan's command were engaged, as Lieutenant Colonel Jackson did not arrive from the rear until after the action had terminated. The enemy lost forty-three killed and one hundred and fifty wounded. Colonel Doniphan had but seven men wounded, all of whom recovered, and none killed. Besides the howitzer, there were also captured a number of carbines, and a quantity of provisions.

The Americans anticipated having another encounter with the enemy before entering El Paso, and were accordingly on the alert. On the night of the 26th they encamped within a short distance of the city, and entered it on the ensuing day without opposition. This town is situated on the right bank of the Rio Grande, three hundred and ten miles below Santa Fé, and was founded by a body of Spanish refugees, driven from the latter place by the Indians in 1680, who crossed the river at this point in order to elude pursuit, from which circumstance the name is derived. El Paso contains about five thousand inhabitants, and there is a large population in the rich valley extending above and below the town. When Colonel Doniphan visited it with his troops, the vineyards were in " the sere and yellow leaf," yet they afforded the promise of an abundant harvest. Most of the Pasénians retired on the approach of the Americans, but they shortly after returned to their homes. Those who remained manifested feelings of friendship; and when the soldiers marched through the streets, baskets of most luscious fruit, the produce of the past season, were forced upon their acceptance.

On his arrival at El Paso, Colonel Doniphan learned from the prisoners taken, and from other sources, that

General Wool had not advanced upon Chihuahua. In this condition of things, a forward movement was deemed extremely hazardous, but he resolved to undertake it as soon as he was joined by the artillery. Major Clark arrived at El Paso on the 5th of February, 1847, with about 120 men of his battalion, and the six pieces of artillery ordered from Santa Fé; and on the 8th instant, Colonel Doniphan proceeded on the road to Chihuahua, escorting the merchant train or caravan which had accompanied him from Doña Ana.* A few miles below El Paso is the Presidio de San Elecario, originally a strong fortification, covering nearly eight acres of ground, and containing a neat church within its walls. This was not occupied by the enemy, and the only instrument of war found in it was a stone mortar, which the Americans took with them. They left San Elecario on the 11th of February, and after crossing several desolate and tedious jornadas, they arrived at the Laguna de Encenillas, a shallow brackish lake, two hundred and seven miles below El Paso, and seventy-four miles from Chihuahua, in the afternoon of the 25th instant. Rumors that the enemy were in force upon the road had previously reached them, and they were now informed by their spies that a body of troops were at Inseneas, the country-seat of Angel Trias, Governor of Chihuahua, about twenty-five miles in advance. They arrived there on the following day, when they found that the enemy had retired. On the 27th they reached Sauz, where they learned that the Mexicans had fortified the pass of Sacramento, twenty miles north of the city of Chihuahua.

The approach of the American troops had been for a long time anticipated by the authorities of Chihuahua,

* The force under Colonel Doniphan now consisted of 924 men.

and preparations were made to obstruct their advance by Governor Trias, and General José Heredia, the commandant general of the district.* At a meeting of the legislature of the department, the governor presiding, it was decided that when Doniphan's men should be taken, they were to be stripped of their money and arms, and sent on foot to the city of Mexico; and a quantity of cord was cut in suitable lengths for tying the prisoners, which was afterwards captured at the battle of Sacramento. General Heredia, with Generals Justiniani, Garcia Conde, and Ugarté and Governor Trias, who acted as a brigadier general, advanced to the pass of Sacramento about the middle of February, with near 4,000 troops, regulars and militia, ten pieces of field artillery, and six culverins, or rampart pieces.† The position was skilfully and strongly fortified, under the direction of General Condé, who was afterwards detached with 800 cavalry to observe the Americans, and on the approach of Colonel Doniphan fell back to the main body.

The road from Sauz to the rancho of Sacramento, in front of which the enemy had fortified themselves, follows the course of an open level valley, bounded on either side by ranges of sterile mountains. About seven

* General Cuilte was posted at San Rosalia, in December 1846, to intercept General Wool; but the post was abandoned when it was ascertained that he had taken another route.

† According to General Heredia's official report, dated March 2nd, 1847, he had but 1,575 men, and ten pieces of artillery. In this estimate he could not have included all the militia and rancheros who were present at the battle, and the Americans certainly captured more than that number of guns, including the culverins. Colonel Doniphan, in his report, dated March 4th, says that "the force of the enemy was 1,200 cavalry from Durango and Chihuahua, with the Vera Cruz dragoons, 1,200 infantry from Chihuahua, 300 artillerists, and 1,420 rancheros, badly armed with lassoes, lances, and machetoes, or corn knives."

miles from the Rio Sacramento, a branch of the Rio Conjos, one of the tributaries of the Rio Grande, the country begins to slope gently down to that stream. The position occupied by the Mexicans was upon an elevated plain, in the centre of a peninsula formed by the Arroyo Secô and Arroyo Sacramento, the two principal branches of the Rio Sacramento, which have their rise in the mountains on the right of the valley, at this point nearly four miles wide, and cross it in an easterly direction nearly parallel to each other. The Arroyo Secô, on the north, inclines to the south when it reaches the eastern range of mountains, and, uniting with the Arroyo Sacramento, they together form the main river. The road to Chihuahua crosses this peninsula from north to south; on its left the plain rises abruptly in a bench, fifty feet high, sloping upwards from every side towards the north-east corner, where it culminates in a rocky knoll called the Cerro Frigolis, one hundred and fifty feet above the plain; but on the right it is smooth and unbroken, descending gradually from the hilly bench, along the base of which the road passes. On the southern bank of the Arroyo Sacramento there is a range of sierras, separated by deep gullies, and forming right angles with the course of the stream. The easternmost ridge is the Cerro Sacramento, which rises on the right of the road, just in rear of the rancho Sacramento. Below the Cerro Sacramento on the east is the valley of the Rio Sacramento, about one mile wide through which winds the road to Chihuahua.

Upon the Cerro Frigolis, was a redoubt and battery, with a stone wall, and abattis in its rear, extending across the bed of the Arroyo Secô to the mountains on the opposite bank. Seven hundred yards west of the Cerro Frigolis there was another redoubt. There was a redoubt also at the north-west corner, and one at the south-west corner of the bench on the left of the road, with three other redoubts at intervals between them. Near the ford of the Arroyo Sacramento was a stone câral, or inclosure, surrounding a spring. The câral and the redoubts were all connected, with the exception of short intervals, by breastworks of stone and trenches for the protection of infantry, thus forming an unbroken line of fortifications, overlooking and commanding the gorge of the Arroyo Secó, and the road across the peninsula throughout its whole extent. On the Cerro Sacramento there was a strong battery, which commanded the road as it approached the ford below it. About three miles west of the ford, on the Arroyo Sacramento, was the hacienda of Torreön, from which another road led through a cañon in the mountains to the main route to Chihuahua.

Colonel Doniphan left Sauz with his command at sunrise, on the 28th of February. The teamsters were armed, and placed under the orders of Major Owens, one of the traders, under whose direction the wagons were arranged in four parallel lines, with intervals of fifty feet. The artillery marched in the interval of the centre; and the remainder of the troops, except two hundred cavalry proper, who were in the advance, marched in the intervals on the right and left. By this means the strength of the force was concealed, and its position masked.* On arriving within three miles of the enemy's fortifications, a reconnaissance was made by Major Clark, who discovered that the Mexican infantry occupied the batteries and redoubts, and that the cavalry were drawn up in front. The column now con-

* Another object of this arrangement was, to have the wagons serve as a breastwork to the troops in case of an attack.

tinued its course along the road about a mile and a half, and the cavalry still further, when they suddenly diverged to the right, for the purpose of gaining the level portion of the plain fronting the position of the Mexicans on the west. The movement was soon perceived by the enemy, and General Condé advanced with a body of cavalry, masking four pieces of artillery, to prevent the Americans from gaining the elevation. The manœuvre was executed too rapidly to render that possible, and Colonel Doniphan formed his men, and the advance column of the wagons was cârallêd before the enemy came within reach of his guns.

The Americans were all dismounted, except three companies, under Captains Reid, Parsons, and Hudson. Major Clark occupied the centre with his artillery; the first battalion on the right was commanded by Lieutenant Colonels Mitchell and Jackson, and the second battalion, on the left, by Major Gilpin. The action was commenced about three o'clock in the afternoon by a brisk fire from the American battery, which was returned by the enemy. At the third discharge the Mexican lancers gave way, and retired behind the redoubts with their artillery, having lost several men killed and a number wounded. Anxious to improve the advantage gained, Colonel Doniphan ordered a charge upon the enemy's line of intrenchments and batteries. At the word, his men sprang forward with cheers and shouts. Captain Weightman advanced with the howitzers at full speed,* upon the redoubts at the south-

* A statement has been extensively circulated by the public press, to the effect that the American artillery at the battle of Sacramento was drawn by oxen. This is entirely erroneous. Four of the carriages were drawn by American horses, and the remaining carriages and caissons by mules obtained in the country.—Official report of Major Clark, March 2nd, 1847.

west corner of the bench, supported by the cavalry under Captains Reid, Parsons, and Hudson; Major Clark followed the movement as fast as practicable a little further to the left; and the remainder of the troops dashed rapidly forward on foot. While they were advancing, the enemy's cavalry were twice rallied for a charge upon the left flank of the wagons following in the rear of the American line, but they were easily dispersed by the fire of Major Clark's guns. Captain Weightman unlimbered his pieces within fifty yards of the redoubts, and the cavalry and infantry rushing boldly up to the breastworks, drove the enemy before them with their sabres and rifles.

As the Americans entered the line of intrenchments east of the road, a warmer and more effective fire was opened from the battery on the height of Cerro Sacramento, which had been constantly playing upon them, and where a large body of Mexicans had now rallied. Major Clark promptly placed his pieces in position, in the redoubt at the south-west corner of the bench, twelve hundred yards distant, and in a short time silenced the enemy's guns. Meanwhile Lieutenant Colonels Mitchell and Jackson, with the first battalion remounted, and Captain Weightman's howitzers, had bravely charged up the hill, followed by Major Gilpin with the second battalion on foot. Before they reached the battery the enemy had abandoned it, and their entire force was scattered in flight. The cavalry and the howitzers immediately pushed forward in hot pursuit. The road was strewed with the arms and accoutrements which the Mexican soldiers had thrown down as they hurried towards Chihuahua. Governor Trias was among the first to reach the city, and the seat of government was instantly ordered to be removed to Parral.

Night put an end to the carnage. The enemy lost all their artillery, ten wagons, and large quantities of provisions; they had three hundred killed, about the same number wounded, and there were forty taken prisoners. Several national and regimental standards were also captured, and among the colors was the black flag exhibited at the Bracito. Colonel Doniphan had but one man killed, and eight wounded, some of them mortally.*

The way was now opened to Chihuahua, and on the 1st of March Colonel Doniphan took formal possession of it in the name of his government. This city was the residence of the Captains-general of the internal provinces, under the vice-regal government of Spain, and is pleasantly situated on a branch of the Rio Conjos, in the centre of the rich mining district in northern Mexico. It contains about thirty thousand inhabitants, and is surrounded by a fertile country, disfigured but slightly by occasional piles of scoriæ and basaltes. On entering the town the American soldiers took up their quarters in the Plaza de Toros, in front of which was the Alameda. Here, in the enjoyment of the luxuries and hospitalities which almost caused them to forget the hardships they had endured, they remained for several weeks, without the occurrence of any incident of extraordinary moment.

On the 5th of April the artillery, and one battalion of the 1st Missouri, were ordered to proceed to Parral, where Governor Trias had established his government; but, on the third day out, the detachment learned that his excellency had again fled in alarm, and they therefore returned to head-quarters. Colonel Doniphan was not desirous of remaining any longer as a wagon guard

* Major Owens accompanied Captain Reid in the charge, and was killed in storming the enemy's redoubts.

for the traders, and he saw that his men would eventually be ruined by improper indulgences if they remained at Chihuahua. Most of his officers preferred staying in that city; but he determined to send a party of twelve men to General Taylor for orders.* They returned, on the 24th instant, with instructions to join the latter forthwith, by the way of Parras, Buena Vista, and Saltillo.

Preceded by Lieutenant Colonel Mitchell with his escort, the Americans left Chihuahua on the 25th of April, 1847, still accompanied by the traders. Again traversing the weary jornadas on their route, and passing through the dismal muskeet forests of Mapimi, they arrived at the rancho of El Paso, four hundred and nine miles from Chihuahua, and two hundred and seven miles from Monterey, on the 13th of May. Near this place a most gallant exploit was performed by Captain Reid, and a party of officers and men, about twenty-five in number, belonging to Colonel Doniphan's command. At the request of the owner of the rancho, who furnished the party with horses, they attacked a band of sixty Lipan warriors, a branch of the Camanches,

* "While we were in the city, [Chihuahua] a council of war was called. We had expected to have here met and joined General Wool; however, we had done our work without him; but what course were we now to take? for there was danger at all points! A few of the officers proposed staying in Chihuahua, others were for trying to join General Taylor, and some suggested a retrograde march to Santa Fé; most, however, were in favor of pressing home by way of Monterey. No ultimate decision was at that time had; but a short time afterwards, another council was held, and, at this time, most of the officers were for remaining in quarters. Doniphan heard them for some time, but with impatience, and at last, bringing his heavy fist down on the table, he gave the board to understand that, they might possibly have found *fair* reasons for staying; 'But, gentlemen,' added the Colonel, '*I'm for going home to Sarah and the children!*' The reader may be assured that we caught up these words, and often afterwards spoke of going home to Sarah and the children."—Edwards' Campaign in New Mexico.

who had been prowling for several days in the vicinity killed a number of the savages, rescued eighteen Mexican captives, and recaptured considerable plundered property. This act did not go unrewarded,—the proprietor of El Paso presented each one of the party with the horse which he had rode, and the prefect of the department of Parras gave Captain Reid an official acknowledgment of the gratitude and thanks of his fellow citizens.

In the tattered uniforms which they had worn from St. Louis and Fort Leavenworth, Colonel Doniphan and his men presented themselves before General Taylor, in his encampment at Walnut Springs, on the 26th of May. They were very desirous of seeing a little more service under his immediate command, but he was unable to gratify their wishes.* Leaving the artillery which they had brought from Santa Fé, and taking with them the captured guns, they marched to the Brazos, where they embarked for New Orleans. At this city they were mustered out of service, and returned to their homes in Missouri; having travelled, during their absence, more than five thousand miles; nearly two thousand miles more than the famous march of Xenophon and the Greeks in their retreat from Asia, the record of which, written by the same skilful hand which pointed out the route, has survived the ravages of so many centuries.

* The *sobriquet* of 'Rough and Ready' has long been familiarly given to General Taylor. Colonel Doniphan's men thought they could make the alliteration more complete, by applying it, with a trifling addition, to themselves; for they might justly be considered, *Rough, Ready, and Ragged!*

CHAPTER XI.

REVOLT IN NEW MEXICO.

Disaffection among the inhabitants of New Mexico—Murder of Governor Bent and others—March of Colonel Price—Defeat of the enemy at Cañada—Affair at Moro—The Pass of Embudo—Storming of Puebla de Taos—Suppression of the Revolt—Depredations in the valley of the Moro—Skirmishes with the Marauders—Quiet restored in the Province.

SANTA FÉ came very near proving a Capua to the American soldiers. Colonel Price,* of the 2nd Missouri mounted volunteers, who remained in command of the troops in that quarter, does not appear to have been a martinet in discipline, although he certainly displayed both ability and energy as an officer in the field. Relaxation and excess were more frequently witnessed than subordination and good order, and the wholesome restraints imposed by General Kearny were, one by one, disregarded. During the fall of 1846, and the ensuing winter, the soldiers were employed in the construction of a fort on a high hill commanding the town and the surrounding country, which was named Fort Marcy, in honor of the head of the War Department. There was a great deal of leisure time, however, neither wisely nor profitably spent; and many of them fell victims to diseases engendered by unreasonable indulgences, and the unfriendliness of the climate.

* Colonel Price was appointed a brigadier general of volunteers, July 20th, 1847.

Frequent altercations occurred between the Mexican inhabitants and the soldiers ; the former were naturally jealous of foreign interference ; many of the disbanded troops of Governor Armijo lingered in the vicinity of Santa Fé, in readiness for employment, if an opportunity was presented ; the civil officers who had been displaced, viewed their successors, appointed under the newly-established government, with emotions of hatred and ill will ; the Puebla Indians were violently hostile to the Americans ; and the most prominent and influential citizens in the province labored to foment the disaffection rapidly gaining ground. About the 15th of December, Colonel Price was informed that an insurrectionary movement was in contemplation. Several persons supposed to be implicated were arrested, and an investigation was had, in the course of which it appeared that a plan had been formed for a general rising on Christmas eve. The principal leaders in the affair, Ortiz and Archuleta, escaped in the direction of Chihuahua,* the project was further frustrated by the arrests which had been made, and in a few days the alarm entirely subsided.

Subsequent events showed that the revolt was not effectually suppressed. On the 14th of January, 1847, Governor Bent left Santa Fé for San Fernando de Taos, accompanied by a number of civil officers. In the night of the 19th instant, the governor, the sheriff, the district attorney, and three other persons, were seized by a band of Mexicans and Puebla Indians, and put to death in the most inhuman manner.† On the same day

* The individuals concerned in the revolt in New Mexico anticipated aid from Chihuahua, but the defeat of the Mexican force at Bracito, by Colonel Doniphan, prevented their receiving any assistance.

† It is suggested, in Edwards' Campaign in New Mexico, (p. 103,)

seven Americans were murdered at Arroyo Hondo, eight miles from Taos, in the valley of the Moro, and two others on the Rio Colorado; and on the 20th instant, eight or nine persons were killed at the upper Moro. The leaders of the insurrection were Tafoya, Pablo Chavis, Pablo Montoya, Cortés and Tomas, a Puebla Indian; and their main object seemed to be, to cut off every American and Mexican who had accepted office under the new government. This movement was confined to the northern part of New Mexico, but the disaffected from other quarters, to some extent, participated in it. Intelligence of the murders committed by the revolters reached Santa Fé on the 20th of January, and circulars were also intercepted, written by them, calling upon the inhabitants along the Rio Abajo for aid. All the towns in the valley of the Moro declared in favor of the insurrection, except Qucoloti and Las Vegas—an attempt to excite the population of the latter being defeated by the timely presence of Captain Hendley, of Lieutenant Colonel Willock's battalion, with a portion of his grazing detachment. It was now ascertained that the enemy designed to advance upon the capital of the province, as soon as they had concentrated their forces, which were coming together as fast as possible. The garrison of Santa Fé was considerably reduced, in consequence of a number of the mounted men having been sent off in different direc-

that the murder of Governor Bent was instigated entirely by his wife, a Spanish woman, from whom he had for some time been separated, and who was concerned in the insurrectionary movement. She may have connected herself with the revolt, for the purpose of gratifying her private malice; yet it is hardly to be supposed, that the head of the government would have been overloooked, when so many were murdered who occupied subordinate stations. Nor is it at all probable, that they were put to death, because of their temporary association with him.

tions to graze their horses; but Colonel Price immediately dispatched orders to Major Edmonson, at Albuquerque, to return to head-quarters with the detachment of the 2nd Missouri under his command, and to Captain Burgwin, commanding a squadron of the 1st regular dragoons, stationed at the same place, to join him with one troop, and to leave the other at Santa Fé. Having made these preparations for securing the post, and leaving Lieutenant Colonel Willock, of the separate battalion of Missouri mounted volunteers, in charge, Colonel Price marched to the north to suppress the revolt, on the morning of the 23rd of January, at the head of five companies of the 2nd Missouri, Captain Angney's battalion of infantry, and a company of Santa Fé volunteers commanded by Captain St. Vrain, in all 353 men, together with four twelve-pounder mountain howitzers, under Lieutenant Dyer of the ordnance.

The company under Captain St. Vrain, who were alone mounted, moved in the advance, and early in the afternoon of the 24th instant the enemy were discovered, about 1,500 strong, occupying an advantageous position upon the heights east of the town of Cañada, situated on a small branch of the Rio Grande, which commanded the road to that place. They were also in possession of three houses at the bases of the hills, from which a warm fire was kept up. The howitzers were at once pushed forward on the left flank beyond the creek, and opened on the houses, while the dismounted men endeavored to gain a position where they would be sheltered by the high bluff bank of the stream from the fire of the Mexican force. The troops had advanced with so much rapidity, when the word was passed that the enemy were in front, that the wagon-train was left nearly a mile in the rear. Upon discovering this, the enemy detached a party to cut it off, but the manœuvre was quickly checked by Captain St. Vrain, with his company. When the train came up, Captain Angney dislodged the Mexicans from the house opposite the right flank with his battalion of infantry, and a general charge was then ordered. Captain Angney, supported by two companies of the 2nd Missouri, moved up one hill, and at the same time Captain St. Vrain was ordered to fetch a circuit with the horse, and turn it, in order to intercept the retreat of the enemy. The artillery, supported by the remaining three companies of the 2nd Missouri, took possession of some houses further to the left, inclosed by a strong câral densely wooded with fruit-trees, and of the heights beyond them. In a very few minutes the enemy were dislodged at all points, and flying over the hills.

The broken character of the ground rendered a pursuit impossible, and Colonel Price took up his quarters in the town. In the morning the enemy again showed themselves on the distant heights, and he marched out to attack them, but they retreated so hastily that they could not be overtaken. The American loss in the affair at Cañada was two killed and six wounded; that of the enemy, was thirty-six killed and forty-five wounded.

Although the attempted outbreak at Las Vegas, seventy-five miles north of Santa Fé, on the road to Independence, was prevented by the prompt interference of Captain Hendley, he thought it advisable to concentrate his force at that point, and the various parties of his grazing detachment were ordered to join him forthwith. On the 23rd of January he learned the particulars of the murderous transaction at Moro on the 20th instant, and in the morning of the following day he started for that place with 80 men. One hundred and fifty or two hundred of the enemy had assembled here under the lead of Cortés, and on approaching the town Captain Hendley ordered his men to charge upon them. The Mexicans fired two or three volleys, and retreated to their rude fort. The Americans returned their fire for some time, and then commenced burning and tearing down the houses. Captain Hendley had just succeeded in getting into one end of the fort with several of his men, when he fell mortally wounded. It was now getting late, and the Americans feared that a party of between three and five hundred men, who, it was said, had left Moro that morning for Santa Fé might return; they therefore concluded to retire to Las Vegas, taking with them fifteen Mexican prisoners. They had three men wounded, besides their commander, and they killed fifteen of the enemy. The whole detachment being collected, they soon after returned to Santa Fé.

Colonel Price remained at Cañada until the 27th of January, when he advanced up the Rio Grande as far as Luceros, where he was joined on the 28th by Captain Burgwin, with his company of the 1st dragoons dismounted, and another company of the 2nd Missouri. Lieutenant Wilson, of the 1st dragoons, also came up with a six-pounder gun which had been sent for from Cañada. The whole force now consisted of 479 rank and file, and on the 29th they marched to La Joya, where they learned that a party of sixty or eighty Mexicans had posted themselves on the steep slopes of the mountains on either side of the Cañon leading to Embudo. Finding that the road through the gorge was impracticable for artillery or wagons, Captain Burgwin was detached with a party of 180 men, consisting of his company of dragoons, the volunteer company of Captain St. Vrain, and one company of the 2nd Missouri under Lieutenant White, to dislodge the enemy.

Pushing rapidly forward, Captain Burgwin found between six and seven hundred of the enemy, Mexicans and Indians, occupying both sides of the gorge, at a point where it scarcely admitted of the passage of three men marching abreast. They were likewise protected by dense masses of rock, and the bushy cedars covering the hills, whose sides were so precipitous as to be almost impossible of ascent. Flanking parties were thrown out on either hand, and the Americans advanced boldly upon the enemy, springing up the rugged acclivity, and clinging with one hand to the branches of the trees, as with the other they fired the rifles whose unerring balls hurtled through the pass. During the action Captain Slack, of the 2nd Missouri, arrived from La Joya, where the firing had been heard, with twenty-five of his men mounted, the horses of this company having joined them at Cañada. A more vigorous onset was now made, when the Mexicans abandoned their position and retreated in haste beyond Embudo, with the loss of twenty men killed and sixty wounded. The Americans lost one man killed and one wounded. Captain Burgwin entered the town without opposition, and on the 30th instant proceeded to Trampas, where he awaited the arrival of the main body.

Colonel Price left Trampas on the 31st of January, with his whole command. Crossing over the Taos mountain, through roads filled with new-fallen snow—the soldiers marching in front of the artillery and wagons, with unwearied patience and constancy, in order to break the way, and many of them being frost-bitten on the route,—they entered San Fernando de Taos on the

3rd of February. At this place they ascertained that about seven hundred of the enemy were posted in Puebla de Taos, a short distance in the advance. This was a strongly fortified Indian village, surrounded by adobé walls and pickets, flanked by projecting buildings.* Within the inclosure, and near the northern and southern walls, there were two large structures of an irregular pyramidal form, and seven or eight stories in height, each capable of sheltering five or six hundred men. In addition to these, there were a number of smaller buildings, and in the north-western angle there was a large church, with a narrow passage between it and the outer wall. The inclosed buildings and the exterior walls were pierced for rifles.

A reconnaissance was made, and Lieutenant Dyer took position with the artillery on the western side of the village. A warm fire was kept up till sunset, when, as the ammunition-wagon had not arrived, and the troops were suffering from the inclemency of the weather, they returned to San Fernando. With the first glimmering of light on the morning of the 4th, they were again in motion. On approaching the town, Captain Burgwin was stationed within two hundred and sixty yards of the western flank of the church, with his company, and two howitzers, in command of Lieutenant Hassendaubel, of Major Clark's artillery battalion. Lieutenant Dyer was ordered to take post with the six-pounder and the remaining two howitzers, about three hundred yards from the northern wall, so as to obtain a cross fire upon the church, the most feasible point of

* These fortified villages are frequently to be met with in the northern part of Mexico. They are constructed by the half-civilized Mexican Indians, to protect themselves and property against the more savage tribes. The *adobé* walls are formed of bricks dried in the sun

attack. The mounted men, under Captains St. Vrain and Slack, moved round to the eastern side of the town, to intercept any fugitives who might attempt to escape in that direction, and the remainder of the troops were directed to support Lieutenant Dyer. The batteries opened at nine o'clock, and at the expiration of two hours no breach had been effected in the walls of th church. Orders were therefore given to storm the building. Captain Burgwin advanced on the western side with the dragoons and one company of the 2nd Missouri, while Captain Angney approached the northern wall with his battalion, and two companies of the 2nd Missouri.

The enemy held out manfully, and poured a terrible fire upon the assailants, who succeeded in gaining the cover of the wall on the western side of the church. As soon as the Americans had established themselves, they commenced plying their axes in the attempt to effect a breach. A temporary ladder was also constructed, by the aid of which the roof was fired. Captain Burgwin, and a small party, penetrated into the câral in front, and endeavored to force the door of the church. They found the attempt fruitless, and, being fully exposed on all sides to the fire of the enemy, the party were compelled to retire to their former position, carrying with them their daring leader mortally wounded. In the meantime several holes had been cut in the western wall, through which shells were thrown in by hand, doing good execution. Lieutenant Wilson now came round with the six-pounder, and poured a heavy fire of grape into the town. Between three and four o'clock in the afternoon the gun was run up, and opened on the church within sixty yards, the enemy still continuing their deadly volleys. After firing several rounds, one of the holes cut with the axes was widened into a practicable breach. The six-pounder was further advanced within ten yards,—a shell and three rounds of grape were thrown into the opening,—and ere the echoes had died away, a party of stormers, headed by Lieutenant Dyer, of the ordnance, and Lieutenants Wilson and Taylor, of the 1st dragoons, sprang through the smoke and falling ruins into the centre of the church. The enemy fled before them, and shortly after abandoned the whole western part of the town. Some took refuge in the houses on the east, and others attempted to escape to the neighboring hills, but were cut down by the mounted men under Captains St. Vrain and Slack.

The American troops were quietly quartered in the houses on the western side of the village, during the night of the 4th, and early in the next morning the aged men and women of the enemy appeared before Colonel Price as suppliants, bearing their children, their images and crosses, and humbly sued for peace. Their request was granted on condition that Tomas, the Puebla Indian, should be delivered up to him. This was done, and he then returned to San Fernando with his command. In this affair the Americans had seven killed and forty-five wounded, many of them mortally. One hundred and fifty of the enemy were killed, and the number of their wounded was still greater. The prompt action of Colonel Price put an end to the insurrection. All the leaders of the movement, with the exception of Cortés, were dead;* and, although the American forces remained for

* Tafoya was killed at Cañada; Chavis fell at Puebla de Taos; Tomas was shot in an altercation with a private soldier, in the guard-room at San Fernando; and Montoya was hanged at the latter place on the 7th of February. It will be recollected that General Kearny assumed to transfer the allegiance of the inhabitants of New Mexico, from their own government to that of the United States. If this could

several days at San Fernando, they discovered no more indications of disaffection, and therefore returned to Santa Fé.

Symptoms of revolt had been manifested at the capital, but the severe defeat sustained by the insurrectionists in the north, prevented any attempt openly to resist the authority of the United States. A greater degree of vigilance was afterwards observed, and every thing remained peaceful and quiet until the month of May, when bands of Mexicans and Indians, many of whom came from Taos, were embodied in the valley of the Moro, for the purpose of attacking the supply trains on their way from Fort Leavenworth, and capturing the horses of the grazing parties which Colonel Price had again distributed through the country.

On the 20th of May, the camp of Captain Robinson, of Lieutenant Colonel Willock's battalion, was surprised; one man was killed and two wounded, and over two hundred horses and mules were driven off. Major Edmonson, then in command at Las Vegas, immediately started in pursuit with about 80 men. Upon his arrival at the Wagon Mound, where Captain Robinson was encamped, he learned that a wagon-train had been attacked at Santa Clara springs, on the 23rd instant, by the same party of marauders, supposed to be between three and four hundred strong, commanded by Cortés. Following closely upon the enemy's trail, in the after-

have been done, which it could not, under the laws of nations, the revolters were all guilty of treason, and the execution of Montoya would therefore have been justifiable. Colonel Price seems to have regarded the matter in this light; but a few weeks later he was advised that his government had disapproved the official acts of General Kearny, transferring the allegiance of Mexican citizens, and an individual by the name of Trajillo, then recently convicted of treason, was ordered to be set at liberty.

noon of the 26th he found them posted in force, on the heights overlooking a deep cañon leading down to the Red River. A desultory and spirited contest ensued, which was kept up till dark, when Major Edmonson withdrew his men to a more open position, and encamped for the night. On the following day he re-entered the cañon, but found it evacuated. The pursuit was continued for several miles, until the track was lost amongst the large herds of wild horses on the plains. The check was effectual, however, for the time; the enemy having lost forty-one killed and a large number wounded. The Americans lost but one man killed and three slightly wounded.

Lieutenant Brown, of the 2nd Missouri, left Las Vegas on the 27th of June, with two men and a Mexican guide, in pursuit of some horses which had been stolen at that place. He found the animals at Las Vallas, fifteen miles distant; but, upon his seizing them, the Mexicans murdered the whole party. On being informed of the massacre, Major Edmonson made a forced march from Las Vegas with sixty men and two howitzers, surprised the town, shot down a few who attempted to escape, and took about forty prisoners. On the 6th of July the camp of Captain Morris, of the separate Missouri battalion, was attacked; Lieutenant Larkin and four men were killed, and there were nine wounded. All the horses and property were captured by the marauders. A portion of the detachment took shelter under the banks of the Cienega, near which they had been posted, and maintained their position until the arrival of Captain Shepherd with his company, when the enemy retired. Lieutenant Colonel Willock, commanding at Taos, pursued them some distance, but could not overtake them.

In July, there were frequent rumors of an approaching insurrection, and the troops were ordered to be in readiness for any emergency. The presence of an additional force ordered to New Mexico, had the tendency to check any movement, if one was in contemplation. Occasional depredations were committed by the Indians, but the Mexicans busied themselves for the most part in securing their crops, and nothing of extraordinary interest occurred during the remainder of the summer, or of the ensuing autumn.

CHAPTER XII.

CONTRERAS AND CHURUBUSCO.

Route from Puebla—The Valley of Mexico—Fortifications—Turning Lake Chalco—Affair at Oka Laka—March of Major Lally from Vera Cruz to Jalapa—Arrival of the American army at San Augustin —Attempt to reach the San Angel road—Crossing the Pedregal—The Night Bivouac—Storming the Intrenchments at Contreras—The Enemy driven from San Antonio—Battle of Churubusco—The Victors at the Gates of the Capital.

General Scott left Puebla, in person, on the 8th of August, and on the same day overtook, and then continued with, the leading division under General Twiggs. The different corps of his army moved forward, *en echelon*, being at no time beyond five hours, or supporting distance, apart. The city of Mexico is something more than ninety miles from Puebla. The road ascends gradually through a fertile rolling country, checquered with beautiful gardens and hedges of cactus, with fields of maize and plantations of the aloe, until it reaches the *tierra fria*, or cold region, "the third and last of the great natural terraces into which the country is divided."* Here the feathery palm gives place to the evergreen, and the fruits and vegetation of the tropics, make room for those usually found in more northern climes. Leaving Cholula to the south, on the third day of their march the Americans arrived at the pass of Rio Frio, ten thousand feet above the level

* Prescott's Conquest of Mexico, vol. i. p. 8.

of the ocean. Far away to the north extended the mountain crests of Anahuac, and on the other hand rose the lofty peak of Iztaccihuatl, and still further to the left, and towering still higher into the clouds, "the great *volcan*," Popocatepetl,—the cold bleak winds of winter ever whistling about their summits, and the gentle breezes of an unending summer sporting and playing with the shrubs and flowers that blossom at their feet.*

From Rio Frio the descent is rapid. Shortly after the advance of the army emerged from the pass, and on turning an angle of the mountains, which left their view to the westward entirely unobstructed, the Valley of Mexico burst upon them like some vision of enchantment. Spread out before them, and beneath them, lay the gorgeous panorama, of hill and mountain, grove and forest, river and lake, hamlet and city,—upon which they gazed with emotions similar to those with which Hannibal and his followers looked down from the Alps, over the fair plains of Italy; or those that animated the mail-clad warriors of Cortés, when they sounded their cheering war-cry of "San Jago and San Pedro!" through these wild gorges, or, flushed with victory and conquest, turned their eyes upon the same glorious scenes, beholding, "in the midst,—like some Indian empress with her coronal of pearls,—the fair city of Mexico, with her white towers and pyramidal temples, reposing, as it were, on the bosom of the waters,—the far-famed 'Venice of the Aztecs!' "†

The Valley of Mexico, or Tenochtitlan, as it was called

* These two mountains, in former times, were looked upon by the Indians as divinities; Iztaccihuatl, "the white woman," as the name signifies, being regarded, according to their superstition, as the wife of Popocatepetl, or "the hill that smokes." During the past century the latter has rarely been in a state of activity.

† Prescott's Conquest of Mexico, vol. ii. p. 51.

by the ancient inhabitants, in which the capital is situated, is an irregular, oval basin, about two hundred miles in circumference, inclosed by walls of porphyritic mountains, and surrounded by some of the highest peaks of the Cordilleras. Lying in the centre of the great table land of the country, it is protected alike from the fierce *norte*, and the rude breezes of the east, by the bold sierras that encircle it. Favored with a most genial temperature, this sunny spot teems with the valuable products, quickened into existence by the warm breath of the tropics, and watered by copious showers of rain, and the torrents that gush forth from the fissures of the neighboring cliffs. Forests of oak and pecan trees adorn the more elevated ground. Here a copse of sycamores, and there a group of tall cypresses, fling their broad shadows over the landscape. lighted by the rays of the burning sun, or the soft bright moon. The glossy leaves of the myrtle nestle close beside the pepper tree, whose scarlet berries cast a rich flush over its delicate foliage. Aromatic shrubs load the air with the intoxicating odors that invite the senses to repose, and an endless variety of flowers add their gay and brilliant colors to enhance the beauty of the scene.

Just beneath the range of mountains on the east, is the series of lakes which form the most picturesque attraction of the valley, looking up, like the blue eyes of the turquoise, to the azure heavens above them, whose glory they reflect. Pretty gardens are scattered lavishly around them, and smiling villages and haciendas peep out in every direction from the groves in which they are imbosomed. But, conspicuous above all, is the city of Mexico,—containing a population of two hundred thousand souls—the most ancient, as it is the most splendid capital on the Western Continent! Her white domes, her Gothic churches, her shady paséos, and her beautiful Alameda; her noble cathedral, whose fretted roof, and groined arches, echo daily with the swelling notes of old *Te Deum;* and her lofty palaces, with their sculptured façades, and porticos embellished with porphyry and jasper, are the first to attract attention—the first to elicit admiration.

As there is no happiness without its alloy, so there are patches covered with rocks of lava, or masses of scoriæ, occasionally to be found in this lovely valley; and now and then a dark buttress, destitute of vegetation,—save, perhaps, a stray creeper, rooted in some crevice, and clambering up its rugged sides,—may be seen projecting from the mountains. Still, it may be questioned, whether these do not, by the very contrast they exhibit, serve to add to, rather than diminish, the beauty that surrounds them. The *chinampas,*—those floating wildernesses of sweets and blossoms, far surpassing the Alcinas and Morganas of the Italian poets—which dotted the lakes in the time of the conquest, have nearly disappeared.* The clearing away of the primeval forests, too, and other influences connected with the improved condition of the country, have caused their waters to recede from their original limits, and

* The *chinampas*, or floating gardens, were rafts formed of reeds and rushes, and the branches of young trees woven firmly together, which were covered, to the depth of three or four feet, with the alluvial wash of the streams, and the black mould drawn up from the bottom of the shallow lakes. Vegetables, flowers, and small trees, were raised in them, and sometimes they were capable of sustaining a hut for the residence of the gardener. Although they could be pushed through the water without much difficulty, they were usually moored near the shore for safety. This was certainly a rare device to insure the presence of sufficient moisture to counteract the burning heat of a tropical sun.—Humboldt's Essai Politique, tom. ii. pp. 87, 153.—Murray's Encyclopedia of Geography, pp. 323–4.

some of them are now girded by barren strips of land, covered with white sand, or incrusted salts.* Standing close beside them, they appear much less beautiful than in former days, but seen in the distance, with the sunlight streaming over them, they appear like a cluster of rich jewels in a framework of silver.

The principal lakes in the valley are five in number. The salt lake, Tezcuco, occupies the lowest ground, near the centre of the basin; separated from it by a narrow isthmus on the north, is San Christóbal, and further to the north-west is Lake Zumpango; between five and six miles south of Tezcuco, is Xochimilco, and near the eastern extremity of the latter is Lake Chalco. At the period of the conquest by the Spaniards, the city of Mexico was entirely surrounded by the waters of Lake Tezcuco, and connected with the mainland by three massive causeways or dikes, which, at this day, form important avenues to the capital. For a long time it was liable to frequent inundations, when the great central reservoir, which received the surplus waters of the other lakes, was swollen beyond its ordinary height. The elevation of the site by the ruins of the ancient dwellings of the Aztecs, thrown down by Cortés during the siege,—the subsidence of the waters —the building of embankments and sluices,—and the construction of the great drain of Huehuetoca, in the seventeenth century,—have entirely obviated the danger. The *plaza mayor*, or great square, is now four feet higher than the average level of Tezcuco; but the

* The waters of Lake Valentia, in the valley of Aragua in Venezuela, similarly situated with those in the vicinity of Mexico, have subsided in like manner. The same is also true of the lakes of Switzerland, and of those near Ubaté, in New Granada. The reader will find this subject,—the influence of agriculture on the quantity of running water of a country,—discussed, at length, in Boussingault's Rural Economy.

environs of the city, though more or less cultivated, are quite wet and marshy, especially during the rainy season, that commences towards the latter part of June, and terminates in September.

The modern city,* which is over 7,600 feet above the level of the sea, lies about three miles west of Lake Tezcuco, and near six miles from the north-western point of Lake Xochimilco. It is approached by six great roads, terminating in stone causeways, from one and a half to three miles in length. The National Road, from Vera Cruz, along which the reader has followed the march of General Scott and his army, skirts the southern shore of Tezcuco, and enters the capital from the east. The Acapulco road, which terminates in the San Antonio causeway, approaches it from the south; the road from Toluca,—entering upon the Tacubaya causeway, with a lateral branch leading to the causeway of San Cosmé, from the south-west; and the great western, or San Cosmé road, from the west. The other two roads enter the city from the north. Between these principal roads are smaller ones, also terminating in causeways, which lead to the different towns in the valley and its neighborhood.

Few soldiers have ever wooed fortune for the smallest of her favors, so assiduously, and with such poor encouragement, as Santa Anna, the provisional President of Mexico, and General-in-chief of her armies. His military career, subsequent to the overthrow of the federal constitution, presents but a series of disasters; yet, in the midst of his reverses, he seems never to have been absolutely discouraged or disheartened. With the recollections of Angostura and Cerro Gordo fresh in his remembrance, he

* Mexico was rebuilt by Cortés, on the site of the ancient capital of the Aztecs

still hoped for the best. A majority of his countrymen appeared to be with him, heart and hand ;* the clergy, who possessed the means, contributed from their vast wealth for the national protection ; new levies were made, and large numbers of citizens enrolled in the National Guard ; and he never suffered his energies to relax, nor his spirits to be dampened, after the avowal of his determination to prosecute the war to the uttermost. One triumph,—one repulse,—but a single check given to the unbroken tide of victories sweeping in advance of General Scott, as he progressed towards the capital,—would be sufficient to place him on that proud pinnacle of power to which his aspirations were directed, and enable him, and those whom he served, to proffer, instead of accepting, terms of peace to the enemy, without humiliation, and without dishonor.

Early in the month of August, 1847, Mexico was placed in a tolerable condition of defence. The main avenues leading to the city, on the south and east, by one or other of which it was supposed the American army would approach, were strongly guarded. Sweeping away, in a wide semicircle, from the southern border of Lake Tezcuco to the western mountains, a chain of bristling fortifications met the eye. About seven miles from the capital, in a south-easterly direction, is El Peñon, an isolated hill, three hundred feet high, having three plateaus of different elevations, each of which was garnished with a tier of guns, and infantry breastworks. Directly at its base, on the north, is the National Road, passing along a causeway con-

* In the month of July a coalition was formed by the authorities of the five states of San Luis Potosi, Mexico, Zacatecas, Jalisco, and Queretaro, who declared that they would be bound by no treaty so long as the army of the United States threatened the capital, or occupied any part of the Mexican territory.

structed upon the very verge of Lake Tezcuco. The height was completely surrounded by a deep ditch, flooded by sluices from the lake. There was a strong battery, also, on the causeway, four hundred yards in advance of the hill, another by its side, and a third, about a mile from the gate of San Lazaro. Three miles in front of El Peñon, at the hamlet of Los Reyes, a second road, though but an indifferent one, branches off to the south-west, to the village of Mexicalcingo, situated at the foot of Lake Xochimilco, on the outlet or canal leading to Mexico, from which it is about five miles distant. The ground in the vicinity of the village is low and boggy, and the bridge over the outlet was fortified, and flanked to the right and left, by powerful batteries.*

Two miles south-west of Mexicalcingo, upon the opposite shore of Xochimilco, is CHURUBUSCO, on the Acapulco road—the first high ground west of the lake. A short distance north of the village, the road, or causeway, crosses the river Churubusco, over a large stone bride. This was protected by a *tête du pont*, with bastioned fronts regularly proportioned, and a wide ditch. The outer face of the south front was seventy five yards in length:—the eastern front was one hundred yards, and the western nearly the same. Between two and three miles south of Churubusco, at the village of San Antonio, there were strong fieldworks, containing seven batteries, with twenty-four heavy guns, and two infantry breastworks, which commanded the approaches in that direction.

Five miles north-west of Churubusco, where the

* At El Peñon there were twenty batteries, mounting 51 guns, and fifteen infantry breastworks; and at Mexicalcingo, eight batteries, mounting 38 guns, and one breastwork for infantry.

mountains on the west incline nearer to the city, is "the royal hill of CHAPULTEPEC,"*—once washed by the waters of Lake Tezcuco—in ancient times the favorite retreat of the mild Montezuma and his royal ancestors. At a later day it was crowned with the splendid palace of the Viceroy Galvez—subsequently converted into a military school and fortification. The main structure and terre-plein, covering about four hundred square yards, and provided with heavy armaments, occupied the summit of a rocky acclivity, one hundred and fifty feet above the adjacent meadows, near the east end of an oblong inclosure, surrounded by a stone wall ten feet high, four hundred yards broad, from north to south, and nine hundred yards in length, from east to west. On the rising ground, beyond a gentle slope inclining towards the west from the base of the acclivity, and adorned with a magnificent grove of cypress trees, twelve hundred yards distant from Chapultepec, was EL MOLINO DEL REY, "the Mill of the King," a long range of stone buildings, with towers at the end, originally, as the name implies, used as a mill; but when the Americans entered the valley, it was occupied by the Mexican troops. From four to five hundred yards further to the west, upon a ridge, and nearly on a line with the northern face of El Molino del Rey, was Casa de Mata, an old square building, with thick stone walls, surrounded by ditches and bastioned intrenchments, erected for a fort, but afterwards occupied as a dwelling. Ditches, batteries, redans, and breastworks, varying in form and extent, were constructed in and about this group of fortifications.†

* The Hill of Grasshoppers.

† There were seven batteries at Chapultepec, mounting 19 guns, and seven infantry breastworks.

Less than a mile south of Chapultepec, and within range of its guns, is the village, or hermitage of Tacubaya, containing the palace of the archbishop, and a number of fine country seats. At the south-eastern angle of the inclosure, the Toluca road intersects the causeway, leading direct, one and a half miles, in a north-easterly course, to the gate of Belén. Here also commences the branch conducting to the San Cosmé causeway, about two miles further north. The Tacubaya causeway,—the branch, from the north-eastern angle of the wall encompassing the heights of Chapultepec,—and the San Cosmé causeway, from its intersection with the latter,—are double roadways, on either side of massy elevated aqueducts, supported on heavy arches and pillars, which supply the city with fresh water. The causeways are all flanked by deep ditches, and marshy grounds.

Within this exterior chain of defences, which mounted, together, over one hundred pieces of artillery, there was also an interior line scarcely less formidable. A wide and deep navigable canal, intended for drainage and for custom-house purposes, and extremely difficult, if not impossible, to bridge in the face of an active enemy, surrounded the city throughout its greater extent. There were eight main entrances, at each of which there was a garita, or large fortified gateway, where duties were collected, as in many European towns.

On the left of the Tacubaya causeway, but a short distance in rear of the garita Belén, was the Ciudadela, or citadel, a solid rectangular work, between two and three hundred yards square. Batteries and redans were built upon and near the causeways and garitas, and in the intervals between them; and preparation.

were made to connect the works by a continuous line of breastworks and redoubts, and to barricade the heads of the streets leading into the principal thoroughfares. The losses sustained by the Mexicans during the progress of the war had occasioned a great deficiency in artillery, and the interior line of defence was but poorly supplied with guns; it having been the intention, probably, of Santa Anna, if forced to retreat, to withdraw his artillery from the exterior line, and employ it in defending a new position.

The army under the immediate command of the Mexican President and General-in-chief, numbered over 30,000 men, who were well provided with arms, and well disciplined. The various fortifications south and east of the city were garrisoned, and General Valencia was thrown forward with his division, on the road to Puebla, to hold that route in observation. Santa Anna took post with the main body of his troops, in the vicinity of the capital, in readiness to succor any point that might be menaced. General Valencia advanced as far as the pass of Rio Frio, where the mountains close down upon, and overhang the road, for nearly a mile. Trees were felled, and embankments thrown up, but on the approach of General Scott, he fell back towards Mexico, and the march of the former was entirely unobstructed.

Rumors of resistance were quite frequent as the Americans advanced into the interior; but they encountered no obstacle worthy of mention, and saw no enemy, except, it might be, an occasional guerillero flitting away over the distant cliffs, with the speed of the wild deer chased by the hunters. Major Sumner, with the companies of the 2nd dragoons, and one company of mounted rifles, led the advance; and on approaching the foot of the mountains, he discovered a body of the enemy's lancers posted about a mile in his front, near the hacienda of Buena Vista. Promptly ordering a charge, the Mexicans were compelled to make a hasty retreat. General Twiggs reached Ayotla, fifteen miles from Mexico, on the 11th of August, where he halted with his division. The other divisions of the army soon came up, and encamped in his rear, about the head of Lake Chalco.

There were three different routes that suggested themselves to General Scott, by which the city could be approached; the first, to make the circuit of Lake Tezcuco, and enter it by way of Guadalupe, from the north; the second, to proceed straight forward upon the National Road; and the third, to turn Lakes Chalco and Xochimilco, and approach it on the south. The first was ascertained to be too tedious and too circuitous to be undertaken. Close and daring reconnaissances of El Peñon were made on the 12th and 13th, which disclosed the strength of the position, and convinced the American commander that the work could not be carried except at a great sacrifice of life. Several skirmishes took place with the enemy's advanced corps, while these reconnaissances were being made, and on the 13th a superior force of Mexican cavalry were attacked and routed by a small party of dragoons escorting Lieutenant Hamilton, aid-de-camp to General Scott, who was ordered to make an examination of a foundry near Mil Flores, a small town five or six miles beyond Chalco. On the 13th instant, another reconnaissance was directed upon Mexicalcingo, when it was found that, masking El Peñon, the passage of the bridge at that place could be forced. But it was also ascertained that the causeway beyond the bridge was very narrow, and flanked on both sides by water and marshes. To proceed by either of the routes on the east, was, therefore, deemed unadvisable, if a more feasible one could be found.

General Scott had long entertained the project of passing around Lakes Chalco and Xochimilco, in order to gain the harder and firmer, though more uneven ground, to the south, and south-west of the capital.* On the 14th of August, Captain Mason, of the engineers, supported by a party commanded by Lieutenant Colonel Duncan, reconnoitred the southern route, and discovered that there was a practicable road for artillery, by which the strong fortifications east of the city could be avoided. Orders were immediately issued for putting the columns in motion. The order of march was now reversed. General Worth's division, with Colonel Harney's brigade in the advance, marched in the afternoon of the 15th instant. Generals Pillow and Quitman followed the movement closely with their divisions, and on the 16th General Twiggs brought up the rear with his command. At the hacienda of Oka Laka, about half a mile south of the National Road, General Twiggs encountered the division of General Valencia, formed, as he thought, to cut him off from the leading columns. His men were quickly and handsomely arrayed in line of battle, and then moved forward to meet the enemy. Captain Taylor at the same time opened upon them with his guns, but they judged it prudent to retire before the American infantry came within range. They were driven nearly two miles from the road, by the fire of the battery, leaving several of

* This was, mainly, the route taken by Cortés, on his second visit to the capital of the Aztecs. During the siege, his head-quarters were at fort Xoloc, on what is now the San Antonio causeway.

their dead on the field, and General Twiggs then continued on his course unmolested.

Following the miserable trail that wound its devious way around Lake Chalco, the Americans once more came in sight of the glittering spires of the capital, as they reached the southern borders of Xochimilco, no longer, as its name imports, "the field of flowers." The road was almost impassable; in some places being nearly covered with water and excessively muddy; and in others running beneath frowning cliffs, or across deep rocky gulleys. A few straggling parties of the enemy were discovered, but no attempt was made to impede the progress of the American columns, til the 17th instant. General Worth then found the narrow road, beyond the hacienda of San Gregorio, badly cut up and filled with rocks. These obstructions considerably retarded his advance, as it became necessary to remove them before the column could proceed. Near Santa Cruz a scattering fire was opened upon the head of the division, by a body of Mexicans, posted on the hills above the road on the left, who were quickly dispersed by the light battalion under Lieutenant Colonel C. F. Smith, and the 2nd artillery under Major Galt. At La Novia, also, the American advance had a skirmish with one of the enemy's pickets, which was driven in.

After the evacuation of Jalapa by the American troops, on account of the inability of General Scott to garrison so many posts on the road to Vera Cruz, that city became the head-quarters of the guerilla chiefs, whose bands had infested the road. The severe chastisement the latter had received from Generals Cadwalader and Pierce had produced a deep impression, and it required some powerful attraction to draw them in very great numbers from their hiding-places. On the

6th of August Major Lally, of the 9th infantry, left Vera Cruz with about 1,000 men, consisting of nine companies of infantry, belonging to different regiments, two companies of voltigeurs, one company of Georgia mounted volunteers under Captain Loyall, and a battery of two six-pounders, commanded by Lieutenant Sears, of the 2nd artillery. The command escorted a train of sixty-four wagons, which, it was erroneously reported, contained one million of dollars in specie. The opportunity of reaping this golden harvest was not lost by the guerilleros. The intelligence was conveyed with great rapidity through the country, and General Soto, governor of the state of Vera Cruz, in connection with the guerilla leaders, Padre Jarauta, Señor Aburto, and others, succeeded in collecting together between twelve and fifteen hundred men, with several pieces of artillery.

Anticipating an encounter with the banditti upon the road, Major Lally placed the left wing of his detachment, under Captain Winans, of the 15th infantry, in front of the train, and the right wing, under Captain Hutter, of the 6th infantry, in the rear. The centre guard, of two companies, was commanded by Lieutenant Lear, of the 5th infantry, and mounted flankers were thrown out on either side. The enemy were first discovered, on the 10th of August, at Paso de Ovejas, where they attempted to harass the American troops, by firing at long distances, for the purpose of drawing them into the chaparral in a fruitless search. Their object was soon understood, and the command continued steadily on their route. About two o'clock in the afternoon, the principal attack was made from behind the ruins of a stone house, upon a hill on the right of the road in front. Lieutenant Sears opened an effective fire of grape and ball on the house, and Captain Alvord, of the 4th infantry, seconded by Lieutenant Leigh, of the voltigeurs, gallantly stormed the height with a party, and drove the enemy before them. In the meantime an attack was made on the head of the train, which was repulsed by Captain Winans. Daring assaults were also made on the centre and rear that were promptly met by Lieutenant Lear and Captain Hutter.

Major Lally immediately dispatched a messenger to Colonel Wilson, in command at Vera Cruz, with the intelligence of his rencontre with the guerilleros, and on the 13th instant Captain Wells, of the 12th infantry, was ordered to reinforce him, with two companies of infantry and one company of the Louisiana mounted volunteers, under Captain Fairchild. Meanwhile Major Lally had proceeded with his detachment, having been joined, on the 11th instant, by a company of Louisiana cavalry under Captain Besançon. On the 12th, he discovered the enemy, posted in force, at the Puente Nacional. As usual, the bridge was barricaded, and a terrible fire from the Mexican escopetas was poured upon the command, from the fort, and the heights on the right of the town beyond the stream. Lieutenant Sears attempted to breach the barricade with his guns, but could not bring them to bear in such an exposed position. They were then withdrawn, and the fire of one piece was turned upon the fort, while the other, from a hill on the right, opened on the heights near the town. At the same time Lieutenants Wilkins and Doyle, of the 15th infantry, and Lieutenant Loring, of the 11th infantry, with parts of their companies, advanced to the parapets of the bridge, from which they kept up a constant fire. Lieutenant Loring succeeded in passing the barricade with a small party, and was instantly followed by a body of foot and horse. The artillery had now dislodged the enemy from the fort and the heights; the bridge was cleared; and at sunset Major Lally was in possession of the town, where he remained until the morning of the 14th instant, to give time for any reinforcements that might be sent from Vera Cruz, to come up with him.

Captain Wells found the road swarming with guerilleros, and was compelled to fight his way, foot by foot, to the National Bridge. He attempted to cross the river, but found all the adjacent heights occupied by the enemy. Repeated efforts were made to effect the passage of the stream, though without success. Nearly all the mules attached to the wagons were killed, and being destitute of artillery, the party were eventually forced to retire, with the loss of ten or twelve men killed and wounded. All the wagons, with one exception, containing the baggage of the officers and knapsacks of the men, fell into the hands of the Mexicans.

Before his arrival at the National Bridge, Captain Wells had detached thirteen men of Captain Fairchild's company, to inform Major Lally of his approach. The party succeeded in joining him on the 15th of August, at the Plan del Rio, whither he had advanced on the previous day. His forage having been exhausted, Major Lally left his train at this point, under a strong guard, and moved forward with the main body of his command to the pass of Cerro Gordo, which, as he had anticipated, was occupied by the guerilleros, who still clung with the utmost tenacity, to the hope of securing the glittering prize promised by their leaders. Three hundred yards below the main height of Cerro Gordo a barricade, four feet thick, was thrown across the road; and the hills and thickets of chaparral on the right, between the National Road and the road cut by General Twiggs, and the intrenchments and breastworks on the series of bluffs upon the left, were filled with Mexicans. As the Americans approached, the enemy commenced firing from the hill-side and wooded ravines on the right, and Lieutenant Sears immediately brought his guns to bear upon them. The fire was continued for some time, when Captain Hornsby, of the 12th infantry, was ordered to dislodge them with three companies of infantry and one of voltigeurs. Moving rapidly through the chaparral, he scaled the height, and drove the enemy from their position in a few moments. On the left of the road, Lieutenant Ridgely, of the 4th infantry, with three companies, boldly stormed the intrenchments on the central bluff, notwithstanding a destructive fire of musketry, and of canister from a nine-pounder gun, which the enemy poured down upon his party. The work was carried, and two nine-pounder guns and nine thousand musket cartridges captured from the enemy. Lieutenant Ridgely now turned his fire upon the other positions occupied by the Mexicans, and they soon after fled at all points. The hills along the road were at once ordered to be occupied by detachments of the command, and Captain Besançon was then dispatched, with fifty mounted men, to communicate with Captain Wells.

Captain Besançon learned that the National Bridge was in possession of the enemy, and rightly concluded that the reinforcement had been driven back. Upon receiving this information, Major Lally pushed forward with his train, on the 17th instant. The guerilleros had become very much dissatisfied with their ill fortune;—

the American artillery at the Puente Nacional had committed sad havoc among them, and the heights and gorges of Cerro Gordo were covered with their dead comrades. In such a service, where the pay was booty, and that only to be reached through torrents of cannon balls, and over the bayonets of a firm and unflinching infantry, there were few inducements for an army of bandits. Large numbers of them dispersed to their homes; but in the afternoon of the 19th instant, Major Lally was again assailed by the remnant of the band, at Las Animas, one and a half miles from Jalapa, who had posted themselves behind a stone fence on the left of the road. Several rounds of canister discharged upon them, and a vigorous charge of infantry, speedily cleared the road. The Americans were delayed but little more than an hour, and entered the suburbs of Jalapa in the evening, where they rested on their arms until daylight, on the following morning, when they took possession of the town without opposition.

This hazardous march was accomplished with the loss of but one hundred and five men killed, wounded, and missing.* Not a single wagon was left upon the road, or captured by the enemy. Shortly after he reached Jalapa, Major Lally was joined by Colonel Wynkoop,† who had heard of the affair at Cerro Gordo,

* In the affair at the National Bridge, Mr. George D. Twiggs, acting as an officer, and expecting a commission and an appointment on the staff of his relative, General Twiggs, was killed.

† An amusing incident connected with the guerilleros, in which Colonel Wynkoop performed a prominent part, took place subsequent to the evacuation of Jalapa, upon the advance of General Scott from Puebla. When the American garrison was withdrawn from the city, four sick and wounded officers, not sufficiently recovered to travel, were left behind in care of the chief alcalde, who treated his guests with great kindness and humanity. But a few days afterwards he was compelled, by

with about three hundred men. The former concluded to remain temporarily at Jalapa, to recruit his command, and Colonel Wynkoop returned to Perote.

The tedious march of General Worth's division, rendered far more fatiguing in consequence of the labor required to fit the road for the passage of their wagon train and artillery, was terminated on the 17th of August, by their arrival at San Augustin, on the Acapulco road,—twenty-seven miles from Ayotla, by the route traversed by the American army, and nine miles south of the city of Mexico. Captain Blake, of the 2nd dragoons, in command of the advance guard, had a slight skirmish with the enemy's pickets, as he entered the town, in which the latter were easily routed. General Scott came up early in the morning of the 18th, and General Worth was then ordered to move along the causeway, towards San Antonio, two and a half miles further north, to make room for the other divisions to close on him. On approaching San Antonio, it was discovered that the fortifications at that point commanded the causeway and the marshes on the left, as far as Lake Xochimilco. The right was protected by a *pedregal*, or field of volcanic rocks, impassable for cavalry or artillery, and nearly so for infantry, extending some four or five miles westward, to the San An-

threats of violence, to deliver them up, though very reluctantly, to four guerilla chiefs, two of whom were said to be natural sons of Santa Anna, whose bands were in the vicinity. When this was made known to Colonel Wynkoop, he formed a project for the capture of four leaders of the marauding parties, in order to exchange them for the American officers. The expedition was undertaken with secrecy, and was eminently successful. Four of the guerilla chiefs, and, as it proved, the identical persons who had coerced the alcalde, were captured. It is unnecessary to add, that they were quite willing to regain their liberty by an exchange.

gel road, which left the San Antonio causeway near the *tête du pont*, and continued up the valley of the Churubusco river, in a south-westerly course, by way of Cojohuacan, or Coyoacan, as it is now usually written, and San Angel, to the factory of Magdalena, about nine miles from Churubusco.

General Worth halted his column at a hacienda, within fifteen hundred yards of the enemy's works at San Antonio, and Captain Mason, assisted by Lieutenants Stevens and Tower, all of the corps of engineers, was sent forward to reconnoitre, supported by Captain Thornton with his company of the 2nd dragoons. The Mexican batteries opened on the party, when they came within range; the first shot killing Captain Thornton, and severely wounding the guide. No practicable route, even for infantry, could be discovered to turn the position on the right, and none on the left, except by crossing the pedregal. An assault in front could only be made by battering in breach, and the use of scaling-ladders and fascines. In the meantime a reconnaissance was made by Captain Lee and Lieutenant Beauregard, of the engineers, of a mule path leading through the pedregal, and intersecting the San Angel road about four miles directly west from San Augustin. Lieutenant Colonel Graham, with the 11th infantry, and Captain Kearny, of the 1st dragoons, with his troop, covered the reconnaissance. A large body of observation was discovered in that direction, with the advance corps of which the supporting party had a successful skirmish. A second reconnaissance of this route was made in the morning of the 19th, and Major J. L. Smith, the senior engineer officer with the army, also made a careful examination of the different approaches to the city. These reconnaissances rendered it certain that the mule path could be made practicable for artillery, and General Scott at once determined to gain the San Angel road, and then move round to the attack of San Antonio in rear.

As soon as it became known that the American army had changed their course, and were proceeding south of Lake Chalco, to reach the Acapulco road, Santa Anna moved the greater part of his forces to the San Antonio causeway and its vicinity. The works at San Antonio were garrisoned with 3,000 men. Eight guns were mounted in the *tête du pont* at the Puente del Rosario, the fortified bridge near Churubusco. A strong field-work was thrown up around the southern front and angles of the stone church of San Pablo, from three to four hundred yards to the right and front of the *tête du pont.* This work, which was also surrounded by a high wall, commanded the San Angel road, and a cross-road extending about half a mile to the south, where it intersected a similar road leading from the San Angel road to the San Antonio causeway. Seven guns were placed in battery at San Pablo, the garrison of which was commanded by General Rincon. General Valencia was posted on the San Angel road with 7,000 men, said to have been "the flower of the Mexican army," and twenty-four pieces of artillery, half of which were of heavy calibre. Santa Anna remained near Coyoacan, with the main body, between twelve and fourteen thousand strong, and General Perez, in command of the reserve, occupied the hacienda of Portales, three-fourths of a mile in rear of Churubusco, on the San Antonio causeway. In the morning of the 18th of August, General Valencia was directed to fall back on Coyoacan; but in violation of his orders, as subsequently stated by

Santa Anna,* he proceeded to the HILL OF CONTRERAS where he was permitted to remain, something more than two miles beyond San Angel, upon which he intrenched himself, and planted his guns. The troops under his command were those discovered by Captain Lee on the 18th instant. The hill on which they were posted lies in a bend of the San Angel road, that winds around its northern and eastern faces, and fronts the opening of the mule path along which General Scott decided to advance. East of the hill and San Angel road, and between the latter and the pedregal, is a broad and deep ravine, which it was necessary for a party assailing the position in front, to cross under a plunging fire. The guns on the left flank of the intrenched camp enfiladed the road descending towards San Angel, for more than a mile.

In conformity with the determination of General Scott, the division of General Pillow, and the company of sappers and miners, commanded by Lieutenant G. W. Smith, were advanced on the morning of the 19th, under the direction of Captain Lee of the engineers, to open the mule path leading to the San Angel road, and General Twiggs was ordered to cover the movement in front, with his division. The route was quite hilly, and lay partly through fields of corn, and hedges of chaparral, growing in the rich intervals of the barren and rocky waste, and over ditches filled with water, and lined with maguey and prickly pear. General Twiggs moved forward with his command—both officers and men picking their way on foot—within one mile of the

* Manifesto of Santa Anna, dated at Mexico, August, 23rd, 1847.—The private correspondence between Santa Anna and Valencia, on the 18th and 19th of August, intercepted by the Americans, corroborates the statement in the Manifesto.

enemy's position. Captain McLellan of the engineers proper, and Lieutenant McLellan of the topographical engineers, being sent forward to reconnoitre, they were fired upon by the enemy's skirmishers, now occupying the ground in front. The rifles, under Major Loring, were brought up to clear the road. This done, General Pillow detached from his division Captain Magruder, with his field-battery, and the rocket and mountain howitzer battery of the voltigeurs, in charge of Lieutenant Callender, of the ordnance. After much severe labor in dragging the artillery over the rocks, Captain Magruder placed his guns in battery at nine hundred yards distance from the Hill of Contreras, and Lieutenant Callender planted three of his pieces on the left,—Lieutenant Reno, also of the ordnance, moving still further to the left, with the rocketeers. Colonel Riley, with the second brigade of General Twiggs' division, received orders to cross the pedregal on the right, and having gained the San Angel road, to attack the enemy in rear. General P. F. Smith moved to the left and front of the batteries with his brigade, and General Pierce, in command of the first brigade of General Pillow's division, took post on the right.

At three o'clock in the afternoon, the American guns opened a lively and well-directed fire on the Mexican position, though but partially covered, by ledges of rocks, from the incessant shower of balls and howitzer shells which fell among them. A fierce cannonade was kept up for hours, during which the men at the batteries, and the brigades of Generals Pierce and Smith, occasionally engaged with the enemy's skirmishers, suffered severely. While the battle was raging at this point, General Pillow sent General Cadwalader to the support of Colonel Riley, with the second brigade of his division. General Scott arrived at the scene of action a few minutes later, and immediately ordered Colonel Morgan, of the 15th infantry, belonging to General Pierce's brigade, till then held in reserve, to move in the same direction.

The severity of the fire, so long gallantly sustained by the batteries of Captain Magruder and Lieutenant Callender, and the other troops in front, was not abated for a moment. General Smith saw that the slope and ravine, intervening between his position and that of the enemy, could not be crossed except at the imminent hazard of the entire destruction of his force. To remain longer in this position was useless. He therefore moved round to the rear of Captain Magruder, and leaving three companies of the 3rd infantry under Captain Craig, a detachment of the rifles under Captain Sanderson, and a small party of the 1st artillery, to support the battery, he also entered the pedregal. Subsequently General Shields came up with his brigade of General Quitman's division, and was directed, by the General-in-chief, to follow the same intricate and difficult path over the field of lava,—perhaps resembling nothing so much, as what one might fancy, the fabled battle-ground of the Titans. The route being wholly impracticable for artillery, Captain Taylor, of Twiggs' division, was forced to remain behind with his battery.

The different corps ordered to cross the pedregal, were at no time out of range of the heavy guns of the intrenched camp of General Valencia. Divested of their knapsacks—the officers being dismounted—with buoyant and manly strides they sprang from rock to rock,—tearing their way through closely matted thickets of chaparral, climbing over jagged precipices, and leaping across wide fissures, and deep chasms. The distance to the further side of the pedregal was nearly a mile, and, on emerging from the rocks, Colonel Riley crossed a ravine, at the bottom of which was a small stream. On ascending the opposite slope, he came upon the San Angel road, at the hacienda of Ensaldo, about fourteen hundred yards north of the Hill of Contreras. Passing another ravine, also the bed of one of the tributaries of the Churubusco, he gained a second slope or elevation, upon which was the hamlet of San Geronimo, or Contreras, four hundred yards west of the main road, and connected with it by a narrow lane. Beyond the village was a third ravine, to which he extended his line, for the purpose of sweeping through the hamlet, and driving back the enemy's cavalry, large bodies of which had been dispatched by General Valencia to check the attempt to gain his rear.

Repeated attempts were made by the enemy's lancers to force Colonel Riley to retire, but they were always repulsed with loss. Having driven them back upon their support, he sheltered his brigade, temporarily, from the fire of the Mexican guns, in a ravine south and west of San Geronimo. Upon the arrival of Generals Cadwalader and Smith, with their brigades and the 15th infantry, a heavy force of cavalry and infantry, supported by six pieces of artillery,—afterwards ascertained to consist of 12,000 men, commanded by Santa Anna in person,—were discovered advancing from San Angel, and occupying the slopes west of the road. Colonel Riley now joined the other corps, and General Smith, as the senior officer present, took command of the united force, at most, but 3,300 strong.

General Smith commenced making his dispositions for attacking the enemy's columns in the direction of San Angel; but the delay in the transmission of his instructions, in consequence of the officers being without their horses, prevented their completion till long after sunset, and his orders were then countermanded. The night set in dark and lowering, gloomy and inauspicious. The cold rain began to pour down in torrents. The American soldiers were posted in the lanes and orchards, in the gardens and groves of San Geronimo. Feeble in numbers, ignorant of the country around, with no fires to cheer them, cold, wet, and hungry,—they were still sustained by the ambition and emulation that had achieved so much, and the soldierly pride and daring ready for any enterprise of danger or peril. Some few were sheltered in the church, and other buildings of the hamlet; others sought the friendly cover of a shrub or tree; but many lay down on the damp ground, wholly unprotected from the pelting storm. To all it was a lonely bivouac. Those who watched were well nigh overpowered with fatigue, and those who slumbered, awoke unrefreshed, to listen to the wild howlings of the blast!

On the other side of the pedregal, all was anxiety and suspense. General Pierce marched the remainder of his brigade to the left of the batteries, which ceased firing after nightfall. Generals Pillow and Twiggs made ineffectual efforts to cross over to the San Angel road, and seven different officers, dispatched by General Scott to communicate instructions to the troops at San Geronimo, lost their way in the darkness and were compelled to return.

In the meantime General Smith and his officers had assembled in consultation. They were obviously in a critical position, and liable at any moment to be surrounded by an overwhelming force. Had they been opposed by an active enemy, they would not have remained unmolested. A few shots and shells were thrown into the hamlet, but without occasioning any injury. During the night, two pickets were captured, and several Mexicans, who attempted to pass along the road, were also taken prisoners. General Valencia fancied he had completely repulsed the attack on his position, and while he and those around him were holding high revel over their imaginary victory, or dozing away the precious hours of darkness, the Americans were examining the ravines and passes around his camp. Lieutenant Tower twice carefully reconnoitred the ravine between San Geronimo and the hacienda of Ensaldo, which extended up in rear of the hill, and reported that it was practicable, though difficult, for infantry. A prompt decision was now made, and orders were issued to the officers commanding brigades, to have the heads of their columns formed on the path leading through the village to the ravine, at half-past two o'clock on the following morning, in readiness for storming the height of Contreras.

But there was yet one difficulty,—to hold in check the large force hovering on the road to San Angel. The enterprise must not fail, and the troops required for this purpose could not well be spared from the storming party. At this juncture, the aid of General Shields arrived, with the information that his commander had crossed the pedregal with his brigade, consisting of about 600 men. About midnight, General Shields reached San Geronimo, and on being informed of the arrangements for the morning, though the senior officer present, he magnanimously declined interfering with the plans of General Smith, but reserved to him self the double task of cutting off the retreat of General Valencia, and holding the other force in check.—

Captain Lee was dispatched to General Scott to request that a diversion might be made in front, simultaneously with the attack in rear. He succeeded in crossing the pedregal, and the necessary instructions were issued for a compliance with the request.

At three o'clock in the morning of the 20th, the movement under General Smith commenced. It was still raining, and so dark that an object could not be seen at the distance of six feet. The men were ordered to keep within touch, that the rear files might not go astray. Moving along the narrow path, through clayey mud, and over slippery rocks, they cautiously approached the Mexican position. Lieutenant Tower headed the column; Colonel Riley led the advance with his brigade; General Cadwalader followed; and the brigade of General Smith, temporarily commanded by Major Dimmick, of the 1st artillery, with the company of sappers and miners, brought up the rear. As the columns marched by a flank, the line was so extended, that the morning began to dawn before the head of General Cadwalader's brigade had reached the ravine.

The day broke heavily. Dark masses of clouds drifted across the sky, or rested gloomily over the distant mountains. The dusky lines of the force under Santa Anna were soon discovered making preparations to beat off the attack which they had anticipated. General Shields occupied the hacienda of Ensaldo and the hamlet of San Geronimo, and directed his men to build their fires, as if to cook their morning meal. The enemy in front were thus kept in ignorance of the movement going on in his rear, until it was too late to make a successful diversion.

Having reached a favorable point nearly in rear of

the intrenched camp of Valencia, General Smith ordered a halt, and directed the brigades to close up. It was now six o'clock. The men examined their pieces, and replaced the loads which had been wetted. Colonel Riley formed his command into two columns, and advanced further up the ravine. He then gave the word, and in an instant his men ascended the bank on their left. A slight acclivity still remained between him and the enemy. That was surmounted,—and the camp lay beneath him. Throwing out his leading divisions as skirmishers, with a swoop, like that of the eagle darting on its prey, he dashed down the slope. The sappers and miners, and the rifle regiment, had been thrown across an intervening ravine under the brow of the slope, and now swept it in front of his column. General Cadwalader hastened to the support of Colonel Riley, and Major Dimmick, with the remaining regiments of General Smith's brigade, was ordered to face to the left, and engage a body of the enemy's cavalry under General Torrejon, hastily forming on that flank.

The boldness and daring of this manœuvre took the enemy by surprise. Colonel Ransom, of the 9th infantry, in command of the brigade of General Pierce, who had been severely hurt by a fall from his horse among the rocks, on the 19th instant, together with the detached companies of the rifles and the 3rd infantry, diverted their attention in front, until Colonel Riley appeared above the crest of the hill in rear, when they also sprang forward to join in the attack. Pouring a heavy fire into the enemy's camp, as they rushed down the declivity, Colonel Riley and his men gained the intrenchments, unchecked by the torrents of grape and musketry which they encountered. Portions of the other commands likewise joined in the immediate assault. The contest was brief but bloody. In the short space of seventeen minutes the work was carried. Major Dimmick drove back the cavalry by a vigorous charge, and at the same moment the brigade of Colonel Riley leaped over the breastworks, sweeping the enemy before them with fixed bayonets, and taking possession of their loaded guns. Captain Drum, of the 4th artillery, was the first to discover, among the pieces in the camp, the two guns captured from another company of his regiment at the battle of Buena Vista. As the word was passed, the officers and soldiers of the 4th artillery gathered around the trophies, and rent the air with their shouts and cheers.*

The road to San Angel was now blocked up with a crowd of fugitives hastening from the scene of their disaster, and General Shields promptly interposed his command to intercept the retreat. Many were killed by the fire of the guns from the camp, which were turned upon them as they fled; General Valencia and a considerable portion of his troops escaped towards the mountains; and large numbers were taken prisoners. Twenty-two pieces of artillery,—seven hundred pack mules and many horses,—and great quantities of shells, ammunition, and small arms, were captured. Seven hundred of the enemy were killed, one thousand wounded, and eight hundred, including four general officers, taken prisoners. The Americans lost but sixty, killed and wounded, in the assault.

General Scott had directed General Worth to leave one of his brigades to mask the position at San Antonio, and to join him with the other early in the morning

* These two guns, with other captured pieces, were organized into a battery, and placed in charge of Captain Drum, and his company of the 4th artillery.

GENERAL SMITH.

of the 20th, intending to move forward to support the assault of the intrenched camp of Valencia. General Quitman, who had previously occupied San Augustin, the general dépôt of the army, with the 2nd Pennsylvania, and the battalion of marines, constituting his second brigade, received similar instructions; and Colonel Harney was ordered to garrison San Augustin with the cavalry. These orders were executed; and while General Scott was advancing in the direction of Contreras, he received the cheering intelligence that the work had been already carried. General Worth was now sent back to threaten San Antonio, and attack it in front, when the General-in-chief had moved round through San Angel and Coyoacan, with the troops on that road, and had made his appearance in the rear. General Quitman returned to San Augustin with his command, and the cavalry brigade under Colonel Harney followed General Scott to the San Angel road.

Immediately after the works on the hill of Contreras were carried, the Mexican reserves commanded by Santa Anna, began to retire towards Churubusco. Major Gardner, with the 4th artillery, and detachments from other regiments, was left in charge of the prisoners, and the American troops were forming for the pursuit, when General Twiggs arrived, and ordered them to move rapidly forward. At San Angel General Pillow assumed the command. The rifle regiment, in the advance, had repeated skirmishes with the enemy's rear, upon which they kept up a galling fire. At Coyoacan the columns were halted to await the arrival of General Scott, and receive further instructions.

In none of the actions that took place during his campaign in Mexico, was the old war spirit of General

Scott, which shone so brightly on the plains of Niagara, more fully aroused than on this occasion. Arrived at Coyoacan, the whole scene of action lay before him. In a few seconds all the officers of his staff were hurrying with his orders to different parts of the field. General Pillow, with the brigade of General Cadwalader, following a reconnaissance by Captain Lee, supported by the rifles, was directed to attack San Antonio in rear. General Twiggs, accompanied by Major Smith, of the engineers, was ordered to follow the company of sappers and miners, supporting Lieutenant Stevens in a reconnaissance, and attack the church of San Pablo, with the brigade of General Smith, and Captain Taylor's battery, followed by the brigade under Colonel Riley. After a brief interval, General Pierce, though suffering severely from the injury he had received, but still able to keep the saddle, was dispatched by a third road, further to the left, to turn the right flank of the enemy, and gain their rear, with his brigade, and the howitzer and rocket battery, now commanded by Lieutenant Reno; and immediately thereafter, General Shields, with the New York and South Carolina volunteers, forming the brigade under his command, was sent in the same direction, with orders to take command of the left wing. The troops were now all employed; and, almost alone and unattended, General Scott followed closely after the division of General Twiggs for protection.

The orders issued to General Pillow were anticipated by the prompt and energetic movements of General Worth. On returning to his position in front of San Antonio, he determined forthwith to advance upon the works. The first brigade, under Colonel Garland, consisting of the 2nd artillery, Major Galt, 3rd artillery, Lieutenant Colonel Belton, and the 4th infantry, Major Lee, with the battery under Lieutenant Colonel Duncan, moved slowly along the causeway to an angle which partially masked them from the enemy's fire, and, at the same time, Colonel Clarke made a détour to the left, with the second brigade, and the light battalion, under Lieutenant Colonel Smith, through thickets of chaparral, and across the wide bed of lava, to envelope the right of the position, and cut off the retreat of the enemy. Before the movement could be completed, the garrison at San Antonio, alarmed at the capture of the intrenched camp of Contreras, commenced evacuating the works. Guided by Captain Mason, of the engineers, Colonel Clarke performed his weary march, of more than two miles, in a very short time ; but, on approaching the causeway, twelve hundred yards in rear of San Antonio, the enemy were discovered in full retreat towards Churubusco. Preceded by two companies of the 5th infantry, under Lieutenant Colonel Scott, the brigade advanced upon the road and cut the Mexican column in two—one portion continuing their retreat upon Churubusco, and the other filing off to the hamlet of Dolores, between the causeway and Lake Xochimilco. As soon as Colonel Clarke opened his fire, Colonel Garland advanced rapidly in column upon San Antonio. The enemy had withdrawn most of their guns. Five pieces, however, which they had abandoned, large stores of public property, and a number of prisoners, among whom was one general, were captured.

Six hundred yards in advance of San Antonio, General Worth reunited his division, and pressed forward with alacrity upon the strong fortifications at Churubusco. Santa Anna had now concentrated his forces, at least 25,000 in number, at the *tête du pont* and the fortified church of San Pablo, and upon their flanks, and in the interval and rear. The cornfields were filled with his skirmishers, and the wall around the church, its roof and towers, and the tops of the adjoining convent, and other buildings along the line of battle, were crowded with dense masses of infantry.

Approaching Churubusco, General Worth detached the first brigade and the light battalion, obliquely to the right, to drive the Mexican infantry from the cornfields and marshes, and approach the fortified work at the bridge on that flank. The 6th infantry, under Major Bonneville, moved directly along the high road to storm the *tête du pont* in front, exposed, meanwhile, to a raking fire of grape, canister, and musketry. The remaining regiments of the second brigade—the 5th and 8th infantry, under Colonel McIntosh and Major Waite—advanced immediately upon the right of the road, to co-operate in the assault. Lieutenant Colonel Duncan, being unable to counter-batter the heavier metal in front, remained in reserve.

While giving directions to his battalions, General Worth was joined by General Pillow. The latter had turned to the left on hearing of the fall of San Antonio, had crossed over two deep ditches, with the brigade of General Cadwalader—the rifle regiment having rejoined their brigade—and was advancing against the enemy in his front. The officers of his command were all dismounted, and struggled, with their men, through the marshes, on foot. Such was the spirit of enthusiasm manifested by the troops, that the feeling was communicated to those the least liable to be moved by it; and Chaplain McCarty, of Colonel Clarke's brigade, was the first to assist in pulling down the growing corn, to fill up a ditch foi the passage of the troops under Generai Pillow.

The brigade of General Smith, with which General Twiggs moved upon the defences of San Pablo, was soon warmly engaged. One of the most terrific fires ever witnessed, was poured upon the column from both musketry and artillery. The leading companies of the 1st artillery were almost swept away. Captain Taylor brought his battery up, and opened on the enemy—persisting in holding his position, though fearfully exposed, regardless of the carnage produced around him.

Having advanced far enough on the road which he was directed to follow, to gain the Mexican rear, General Pierce turned to the right with his brigade. Making their way through the fields of corn, and floundering through the difficult morasses, his troops approached the enemy at the hacienda of Portales. General Shields arrived in a short time with his command, and moved further to the left. Sheltered by the stone buildings upon and near the causeway, the Mexicans delivered a most effective fire upon the two columns, and the action now became general along the entire line.

For more than two hours a continuous roar of artillery shook the earth. The sharp roll of musketry was incessant. Broad torrents of flame rolled down from the enemy's fortifications. Lurid columns of smoke shot up towards the sky, and mingled in a heavy canopy over the field of combat. The air seemed "full of daggers."

The clangor of the battle was wild and high, and the voices of the officers could no longer be heard in the din. Numbers fell at every discharge,—yet, resistless and impetuous as the waters of the ocean, on swept the American soldiers, wave upon wave, bearing every thing before them.

The Mexican left was first agitated and thrown into disorder. The 8th and 5th infantry—the latter now led by Lieutenant Colonel Scott, Colonel Clarke having been wounded, and Colonel McIntosh taking command of the brigade—crossed the ditch, and carried the *tête du pont* with the bayonet. The 6th infantry was not far behind, and the 11th and 14th infantry, under Lieutenant Colonel Graham and Colonel Trousdale, followed immediately thereafter. About the same time, the Mexican infantry, opposed to Colonel Garland's brigade and the light battalion, began to waver and break, and retreated towards the causeway, with the victors dashing after them in pursuit.

At San Pablo the enemy still held out. Captain Taylor's battery had been sadly crippled, and was ordered out of range. Captain L. Smith, and Lieutenant Snelling, of the 8th infantry, instantly turned the fire of one of the guns captured in the *tête du pont*, upon the church; and a section of Lieutenant Colonel Duncan's battery, supported by the voltigeurs under Colonel Andrews, was also brought to bear upon the principal face of the work, at a short range, from the San Antonio causeway. This determined the contest. The 3rd infantry, under Captain Alexander, followed by the 1st artillery, under Major Dimmick, now pressed forward for the assault, and Colonel Riley was moving against the left flank of the position, with the 2nd infantry, under Captain Morris, and the 7th infantry, under Lieutenant Colonel Plympton. Captain Smith and Lieutenant Shepherd, with their companies of the 3rd infantry, gallantly entered the work, and planted the regimental colors, as the enemy threw out white flags, on all sides of the church, as signals of surrender. General Rincon, the commanding officer, and a large number of other officers and soldiers, among whom was a battalion, mostly foreigners, composed of deserters from the American army, were made prisoners. General Scott, who had been wounded by a grape shot, arrived at the church soon after the surrender, and was greeted with deafening cheers by his brave troops.

On the extreme left, the brigades of General Shields and Pierce had sustained themselves manfully. Fainting from pain and exhaustion, General Pierce was borne from the field. The 9th infantry under Colonel Ransom, the 12th under Captain Wood—Lieutenant Colonel Bonham having been wounded in the morning—and the 15th under Colonel Morgan, advanced against the enemy with the steadiness of veterans. Colonel Morgan was severely wounded, and transferred the command of his regiment to Lieutenant Colonel Howard. Colonel Butler, of the South Carolina volunteers, fell dead in the thickest of the fight, and Lieutenant Colonel Dickinson also receiving a mortal wound, Major Gladden assumed the command. Colonel Burnett was likewise dreadfully wounded, and Lieutenant Colonel Baxter took charge of the New York regiment. It was a noble sight to witness the strife between the Palmettos and the New Yorkers. Side by side, and shoulder to shoulder, they moved against the enemy, each striving to be foremost in the encounter. Twice were the colors of the New York regiment shot down, but they were snatched again by some brave spirit, ready to peril all in their defence. Both regiments lost more than one-third of their number in this fearful struggle, and the clothing of the survivors was literally riddled by the bullets. At length, the fire of the American muskets, and the howitzer battery actively served by Lieutenant Reno, aided by the panic communicated by the troops giving way in front, and followed by a charge with the bayonet, caused the enemy's infantry to falter, and with their supports of cavalry, to retreat towards the capital. General Shields instantly followed, and succeeded in taking a number of prisoners. Major Sumner had been ordered to support the left wing, understood to be hardly pressed, with the rifles, previously held in reserve, and a troop of the 2nd dragoons under Captain Sibley, but he did not come up until the contest was over.

The Mexicans no longer made serious resistance The causeway was covered with the masses of the retreating troops; and General Shields, with his command, meeting the forces of Generals Worth and Pillow in the road, joined them in the pursuit. At the special request of Colonel Harney, the way was cleared, and he was permitted to follow the enemy with a part of his brigade, up to the gate of San Antonio, interchanging sabre-cuts with the Mexican lancers, and cutting down all who refused to surrender. The recall was sounded when the battery at the garita opened on the pursuing force; but Captain Kearny, of the 1st dragoons, who headed the charge with his troop, and that of Captain McReynolds of the 3rd, persisted in remaining until Major Mills, of the 15th infantry, who accompanied him, was killed, and most of the officers of the squadron, himself among the number, were badly wounded.

The trophies of this memorable day, which had witnessed such a series of brilliant triumphs, including the captures at Contreras, were thirty-seven pieces of siege and field ordnance; large numbers of small arms, standards, pack mules and horses; and vast quantities of shot, shells, and ammunition. The enemy lost 4,000 men in killed and wounded, and there were 205 officers and 2,432 rank and file, taken prisoners. Among the captured officers were Generals Garey, Anaya, Salas, Mendoza, Blanco, Garcia, Arellano, and Rincon. The first two being members of the Mexican Congress, were unconditionally released, by order of General Scott.* Generals Frontera and Mexia were killed.

The American loss, though much less in proportion, was still very severe. There were 137 killed, embracing some of the bravest and most estimable officers, 879 wounded, and 40 missing.†

At sunset the battle was ended. Taking advantage of the panic that prevailed, General Scott might, perhaps, have immediately forced his way into the capital. He had but 8,000 effective men, most of whom had been fasting, and fighting with the elements and the enemy, for the last thirty-six hours; and the enterprise was too hazardous to be undertaken. The powers of endurance of his men might have sustained them still further; but had they proved unequal to the task, the morning sun would have smiled on their folly and lisgrace.

* Report of Lieutenant Colonel Hitchcock, acting Inspector General, lugust 25th, 1847.

† Nineteen American officers were killed, or mortally wounded, durng the operations of the 18th, 19th, and 20th of August, viz:—Captain Thornton, 2nd dragroons; Captains Capron and M. T. Burke, and Lieutenants Hoffman, Irons, and Johnstone, 1st artillery; Captain J. W. Anderson and Lieutenant Easly, 2nd infantry; Lieutenant Bacon, 6th infantry; Captain Hanson, 7th infantry; Major Mills, Captain Quarles, and Lieutenants Goodman and Goodloe, 15th infantry; Lieutenant Chandler, New York Volunteers; and Colonel Butler, Lieutenant Colonel Dickinson, and Lieutenants Adams and Williams, of the South Carolina volunteers.

CHAPTER XIII.

EL MOLINO DEL REY.

The Armistice—Fruitless attempt at Negotiation—Bad faith of the Mexican authorities—Political dissensions—Violation and Rupture of the Truce—Correspondence between General Scott and Santa Anna—Reconnaissances—Assault of El Molino del Rey and Casa de Mata—Severity of the Action—The enemy driven from their Position.

WITH a victorious enemy knocking at the gates of the Capital, and the booming thunder of their artillery echoing through the valley, the Mexican government and people had cause for alarm and apprehension. Their last stronghold was at the mercy of the conqueror. They had been steadily driven from one defence to another,—and the final overwhelming defeat at Contreras and Churubusco, filled the city with consternation. In this season of tribulation there was no lack of counsellors. Some, mindful of the heroism displayed by their gallant kinsmen at Saragossa, exhorted their countrymen to convert every house into a fortification, and, if summoned to surrender, to return, as their only answer, "War, to the knife!" Others appealed to the memories of Iturbide, Hidalgo, and Morelos, the heroes of Mexican Independence, and entreated their descendants to imitate their bravery and daring.

The enemies of Santa Anna attributed the disasters which had befallen the armies of the republic, to his incompetency as a commander; but this was no time for unavailing complaints. The peril was imminent,—the crisis immediate. There was but one alternative:—

.ney must either abandon the indefensible position which they had hitherto occupied,—that of refusing to hear any proposition from the American government,—or prepare to meet her soldiers, foot to foot, for a last struggle, like the dauntless Guatemozin and his brave Aztecs, at their own firesides.

Santa Anna and his ministers instantly decided upon procuring a cessation of hostilities,—not so much with the hope of concluding a peace, unless it would leave him firmly seated in power, as for the purpose of gaining time to revive the spirits of his soldiers, and to strengthen the defences of the city. At his instigation, the British Consul, with other foreign residents, visited General Scott, on the night of the 20th of August, while the smoke of the conflict still lingered over the battle field, and admonished him not to be too precipitate, lest a spirit of national desperation should be aroused, and the war unnecessarily protracted. They also represented, that the Mexican President was disposed to enter into negotiations, but that the influence of his enemies was so great, and the popular prejudices were such, that he was unable to make the first advances. Remembering that his mission was to conquer, not the country, but a fair and honorable peace, General Scott had already determined to give the enemy time for reflection, and to sacrifice to patriotism, " the *eclat* that would have followed an entrance, sword in hand, into a great capital."* Though nothing definite was decided on at this interview, his visitors parted from him with the assurance, that he would do nothing derogatory to the character he had exhibited throughout the campaign,—that of a magnanimous victor.

* Official report of General Scott to the Secretary of War, August 28th, 1847.

While making his preparations at Coyoacan, on the morning of the 21st, to take up the necessary battering or assaulting positions, to authorize him to summon the city to surrender, General Scott was waited on by General Mora y Villamil, who came out to propose a truce. The terms which were suggested being unsatisfactory, the American commander dispatched his contemplated note to Santa Anna, omitting the summons to surrender, and signifying his willingness to consent to an armistice with a view to negotiation.* On the same day a reply was received from Alcorta, the Mexican Minister of War, accepting the proposition, and stating that Generals Mora y Villamil and Quijano had been appointed Commissioners on the part of the Mexican government, to settle the terms of the armistice. Generals Quitman, P. F. Smith, and Pierce, were selected by General Scott to represent the American army; and on the 24th instant, the armistice, signed by the Commissioners, was duly ratified by the commanders of the two armies.

* The note written by General Scott was as follows:

"Head Quarters, Army U. S. America,
Coyoacan, August 21, 1847.

"To his Excellency, the President and General
in Chief of the Republic of Mexico.

"SIR:—Too much blood has already been shed in this unnatural war between the two great Republics of this Continent. It is time that the differences between them should be amicably and honorably settled; and it is known to your Excellency, that a Commissioner on the part of the United States, clothed with full powers to that end, is with this army To enable the two Republics to enter on negotiation, I am willing to sign, on reasonable terms, a short armistice.

"I shall wait with impatience until to-morrow morning for a direct answer to this communication; but shall, in the meantime, seize and occupy such positions outside of the capital, as I may deem necessary to the shelter and comfort of this army.

"I have the honor to remain, with high consideration and respect, your Excellency's most obedient servant.

"WINFIELD SCOTT."

The convention thus agreed upon,—which was to remain in force while negotiations were in progress, or until formal notice should be given, by either commander, of its cessation, and for forty-eight hours thereafter,—provided, among other conditions, that neither army should be reinforced during its continuance; that nothing should be done to enlarge or strengthen any work of offence or defence, within thirty leagues of the city of Mexico; that no new work of that character should be commenced; that the passage of supplies from the country into the city, and from the city or the country into the American camp, should not be obstructed; and that trade should remain unmolested.*

Immediately after the conclusion of the armistice, Generals Herrera† and Mora y Villamil, and Señores Conto and Atristain, were appointed Commissioners by the Mexican authorities, to treat with Mr. Trist, the American Commissioner, who had accompanied General Scott from Puebla. The mission of the latter was solely a precautionary measure, adopted in consequence of the distance from the seat of war to the capital of the United States; and as the confidential agent of the Executive, with very little discretionary power, he took with him the projêt, or outlines, of a treaty prepared at Washington.

* Senate Exec. Doc. 1, (p. 356,) 1st session, 30th Congress.

† Herrera, at first, declined the appointment, upon the ground that he had been ostracized, on a former occasion, for expressing a willingness to hear the propositions of Mr. Slidell. Though ready enough to connive at the fraud about to be practised on the American army, he did not care to be an active participator in the transaction. Subsequently, however, he was persuaded to accept,—influenced, probably, by the fact, that under the full instructions prepared by Santa Anna and his cabinet, who assumed all the responsibility, the Commissioners were the mere passive agents of the Executive.—Senate Exec. Doc. 1, (p. 41,) 1st session, 30th Congress.

‡ Letter of Mr. Buchanan to Mr. Trist, July 13th, 1847.

Several conferences were held between the Commissioners of the two governments, and on the 27th of August, Mr. Trist submitted a proposition, in accordance with his instructions, which provided, in substance, that there should be a firm and universal peace; that all forts, with their armaments, and all territories and possessions, captured by the American army, belonging to Mexico, under the terms of the treaty, should be restored to her; that the boundary line between the two republics should be the Rio Grande, to its intersection with the southern boundary of New Mexico, and thence to run along such boundary, and the western line of New Mexico, to the first branch, or to some point nearest the first branch of the Rio Gila, and thence down the Rio Gila, the Rio Colorado, and the Gulf of California, to the Pacific ocean; and that, as a consideration for this extension of the boundaries of the United States, the latter should satisfy the claims of her citizens against the Mexican government, and, in addition thereto, pay to Mexico a certain sum of money, to be fixed upon before signing the treaty.*

It was well understood by the Commissioners of both countries, that Mexico was without the means to discharge the American claims, and indemnify the United States for the expenses of the war, except by the cession of some part of her territory. But the Mexican Commissioners were unwilling to adopt the Rio Grande as a boundary line, or to cede any thing, except an inconsiderable portion of California. Prevarication and delay characterized their proceedings, as they had for-

* Senate Exec. Doc. 20, (p. 4,) 1st session, 30th Congress.—By an act of Congress, passed at the session of 1846-7, the sum of three millions of dollars was placed at the disposal of the President of the United States, to be employed, if necessary, in the negotiation of a peace.

merly done those of other Mexican negotiators. At a conference held on the 2nd of September, Mr. Trist stated to the Mexican Commissioners, that if they would submit to him a proposition,—providing that the boundary line should follow the course of the Nueces to the Laguna de las Yuntas—thence running westward to the Rio Puerco—thence up that river to the parallel of latitude, six geographical miles north of the fort at El Pasa del Norte, on the Rio Grande*—thence west along that parallel to the western boundary of New Mexico—thence, following the line prescribed in his first proposition, to the mouth of the Rio Gila—thence up or down that river to the thirty-third parallel of latitude—and thence along that parallel to the Pacific ocean; and that the territory between the Rio Grande and the Nueces should remain forever neutral, to be occupied by the citizens of neither republic,—he would transmit it to his government by express, and await its action.†

The Mexican Commissioners were willing to submit this proposition, or rather they professed a willingness to submit it, but refused to grant the necessary time for

* This is, very nearly, the southern boundary of New Mexico; consequently, the proposed line would have embraced almost the whole of that province.

† Senate Exec. Doc. 20, (p. 8,) 1st session, 30th Congress.—The invitation of Mr. Trist to the Mexican Commissioners, to submit this proposition, was unauthorized by the President of the United States, and was promptly disapproved.—Special Message of President Polk, February 2, 1848. Had not this novel idea,—of a boundary, to consist of a neutral strip of land,—been countenanced by many eminent statesmen, it would have very little to recommend it to favor. No government, and, least of all, one whose highest aim it ought to be, to *avoid* all causes of contention, should desire to be bounded by neutral territory, which must necessarily become, in spite of laws and regulations, the refuge and hiding-place of outlaws and bandits,—and the theatre of incessant broils and strifes, in which, sooner or later, the contiguous governments would be involved.

Mr. Trist to communicate with his government. The insincerity of the professions of the Mexican authorities in relation to their desire to conclude a peace, was now made manifest; but, on the 6th of September, their Commissioners, aware that they must submit some formal proposition, in order to preserve appearances, presented to Mr. Trist a counter-projét, in which it was required that all forts, with their armaments, and all territories and possessions captured by the American army, and all the artillery taken outside such forts, should be restored; that the dividing line between the two republics should be the Nueces to its source,—thence to run, in a straight line, to the east-south-east frontier of New Mexico—thence along the boundary of New Mexico, on the east, north, and west, to the thirty-seventh degree of latitude—and thence along that parallel to the Pacific ocean—Mexico undertaking not to found any new settlements or colonies in the territory lying between the Nueces and the Rio Grande; that the United States should pay the American claims, and also make a pecuniary compensation to Mexico; and further, that the claims of Mexican citizens, for injuries sustained in the prosecution of the war by the American army, should be satisfied by the government of the United States.*

Leaving out of view the other objectionable features of the counter-projét of the Mexican Commissioners,—the surrender of the artillery captured outside of the permanent fortifications of Mexico, and the indemnity to be paid to her citizens,—which could never have been submitted to with honor, the territory proposed to be ceded was of comparatively insignificant value. The boundaries specified by the Mexican Commissioners

* Senate Exec. Doc. 20, (p. 12,) 1st session, 30th Congress.

embraced only a small portion of California, including, it is true, the bay and harbor of San Francisco; but, without some portion, or all of New Mexico, the territory thus acquired would have been, in effect, isolated from the other American possessions. Mr. Trist therefore informed the Mexican Commissioners, on the 7th of September, that the terms proposed by them were wholly inadmissible, and the negotiations were here closed.* Previous to this time, however, the armistice conceived and concluded, on the part of Santa Anna, in bad faith, had been finally violated without excuse or justification.†

The foreign residents of Mexico, and the wealthier citizens, whose property was liable to be injured by an assault or bombardment, were averse to a continuation of the war; but the political opponents of Santa Anna, Herrera and the leading federalists among the number, preferred hostilities, to the conclusion of a peace under his auspices; the followers of Paredes, aware of his return to Mexico, and influenced by similar motives, were also clamorous against peace;‡ the friends of the Mex-

* Senate Exec. Doc. 20, (p. 14,) 1st session, 30th Congress.

† Among the papers found in the National Palace of Mexico, after the capture of the city by the American army, was a letter addressed by Santa Anna, on the 31st of August, 1847, to Rejon, then at Queretaro, in which he assures his friend, that he assented to the application of General Scott for an armistice, because it would "give his troops rest, re-establish their *morale*," and afford him "an opportunity to collect the dispersed," and enable him "to adopt other measures to insure a re-action." It is possible, however, that Santa Anna may have really desired peace, provided he could maintain himself in power; and hence, probably, with a hope of preserving his own influence at home, rather than for any other purpose, the conditions and instructions prepared by him and his cabinet, for the government of the Commissioners, upon which their counter-projét was based, assumed that Mexico was the triumphant party to the war.

‡ Paredes returned from his exile at Havana, and was landed at Vera

ican President, as well as himself, saw that the parchment on which a treaty should be written, would not become dry, ere he would be hurled from power ; and the clergy were obliged to favor the prolongation of the contest, through fear lest, if they refused, their churches would be plundered by the military demagogues, who could not forget their animosities, even when their country was in peril.

At a previous session of the Mexican Congress, a resolution had been passed, providing for the removal of that body to Queretaro when the capital should be in danger. Disregarding the spirit of this resolution, on the 21st of August, Santa Anna called a meeting of Congress, to be held in the city of Mexico, while the negotiations were in progress, in order that the members might be conveniently situated to act on any proposition, having reference to such negotiations, that might be submitted to them. This furnished a pretext for complaint, of which his enemies were prompt to avail themselves. On the 22nd of August, the deputies of Mexico, Jalisco, and Zacatecas, mainly federalists, or monarchists, like Paredes, signed a protest denouncing, in advance, any treaty, concluded or ratified under the guns of the enemy. The "Diario del Gobierno" insisted, on the following day, that the proposition of General Scott for an armistice, was acceded to, "without abatement of Mexican honor—tried, yet not cast down by the most disastrous fortune ;"—but the opponents of Santa Anna, though willing that he should continue the war until his military reputation was forever destroyed,

Cruz, in violation of the blockade, on the 15th of August, 1847, from the British steamer Teviot, one of the vessels of the Royal Mail Steam Packet Company. In justice to the company it must be added, that upon a representation of the facts, the board of directors promptly dismissed the captain of the steamer from their service.

were opposed to his concluding a peace with the enemy, and were powerful enough to prevent it. Seventy members of Congress retired to Toluca, declaring their unwillingness to deliberate in the capital; and on the 30th of August, the Congress of the State of Mexico, in session at Toluca, pronounced against peace. Similar sentiments were heard from the rabble in the streets, instigated by the clergy and the disaffected; the passage of supplies to the army of General Scott, was repeatedly obstructed by the populace, and soldiers in disguise; American traders, long residents of the city, were molested; and the Mexican authorities did not, or dare not, interfere to prevent those violations of the armistice.

Matters were thus unfavorably situated, when Mr. Trist invited the Mexican Commissioners to submit to him the proposition laid before them on the 2nd of September. This was regarded as his *ultimatum* on the subject of boundaries, and as soon as it had been considered in a council of ministers and others, before the Mexican Commissioners presented their counter-projét, and without notice to the American commander, Santa Anna, under cover of the darkness, and in violation of the armistice, actively recommenced strengthening the defences of the city,—alleging, subsequently, in a note to General Scott, that the works already constructed had been merely repaired, so as to place them in the same condition they were in on the conclusion of the armistice.* Determined no longer to place any reliance on the Punic faith of the Mexican

* Official Report of General Scott to the Secretary of War, September 11th, 1847.—Reply of Santa Anna to General Scott, September 6th, 1847.—At the council convoked by Santa Anna, it was determined that hostilities should be recommenced on the 9th instant.

government, General Scott, who had removed his headquarters to Tacubaya, notified Santa Anna on the 6th of September, that, unless full satisfaction was given for the violation of the armistice, before twelve o'clock, meridian, on the following day, he should consider it at an end from and after that hour. The reply of the Mexican President, dated on the same day, but received on the morning of the 7th, was pronounced by General Scott to be "absolutely and notoriously false, both in recrimination and explanation."*

So careful had General Scott been in regard to infringing the armistice, that the engineer officers had suspended their reconnaissances, while his troops remained quietly cantoned in Tacubaya, and the neighboring villages. The city and its fortifications had, therefore, yet to be reconnoitred, before any definite plan of attack could be laid down. The enemy being reported to be manœuvring on the San Antonio causeway, on the morning of the 7th of September, Captain Lee was dispatched to observe their movements, but found all quiet in that quarter, and on the Niño Perdido and Piedad causeways, intervening between the San Antonio, and Tacubaya, or Chapultepec, causeways. Two days previous, General Scott had been informed, that a number of church-bells had been sent out from the city to El Molino del Rey, where there

* Senate Exec. Doc. 1, (pp. 355, 359, 360,) 1st session, 30th Congress. Santa Anna charged the American army, in his reply to General Scott, with plundering the Mexican churches, and offering violence to their women. Nothing could have been more false or groundless. No disrespect was ever shown to the religion of the Mexican people, or to their places of worship, which went unpunished, if brought to the knowledge of the American officers; and at Vera Cruz, a soldier was hung for committing an outrage upon a Mexican woman,—General Scott firmly refusing to pardon the offence.

was said to be a cannon foundry, to be cast into guns. It was also known, that there was a large deposit of powder in Casa de Mata,—that the ammunition was much needed by the enemy,—and that, without the manufacture of new pieces, they would be unable to arm all the works at the different gates.

In the forenoon of the 7th instant, Captain Mason made a reconnaissance of El Molino del Rey,—approaching near enough to the Mexican lines to converse with the officers,—and discovered a large body of troops in the vicinity. General Scott accordingly determined to leave the general plan of attack upon the city for full reconnaissances, and, as it was impossible to cut the communication with the mill, without first carrying the fortifications on the heights of Chapultepec, for which he was not yet quite prepared, to drive the enemy from Casa de Mata and El Molino, seize the powder, and destroy the foundry. The performance of this service, to be executed under the formidable guns of Chapultepec, was assigned to the veteran division of General Worth, then quartered at Tacubaya, reinforced by the brigade of General Cadwalader, from General Pillow's division; three squadrons of the 2nd dragoons, one troop of the 1st dragoons, part of a troop of the 3rd dragoons, and a company of mounted rifles, under Major Sumner; a small party of sappers under Lieutenant Foster, of the engineers; two twenty-four pounders from the siege train, with a detachment of ordnance men, under Captain Huger, acting chief of ordnance;* and three pieces of field artillery, under Captain Drum, with his company of

* There were two batteries in Mexico, during the war, served by ordnance men, with several officers.

the 4th artillery. The whole force, in the aggregate, numbered 3,447.

A second reconnaissance was made by Captain Mason, in company with Lieutenant Colonel Duncan, and Lieutenant Hardcastle, of the topographical engineers, in the afternoon of the 7th. Generals Scott and Worth also carefully reconnoitred the enemy's line of defences, and the necessary orders were then given for making the attack at daylight on the following morning. A night attack had been in contemplation, but this was abandoned, on account of the uncertain knowledge derived from the reconnaissances, daring as they were. The configuration of the ground, and the extent of the enemy's force, were ascertained, but a very imperfect idea could be formed of the nature of their defences, which were skilfully masked.

In the evening of the 7th, General Worth ordered one of Captain Drum's pieces, an eight-pounder, in charge of Lieutenant Benjamin, to be sent to the picket in front of Chapultepec. The enemy evidently anticipated a movement of some kind, and scouting parties were frequently sent out during the night. The advance guard of the American picket was once driven in, and several shots were fired ; but, on seeing the port-fire lighted near Lieutenant Benjamin's gun, no further attempt at molestation was made, and every thing remained quiet till three o'clock in the morning of the 8th, when the troops were ordered under arms.

During the reconnaissances of the previous day, the enemy had presented an extended line of cavalry and infantry, with their right resting on Casa de Mata, and their left on El Molino del Rey. Midway between the two was a battery of four pieces of field artillery, supported by masses of infantry. In the course of the night the guns were removed to a position nearly in front of the mill,—thus making El Molino del Rey the strong point of the position, and the centre the weak one. About four hundred yards west of Casa de Mata, there was a deep ravine, impassable except near the enemy's line, extending some distance to the south, and flanking the broad plain in front. On the south side of the plain the ground rose into a ridge, falling away gradually as it approached Tacubaya, something more than a mile from El Molino,—which consisted of a long range of buildings facing the plain. Thirty or forty yards in advance of Casa de Mata and El Molino del Rey, both of which were slightly elevated above the plain, there was a dry ditch, with a breast-height for the protection of infantry, reaching, in a semicircle, from the mill to the ravine. Casa de Mata being upon a retired line, a column approaching over the plain would necessarily be subject to a severe converging, or flank fire, in addition to that in front; except that, as the road to Tacubaya formed the prolongation of the enemy's left, an attacking force moving forward upon that route would be less exposed, and possess the advantage of having an enfilading fire on that flank.

Quietly and orderly the American troops fell into their places, before daylight on the 8th of September; and when objects could be first discovered, in the gray of the morning, they were seen drawn up in readiness for action, within six hundred yards of the Mexican line. Captain Drum, with the two six-pounders lost at Buena Vista, but recovered at Contreras, was posted on the road leading north from Tacubaya, past the western front of El Molino del Rey. Colonel Garland was ordered to support the battery, and in time assault the enemy's left, with his brigade. The 2nd artillery moved out under Captain Mackenzie; and the 3rd under Captain M. Burke,—Lieutenant Colonel Belton being temporarily absent on detached service, but arriving in time to lead his regiment near the close of the action. Three hundred yards west of the road, on the ridge, were the heavy battering guns of Captain Huger, supported by the light battalion of General Worth's division, under Captain E. Kirby Smith, of the 5th infantry,—Lieutenant Colonel C. F. Smith being sick. A little to the left of Captain Huger's battery was an assaulting column of five hundred picked men, with twelve officers, taken from the different regiments of the division, commanded by Major Wright, of the 8th infantry, who was ordered to force the enemy's centre as soon as an impression had been made by the batteries. The second brigade, commanded by Colonel McIntosh, in consequence of the illness of Colonel Clarke,—Lieutenant Colonel Scott taking charge of the 5th infantry—was posted, with Duncan's battery, still higher up the ridge, opposite to the enemy's right, to make the attack on that flank, or sustain the other corps, as might be necessary. Major Sumner was ordered to envelope the extreme left with the cavalry, and be governed by circumstances; and General Cadwalader was held in reserve with his brigade, between the battering guns and the second brigade of the first division.

The enemy were by no means unprepared for the attack. Their long lines of infantry, tastefully arrayed in blue and white uniforms, filled the breastworks in front of the position, the roofs of Casa de Mata and El Molino del Rey, and the space between them. The artillery was placed at intervals, amongst the infantry, just to the left of the centre, and the lancers, under General Alvarez, with their gay ensigns and curveting steeds, their yellow cloaks and scarlet caps and jackets, hovered on the flanks and in rear of the infantry. General Perez occupied Casa de Mata with 1,500 regular troops, and General Leon was posted in El Molino del Rey, with several large battalions of the National Guard. Santa Anna remained further in the rear, between Mexico and Morales, with a heavy reserve.

At early dawn General Worth ordered Captain Huger to open his guns on El Molino del Rey, which was the signal for the action to commence. Having an oblique fire on the enemy's battery and right wing, Captain Huger served his pieces with such rapidity and effect, that the Mexicans were obliged to abandon their guns, and portions of their infantry took shelter in the mill, whose walls trembled at every discharge from the twenty-four pounders. The assaulting column under Major Wright, headed by Captain Mason, Lieutenant Foster, and the sappers with their forcing tools, had gallantly dashed forward, in the direction of the Mexican battery, at the opening of the fire. Unshaken by the galling torrents of musketry and canister poured upon them, they reached the guns, drove back the artillerists and infantry who lingered near them, with their bayonets, and commenced trailing the pieces on the retreating masses of the enemy. Captain Huger's battery was now masked; and discovering the feebleness of the force that had daringly advanced under the very walls of El Molino, General Leon ordered the rally to be sounded, and bravely led his men to the rescue.

A most terrific fire of musketry was at once opened upon the assaulting party. Major Wright, Captain Mason, and Lieutenant Foster, were wounded, and eight of the remaining eleven officers attached to the command, were either killed or wounded. Non-commissioned officers and men were cut down in proportion. Staggered, but not yet beaten, the remnant under Captain Bomford, of the 8th infantry, manfully stood their ground. Leaving Lieutenant Elzye, of the 2nd artillery, to cover the heavy battery with his company, Captain E. K. Smith instantly advanced, in double-quick time, at the head of the light battalion; and in a few moments Lieutenant Colonel Graham, of General Cadwalader's brigade, was ordered to follow the movement with the 11th infantry.

Meanwhile the first brigade, under Colonel Garland, with the two pieces of artillery commanded by Captain Drum, had been moving forward on the Tacubaya road. A slight bend allowed them to approach within two hundred yards of the breastwork in front of El Molino, without being seen. Whilst unlimbering his guns, Captain Drum encountered a severe fire of grape from the enemy's battery, which disabled a number of his horses. The animals becoming frantic from their wounds, he cut the traces and worked his guns by hand, assisted by officers and men of different corps. Having fired once with round shot, he ran his guns forward to within one hundred yards of the breastwork, and opened on the enemy with canister. The light battalion, led by their intrepid officers, were the first to break through the Mexican lines, and gain an archway under the buildings of El Molino del Rey. Being joined by the first brigade, they sprang to the roofs of the adjoining sheds, and commenced a warm and animated contest for the possession of the mill. A foothold being gained, the Americans would not be driven back. The Mexican troops fought bravely, but they could not long withstand the fierce onset of soldiers whose spirits appeared to rise with the severity of the action.

Blackened with smoke and gunpowder, the assailants drove the enemy from room to room. Aided by the fire of Captain Drum's battery, Captain E. K. Smith headed a second charge on the enemy's guns, temporarily recaptured, in which he fell mortally wounded, and Captain Reeve, of the 8th infantry, took command of the light battalion. Lieutenant Colonel Graham also advanced upon the same point with the 11th infantry. This determined perseverance decided the contest on this flank. The guns wese once more taken, and immediately manned by Lieutenant Peck, of the 2nd artillery, and Lieutenants Harley, McClelland, and Scott, of the 11th infantry. Captain Drum then fired a few rounds on a body of the enemy in the mill, when they exhibited a white flag, and surrendered themselves prisoners of war.

On the American left the conflict had been still more bloody and severe. At the commencement of the action, Lieutenant Colonel Duncan opened a vigorous fire from his battery, on the Mexican right, which was kept up for a short time, when Colonel McIntosh was ordered to assault Casa de Mata with the second brigade. Lieutenant Colonel Duncan continued to play with his guns, over the heads of the advancing column, until they were completely masked. He then moved his pieces to the extreme left, supported by the voltigeurs under Colonel Andrews, to check a large force of cavalry and infantry, moving rapidly down the slopes west of the ravine, to reinforce the enemy's right. Major Sumner also dashed to the front, changed direction in an instant, and crossed the ravine within range of Casa de Mata, under an appalling fire which, in a very few seconds, killed or wounded between forty and fifty of his officers and men, and over one hundred horses Successive charges were made by General Alvarez with his lancers; but they were always checked by the fire of Duncan's battery and the voltigeurs, from the other bank of the ravine, and of one of the twenty-four pounders, turned in this direction, and actively served by Lieutenant Hagner, of the ordnance; and by the prompt and skilful evolutions of Major Sumner, who remained on this flank with the cavalry until the close of the engagement.

Instead of an ordinary field intrenchment, as was supposed, Casa de Mata proved to be a strong stone citadel, recently repaired and enlarged, with bastions and impassable ditches. With a step as blithe and free as if moving on parade, the column under Colonel McIntosh advanced against the position. Dense masses of Mexican infantry crowded the roof and adjacent breastworks. Closer and closer the Americans, now deployed in line, pressed upon them. Within one hundred yards they encountered a destructive fire. Promptly returning it, they rushed forward with charged bayonets. The enemy fell back from their first line, at the breastwork, and rallied on the second. Exposed to a murderous discharge of musketry from Casa de Mata, and to a raking fire from El Molino, the assailing troops continued their advance until they reached the ditch and breast-height, within thirty yards of the Mexican position. Here the carnage was terrible. Partly sheltered by the stone wall, the Americans calmly loaded their guns, and picked off their men. At length many of their pieces became foul, their ammunition was nearly expended, and their ranks fearfully thinned. A scathing torrent of flame rolled down upon them, through which it was impossible to pass with life.

Colonel McIntosh fell mortally wounded; Lieutenant Colonel Scott was killed while urging his men to cross the ditch;* and Major Waite, commanding the 8th infantry, was also severely wounded. The 5th infantry was nearly deprived of officers, and Assistant Surgeon Roberts received a mortal wound while acting, as a volunteer, in that capacity. The 6th infantry suffered in like manner; three color bearers of the 8th were killed, and the fourth badly wounded. One-third of the brigade, including one half the officers, were killed or wounded. Confusion became unavoidable; and the column retired to the left of Duncan's battery, leaving behind them several wounded officers and men, who, though helpless and unresisting, were cruelly butchered by the enemy. Having assisted in driving away the lancers on the left, Lieutenant Colonel Duncan now turned his guns on the masses of Mexican infantry crowding in and around Casa de Mata, and rained upon them a constant shower of cannon balls.

At the same time, Lieutenant Colonel Graham, after the enemy's centre had been forced, directed Major Hunter to enter El Molino with a portion of the 11th infantry, and advanced against Casa de Mata with the remainder of his command. Already twice wounded,

* The death of no officer was more deeply deplored than that of Lieutenant Colonel Scott. He had advanced to the breast-height, and, desirous of encouraging his men by his example, refused to shelter himself behind it. A brother officer near him entreated that he would not expose himself unnecessarily. His reply was characteristic:—"Martin Scott," said he, "has never yet stooped!" The next moment a ball entered his heart. He fell upon his back, deliberately placed his cap on his breast, and died. Commanded by officers like him, it is not to be wondered, that the American soldiers should dare any peril.

he urged forward his men, till he was struck from his horse by two additional and mortal wounds; exclaiming as he fell—"Forward, my men!—my word is always, forward!"—The enemy did not wait to encounter men led by such officers, but abandoned the position in haste, followed, at full speed, by the light battery of Lieutenant Colonel Duncan, who did not cease playing upon them until they were out of reach.

The brave stand maintained by General Worth and his men, their daring and sustained efforts, though encountering obstacles which they had never anticipated, decided the fate of the day. The enemy's whole line, which had been repeatedly reinforced from the reserve, was broken; but, in a few minutes, they attempted to rally on the left, under the guns of Chapultepec, to recover possession of El Molino del Rey. The 6th and 8th infantry, commanded respectively, by Captain Hoffman and Major Montgomery, were ordered, under Major Bonneville, to move to that flank,—the 5th infantry, now commanded by Captain Chapman, remaining behind, to mourn the loss of the best and bravest of their officers and men. Lieutenant Stone, of the ordnance, also advanced in the same direction with the remaining twenty-four pounder, and placed his gun in position near the southern end of the mill, where he aided Captain Drum, with one of his pieces, in driving back a large force of the enemy advancing from Chapultepec, and in silencing a battery of one gun in the road leading to the castle, whose fire had seriously annoyed the American infantry in El Molino. The captured guns were planted in the road north of the mill, and supported by the 4th, 6th, and 8th infantry. A brief engagement took place at this point; but the enemy soon abandoned their attempts to regain the ground which they had lost, and retired towards Chapultepec, closely pursued by the Americans for several hundred yards.

In the meantime the work of demolition had been going on. Casa de Mata was blown up, and the useless captured ammunition was destroyed. Lieutenant Colonel Hébert entered El Molino with a battalion of the 14th infantry, and, under his orders, four moulds for casting cannon, eight platforms for heavy guns, and a number of muskets, were broken in pieces; and the combustible parts of the mill, and adjacent buildings, were set on fire. The main action had continued a little over two hours, but the enemy continued to keep up a straggling fire while the works were being destroyed.

General Scott had anxiously watched the changing scenes of the contest, though not interfering with the plans of General Worth; but when the enemy were discovered to be repeatedly reinforcing their line, anticipating a general engagement, he had ordered up General Pillow, from a distance of three miles, with the brigade of General Pierce, and, shortly after, Colonel Riley's brigade of General Twiggs' division. The battle was won, however, just as General Pierce reached the ground, and interposed his troops between the division of General Worth, and the discomfited enemy. Having removed their dead and wounded, the Americans retired to their lines, leaving the walls of El Molino scarred and blackened, and Casa de Mata in ruins.

The battle of El Molino del Rey was the hardest-fought, and the bloodiest engagement of the war. In no action was the heroic ardor of the American soldiers more conspicuous; in none was their desperate valor submitted to a severer ordeal, or more signally triumphant. The plain in front of the enemy's position was deluged with their blood, poured out freely like water. General Worth lost one-fourth of his division, and the other corps sustained a severe loss. Less than 3,500 men, including officers, engaged between twelve and fourteen thousand, either in action, or immediately in reserve, and accomplished their object, with the loss, however, of 784 officers and men.*

It need not be disguised, that the Americans were deceived as to the importance of the enemy's position, and the foundry in El Molino; and as to the strength of their defences;—yet, it is not the least that may be said in their commendation, that they were able to sustain themselves, and finally to triumph, against such odds. Three of the enemy's guns were captured, and the fourth was spiked. Large quantities of small-arms and ammunition, and grain and flour were also taken, and 685 prisoners, including 53 commissioned officers. Over two thousand Mexicans were killed or wounded, and about the same number deserted after the rout. General Leon, and Colonels Balderas, Huerta, and Gelati, were among the killed. But, what was more important than all, the infantry arm of the Mexican service, so essential to the protection and support of

* The Americans lost 125 killed, 649 wounded, many of them mortally, and there were 10 missing. Among the number killed and wounded were 58 officers, 17 of whom died on the field, or shortly after the battle. The officers who fell in this engagement were, Lieutenants Shackelford, Armstrong, and Daniels, of the 2nd artillery; Captain Ayres, and Lieutenant Farry, 3rd artillery; Colonel McIntosh, Lieutenant-Colonel Scott, Captains Merrill and E. Kirby Smith, Assistant Surgeon Roberts, and Lieutenants Burwell and Strong, 5th infantry; Lieutenant Ernst, 6th infantry; Lieutenants Burbank and Morris, 8th infantry; and Lieutenant Colonel Graham, and Lieutenant Johnson, of the 11th infantry. The total number of officers present in this action was 196; consequently nearly one-third were either killed or wounded.

their artillery, was nearly paralyzed by the result of this action. The 11th and 12th regular regiments, under General Perez, were almost annihilated; and, from that time forward, as we shall see, their infantry dared not stand before the destructive fire of the American artillery, or meet the charge of the American bayonet.

CHAPTER XIV.

CAPTURE OF MEXICO.

Preparations for a final attack on the City and its defences—Heavy Batteries planted—The Cannonade—Storming of Chapultepec—Advance of General Quitman to the Garita de Belén and the Ciudadela—Operations of General Worth on the San Cosmé Causeway—Flight of Santa Anna and his Army—Entrance of General Scott into the Capital—The Leperos—Quiet restored in the City—Change in the Mexican Administration.

Night and day the Mexicans labored to complete the fortifications of the Capital. The dull heavy sound of the mattock and spade, employed in digging ditches and throwing up breastworks, was continually heard. Men, women, and children, were constantly employed in the construction of additional defences. Alarm pervaded every breast, and was depicted on every countenance. Anxious groups were collected in the Plaza, and at the corners of the streets—each man eager to put forth the same inquiry, which rushed unbidden to his lips. Even those, who, with folded arms, had hitherto complacently regarded the progress of the war at a distance,—now that the banners of the beleaguering army could be discovered from their balconies and housetops, shared in the general feeling, that something must be done, and that promptly, to avert the impending danger. Letters had been addressed by the Secretary of State to the Governors of the states of Puebla and Mexico, calling for a levy *en masse*, to attack and harass the enemy, by every means which it was practicable to employ, "in the annihilating of an invading army." Circulars were sent by General Herrera, as military commandant of the city of Mexico, on the 7th of September, to the clergy, exhorting them to incite the people to resistance; Olaguibel,* the governor of the state, also appealed to his fellow-citizens, to rally around the standard of their country in this emergency; and the alcaldes and magistrates employed the strong power of the law, to reinforce the army, and compel non-combatants to work in the trenches. The conviction and execution of a number of the deserters taken on the 20th of August, furnished a powerful argument to excite that fiercest and most vindictive of all passions—religious prejudice—among the populace; who were told that these men had been persecuted, solely because they were Roman Catholics, like themselves.†

* In the National Intelligencer of the 25th of October, 1847, there is a letter, dated on the 15th of the same month, signed "T," and extolling, in the highest terms, the patriotism of Olaguibel. The position of the writer—understood to be Mr. Waddy Thompson, formerly minister to Mexico—and his facilities for obtaining information, give great weight to his opinions; and, if these encomiums have reference to the ardent attachment of Olaguibel to a republican form of government, and his opposition to centralism, and the monarchical tendencies of the administrations of Santa Anna and Paredes, they are both deserved and appropriate. In time of war, however, with a foreign enemy, there is, or should be, a different kind of patriotism than mere party devotion; and there is no evidence, that the leading federalists of Mexico, Olaguibel not excepted, rendered a hearty support to Santa Anna in the prosecution of hostilities, or that they did not rejoice, when his defeat and overthrow removed another opponent from the political arena. While our sympathies as American citizens, must naturally go with the Mexican federalists, we cannot be blind to the fact, that their errors have aided to produce that state of turmoil and confusion which has so long existed in the country, and to which, mainly, her difficulties with foreign powers may be attributed.

† Twenty-nine deserters were convicted and sentenced to death, by a

But there was no heartiness in the ebullitions of patriotism thus aroused, and thus manifested. The feeling was short-lived and transient. There was a great want of discipline in the disorganized mass, composing the Mexican army, of which their officers could not remain ignorant. Supplies were furnished slowly, and with a sparing hand. Santa Anna struggled, in vain, against his destiny; and equally futile were the efforts of his countrymen, now forced to experience the bitter consequences of their party strifes and dissensions, to prevent the triumphant entrance of the American soldiers into their capital.

The utmost activity prevailed in the camp of General Scott after the battle of the 8th of September; and the busy hum of preparation was heard at every hour of the day. Colonel Riley had been stationed at the village, or church, of Piedad, nearly two miles south of the city, with his brigade, and on the 9th instant, the division of General Pillow was also ordered thither. Covered by these corps, the engineer officers made their reconnaissances. In the afternoon of the 8th, Captain Lee, and Lieutenants Beauregard and Tower, proceeded along the Piedad causeway, to a barranca, or ravine, crossing that road, and the Niño Perdido and San Antonio causeways, a little over a mile from the city, and

court-martial over which Colonel Riley presided; and thirty-six by a court over which Colonel Garland presided. Several of the number having deserted previous to the existence of actual war, or presenting circumstances in mitigation of their offence, their sentences were commuted by General Scott. Sixteen were hung at San Angel, on the 10th of September; four at Mixcoac, on the 11th; and thirty, at the same place, on the 13th instant. The execution at Mixcoac, on the 13th, took place while the Americans were storming the height of Chapultepec; and the deserters were required to stand on the gallows, until the colors which they had abandoned were displayed from the castle.

discovered the enemy in force on the two roads upon their right. On the 9th, General Scott, accompanied by Captain Lee, made an examination of the enemy's defences at the garita of San Antonio, and, on the following day, a thorough reconnaissance, in that quarter, and of the Paséo de las Vigas, connected with the San Antonio causeway by a road practicable for artillery, was executed by Lieutenants Beauregard, Stevens, and Tower. On the morning of the 11th, Captain Lee and Lieutenant Tower made another, and final examination, of the works commanding the southern approaches to the capital; the result of which was reported to the General-in-chief, at a council of war, held on the same day, at the church of La Piedad.

No serious collision took place with the enemy's forces during the execution of these reconnaissances. An occasional shot was thrown from the Mexican batteries at the garita of San Antonio; Lieutenant Colonel Duncan and Major Sumner had a slight skirmish with a small body of lancers, near Morales, on the morning of the 11th, in which two or three of the enemy were killed; and, in the afternoon, Captain Magruder fired upon a party of cavalry, about 500 strong, who were moving round the American right, in order, as was supposed, to discover their position and force. A number of shot and shells were thrown from his battery, planted in the hermitage at the end of the Niño Perdido causeway, and perfectly screened by rows of maguey, which caused the enemy to countermarch in haste, and retire under cover of their heavy guns.

General Scott now resolved to put in execution a project which had been some time in contemplation. Including the works at the eight garitas, or principal entrances, there were forty-seven batteries around the city, prepared for 177 guns, and seventeen infantry breastworks; all of the batteries, however, could not be manned at the same time, in consequence of the deficiency in artillery. It was impossible to gain an admittance into the capital, with an army, except by passing along the elevated causeways,—flanked, as has been described, by deep ditches and low marshy grounds —and through the fortified gates. South and west of the city,—the quarter to which the operations of General Scott were confined,—there were five causeways. The San Antonio causeway led directly from San Antonio, through Churubusco, to the *plaza mayor*. About one thousand yards further west, was the causeway of Niño Perdido, and rather more than that distance beyond it, was the Piedad causeway, both running parallel to the causeway of San Antonio. The Piedad causeway intersected the Tacubaya, or Chapultepec causeway and aqueduct, at the south-western angle of the city; and the San Cosmé causeway and aqueduct, with the aqueduct and causeway leading from the height of Chapultepec, approached from the west, at right angles with the southern causeways, and, at its entrance into the capital, was nearly one mile distant from the Chapultepec causeway. At the intersection of the Piedad with the Chapultepec causeway, was the garita of Belén; and there was a garita also, on each of the other causeways mentioned. Besides these main causeways, there was a smaller one, called the Paséo de las Vigas, with a garita, about eight hundred yards east of the San Antonio causeway.

The enemy anticipated that an attempt would be made upon the city, from the causeway of San Antonio, and their efforts were principally directed to the strengthening of the fortifications in that quarter, although the other approaches were not neglected. The garita of San Antonio was about a mile in advance of that on the causeway of Niño Perdido, and, between the two, there were three batteries, and a trench traversing diagonally the grazing grounds. On the east, between the garita of San Antonio and the Paséo de las Vigas, there were two batteries. These batteries were well supplied with heavy guns, which, being placed in position, could not be counter-battered with much hope of success, by the lighter pieces of the Americans planted in the open and unprotected ground. Near the Mexican lines there was also not far from 12,000 infantry, stationed there to support the batteries and repel an assault. From three to four hundred yards in advance of the Belén gate, on the Piedad causeway, was a battery without guns, with a breastwork for infantry, facing the west, intervening between it and the garita. At the gate there was a battery of three guns, with another battery of four guns eight hundred yards in its front, on the Chapultepec causeway. East and north of the garita of Belen, was the citadel with its fifteen guns, near the northwestern angle of which, on a paséo running north from the gate, was a battery of two guns. At the San Cosmé gate there was a battery mounting one heavy gun and a howitzer, and there were several other batteries, without guns, in advance of it, and on the branch causeway leading from the heights of Chapultepec. Some six or seven thousand Mexicans, cavalry and infantry, besides the permanent garrison of Chapultepec, were posted in its vicinity, and on the slopes south and east of Morales.

The route by the San Cosmé causeway was the most feasible of all; but, in order to reach it, it would be necessary to make a wide and hazardous circuit, unless the fortress on the steep and rocky bluff of Chapultepec should be first carried. General Scott, however, decided to storm the castle, and to approach the city by the Chapultepec and San Cosmé causeways,—designing to make the main attack by the latter road. But to accomplish this without too great loss, it was requisite that the enemy should be kept in ignorance of the movement up to the latest hour, and that, when discovered, they should mistake it for a feint, and be led to suppose that the Americans intended to return and assault the formidable batteries of San Antonio.

In pursuance of this plan, the details of which were settled at the council held on the 11th instant, General Quitman was immediately ordered to join General Pillow, by daylight, before the southern gates, with his division, previously stationed at Coyoacan. After dark, on the night of the 11th, both generals, with their divisions, proceeded to Tacubaya, where General Scott was quartered with the division of General Worth. General Twiggs remained at Piedad,—two miles east of Tacubaya, and, within a few hundred yards, as far north as the garita of San Antonio,—with the brigade of Colonel Riley, and the batteries of Captains Taylor and Steptoe, to make false attacks, or threaten the works on the southern side of the city, and thus deceive the enemy. General P. F. Smith was left at San Angel with his brigade, but received orders to join General Quitman early in the morning of the 13th. Major Sumner was directed to march to Tacubaya at daybreak on the 12th, with six companies of the 2nd dragoons, one of the 1st dragoons, and one company of mounted rifles. The remainder of the cavalry, with the 12th infantry, Lieutenant Colonel Bonham, one company of the 3rd and one of the 7th infantry, the whole commanded by Colonel Harney, were ordered to garrison Mixcoac, now the general dépôt of the army.

During the night of the 11th, and in the morning of the 12th, four batteries were traced and established near the height of Chapultepec, by Captains Huger and Lee, with the assistance of other ordnance and engineer officers, and working parties detailed for the purpose. Number 1, mounting two sixteen-pounders, and one 8-inch howitzer,* was placed on the Tacubaya causeway, to fire on the south side of the castle; number 2, mounting one twenty-four pounder, and one 8-inch howitzer, on the ridge south of El Molino del Rey, and opposite the south-west angle of the castle; number 3, which received, in the course of the day, one sixteen-pounder and one 8-inch howitzer, near the mill, some three hundred yards to the north and east of number 2, having the wall of the aqueduct as a parapet; and number 4, mounted with a 10-inch mortar, at El Molino, under cover of the high wall formed by the aqueduct, and opposite the west front of the castle. Numbers 1 and 2 were well masked by bushes, and ready to commence cannonading the castle, at an early hour on the 12th.

An unusual degree of alarm pervaded the city on the afternoon of the 11th, when General Quitman was discovered advancing along the Piedad causeway with his division; but, as no further movement was perceived, it soon subsided. All was yet still on the ensuing day, when the rising sun first threw his golden

* These were captured guns; and the 16-pounders, being French pieces, were equal to our 18s.

beams over the bristling peaks of the Cordilleras,—which fell tremblingly upon the lakes of the valley, and the cool jets of crystal water gushing up from the fountains in the Alameda, and suffused palace and convent—dome, and spire, and cross,—with waves of sparkling sheen. It was the last hour of quiet enjoyed by the residents of the capital, until the American flag, tattered and torn in many a perilous conflict, but floating proudly as ever, waved in triumph over the Palacio of Mexico.

Having placed his battery of twelve-pounders in an advantageous position, near Piedad, Captain Steptoe opened a brisk and intense fire, at daylight on the 12th, on the enemy's works at the southern gates, which was kept up steadily throughout the day, and silenced the battery at the garita of San Antonio, whose guns were driven within the walls of the city. The Mexicans returned his fire, and the alarm-bells commenced ringing. Peal upon peal resounded through the streets, rousing the inhabitants from their slumbers, and calling them, in crowds, to the azoteas, or flat roofs, of their dwellings. Jalousies were flung open in haste, and the flashing eyes of the Castilian gazed anxiously forth, through the clouds of morning mist and sulphurous smoke, momentarily lighted by the glare of artillery. Squadrons of lancers dashed to and fro, and the paséos were soon thronged with groups of soldiers and citizens hurrying hither and thither. Scarcely an hour passed, when batteries 1 and 2, opposite Chapultepec, supported by the division of General Quitman—the former served by Captain Drum, assisted by Lieutenants Benjamin and Porter, with his company of the 4th artillery; and the latter by a detachment of ordnance men, under Lieutenant Hagner—joined in the fierce cannonade.

The furious storm of missiles poured from the American batteries upon the castle of Chapultepec and its defences, drove the enemy's light troops and skirmishers from the grove in the surrounding inclosure, and compelled most of the supporting force, stationed in and near the fortress, to retire out of range. At the same time the fire of the guns in the castle, which had vigorously answered the attack, was sensibly slackened. Availing themselves of the favorable moment, the American ordnance and engineer officers prepared batteries 3 and 4 for action. Number 3 was manned by Captain Brooks, of the 2nd artillery, with his company, who was relieved, in the evening, by another company of the same regiment, under Lieutenant Anderson, assisted by Lieutenant Russell, of the 4th infantry :—during the fire, the stock of the sixteen pounder was broken, leaving only the 8-inch howitzer in the battery; but the broken piece was subsequently replaced by a twenty-four pounder gun. Number 4 was served by a detachment of ordnance men under Lieutenant Stone.

Shortly after daybreak, on the 12th, Lieutenant Colonel Hébert had taken possession of El Molino del Rey, under a severe shower of shot and shell from the Castle of Chapultepec, with a force organized for the purpose, and General Cadwalader afterwards occupied it with his brigade. General Pillow displayed the remainder of his division, including Magruder's battery, and excepting the 12th infantry, which constituted part of the garrison of Mixcoac, on the battle-field of the 8th instant, with the cavalry command of Major Sumner on his left, both to support batteries 3 and 4, and to hold in check the Mexican lancers and infantry, under Generals Alvarez and Rangel, occupying the slopes north and west of Chapultepec. Several feints were made by the enemy, but they did not attempt to molest General Pillow.

The permanent garrison of Chapultepec probably did not much exceed 1,000 men, commanded by General Bravo;* but there was a force at least 6000 strong in the adjoining grounds, and within supporting distance, on the outside, in rear, and towards the city. The elèves of the military school, under their superintendent, General Monterde, also aided in the defence of the post. There were ten pieces of artillery in the castle, some of which were of very heavy calibre. The heights were dotted all over with bastions, parapets, redoubts, and batteries. There was a battery of three guns on the Tacubaya road, at the south-east angle of the inclosure, flanked by a one-gun battery, sweeping the low grounds between it and the causeway, a short distance to the west; and a few hundred yards beyond the latter, there was another battery. About four hundred yards east of the mill, on the road passing along the north side of Chapultepec, there was

* General Bravo, in his official report dated September 14th, 1847, states that the garrison of Chapultepec numbered only 832, many of whom deserted before the assault; and that, although he repeatedly applied to Santa Anna and General Rangel for assistance, none was rendered. It is extremely difficult, as is the case with most accounts of the Mexican officers, to reconcile this statement with facts about which there can be no question. Nearly five hundred dead bodies were found after the assault, in the castle and outworks of Chapultepec; numbers were seen to escape over the northern and eastern walls; and there were over seven hundred taken prisoners, including, with the commander, five generals, and more than a hundred subordinate officers. The actual garrison may not have exceeded 1,000 men, but the supporting force certainly could not have remained inactive.

a battery of two guns, and a second one where the aqueduct and causeway lead off to the San Cosmé road.

The castle suffered terribly from the fire of the American batteries on the 12th. The guns were aimed with such precision that the flag-staff was several times carried away; the lofty dome surmounting the magnificent pile was shivered; the light woodwork of the apartments appropriated to the school was torn into splinters; embrasures were shattered; thick stone walls crumbled away; sodded rampe and terrace were furrowed by the ploughing shot; and a wide breach was effected in the southern wall near El Molino del Rey. Howitzer shells fell hissing and sputtering into the pools of water in the wet and springy grove at the western base of Chapultepec, and whirling balls came thundering and crashing down upon the heads of the men in the breastworks. Both the garrison and the supporting force sustained a severe loss; discipline scarcely remained among the terrified soldiers; the confidence based on superior strength, in numbers and position, was nearly gone; they were already cowed and disheartened; and numbers deserted on the night of the 12th, anxious but to escape the horrors of the assault which they anticipated would soon be made.*

At dark, the Americans, who had been comparatively unharmed, suspended their fire, and General Pillow drew his whole force down to the mill. The enemy's works were now well crippled, and, at another meeting of his officers, General Scott made his final arrangements for storming the castle on the morning of the 13th. The bombardment was ordered to be continued for two or three hours after sunrise, and the momentary cessation of the fire was to be the signal for the assault. General

* Official Report of General Bravo, September 14th, 1847.

Quitman was directed to make the attack with his division on the south and east, where the hill, though steep and rocky, was accessible; and General Pillow was to advance, at the same time, with his column, from the west. On the north the height was so precipitous that it could not be approached from that quarter. Storming parties, mostly volunteers for the attack, each containing about 250 rank and file, were selected from the divisions of Generals Worth and Twiggs, to lead the assaulting columns. The party furnished from Worth's division was commanded by Captain Mackenzie, of the 2nd artillery, who joined General Pillow; and that furnished from Twiggs' division, by Captain Casey, of the 2nd infantry, who reported to General Quitman. A second storming party of 120 men, under Major Twiggs, of the marines, was organized by General Quitman from his division. Pioneer parties were also selected, to accompany the stormers with ladders, fascines, picks, and crowbars. General Worth was ordered to hold his division in reserve, near El Molino del Rey, to support General Pillow, and General Smith was directed to support General Quitman with his brigade.

During the night of the 12th, Captain Paul, of the 7th infantry, in command of an advanced picket of fifty men, established on the road to Chapultepec, had a brisk skirmish with one of the enemy's outposts, which was driven back. Apprehensive that this demonstration was intended to cover the passage of reinforcements into the castle, General Quitman ordered Lieutenant Andrews, of the 3rd artillery, to advance a piece of artillery, and rake the road with several discharges of canister. This being done, every thing remained quiet till the early dawn, when General Twiggs was again heard thundering at the southern gates. The batteries near Chapultepec,—Lieutenant Andrews relieving Captain Drum, for a short time, with his company of the 3rd artillery,—and the guns of the fortress, were instantly at work. The cannonade soon swelled into a continuous roar, and the solid earth shook with the dreadful concussion. The batteries were kept playing for about two hours, in which time one of the sixteen-pounders, in battery number 1, was disabled; and showers of grape, canister, and shells, were then thrown into the groves and shrubbery around the castle. At eight o'clock, the order to cease firing was given, and the attacking columns moved forward,—the guns once more opening, immediately after the advance, and keeping up an incessant fire, over the heads of the assailants, till they were masked.*

The American troops had mostly slept on their arms. Though somewhat fatigued, and entertaining, it may be, considerable anxiety as to the result of the approaching struggle, a bright glow was imparted to their cheeks by the confidence and courage that continued to animate them. There were no laggards,—none to falter; and a beaming light sparkled in the eye of him who shook his comrade's hand at parting, and a high-souled daring curled his lip, when he went forth to battle, bearing with him the premonition of an early death, which, though it saddened the heart, had no enervating power. All felt the importance of the movement. But little over ten thousand in number, they had precipitated themselves into a valley swarming with enemies. Fighting their way through rivulets of blood,—through the intrenchments of Controras, San Antonio,

* Over 500 round shot, near 300 shells, and 50 rounds of canister, were thrown into the castle and outworks during the bombardment.

and Churubusco,—victors, too, at Casa de Mata and El Molino,—a sadly diminished band of less than 8,000 effective men,--their communications with the sea-coast obstructed or cut off,—they now stood before a hostile city, every house, with its flat roofs and parapets, and every convent, church, and public edifice of which, could be converted into a fortification, containing 200,000 inhabitants, and defended by a frowning castle, by powerful batteries, and an army 25,000 strong. It was, indeed, a last stroke,—but life, death, every thing, depended on the issue!

General Pillow had placed one section of Captain Magruder's battery, inside the extensive range of buildings of which El Molino formed a part, to clear a sand-bag breastwork constructed by the enemy, outside the southern wall of the inclosure around Chapultepec, to command the breach made by the siege guns. The mountain howitzers of the voltigeurs, under Lieutenant Reno, were also planted in battery, in rear of the mill, to aid in driving the Mexican light troops from the grove, and from a strong intrenchment extending nearly across its front. These batteries were admirably served, and effected good execution. When the order was given to advance, Lieutenant Colonel Johnstone rushed forward, with one battalion of voltigeurs, on the south side of the main wall, under a brisk fire from the lunette, and sprang through the breach. Deploying at a run, they drove the enemy from the parapet before the rear companies were in line. Meanwhile Colonel Andrews and Major Caldwell had passed through a narrow gateway, opening from the rear of the mill, with the remaining battalion of the voltigeurs, and advanced on the left of Lieutenant Colonel Johnstone's command. Darting from tree to tree, covered by the bolls of the huge cypresses, the regiment made the wood ring with the sharp crack of their rifles, and the howitzer shells of Lieutenant Reno filled the air with falling leaves and branches, as they scattered the enemy's skirmishers in confusion.

A loud cheer from the voltigeurs soon announced that they had cleared the grove of the Mexican sharp-shooters. The stormers, under Captain Mackenzie, with percussion caps removed, and depending on the bayonet alone, were now ordered forward. The 9th and 15th infantry, under Colonel Ransom and Lieutenant Colonel Howard,—Colonel Morgan being still disabled from his wounds,—followed rapidly, accompanied by General Pillow. On emerging into the open space, from twenty to thirty yards broad, at the foot of the acclivity, the troops became exposed to a terrible fire of shot, shell, and musketry, from the batteries and breastworks of the castle. General Pillow fell severely wounded, though afterwards borne along in the arms of his men, as they pressed onward to secure the victory. Colonel Ransom was shot dead at the head of his regiment, and Major Seymour assumed the command.

General Cadwalader, in the absence of General Pierce, who was yet an invalid, promptly led on the column. The battalion of voltigeurs under Colonel Andrews, and the 9th and 15th infantry, pushed up the height, shouting and cheering as they forced the enemy from shelter to shelter. Balls and shells fell upon them like rain. "There was death below, as well as above ground."* The hill-side was mined;—but, fortunately, it was discovered in time. The men appointed to fire the mines fell before the unerring aim of the voltigeurs,

* Official Report of General Scott, September 18th, 1847.

watering with their blood the trains which they had vainly endeavored to ignite. In their haste, the attacking parties outstripped the stormers, who had moved on more slowly until the ground should be relinquished by their comrades; and when they gained the crest of the counterscarp, they were obliged to wait for the ladders, without which the works could not be carried. They then partially sheltered themselves in the crevices of the rocky acclivity, and poured an incessant fire upon the enemy behind their breastworks and parapets.

At the request of General Pillow, General Worth had detached Colonel Clarke with his brigade, consisting of the 5th, 6th, and 8th infantry, under Captain Chapman, and Majors Bonneville and Montgomery, to support the attack. Portions of these regiments joined the assaulting column, as Captain Mackenzie came up with his command. The delay was of brief duration. The ditch was crossed, and the ladders planted. Hand-grenades and musket-balls were poured upon the assailants, and the first who mounted the ladders fell to the earth, either killed or severely wounded; others took their places, and gained the parapet. The color-bearer of the voltigeurs being shot down, Captain Barnard snatched the flag, scaled the wall with it unfurled, and planted it in advance of any other color. One of the salients of the outer work was in their possession, and the columns moved forward upon the castle.

In the meantime, Lieutenant Colonel Johnstone, with his battalion, accompanied by Lieutenant Reno with two of the howitzers, had passed round to the right, up the paved road leading in a triangular form to the main gate on the south side of the castle. Here he encountered a warm fire from the parapet of the east terrace, and the battery at its base. Lieutenant Reno brought his guns into action, and served them efficiently, until, being wounded at the gateway, he resigned his charge to Lieutenant Beauregard, of the engineers. A vigorous attack was at once made by the command, when the works were reduced.

The column under General Quitman, guided by Lieutenant Tower, had advanced to the assault, along the Tacubaya road, with equal promptitude and enthusiasm. General Smith moved in reserve with his brigade, prolonging his right beyond that flank of the assaulting column, to protect it from skirmishers, and from the enemy's forces lining the causeway leading from Chapultepec to the city. Lieutenant Hunt, who had reported to General Quitman, with a howitzer and six-pounder gun belonging to Duncan's battery, followed the main column, and having gained a position in the road, within easy range of the castle, opened his fire, throwing shell and shrapnel shot that exploded directly over the parapets on the lower part of the hill, from which the enemy's fire seemed hottest, and elevating his pieces as the troops advanced. The storming parties under Major Twiggs and Captain Casey, supported by the battalion of marines, under Lieutenant Colonel Watson, dashed forward, with hearty cheers, upon the battery at the south-east angle of the height. Major Twiggs receiving a mortal wound, Captain Miller, of the 2nd Pennsylvania, took command of his party; and Captain Casey being also disabled, Captain Paul, of the 7th infantry, assumed his place. The contest at the battery was hand-to-hand, and for a short time was stoutly maintained. Parties of the rifle regiment joined the stormers, and entered the works with them. Being unable to withstand the impetuous onset of their antagonists, the enemy abandoned their guns, and retired in haste.

The remaining regiments of General Quitman's division,—the New York and South Carolina volunteers, under Lieutenant Colonel Baxter and Major Gladden, and the 2nd Pennsylvania, under Lieutenant Colonel Geary, Colonel Roberts being confined to a sick bed,—led by General Shields, who had solicited the command of the storming parties, but had been refused on account of his rank, after proceeding about half a mile along the causeway, turned to the left, and making their way through fields intersected by deep ditches, filled with water, under a severe fire of grape and musketry, approached the southern wall of Chapultepec. The Palmettos broke through it, and charged up the height, without firing a gun. Lieutenant Colonel Baxter being mortally wounded, Major Burnham placed himself at the head of the New Yorkers, and entered the inclosure, in company with the 2nd Pennsylvania, through an abandoned battery, to the left. Lieutenant Reid, with his company of the New York regiment, and a company of marines, moving still further to the left, passed through the breach made by the heavy guns, and was soon among the foremost of the parties who had assaulted the work from the west. A portion of the storming party from General Twiggs' division, under Lieutenant Gantt, of the 7th infantry, also ascended the hill.

A simultaneous rush was now made upon the east, south, and west of the castle. Scaling-ladders were applied on all sides. Major Seymour, of the 9th infantry, reached the flag-staff, and hauled down the Mexican standard,—and the national color of the New York regiment, the first on the fortress, was displayed, by Lieutenant Reid,—while the battle was raging at their feet. For a few moments the conflict was terrible. General Bravo and his soldiers made a sturdy defence. The elèves of the military school fought bravely and gallantly. Swords clashed; bayonets were crossed; and rifles clubbed. The cruelty of the enemy at Casa de Mata was not forgotten; and the ramparts and batteries were covered with those who had fallen, some maimed and disabled, but many cold and stiff as the rocks and stones that formed their resting place. Carried away with indignation, for a moment the American soldiers seemed inclined to make no prisoners; but the earnest remonstrances of their officers, checked the exhibition of a feeling, which, though not unprovoked, would have sullied the flag under which they fought. Resistance, however, was in vain; the work was carried;—and General Bravo surrendered himself and men prisoners of war.*

While the assaulting parties were engaged in storming the height of Chapultepec, Colonel Trousdale had moved along the road at the northern base of the height, with the 14th infantry, and a section of Magruder's battery, under Lieutenant Jackson,—Lieutenant Colonel Hébert remaining at the mill, temporarily in charge of the 11th infantry. A destructive fire was opened upon the command from the two-gun battery, which was actively returned by Lieutenant Jackson. The section was dreadfully cut up, and almost disabled; the infantry support lost several men;

* General Bravo, and General Rincon—the latter taken prisoner on the 20th of August—were exchanged for Captains Heady and Clay, and other officers and men captured the previous winter from the column under General Taylor. Majors Gaines and Borland made their escape soon after the Americans entered the Valley, and served as volunteer aids, respectively, to Generals Scott and Worth.

and Colonel Trousdale and some of his officers were badly wounded. Leaving Major Hunter with the 11th infantry, Lieutenant Colonel Hébert hastened forward to take command of his regiment. A demonstration made by a body of the enemy on this flank, was checked by Major Hunter; but their forces, in large numbers, were discovered rallying upon the branch causeway and aqueduct leading to the San Cosmé road, and threatening the section of the battery commanded by Lieutenant Jackson. Captain Magruder pushed on to his assistance with the other section; and, at the same time, General Worth turned the mill and advanced upon the road, with Colonel Garland's brigade,—consisting of the 2nd and 3rd artillery, under Captain Brooks and Lieutenant Colonel Belton, and the 4th infantry, Major Lee,—the light battalion of Lieutenant Colonel C. F. Smith, Duncan's battery, and three squadrons of dragoons, under Major Sumner.

A flank movement of a portion of Colonel Garland's brigade completed the capture of the breastwork, under the fire of Lieutenant Jackson's guns, and General Worth continued his advance, attacking the right of the enemy's line resting on the branch causeway, and driving them before him, at the moment of the general retreat consequent upon the capture of the castle. He then rapidly pursued the routed enemy, in the direction of the San Cosmé road.

As soon as his command could be formed and supplied with ammunition, General Quitman also advanced on the Chapultepec causeway, the more direct route to the city. Meanwhile Captain Drum had brought up a four-pounder captured gun, and was moving along the causeway, pouring a constant fire upon the flying Mexicans. The rifle regiment commanded by Major Loring, formed under the arches of the aqueduct, and the remainder of General Smith's brigade—the 1st artillery and 3rd infantry, under Major Dimmick and Captain Alexander—levelled the parapets and filled up the ditches in the road, so as to permit the passage of heavy artillery. This being done, the whole column was put in motion.

General Scott arrived at the castle shortly after its reduction, and immediately ordered Colonel Clarke, with his brigade, to join his division, and also dispatched the brigade of General Cadwalader to the support of General Worth. The 9th infantry was ordered to follow the movement of General Quitman, and the 15th was designated as the garrison of Chapultepec. Siege pieces were likewise directed to be sent forward to both columns. Having issued these orders, General Scott proceeded along the road taken by General Worth. Two heavy pieces, under Lieutenant Hagner, escorted by a command of New York volunteers and marines, under Captain Gallagher, and two pieces and a 10-inch mortar escorted by the 14th infantry, followed, as soon as they could be got in readiness. Captain Huger also sent heavy guns to General Quitman, and then joined the column of General Worth.

The first obstacle encountered by General Quitman was the battery between the castle of Chapultepec and the garita of Belén. A short, but effective fire, from an 8-inch howitzer, brought up by Lieutenant Porter, directed by Captain Drum; aided by Lieutenant Colonel Duncan's battery,—which had been advanced, by direction of General Worth, from the causeway along which his column was moving, supported by the light battalion, over a cross route, to within four hundred yards of the work,—together with the daring and bravery of the rifle regiment, soon cleared the battery. The column was forthwith reorganized for an attack upon the work at the garita. The rifles, intermingled with the South Carolina volunteers, led the advance, supported by the remainder of General Quitman's division and the brigade of General Smith, and a part of the 6th infantry, under Major Bonneville, who had fallen into this road.

Springing boldly from arch to arch of the aqueduct, the advance moved upon the garita, under a tremendous fire of grape, canister, and round shot, from the battery, and of small-arms from the paséo on their left, and the Piedad causeway on their right. The enemy had been completely deceived by the movements of General Scott, and did not recover from their delusion until the American troops were seen streaming along the San Cosmé and Chapultepec causeways. It was then too late to plant new batteries, or shift their guns. Still a brave defence was made at the Belén garita, by General Terres, who commanded the forces at this point, supported by a strong reserve under General Garey. Santa Anna also hastened thither; and for a few moments the conflict was warm and animated.

Several rounds of canister, thrown from a sixteen pounder gun, pushed forward to the head of the American column by Lieutenant Benjamin, checked the annoying fire of the Mexican infantry on the Piedad causeway, who were soon after driven back by the 4th artillery, under Major Gardner, advancing for the purpose from their position near the church of La Piedad. Both gun and howitzer were then opened on the garita. The rifles, now under Captain Simonson, Major Loring having been severely wounded, from their partial cover beneath the arches of the aqueduct, picked off the artillerists, one by one; the enemy's infantry refused to be led forward; and the removal of their guns was commenced. Discovering this, General Quitman ordered a charge. The Americans sprang forward with eager impetuosity, entered the work at a few minutes past one o'clock in the afternoon, and captured two of its guns. General Quitman was among the first at the garita, and none of the colors having yet come up, attached a silk handkerchief to a rifle, and waved it over the battery, amid the joyous shouts of his brave soldiers.

The garita being taken, the riflemen and South Carolina volunteers rushed on, and occupied the arches of the aqueduct, within one hundred yards of the citadel. The ammunition of the heavy guns having been expended, Captain Drum turned a captured nine-pounder upon the enemy, and served it with good effect, until the ammunition taken with it was also expended. Daring as was the advance of the American column, they had proceeded too far without the necessary siege guns and ammunition. Yet they held their ground firmly under a most appalling fire. Captain Drum, Lieutenant Benjamin, and a number of their men, were killed at the gun which had been run forward in front of the garita, waging an unequal contest with the heavy artillery in the citadel. When the enemy perceived that the Americans had expended their ammunition, they rallied to drive them back from the lodgement which had been effected. Repeated, though ineffectual sallies, were made, and both sides of the aqueduct were swept by the iron shower poured from the citadel, the batteries on the paséo, and the buildings on the right of the garita. An attempt to enfilade the left flank of the column being apprehended, Captain Naylor took possession of a low sand-bag defence, about one hundred yards to the left of the causeway, with two companies of the 2nd Pennsylvania; and held it, under a severe fire, till nightfall, when the Mexican batteries ceased firing.

Sweeping the enemy with the utmost ease, from the two batteries enfilading the route, at which they vainly endeavored to make a successful stand, General Worth arrived at the intersection of the branch causeway with the San Cosmé road, about two miles distant from Chapultepec. Here, on his left, was a formidable work at the Campo Santo, or English burying-ground, but entirely destitute of guns. Leaving the brigade of General Cadwalader at this point to protect his rear, General Worth turned to the right, and moved cautiously along the road towards the garita of San Cosmé, where General Rangel was in command. Several hundred yards further on, the column came upon a strong adobé breastwork, two hundred and fifty yards in front of the garita. The approach to the two defences was in a right line, and the whole space was raked by grape, canister, and shells, from the heavy gun and howitzer in the battery at the gate; in addition to which, an incessant fire of musketry was poured from the tops of the houses and churches, flanking the road. Lieutenant Hagner was ordered forward with his pieces; but, it being found impossible to bring them into action, on account of the nature of the ground, they were withdrawn.

General Worth then decided to vary his mode of operations. Lieutenant Johnson, with a portion of the 6th infantry, moved to the right, in rear of several small buildings, until he reached a large dwelling fronting the street. Having broken into the house, his men tore open the windows, and commenced firing upon the Mexicans behind the breastwork. A similar movement to the left was made by Captain Brooks, of the 2nd artillery, and Lieutenant Grant of the 4th infantry, with small parties. Other troops passing still further up, gained a cross street, and came down on the enemy's rear, when the latter fell back to the garita. An attempt to regain the work was prevented by the fire of a section of Magruder's battery, under Lieutenant Jackson. The brigade of Colonel Garland was now thrown to the right, and that of Colonel Clarke to the left, with orders to burrow their way, from house to house, with picks and bars. A mountain howitzer was also placed on the top of a commanding building on the left, and another on the church of San Cosmé on the right, under Lieutenant Hagner, of the ordnance, and Captain Edwards of the voltigeurs, which soon occasioned considerable commotion among the enemy.

The contest for the possession of the garita—to which Santa Anna had retired, after his unsuccessful attempt to prevent the advance of General Quitman, equally deluded, however, if he hoped to achieve a triumph over the caution, bravery, and skill of General Worth—was spirited, but somewhat desultory; detached parties of the different commands, crossing and recrossing the street, as opportunity served, to enter some narrow lane, or spring through some open gateway. At five o'clock in the afternoon, both columns had reached their positions, and it then became necessary, at all hazards, to advance a piece of artillery to the captured breastwork. This was gallantly done by Lieutenant Hunt, of Duncan's light battery, who lost five, out of nine men, in moving at full speed over a distance of one hundred and fifty yards. Reaching the breastwork, and pointing his gun through one of the embrasures, he came muzzle to muzzle with the enemy. At the same moment, the troops who had burrowed through the houses, sprang to the roofs, doors, and windows. Lieutenant Johnson, with a number of good marksmen from the 6th and 8th infantry, had entered a small adobé shed facing the road; and Major Buchanan had ascended to the top of a house overlooking the garita, with a part of the 4th infantry.

For an instant the street was one blaze of fire. But a single withering volley was sufficient,—and a loud prolonged shout was raised by the victors, as the Mexicans fled from the garita. Captain Mackenzie, with the rem nant of his storming party, and Lieutenant Colonel Belton, with the 2nd and 3rd artillery, and 4th infantry, rushed up the road, and the other troops also darted forward. The heavy gun in the work, a sixteen-pounder, was captured, and turned upon the enemy, by Captain Bomford and Lieutenant Merchant, of the 8th infantry, "to expedite their departure." Lieutenants Sydney Smith and Judah, of the 4th infantry, with Lieutenant G. W. Smith, of the engineers, and a small party of sappers and miners, pursued them nearly half a mile into the city, and captured a gun, and a number of prisoners, among whom was an aid of Santa Anna; and one of them had the gratification of eating a supper prepared for his Excellency.

During the operations of General Worth in front, an effort was made to annoy his left flank by a body of the enemy, cavalry and infantry, who were driven off by Captain Biddle, with his company of voltigeurs, and a mountain howitzer. After the capture of the garita, General Worth placed his division in secure positions on the right and left of the road, and established picket guards. Captain Huger then advanced two siege pieces, and a 10-inch mortar, to the garita, and fired a few 24-pound shot; and, between nine and ten o'clock in the evening, he threw several shells from the mortar in the direction of the National Palace, about sixteen hundred yards distant.

Early in the afternoon, General Scott had returned to Chapultepec. The remaining brigade of General Twiggs, (Colonel Riley's), was ordered from Piedad, to support General Worth; and Captain Steptoe was directed to rejoin General Quitman's division with his battery. Intrenching tools and ammunition were also sent to General Quitman, whose men were busily employed, throughout the night, in constructing two sand-bag breastworks and parapets, at the garita of Belén, upon which two heavy guns and an 8-inch howitzer were placed in battery by Captain Steptoe. Late in the evening General Shields was forced to retire, in consequence of a severe wound received at the storming of the castle, but his place was filled by General Pierce, who reported for duty to General Quitman.

But all these preparations for the reduction of the capital proved to be unnecessary. When the blazing shells thrown by Captain Huger were seen falling into the Plaza, Santa Anna, and his officers and advisers, were convinced that it was useless to struggle longer. They were besought, on every hand, to prevent a bombardment; the inhabitants were fleeing in alarm; and insubordination began to make its appearance in the army. A hurried consultation was held, at which it was decided to evacuate the city. Before midnight the causeways unoccupied by the American troops, were thronged with fugitives; with wagons, tumbrils, gun-carriages and caissons; with ambulances and splendid coaches; horse and foot, officers and soldiers, camp followers and citizens—a motley mass—mingled together in confusion.

At one o'clock in the morning of the 14th, a deputation from the ayuntamiento, or city council, came to the advanced post of General Worth, announcing that the officers of the national government and the army had commenced retiring from the city, and that they were authorized to confer with the General-in-chief of the American forces. On their arrival at the head-quarters of General Scott, they informed him of the evacuation, and demanded terms of capitulation in favor of the church, the citizens, and the municipal authorities. They were promptly informed by General Scott that he would sign no capitulation; that the city had been virtually in his possession, from the time when a lodgement had been made on the previous day; that he regretted the escape of the Mexican troops; that he should levy a moderate contribution for special purposes; and that "the American army should come under no terms not self-imposed—such only as its own honor, the dignity of the United States, and the spirit of the age," demanded and required.*

Upon the termination of the interview with the city deputation, General Scott dispatched orders to Generals Worth and Quitman, to advance slowly and cautiously towards the heart of the city. At six o'clock, the head of General Worth's division had reached the street leading direct from the Alameda to the *plaza mayor*, on which the National Palace, containing the halls of Congress and the executive offices of the national government, is situated; and it would have been the firs to arrive at "that goal of general ambition,"† had it

* Official Report of General Scott, September 18th, 1847. † Ibid.

ENTRANCE OF THE ARMY INTO THE GRAND PLAZA AT MEXICO.

not been halted by direction of General Scott. At dawn of day, General Quitman had taken possession of the citadel, upon the invitation of the civil authorities which was temporarily garrisoned by the South Carolina volunteers; and he soon after moved the remainder of his column, the rifle regiment leading the way, in the direction of the National Palace. Arriving at the great square, he formed his men in front of the Palacio, and at seven o'clock in the morning of the 14th of September, 1847, the American flag,—"the first strange banner which had ever waved over that palace since the conquest of Cortés,"*—was planted by Captain Roberts, of the rifles, and saluted by the whole command, with every demonstration of applause and satisfaction.

General Scott and his staff, in full uniform, entered the capital at eight o'clock, escorted by Major Sumner with his battalion of cavalry. General Quitman was immediately appointed civil and military governor of the city, and General Scott issued an order, cautioning his soldiers to be upon their guard, to commit no disorders, and to avoid straggling from the head-quarters of their respective corps.† Shortly after the troops

* Official Report of General Quitman, September 29th, 1847.

† "GENERAL ORDERS, No. 284. "Head Quarters of the Army, Mexico, Sept. 14, 1847.

"1. Under the favor of God, the valor of this army, after many glorious victories, has hoisted the colors of our country in the Capital of Mexico, and on the palace of its government.

"2. But the war is not ended. The Mexican army and government have fled, only to watch an opportunity to return upon us in vengeance. We must then be on our guard.

"3. Companies and regiments will be kept together, and all stand on the alert. Our safety is in military discipline.

"4. Let there be no drunkenness, no disorders, and no straggling. Stragglers will be in great danger of assassination, and marauders shall be punished by courts martial.

"5. All the rules so honorably observed by this glorious army, in entered the city, and while they were about occupying the most important points, they were attacked by crowds of leperos,* and convicts liberated by the authorities of the state and nation prior to the evacuation of the capital, together with soldiers in disguise, who had not accompanied the army, or had returned after the flight.

Escopetas were fired from half-opened doors and windows, and from the corners of the streets and alleys; and missiles of every description were thrown from the flat roofs of the houses. The Americans suffered considerably at first, from this irregular and annoying fire; Colonel Garland was badly wounded; Lieutenant Sydney Smith and several men were killed; and a number of other officers and men received severe

Puebla, must be observed here. The honor of the army, and the honor of our country, call for the best behavior on the part of all. The valiant must, to win the approbation of God and their country, be sober, orderly, and merciful. His noble brethren in arms will not be deaf to this hasty appeal from their commander and friend.

"6. Major General Quitman is appointed civil and military governor of Mexico.

"By command of Major General Scott.

"H. L. SCOTT,
"Acting Assistant Adjutant General."

* The *leperos* of Mexico correspond, very nearly, to the *lazaroni* of Italian towns and cities. The number in the city of Mexico, in 1823, estimated, in Ward's Mexico, at 20,000. The object of these marauders appeared to be to plunder the wealthy citizens, as much as to harass the American troops. During the disturbance, a party of Mexican lancers penetrated a short distance into the city from the north, but were driven back. They were probably sent by Santa Anna, to learn whether any thing could be gained by a return with his forces. A principal reason for his liberating the convicts may have been, the hope that the Americans would be thrown into such confusion, that he would be able to drive them from the city. If he entertained such an expectation, he was very much deceived in regard to the materials of which the American army was composed.

wounds. The most prompt measures were taken to put an end to these dastardly outrages. Lieutenant Hagner fired upon the houses, occupied by the enemy, with an 8-inch howitzer. The sappers and miners, under Lieutenants G. W. Smith and McLellan, forced their way in with crowbars and axes, and cut down every occupant, found with arms, or weapons, in his hands. Good service was also rendered in clearing the streets, and restoring order, by a detachment of cavalry under Major Sumner; by the 2nd and 7th infantry, under Captain Morris and Lieutenant Colonel Plympton; a battalion of the 4th infantry, under Major Buchanan; and part of the rifle regiment, under Captain Roberts.

This street-contest continued for more than twenty-four hours; but the city became tolerably quiet on the 16th; and on the 18th, the four divisions of the army were posted at or near the four principal gates, viz: San Lazaro, San Antonio, San Cosmé, and Peravillo, or Guadalupe;—and the cavalry brigade, under Colonel Harney, was ordered to occupy the cavalry barracks near the National Palace.

Thus terminated, in the capture of the Mexican capital, a campaign unsurpassed, for the brilliancy of its victories, and the magnitude of its results, in the world's history. About 1,000 of the enemy were supposed to have been killed at the storming of Chapultepec, and the subsequent operations in and near the city; over 1,500 were wounded; and there were 823 taken prisoners.* A number of colors and standards were captured by the Americans, together with small-arms and ammunition, in sufficient quantities to supply an army

* Among the prisoners were Generals Bravo, Monterde, Noriega, Dosamantz and Saldana. General Perez was killed at the storming of Chapultepec.

during a campaign, and nearly 100 pieces of artillery The American loss was 130 killed, 704 wounded, and 29 missing.*

All was not yet entirely tranquil in the city. Sleepless and untiring vigilance was necessary on the part of General Scott and his officers, and they did not fail in the performance of their duty. Stragglers were frequently found assassinated, and dark and terrible threats were uttered. The clergy refused to open their churches for public worship, with a view of preventing the restoration of good order; but when they were told by the American commander, that his protection should be withdrawn from them, and the valuable property committed to their care, unless they continued to discharge their functions, as formerly, they were quite willing to resume them. As a consideration for the protection afforded by his army to the property of the church and the citizens, General Scott levied a contribution of one hundred and fifty thousand dollars upon the capital, which was paid in four equal weekly instalments.† Martial law was also proclaimed in and about all towns and posts occupied by the American

* The Americans lost thirteen officers, either killed or mortally wounded, in the operations of the 13th and 14th of September, viz.:—Captain Drum and Lieutenant Benjamin, of the 4th artillery; Lieutenant Sydney Smith and Rodgers, 4th infantry; Lieutenant J. P. Smith, 5th infantry; Lieutenant Gantt, 7th infantry; Colonel Ransom, 9th infantry; Major Twiggs, marine corps; Lieutenant Colonel Baxter, and Captains Van O'Linda and Pearson, New York volunteers; and Lieutenants Cantey and Morange, of the South Carolina Regiment.

† Twenty thousand dollars of this sum was appropriated to the purchase of extra comforts for the wounded and sick of the American soldiers in hospital, and ninety thousand dollars to the purchase of blankets and shoes for gratuitous distribution among the rank and file of the army; and the remaining forty thousand dollars was reserved for other necessary military purposes.—General Orders, Number 287.

army. The collection of duties at the gates was ordered to be continued;—the proceeds of which were applied, as far as necessary, to the payment of the city expenses, and the remainder as was directed by the General-in-chief. Not long after the occupation of the capital, an extensive conspiracy to surprise the Americans and murder the officers and men, fomented by a number of priests and disguised Mexican officers and soldiers, was frustrated. Timely precautions were adopted; and all Mexican officers in the city, who had not given their paroles, were required to report to Lieutenant Colonel Hitchcock, Acting Inspector General.

The Mexican army enrolled for the defence of their capital, was almost disorganized. Divided into small commands, the largest of which, numbering about 4,000 men, proceeded to Queretaro, under General Herrera, it was soon scattered through the country, under various leaders, uncertain what to do, pursuing no definite plan or object, and for the most part, careless and indifferent as to the further prosecution of the war. On the 7th of September, Santa Anna had issued a decree, ordering that Peña y Peña, President of the Supreme Court of Justice, and Generals Herrera and Bravo, should assume his duties as Provisional President, in case he should fall, or be taken prisoner. After the capture of General Bravo, and the evacuation of the city, he issued a second decree, at Guadalupe Hidalgo, on the 16th of September, renouncing the presidency, and designating Señor Alcorta in the place of General Bravo; the substance of which decree was communicated to the Governors, and Commandants-general, of the different states, by Señores Pacheco and Alcorta, Ministers of Internal and Foreign Relations, and of

War. Accompanied by about 2,500 cavalry, Santa Anna then proceeded to Puebla, to harass the communications of General Scott, and to do every thing, in his power, essential to "the defence of the independence of his country."*

Under the provisions of the Mexican Constitution, the office of Provisional President devolved on Peña y Peña, by virtue of his position as the presiding officer of the Supreme Court, and he immediately entered on the discharge of his duties; refusing, however, to recognize the persons associated with him in the decrees of Santa Anna. This was most probably done with their consent, as they made no attempt to assert their claims, if any they may have had. The acting Provisional President, and most of the leading men of Mexico and the adjoining states, repaired to Queretaro, where the National Congress was ordered to assemble, early in October, to take into consideration the deplorable state of the country. Several of the members passed through the city of Mexico, under a safe conduct from General Scott.

* Official Circular of Pacheco, dated at Toluca, September 18th, 1847. Santa Anna afterwards insisted that his renunciation of the chief magistracy was only of temporary duration, and that he had a right to resume the functions of the office at pleasure.—See his Address to the Mexican people, issued at Tehuacan, October 22nd, 1847.

CHAPTER XV.

THE ARMY UNDER TAYLOR.

The American forces on the line of the Sierra Madre, and in the Valley of the Rio Grande—Correspondence between General Taylor and General Mora y Villamil—The Texan Rangers—Expedition to Huejutla—Part of General Taylor's forces ordered to Vera Cruz—Position of the Troops—The command transferred to General Wool.

THE severe defeat experienced by the Mexicans, at Buena Vista, threw them far back into the interior; and no further attempt was made seriously to molest the American forces on the line of the Sierra Madre, and in the valley of the Rio Grande. Reposing quietly and contentedly on the laurels he had won,—his name potential as that of the Black Douglass in overawing the enemy,—General Taylor remained in his camp near Monterey, not seeking an opportunity to achieve new victories, but prepared, at all times, to maintain and enforce the authority of his government over the territory occupied by the troops under his command. Generals Urrea and Canales hovered in the vicinity with their bands of rancheros, but they were careful not to approach within reach of an arm, which, as they well knew, was not more prompt, than it was powerful, to strike.

In accordance with the directions of General Taylor, most of the ranchos between Mier and Monterey, which had been the harboring-places of the marauding bands who had obstructed his line of communications, were laid waste. This harsh, but necessary measure, in connection with his order requiring an indemnity for property destroyed, secured his trains, in a great degree, from attack; although occasional efforts were made, by small parties of the enemy, to capture some of the wagons, where a train was large, or feebly guarded. The principal object of the banditti appeared to be, to seize the merchants' goods going up under the protection of the army escorts, and General Taylor felt compelled, for the safety of his own supplies, to prohibit their accompanying the trains. Fewer inducements, therefore, were held out to the guerilleros; and consequently there were fewer attacks, and fewer losses sustained.

After the return of Santa Anna to the city of Mexico, General Mora y Villamil held the command, for a short time, at San Luis Potosi; and when the requisition for an indemnification was issued, he addressed a communication to General Taylor, desiring to know, whether his wishes and instructions were, "to prosecute the war in conformity to the laws of nations, and as war [was] conducted by civilized countries, or as barbarous tribes [carried] it on among themselves?" Besides referring to the requisition, he also alluded to several acts of violence committed by some of the Texan rangers, a new regiment of which, under Colonel Hays, had recently been enrolled; and threatened to retaliate, in case satisfaction was not rendered for the grievances specified. General Taylor replied on the 19th of May, 1847, refusing, peremptorily, to give a categorical answer to the inquiry, upon the ground that it was a deliberate insult to himself and his government, yet, nevertheless, assuring the Mexican general, that every possible effort had been made to discover the perpetrators of the acts complained of, in order to bring them to trial and punishment, but without success. In regard to the threat of retaliation, he treated it, as it deserved, and stated that he was ready for any course of policy which the Mexican authorities decided to adopt.*

During the ensuing summer, General Taylor found himself unable to control the lawlessness of the rangers; and so many unprovoked outrages were committed, the authors of which could very rarely be ascertained, that, as an act of justice to himself and to his country, he ordered a number of the more turbulent and refractory among them to be summarily dismissed from the service, regarding them as being wholly unworthy to belong to the American army.† Collisions, growing out of these outrages, frequently took place; but the departments of Tamaulipas and New Leon, with this exception, were generally quiet. The active operations of the war were carried on upon a different

* "It is with pain that I find myself under the necessity of addressing you in a manner to which I am little accustomed; but I have been provoked to do so by the object and the manner of your communication, which is objectionable, in my estimation, as well in its insinuations as in its tone. With respect to the implied threat of retaliation, I beg you to understand that I hold it at its true worth, and that I am at all times prepared to act accordingly, whatever may be the policy or mode of carrying on the war, which the Mexican government, or its generals, may think it proper to adopt."—Extract from the letter of General Taylor.

† Assassinations and outrages, of the most barbarous and revolting Character, that could not have been provoked by the bad conduct of the rangers, were committed by the regular and irregular Mexican troops. The cruelties practised by the Mexicans during the revolution in Texas, and the war with the United States, no doubt instigated the volunteers to some extent; but, however justly the former may have been punished, the cruelty of the rangers was none the less deserving of censure.

theatre, and General Taylor remained strictly on the defensive.*

Early in July, Colonel Gates, of the 3rd artillery, the commanding officer at Tampico, received information that a number of American prisoners, entitled to liberation, were at or near Huejutla, over one hundred miles in the interior of Tamaulipas, where General Garey had established his head-quarters, with a force from twelve to fifteen hundred strong. Being anxious to liberate them as soon as possible, Colonel Gates ordered Colonel De Russey, of the Louisiana volunteers,

* In his letter to General Gaines, before alluded to, dated November 8th, 1846, General Taylor avowed himself in favor of withdrawing the American troops to a defensive line, extending from some point on the Gulf of Mexico to the Pacific, and at the same time enforcing a rigid blockade of the Mexican ports, as the surest mode of conquering a peace. The same idea was advocated by Mr. Calhoun, of South Carolina, in the Senate of the United States, during the session of 1847–48; propositions for a large increase of the army being then before Congress. The Hon. Joel R. Poinsett, formerly Minister to Mexico, and Secretary of War, also approved of that policy, in a letter addressed to Mr. Butler, a senator in Congress from South Carolina, dated on the 12th of December, 1847, and published in the National Intelligencer on the 22nd of January following. Mr. Poinsett instances, in support of his argument the failure of the Russian government permanently to enforce her authority over the Caucasians. But the two cases are hardly analogous. The Caucasians are wild, fierce, and intractable, while the Mexicans are indolent, cowardly, and treacherous,—tyrannical as masters, but slavish as subjects; the former have few or no towns, and when driven from them, they regarded the deprivation as of little consequence, while the latter looked upon their capital, and their principal cities, as their main dependence and reliance; and, more than all, Russia desired to make a permanent conquest, which, of itself, was well calculated to arouse an untiring and undying spirit of hostility.

Had Mexico been inhabited by any other race, except a people descended from a Spanish stock, perhaps the defensive policy would have been the most desirable. Such a policy, however, would have been of little or no avail against the Mexican guerilleros. It was the offensive measures adopted by the American commanders, and those alone, which to proceed to Huejutla, accompanied by an escort of 126 men, in order to communicate with General Garey, and effect the restoration of the prisoners.

Colonel De Russey left Tampico on the 8th of July with his command, consisting of one company of the 3rd artillery, Captain Wyse, with a field-piece; a company of dragoons, under Captain Boyd and Lieutenant Taneyhill; a detachment of Louisiana volunteers, under Captains Mace and Seguine; and a small party of Tampico rangers, a volunteer company organized by Colonel Gates for the defence of the post. Passing up the river Panuco, in steamers, about sixty miles, and then marching by land through Asulwama, the alcalde of which was made acquainted with the friendly purpose of the expedition, and cheerfully furnished the command with supplies, Colonel De Russey arrived at Tantayuka, twenty-five miles from Huejutla, on the 11th instant. The alcalde of this town was also informed of the object of his mission; and on the morning of the 12th he continued his march. So far he had been unable to find a military officer who might accompany him to the head-quarters of General Garey and, although he anticipated that preparations for de

they feared and dreaded. In a speech delivered in the Senate, on the 4th of January, 1848, Mr. Calhoun made use of the following bold and striking figure:—"Mexico is to us as a dead body, and this is the only way [the defensive policy] that we can cut the cord which binds us to the corpse." Had the distinguished senator but enlarged a little upon his idea, and inquired how Mexico became reduced to that situation, would he not have refuted his own argument? She was, indeed, prostrate and lifeless,—but why? Because she was in the grasp of a giant! —The defensive policy would have released her from that grasp, and restored her towns and cities, her base of supplies, and all her most valuable internal resources,—thus inviting a bloody and vindictive warfare, to continue as long as a single man could be found to echo "the wild guerilla's curse" among the gorges of the Sierra Madre.

fence would be made, he intended to rely on the white flag when the enemy should be discovered, in order to prevent a conflict, at least until the pacific nature of his visit should be made known.

About eight miles from Tantayuka, a Mexican Indian was met, who informed Colonel De Russey that General Garey, with a large force, had laid an ambuscade for him, at the Calaboso river, one mile in his front. Captain Boyd was then in advance with his company, and before orders could be sent to him to fall back to the main body, a rapid discharge of fire-arms was heard. Colonel De Russey hurried forward with the remainder of his detachment, and encountered the dragoons in retreat, having already lost Captain Boyd and six of their comrades. On approaching the river, it was found that the enemy, who had displayed considerable sagacity in their choice of position, had cleared the ground from bushes, for the space of one hundred and fifty yards on either side of the road, leaving, beyond the now open ground, a dense hedge of chaparral, in rear of which a fence had been constructed as an obstacle to the movements of cavalry. The main body of General Garey's force were upon the opposite bank of the stream, also protected in their front by thick chaparral.

A charge was instantly made on either flank by Captains Mace and Seguine, with their men, and the enemy retired hastily across the river. Captain Wyse at once opened his fire upon the main body on the opposite bank, which was kept up for nearly an hour, when the enemy manifested a disposition to abandon their ground, and their fire altogether ceased. It was now ascertained that all the cartridges but three had been exhausted, and great numbers of the enemy from the towns through which the Americans had passed, were discovered on the flanks and in the rear, who had succeeded in capturing about ninety mules, laden with the provisions, the money, and clothing of the detachment It was also known that the road to Hueutla lay through a gorge flanked by steep acclivities, and that the prisoners had been removed. In this position of affairs, Colonel De Russey determined to retrace his steps with his small command.

After the retrograde movement commenced, the Mexicans began to harass the American rear, but they were always repulsed, with great loss, by Captain Mace, who poured upon them his volleys of musketry with good effect. On ascending a hill about one mile from Tantayuka, a desperate rush was made by the enemy, and the rear-guard was driven in. Captain Wyse promptly unlimbered his gun, and dispersed the Mexicans with two discharges of canister. In this manner the detachment returned to Tantayuka, keeping up a continued fight throughout the whole distance of nine miles. When they reached the town, the enemy appeared in their front to oppose them. The field-piece was again discharged, and again scattered the enemy in confusion.

Colonel De Russey now posted his men on a mound overlooking the town; powder and ball were procured at the stores; and a number of cartridges were prepared, by using champagne bottles, as a substitute for tin cylinders, which were half filled with balls, and the remaining space packed with earth. Musket cartridges for the infantry were also manufactured, and every preparation was made to defend the position. At nine o'clock on the night of the 12th, a message was received from General Garey demanding the im-

mediate surrender of the force. Colonel De Russey replied that this was impossible, and then informed the bearer of the message of the object of his visit. The latter stated, in answer, that there had been some misunderstanding in regard to the matter, and arranged an interview between General Garey and Colonel De Russey, to take place in a few hours. The Mexican officers failed to keep the appointment, and suspecting treachery, Colonel De Russey ordered his men under arms, and at two o'clock in the morning of the 13th continued his retreat towards Tampico, protected by the darkness. Shortly after daylight the enemy again appeared upon the flanks and rear of the detachment. Whenever they attempted to make a close attack they were driven off by the fire of the field-piece or muskets, though the pursuit was continued for more than fifty miles beyond Tantayuka. The detachment succeeded, however, in reaching Tampico, having lost, in the affair at the Calaboso river, and the subsequent retreat, fifteen killed and mortally wounded, ten wounded, and three missing.* The enemy lost nearly two hundred in killed and wounded.

During the absence of Colonel De Russey, Colonel Gates was informed of his critical situation, and it was also rumored that an attack upon Tampico was contemplated; whereupon, he immediately dispatched a messenger to Colonel Wilson, at Vera Cruz, with a request that he might be reinforced. There being no disposable troops belonging to the army, at that post, Commodore Perry sent a small party of marines to

* Among the killed, or mortally wounded, were Captain Boyd and Lieutenant Taneyhill. Having no surgeon or means of transportation, Colonel De Russey was compelled to leave Lieutenant Taneyhill and two privates, all mortally wounded, at the house of the alcalde in Tantayuka, where every attention was paid to their wants.

Tampico. In the meantime Colonel Gates had ordered a reinforcement of one hundred and fifty men to move up the Panuco to the support of Colonel De Russey, who did not effect a junction with the latter until after the enemy had ceased to molest his command. The alarm at Tampico did not entirely subside for a number of weeks. The ordinary supplies of the market were nearly cut off, and General Garey was reported to be moving upon the town with 3,000 troops. On the 29th of July the schooner Petrel, Lieutenant Moore in command, proceeded up the Panuco, in tow of the steamer Undine, with a detachment of marines on board, and a field-piece in addition to her armament; but she returned without accomplishing any thing, except that the enemy were intimidated from making any attack upon Tampico, if it had been in contemplation.*

Exaggerated rumors of the approach of large bodies of troops constantly reached the American camp at Buena Vista, where General Wool remained in command, during the summer of 1847. General Urrea was known to be at Tula with about 1,500 troops, and after General Valencia was ordered to Mexico, with his division, General Filisola was left at San Luis Potosi with 3,000 men. Canales also roamed about the country with several hundred men, always taking care, however, to keep out of the way of harm. Most of the rumors in circulation had reference to the movements of one or more of these commanders, and par-

* Towards the latter part of November, the Indian population near Huejutla rose against the troops stationed there, and commenced murdering the white inhabitants. The latter were now very willing to implore aid from the American commander at Tampico. Notwithstanding their former treacherous behavior, Colonel Gates humanely sent Captain West, with two companies of the Louisiana volunteers, to their assistance.

ties were frequently dispatched in different directions, to obtain information. In July, a detachment was sent to Parras to capture Señor Aguirre, Governor of the State of Coahuila, but they came back without His Excellency, though bringing with them a quantity of captured provisions.

In the expectation of being ordered to advance into the interior, General Taylor directed a camp of instruction to be formed at Mier, early in the summer, in order to have his troops ready for active duty in the field. The camp was organized by General Hopping, who was placed in command of the upper district on the Rio Grande—Colonel Davenport, of the 1st infantry, being assigned to the lower district. Colonel Belknap, of the 8th infantry, was ordered to take the immediate charge of the camp, but before it had fairly gone into operation, General Taylor received orders to detach a large portion of his troops to reinforce the column under General Scott. The brilliant results which had attended the operations of the General-in-Chief on the line of the National Road, and the necessity of opening his communications with the sea-coast, rendered it as necessary as it was advisable, to strengthen his column without delay. Several new volunteer regiments had previously joined General Taylor, together with three regiments of infantry raised under the ten regiment bill, and a part of the 3rd dragoons.

Instructions were received by General Taylor, in August, to send all his disposable troops to Vera Cruz; and, in accordance therewith, General Cushing, with his brigade, consisting of the 13th infantry, Colonel Echols, and the Massachusetts volunteers, Colonel Wright; and General Lane, with the 4th Ohio, Colonel Brough, and 4th Indiana, Colonel Gorman, forming the brigade under his command; together with five companies of Texan rangers, under Colonel Hays, were ordered to embark forthwith from the Rio Grande. General Marshall was also directed to join General Scott, with two regiments of Kentucky volunteers, recently enrolled, and on their way to Vera Cruz.

After the departure of these troops, General Taylor had about 6,000 men under his command, including ten companies of regular dragoons, belonging to different regiments; and nine companies of regular artillery, also belonging to different regiments, and serving with batteries, or garrisoning the forts on the Rio Grande. Besides the regular cavalry, there were five companies of Texas horse, and four companies of mounted volunteers from different states. The 10th infantry, Colonel Temple, was ordered to garrison Matamoras and Camargo. Colonel Butler, with the companies of the 3rd dragoons, was also stationed on the Rio Grande. Colonel Tibbatts garrisoned Monterey with six companies of the 16th infantry, and the remaining four companies of his regiment occupied Seralvo. Lieutenant Colonel Fauntleroy, with his squadron of the 2nd dragoons, and the battery of Lieutenant Colonel Bragg, were stationed at General Taylor's camp at Walnut Springs. At Buena Vista and Saltillo, were the Virginia and North Carolina regiments, under Colonels Hamtranck and Paine, and the 2nd Mississippi rifles, Colonel R. Davis, with the heavy battery of Captain Prentiss, the light battery of Captain Deas, and several companies of regular and volunteer cavalry, all under the orders of General Wool.

A forward movement from the line of the Sierra

Madre being now abandoned, for the present, General Taylor, at his own request, was permitted to return home in November,—leaving General Wool in command, who transferred his head-quarters to Monterey.

CHAPTER XVI.

THE GULF SQUADRON.

Expedition against Tuspan—Capture of the Town—The Carmelita—Recapture of Tabasco—Repeated Skirmishes with the Enemy—Affair at Timulte—Abandonment of the City—Difficulties in Yucatan.

AFTER his return from Alvarado, Commodore Perry did not allow the vessels belonging to the Gulf Squadron to remain for a long time rolling lazily at anchor in the roadstead of Vera Cruz,—swinging slowly with the ebb and flow of the tide, or tossing uneasily when the breath of the fitful norther swept over the foaming waters. Immediate preparations were made for an expedition against Tuspan, and as soon as every thing could be got in readiness, he left Vera Cruz with the steamers Mississippi, Spitfire, Vixen, and Scourge; the frigate Raritan; sloops of war John Adams, Albany, Germantown, and Decatur; bomb-vessels Vesuvius, Ætna, and Hecla; and the schooners, or gunboats, Bonita, Petrel, and Reefer. Nearly 500 men belonging to the Ohio and Potomac, both of which remained off Vera Cruz, were distributed among the different vessels.

The steamers were obliged to wait, for some days, at the island of Lobos, for the arrival of the sailing vessels; and a brief delay afterwards took place, in consequence of the dispersion of the squadron by a norther. But all was ready for the landing, on the morning of the 18th of April,—the day on which the heights of Cerro Gordo were carried by the troops under General Scott. The Mississippi anchored off the bar of Tuspan river; the small steamers—their masts being taken out, and otherwise lightened—took the gunboats and barges in tow, carrying in all 1,200 men, armed with cutlasses, pistols, and muskets, and two pieces of field artillery; and the other vessels of the squadron remained at anchor under Tuspan shoals, from six to eight miles eastward of the bar.

The Spitfire, under Captain Tatnall, led the way over the bar, followed by the Vixen and Scourge, each having a gunboat in tow. Two of the steamers struck; but they soon ploughed their way over the sand, and dashed through the breakers. At noon the whole flotilla had entered the river. Commodore Perry then hoisted his broad pennant on board the Spitfire, and commenced the ascent of the stream. About five miles from the mouth of the river, two forts were discovered, on the right bank, the guns of which began to play briskly upon the squadron. The small boats were immediately manned with storming parties, and darted for the shore, under cover of a rapid fire from the steamers and gunboats. The Mexicans did not wait to meet the assailants, but retreated down one side of the hill, as the gallant tars from the American vessels sprang up the other, shouting and cheering at the top of their voices. The forts being captured, the flotilla again moved forward.

On approaching Tuspan, another fort erected on a high hill, commanding the town, opened on the squadron. Volleys of musketry were fired, at the same time, from the thickets of chaparral on the bank of the river. Two parties were now landed; one of whom proceeded against the fort, which was carried without serious resistance, and the other entered the town. Most of the inhabitants had fled into the interior, and but very few soldiers were seen, who were brave enough to stand, even for a few moments, before the American fire. Commodore Perry took possession of the town, having lost but seventeen men, killed and wounded, during the day, and ordered the forts on the river to be destroyed.* Those inhabitants who were peaceably disposed, were invited to return and resume their occupations; and on the 22nd instant, the Commodore re-embarked his forces, and set sail for Vera Cruz, leaving the Albany and Reefer, under Captain Breese, to guard the river and town, and also directing one of his vessels to blockade the stream on which the town of Soto de Marina is situated.

The attempt of the Mexican government to annoy American commerce, by the issue of letters of marque, was wholly unsuccessful. Early in the spring of 1846, the Carmelita, a merchant vessel, was seized on the high seas and carried into Barcelona, by an armed vessel, called the Unico, claiming to cruise under Mexican authority. The alleged prize was at once restored by the Spanish authorities, and the captors were imprisoned for trial.† This was the only capture made by the enemy, and the American merchantmen pursued their way, from shore to shore, unmolested, while our

* Several guns of the Truxton, which, it will be recollected, was lost on the bar at the mouth of Tuspan river, in the summer of 1846, were found mounted in the forts. These, with a number of other articles belonging to the same vessel, were all recovered, and taken away by the squadron.

† Annual Report of the Secretary of the Navy, December 6th, 1847.

vessels of war continued the rigid blockade of the Mexican ports.

The next enterprise of any moment, undertaken by Commodore Perry, was a visit to Tabasco, whose citizens had threatened the population of Fronteira with their vengeance, for daring to hold intercourse with the American vessels. The Ætna and Bonita, under Commander Van Brunt, were sent to protect the place soon after the capture of Tuspan, and on the 1st of June the Spitfire left Vera Cruz, and arrived at Fronteira on the 3rd instant, where she remained until the 11th. She then ran down the coast, fringed with the rich Campeachy dye-woods, and adorned with the beautiful forests,—

> "Where the palm tapers, and the orange glows,
> Where the light bamboo weaves her feathery screen,
> And her far shade the matchless *ceiba* throws!—

to Laguna, the highest port of Yucatan,* sixty miles distant from Fronteira. The steamer Scorpion, bomb-vessel Hecla, and a gunboat, under Commander Bigelow, were at Laguna; and on the 12th instant, the Spitfire returned to Fronteira, in company with the Scorpion, to take part in an expedition up the river.

Commodore Perry reached Fronteira with the Mississippi, and the other vessels of the attacking squadron, on the 13th instant; and, at sunset on the following day, the flotilla of small steamers and gunboats weighed anchor, and commenced ascending the stream. Commodore Perry, in the Scorpion, with the brig Wash-

* Yucatan signified her willingness to reunite with the other Mexican States, under the constitution adopted after the return of Santa Anna; but she took very little part in the war. Supplies had been shipped from Laguna, but this could not be continued after the blockade of the port.

ington and bomb-vessel Vesuvius in tow, moved in advance; followed by the Spitfire, with the bomb-vessel Stromboli, and the Bonita; the Vixen, having the Ætna in tow; and the Scourge, with a schooner containing the apparatus of Captain Taylor to lighten the vessels over any obstruction in the river. Each vessel towed from ten to twenty small boats, loaded down to the gunwales with armed sailors and marines, and field artillery. The whole force amounted to about 1,500 men, and the aquatic procession, which was nearly six miles in length, presented a most imposing sight, as it wound up the crooked stream.

At sunset on the 15th, the flotilla arrived within five hundred yards of the "Devil's Bend," near which obstacles had been sunk to prevent the ascent of the river. Here they were suddenly hailed by volleys of musketry fired from the thick screen of mangrove-trees on the starboard bank. Streams of grape and canister were instantly poured upon the enemy, who soon deserted the bushes; and the vessels then came to anchor for the night. A straggling fire was kept up, but no attempt was made to attack the Americans, who had prepared themselves against a surprise.

The morning of the 16th dawned beautifully, and the fragrant and balmy breeze that stole through the branches of the tall palms bending so gracefully over the stream, scarcely disturbed its silvery current. Lieutenant May was now ordered forward with a boat's crew to sound the river, and the other vessels followed to protect him. While engaged in making the soundings, the party were fired upon from a concealed breastwork, which was silenced by the guns of the squadron. Commodore Perry then determined to land a part of his force, and assault the town in rear, while the vessels should move up and attack it in front. At eleven o'clock the commodore put off for the shore, with 800 men in sixty barges, and eight six-pounder guns. An irregular militia force,* under General Bruno, had been organized to defend the approaches to Tabasco, but the landing was not seriously opposed. The Americans sprang up the steep banks of the river, with deafening shouts, dragging the field-pieces after them, and dashed along the road leading to the town, but four miles distant by the land route.†

The vessels remained at anchor for about two hours, when they again moved up the river, running over the bar in nine feet water, and turning up some of the piles which formed the chevaux-de-frise. The drums beat to quarters, and the men all took their stations, anticipating a warm reception from the enemy. On turning the bend below Fort Accachappa, its heavy twenty-four-pounders sent forth a thundering peal, which was promptly answered by the long guns of the flotilla, whose shot and shell told with singular precision. Volleys of musketry were also rained incessantly from the bushes, and the carbines of the Americans were soon actively served. In a few moments the Mexican flag was struck; three or four rounds of short-fused shell and grape were thrown from the Spitfire; and Lieutenant Porter then pulled for the shore with about

* The central government of Mexico made few or no attempts to aid the departments remote from the capital, and left them to rely mainly upon their own resources. Had the inhabitants of Tabasco been more united, the Americans would probably have found greater difficulty in capturing the town, but it has long been the theatre of incessant broils and strifes, and was poorly prepared to resist an invader.

† Commodore Perry landed upon the same spot where Cortés embarked a part of his force, under Avila, previous to his capture of Tabasco.

twenty men, and displayed the stripes and stars on the captured fort. The breastwork was pierced for four guns, three of them twenty-four-pounders, and the fourth a smaller piece. Three six-pounder field-pieces were also found in the fort, which were borne away as trophies,—the other guns being spiked.

In the meantime a party from the Scorpion had landed in the city, about half a mile further up, where they were met by the alcalde, who surrendered the place. A considerable force, under General Garcia, had been stationed in the city for its protection, and disregarding the action of the civil authorities, they commenced firing upon the Americans from the house-tops and corners of the streets. Midshipman Briceland broke a hole through the roof of the Governor's house, and planted the American flag amidst a shower of bullets. Commodore Perry shortly after came up with the land force, having driven the Mexican militia, from thicket to thicket, as he advanced; and the armed parties of the enemy now abandoned the town to the victors.

Leaving the Spitfire, Vixen, Scourge and Ætna, as guard-ships at Tabasco, Commodore Perry returned to Fronteira with the remainder of the flotilla. The Mexicans were not disposed to rest quiet, especially when so feeble a force was left to overawe them. Including the marines, the Americans could muster but 175 men to serve ashore. These were quartered in the main plaza, with three field-pieces, and the guns of the vessels were trained so as to rake the suburbs with shell. The Mexican guerilleros prowled about the town every night, plundering the citizens, and annoying the Americans on shore. During the day they secreted themselves in the thickets and thatched huts on the outskirts of the city, or in the neighboring villages. Several skirmishes took place, in the course of which a number of the light bamboo cottages were burned by the Americans. At length the latter became nearly worn out with incessant watching and fighting, and the Vixen was dispatched to Commodore Perry for assistance. She returned on the 29th of June, with a reinforcement of 100 sailors and marines; and on the 1st of July a force of 200 men, consisting of ninety marines, under Lieutenants Slack, Shuttleworth and Adams, the crew of the Spitfire under Lieutenant Porter, and a number of officers and volunteers, from the Scorpion, Ætna, and Scourge, with two field-pieces, marched against Timulte, a small village four miles from Tabasco. About five hundred of the Tabasco militia, under Generals Chigané and Garcia, were in ambuscade near the town, and fired upon the party as they approached. The contest was brief. The guns were fired but twice before the enemy were seen scattering through the bushes in flight. The sailors and marines pursued them till they were quite exhausted, when orders were given to return to Tabasco, where they arrived at sunset, having captured a large quantity of arms and ammunition, and killed and wounded from seventy-five to one hundred of the enemy, with the loss of only two men killed and four wounded.

Commodore Perry retained possession of Tabasco until the 22nd of July, when he ordered the place to be evacuated, not caring to expose the health of his men by the permanent occupation of the city. Many of the inhabitants, through fear of the ragged and half-starved soldiery, who had previously been quartered on them, accompanied the American vessels to Fronteira, where Commander Van Brunt was directed to remain, with the Scourge, Ætna, and Bonita, to guard the river and protect the inhabitants. Commodore Perry, with the rest of the squadron, returned to Vera Cruz.

During the further continuance of hostilities, the Gulf Squadron was principally employed in enforcing the blockade, and in affording relief to the white inhabitants of Yucatan. The Indian population of the department manifested symptoms of hostility early in the winter of 1847. A disturbance took place at Tzimizin in February, and a second one in July following. Subsequently the Indian population rose in a mass, and commenced an indiscriminate massacre of the whites. The latter were forced to fly to the seaports, and took refuge on board the vessels lying on the coast. Commodore Perry assisted them as far as he was able, and a treaty was finally concluded between the leading men of the two races, when quiet and order were restored.

CHAPTER XVII.

CLOSING SCENES OF THE WAR.

Defence of Puebla—Occupation of the Prominent Points on the National Road—March of General Lane to the Relief of Colonel Childs —Battle of Huamantla—Attack on Atlixco—The Guerilleros—Opening of General Scott's Communications—The Mexican Congress and Government—Negotiations Resumed—The Army in the Capital—Orders for the Collection of Taxes—Expedition to Tehuacan—Affairs in California—Capture of Guayamas and Mazatlan—Defence of La Paz and San José—March of General Price upon Chihuahua—Storming of Santa Cruz de Rosales.

Like the memorable retreat of the British army from Burgos, the evacuation of their capital by the Mexican forces was peculiarly unfortunate. Its consequences were more disastrous than the loss of a dozen pitched battles. The legitimate fruits of insubordination were speedily visible; and the murmur—at first low, but portentous--soon swelled into a loud and general outburst of discontent. There were angry disputes and altercations among the officers; and the leaven of strife, once animated, spread rapidly through the ranks. The National Guard disbanded by companies and regiments,—many of their number returning to the city, to mingle with the populace and excite them to vengeance,—some flying to join the guerilla bands on the line of the National road,—and others, who did not care again to incur the hazards and chances of war, escaping to the more distant sections of the country.

Santa Anna no longer possessed the ability to control the turbulent masses of which his army was composed; the spell, by which he had harmonized the discordant elements, was dissolved; his influence was gone—the wand of the magician broken. Accompanied by from three to four thousand infantry and lancers, he directed his course towards the city of Puebla, already threatened by a large force of irregular cavalry and guerilleros, under General Rea. General Alvarez, with about three thousand men, moved round the valley, into the State of Oajaca; and still another fragment of the once formidable array, consisting of cavalry, artillery and infantry, followed the movement to Queretaro, under General Herrera. While on his way to the new seat of government, the acting President, Peña y Peña, directed an order to be issued at Toluca, requiring Santa Anna to surrender the command of the forces under his immediate orders to General Rincon, until his conduct should be examined into by a military council. Before the order was received, he had once more learned how vain it was, how worse than useless, to struggle against his destiny.

When General Scott moved from Puebla upon the Mexican capital, it will be remembered, Colonel Childs was left in command at the former place, with a garrison composed of detachments from different regiments. His actual effective force numbered about 400, consisting of one company of the 3rd dragoons, under Captain Ford, one company of the 2nd and one of the 4th artillery, under Captains Kendrick and Miller, and six companies of the 1st Pennsylvania, under Lieutenant Colonel Black.* Besides these, however, there were 1,800 sick in the hospitals—a great number of whom

* Colonel Childs had, also, a company of Mexican spies, under Captain Arria, who did good service in the defence of the city.

were convalescent, or became so not long after the departure of the main army, and were capable, either of bearing arms, or of aiding, in some other manner, in the defence of the positions occupied by the garrison,—which was thus increased to near 1,400 men.

During the occupation of Puebla by the American forces, Atlixco became the seat of government of the state; guerilla expeditions, to operate in different directions, were fitted out here; and it was also the head-quarters of General Rea, who commanded the regular and irregular troops in this quarter. A tolerable degree of quiet prevailed in the city of Puebla, subsequent to the forward movement of General Scott, and while the armistice was in force,* except that, on the 26th of August, a large body of the enemy's cavalry appeared in sight, and captured and drove off a number of mules. A small party of twenty-six men, mostly teamsters, immediately mounted and started in pursuit. Within an hour's ride of the city, they were surrounded by the enemy, and nearly annihilated. Ten of the party were killed, several badly wounded, and a few taken prisoners.

After this occurrence, no further open act of hostility took place, although robberies were frequently committed by the guerilleros, in the city and its vicinity, until the night of the 13th of September, when a warm, but desultory fire, was opened from the main street leading to the Plaza, the Tivoli,† and the tops of

* The official dispatches of General Scott, communicating the events of the 19th and 20th of August, which were sent by carriers provided with passports from Santa Anna, while the armistice was in force, did not reach Puebla, in consequence of the guerilleros infesting the road.

† The Tivoli is one of the finest ornaments of Puebla. It is a most beautiful promenade, with three broad avenues, lined with stately trees, each separated by a stream of water.

CAPTAIN WALKER.

some of the neighboring houses, on the citadel of San José, within the protection of which the hospitals had been removed upon the first indications of an outbreak. The fire proceeded from the forces of General Rea, about 4,000 in number, who had entered the town in the course of the day, with a determination, in conjunction with the lower classes of the inhabitants, to force the Americans to abandon their positions.

San José was the head-quarters of Colonel Childs, and the principal dépôt of supplies. The immediate command of the post was intrusted to Lieutenant Colonel Black, who had with him four companies of the 1st Pennsylvania, Captain Ford's company of dragoons, Captain Miller's company of artillery, and a battery of mountain howitzers in charge of Lieutenant Laidley, of the ordnance. Two other prominent points in the city,—Fort Loretto, and the Convent of Guadaloupe,—were likewise garrisoned. The latter is the first object of importance that attracts the attention, as you enter the town by the National road, from the east; it is perched on an eminence, on the right, commanding the approaches in that direction, and has a ditch and revêtted wall around it; but, during the siege, it was in a dilapidated condition. Fort Loretto, on the same ridge, but lower, and further to the west, is a regular work, with four barbette batteries, one at each angle, which commands a great part of the city, and rakes the principal street. This was garrisoned by about 350 men, consisting of Captain Kendrick's company of artillery, Captain Hill's company of the 1st Pennsylvania, and a number of sick who were convalescent, with two twelve-pounder field guns, and a ten-inch mortar—the whole commanded by Major Gwynn, of the 6th infantry. Captain Morehead, of the 1st Pennsylvania, occupied the Convent of Guadaloupe, with one company of his regiment; a number of sick, convalescent; and two mountain howitzers, under Lieutenant Edwards, of the 2nd artillery.

The fire of the enemy on the night of the 13th of September, was briskly returned by Lieutenant Colonel Black, who remained with his command, including the inmates of the hospital able to carry muskets, on the roofs of San José and the adjacent buildings, till the morning of the 14th. At night the firing recommenced with more spirit and warmth, and was continued day after day, and night after night, until the garrison were almost worn out with watching and exposure. The number of the assailants was augmented daily, and their fire grew more intense. On the 22nd instant, Santa Anna arrived with the troops who had followed him from Mexico; and the domes and towers of the cathedral, its dark gray walls of porphyry, and the spires and roofs of the humbler church edifices in the city, were vocal with the merry peals rung forth to welcome his approach. A prompt discharge of shells and round-shot from Fort Loretto, which had several times silenced unusual disturbances in the city, or checked the enemy's fire when it became too hot, soon put an end to the ringing of the bells.

The enemy, with their numerous cavalry, had succeeded, at the commencement of the siege, in cutting off all kinds of supplies; but they vainly attempted to change the current of the stream of water on which the Americans depended. Fortunately, the latter had secured four hundred sheep and thirty head of cattle, the very night before the flocks and herds disappeared from the vicinity. Still, it seemed as if that feeble garrison must fall an easy prey to the numerous army that had invested the posts they occupied. Yet, notwithstanding their precarious position, they were animated by the best spirit, and, with a bold and determined front, an undoubting confidence, and a courage of mailed proof, they awaited the general assault which they supposed would shortly be made.*

On the 23rd instant, a dropping fire was kept up on San José; and a part of the enemy's forces were sent against Guadaloupe, but they were repulsed with severe loss, and retired in great haste and disorder. A second attempt was made on the convent, in the afternoon of the 24th, by a party about 500 strong, under a general officer, who approached within one hundred and fifty yards of the breastwork, and discharged their pieces. A brisk fire dispersed them in a moment, with the loss of ten men killed, and a much greater number wounded. Fort Loretto remained unmolested, though its guns rendered essential service, in checking the constant shower of bullets poured from the streets and balconies, the house-tops and churches, upon the garrison of San José.

On the 25th of September, Santa Anna summoned Colonel Childs to surrender, informing him that there were 8,000 men in his vicinity, but offering to permit him and his command, if they evacuated the city within a certain time, to join General Scott, or the garrison of Perote. But one reply could be given to the summons;—where duty pointed, there inclination led the

* "Never did troops endure more fatigue, by watching night after night, for more than thirty successive nights, nor exhibit more patience, spirit, and gallantry. Not a post of danger could present itself, but the gallant fellows were ready to fill it. Not a sentinel could be shot, but another was anxious and ready to take his place. Officers and soldiers vied with each other, to be honored martyrs in their country's cause."—Official report of Colonel Childs, October, 13th 1847.

way. Colonel Childs assured the Mexican commander, on the same day, that his means were ample; and that, as he had been left to guard the positions held by his troops, he should defend them to the last. He then rode to the different posts, and communicated both the summons and reply to his men, who gave the latter a most cordial and hearty response.

Contrary to the expectations of the American troops, no attack was made on the night of the 25th, or on the following day. On the 27th, the assault was resumed, and a heavy cannonade was opened from San Juan de Dios, and the convents of Santa Rosa, and Santa Monica. A constant fire was now kept up from Fort Loretto, from which the city and the inhabitants suffered severely. Infantry pickets were also detailed from the fort, who became warmly engaged with parties of the enemy. In the morning of the 29th, Lieutenant Lewis sallied out from Guadaloupe, with a party, and attacked a body of Mexicans firing on San José; after a sharp conflict, in which eight of the enemy were killed, and a great number wounded, a shower of rain compelled him to retire. Another successful sally was made from the same point, in the afternoon, by a party under Lieutenant Bryan.

During the night of the 29th, Santa Anna placed two six-pounders in battery, above the Tivoli, protected by a breastwork of cotton bags, which opened with much spirit on San José, in the morning of the 30th instant. In anticipation of this movement, Colonel Childs had thrown up a traverse on the Plaza, and withdrawn a twelve-pounder from Fort Loretto, with which he returned the enemy's fire. Throughout the day the firing was animated and incessant; but, failing to make any impression on the American works, the Mexican guns ceased playing towards nightfall, and on the morning of the 1st of October, Santa Anna marched out from the city with his troops, and three pieces of artillery, to meet the reinforcements understood to be hastening up from the coast, to the relief of Colonel Childs. General Rea remained with his forces, and continued the attack with vigor and zeal.

Reinforcements for the column under General Scott were constantly arriving at Vera Cruz, during the summer and fall, and were dispatched as rapidly as possible into the interior, to open his communications, and, if necessary, to join the main body of the army. Colonel Hughes, of the Maryland and District of Columbia volunteers, left Vera Cruz on the 6th of September, with a battalion of his regiment, one company of the 11th and one of the 12th infantry, and 100 Louisiana cavalry--in all 400 strong—together with two pieces of artillery. The guerilleros were discovered, as usual, at the Robbers' Den; but they did not attempt to impede his march. On the 9th instant, the command approached the National Bridge, when the enemy's heads were seen peeping over the fortifications on the heights. The guns were immediately planted within six hundred yards of the fort, but the Mexicans were found to be posted too high to be reached by their fire; whereupon Colonel Hughes ordered the hill to be carried with the bayonet. Major Kenley moved up in reverse with three companies,—his men laying aside their jackets and knapsacks, and carrying nothing but their arms and canteens. Nearly three hours were spent in climbing the steep ascent, which could only be done by clinging to the roots, and the long trailing vines of the dark purple grape, that were spread all over the hill-side. On reaching the crest, the party paused a few seconds for breath, and then dashed into the fort which the enemy had hurriedly evacuated. Having thus driven the Mexicans from the position, Colonel Hughes established his troops at this point, to keep the road open.

Colonel Collins, of the 5th Illinois, followed the command of Colonel Hughes in a few days, with a part of his regiment, and a detachment of Louisiana rangers, under Captain Fairchild, and took post at the Rio Frio. He was once attacked by the guerilleros, but repulsed them with loss. On the 10th of September, Captain Heintzleman, of the 2nd infantry, left Vera Cruz, with a mixed command of 350 men, and halted, temporarily, at the San Juan river. General Lane took up the line of march, on the 19th instant, with over 1,700 men,—his command consisting of the 4th Ohio, Colonel Brough; 4th Indiana, Colonel Gorman; Captain Lewis' company of Louisiana cavalry; and a detachment of recruits for different regiments of regulars, under Captain Simmons; together with the light batteries of Captain Taylor, of the 3rd artillery, and Lieutenant Pratt, of the 2nd artillery. On approaching the San Juan, a party of guerilleros was discovered near the hacienda of Santa Anna, and Captain Lewis was detached with his company in pursuit; Lieutenant Lilley, with a part of the company, came up with the enemy, and a smart skirmish ensued, in which the Mexicans were severely worsted. On leaving Paso de Ovejas, also, the rear-guard was fired upon by a small guerilla force, and a brief conflict took place, in which Lieutenant Kline, of Captain Lewis' company, was killed. The enemy were again driven off, and the command continued their march, having been joined by the detachment under Captain Heintzleman.

General Lane left a portion of the Indiana regiment, under Major McCoy, at the Puente Nacional; but, upon his arrival at the Plan del Rio, on the 27th of September, he learned that Major Lally, then at Jalapa, had received orders to move forward to Puebla with all possible speed. General Lane instantly sent an express back to the National Bridge, with orders for Major McCoy to join him at once with all the disposable troops at the post, except the battalion of Colonel Hughes' regiment. When Major McCoy came up, the column pressed rapidly forward towards Puebla, through Jalapa and Perote, taking with them the troops under Major Lally and Colonel Wynkoop. At Perote, General Lane was informed that a large force was concentrating in his front, and, on reaching the hacienda of San Antonio Tamaris, on the morning of the 9th of October, he learned that the enemy were at the city of Huamantla, which lies between Perote and Puebla, and a little east of the National road.

Leaving his train at San Antonio Tamaris, guarded by the Ohio regiment, Captain Simmons' detachment, and Lieutenant Pratt's battery, General Lane advanced against Huamantla, where Santa Anna was concentrating his forces, for the last time, as it proved, during the war, to encounter an American commander. The force moving upon Huamantla was something more than 2,000 strong,* and consisted of four companies of the 1st Pennsylvania, under Colonel Wynkoop; Colonel Gorman's Indiana volunteers; the detachments under Major Lally, and Captains Heintzleman and Simmons; four companies of mounted rifles and

* General Lane's whole command numbered about 3,300.

volunteer cavalry, under Captains Walker, Besançon, Loyall, and Lewis; and five pieces of artillery, under Captain Taylor. The Americans arrived near the city about one o'clock in the afternoon, and General Lane then ordered Captain Walker to move ahead of the column with the cavalry companies, but to keep within supporting distance, and, if the enemy were in force, to wait for the infantry to close up.

When within three miles of the city, parties of horsemen were seen making their way towards it, through the fields, and Captain Walker advanced at a gallop:—owing to the dense thickets of maguey lining the road, it was impossible to distinguish his further movements, from the main column; but, in a few moments, a sharp, quick firing was heard in the direction of the town. At the same time a body of lancers, supposed to be over 2,000 strong, commanded by Santa Anna in person, were observed moving rapidly over the hills, in a line parallel with the march of the American troops, as if striving to reach the city before them. General Lane immediately hurried forward, with the remainder of his troops, at a run. Colonel Gorman was directed to enter the west side of the city with his regiment; while Colonel Wynkoop's battalion and the artillery, having Captain Heintzleman's detachment on their right, moved towards the east side. The command of Major Lally was held in reserve.

On gaining the entrance of the city, Captain Walker discovered about five hundred of the enemy, with three pieces of artillery, in the Plaza, and ordered a charge. His men rushed forward gallantly, routed the Mexicans in an instant, and drove them from their guns. While the command were scattered in the pursuit, and conse quently somewhat in disorder, Santa Anna fell upon them with his lancers. A fierce hand-to-hand conflict took place, in which the American cavalry sustained considerable loss. Captain Walker was killed fighting bravely; but his men held the ground manfully, though unable to fire the captured guns, from the want of priming tubes. Colonel Gorman, however, had now arrived with the Indiana volunteers, and opened a well-directed fire on the enemy. Their line soon wavered and broke. Before Colonel Wynkoop and the artillery came within range, they were completely dispersed, the city was in possession of the American troops, and the colors of the Indiana regiment planted on the arsenal. Two of the Mexican pieces were captured; together with a large quantity of ammunition, and a number of wagons, which General Lane ordered to be destroyed. The enemy lost one hundred and fifty, killed and wounded, in this affair; and the Americans thirteen killed and eleven wounded. A number of prisoners were also taken, among whom were Colonel La Vega, and Major Iturbide,—the latter a son of the former Emperor of Mexico.

Having rejoined his train, General Lane proceeded to Puebla, where he arrived on the 12th of October. As his troops approached the city, a rapid firing was heard, which assured him that Colonel Childs was not yet entirely vanquished. Feeling confident, therefore, that his force was strong enough to enter the town at once, he directed Colonel Brough, with the Ohio regiment and Captain Heintzleman's detachment, to proceed along the main road, and Colonel Gorman, with the Indiana volunteers, to feel his way cautiously into the city, further to the east and left.

The attack on the American posts in Puebla, was

continued, without cessation, after the departure of Santa Anna. On the 2nd of October, Colonel Childs availed himself of the reduction of the enemy's numbers, to make a sortie against some barricades and buildings, the fire from which had become very annoying. One of the expeditions was confided to Captain Small, of the 1st Pennsylvania, who passed through the walls of an entire square, by the aid of picks and crowbars, with fifty men, gained a position opposite one of the largest barricades, and drove the enemy from behind it with great loss,—they leaving seventeen dead on the ground. The barricade, consisting of one hundred and fifty bales of cotton, was consumed ; and Captain Small retained possession of a prominent building near it, for twenty-four hours, when it was blown up by Lieutenant Laidley. Another expedition was intrusted to Lieutenant Morgan, of the 14th infantry, with a detachment of marines and Lieutenant Merrifield, of the 15th infantry, with a party of rifles. They attempted to gain possession of certain buildings from which a galling fire was constantly poured, but were only partially successful, and returned again to San José. On the 5th instant, Captain Herron, of the 1st Pennsylvania, was detached with his company to take possession of a building, from which the enemy had been enfilading the Plaza, and accomplished it in a handsome manner. Successful sorties were also made from Guadaloupe, on the 6th and 8th, by Lieutenant Edwards and Captain Johnson, with small parties.

The assailants were largely reinforced on the 8th instant; the supplies of the garrison were growing low; and affairs began to assume a still more critical aspect. Still, there were no symptoms of giving way, and none proposed a surrender. The Mexicans made a close demonstration in the afternoon of the 8th, but were promptly met and repulsed. On the 10th, hostilities were suspended; a few scattering shots were thrown until the night of the 11th; and on the following morning the enemy began to retire from their positions. The movement had already commenced when General Lane arrived with his reinforcements, and opened his fire on the disappointed troops of General Rea. Meanwhile Lieutenant Colonel Black had moved down the main street, with two companies of the 1st Pennsylvania, under Captains Hill and Herron, to silence a warm fire still kept up near the Plaza. At his approach, a body of lancers fled down a cross street, and Captain Herron was directed to move round the square with his company, and cut off their retreat. Whilst hastening to execute the order, Captain Herron was suddenly surrounded by over five hundred lancers, who charged upon him from the lanes and cross-streets intersecting the road along which he was moving; his men fought with the utmost desperation, losing thirteen killed and four wounded; but they were at length rescued from their perilous situation by the timely arrival of Lieutenant Colonel Black, with Captain Hill's company, who had moved upon the enemy in front.

The long-continued siege of the posts occupied by the American troops in the city of Puebla, was now terminated. Their anxiety and suspense were at an end. Although they had lost but nineteen killed and fifty-one wounded during the attack,* and had never doubted their ability to maintain the position; yet, their emotions can be more easily conceived than expressed,

* From the nature of the case, it was impossible to ascertain the extent of the enemy's loss, in the course of the siege. It has been estimated at from 500 to 1,000 killed and wounded.

when they caught sight of the glistening sabres, the flashing bayonets, and the victorious banners of General Lane, as his columns wound through the now almost deserted streets; and when his trumpets sounded their shrill notes of defiance, every man breathed "freer and deeper," and felt prouder of his country, of her honor and fame.

On the evening of the 18th of October, General Lane learned that General Rea was then quartered at Atlixco, about ten leagues distant, with a considerable force, and immediately made preparations for a forced march on that place on the ensuing day. At eleven o'clock in the forenoon of the 19th, he left Puebla with the 4th Ohio, Colonel Brough; the 4th Indiana, Colonel Gorman; a battalion of the 1st Pennsylvania, Colonel Wynkoop; the battalions of Major Lally and Captain Heintzleman; the batteries of Captain Taylor and Lieutenant Pratt; and a squadron of dragoons, under Captain Ford.

General Lane's column pressed forward all day, at a rapid rate, though exposed to the broiling sun, which beat fiercely on their heads; and at four o'clock in the afternoon they reached Santa Isabella, three leagues from Atlixco, where the Mexican advance guard was posted. The enemy's outposts were driven in by the dragoons, who pursued them for more than a mile. They then made a stand on a small hill, and contested the ground warmly, until the American infantry appeared, when they continued their retreat. A running fight was kept up for four miles, and, within a mile and a half of Atlixco, the main body of the enemy were discovered posted on the side of a hill covered with thick chaparral. The American dragoons dismounted, and fought on foot, cutting and hewing the way with their sabres. The contest was severe and bloody, and the hill-side was strewn with the dead bodies of the Mexican guerilleros. The infantry, nearly exhausted, and panting for breath, having strained every nerve for the last six miles, soon arrived, and the enemy again retreated. The artillery took no part in the skirmishing, as the road was intersected by such deep gulleys that they could only advance at a walk.

Although his horses and men were almost overcome, General Lane followed like a sleuth-hound on the track. Notwithstanding their utmost efforts, his troops were unable to reach Atlixco before the night had set in. The moon was shining gloriously, however; and its softened light came down pure and clear, through the highly rarified atmosphere of that elevated clime, throwing out the prominent objects in bolder relief, and enveloping the shadows in still deeper gloom. Several shots were fired upon the Americans as they approached the town, but General Lane deemed it unwise to risk a street fight, in a place of which he and his men were so entirely ignorant. He therefore ordered the batteries to be brought up, and to open their fire. A most picturesque sight was now presented, and it might even have been considered beautiful, were it not for the blazing roofs and tumbling walls, the shrieking women and affrighted children. The cannonade was continued for about three-quarters of an hour, and Colonel Brough and Major Lally were then ordered to advance with care and caution. The ayuntamiento soon made their appearance, and begged that the town might be spared. General Lane listened to their request, and suspended his operations. In the morning search was made for arms and ammunition, quantities of which were found and destroyed.

General Rea made his escape from Atlixco with 400 guerilleros; but the stroke was as effectual, as it was bold and well-executed. The inhabitants of the town had hitherto clamored loudly for a continuance of the war, but, now that its terrors were brought to their own firesides, they began to assume a more pacific tone. General Lane lost but one man killed, and one wounded, during the day;—while the enemy had 219 killed, and about 300 wounded. On his return to Puebla, he learned, when at Cholula, that two pieces of artillery had just been finished at Guexocingo, whither he proceeded with a portion of his command, and destroyed the carriages,—the guns having been previously removed by the enemy.

Bands of guerilleros still hovered in the neighborhood of Puebla, after the arrival of General Lane with reinforcements, and the consequent raising of the siege. The official reports of General Scott were repeatedly intercepted;* and on the 19th of October, Lieutenant Sears, of the 2nd artillery, on his way down from Puebla, with dispatches, escorted by a Mexican spy company, under Captain, or, as he is sometimes called, Colonel Dominguez, was attacked near that city by a large force under General Torrejon. Having beaten off the enemy, he proceeded on his course; but, on encountering another body under Colonel Vamos, within a short distance, he was obliged to return, having lost fifteen killed and wounded in the two engagements. The enemy's loss

* The first information received of the battles in the valley of Mexico, on the 8th, 13th and 14th of September, came through Mexican sources, and, of course, was greatly exaggerated and untrue.

was near one hundred. The escort accompanying the bearer of dispatches was now joined by a part of the 1st Pennsylvania, under Colonel Wynkoop, who proceeded as far as the Plan del Rio, and soon after returned with General Patterson.

But the plundering propensities, and hostile feelings of the guerilleros, were not manifested alone towards the Americans, and those connected with them. On the 8th of November, a train of thirty-six wagons, containing merchandise belonging to merchants in Puebla and Mexico, left the former place on their way to the capital. On reaching San Martin, Generals Rea and Torrejon made a descent upon the train, with a guerilla force, and captured it. Information of this transaction was speedily conveyed to General Lane, at Puebla, who forthwith started in pursuit of the marauders, with a party of cavalry and infantry. At Tlascala he overtook the enemy, who were proceeding towards Queretaro with their booty. Captain Roberts, of the mounted rifles, in command of the cavalry, fell upon a portion of the guerilleros, who were attempting to run off the train, and routed them, with ease,—killing seventeen of their number, and taking thirteen officers prisoners. The wagons, except a number which had been destroyed, together with their contents, were recaptured.

General Patterson arrived at Vera Cruz, with large reinforcements, shortly after General Lane left for the interior. In pursuance of special instructions from the War Department, he took effectual measures to clear the road of the guerilleros, and to open the communications of General Scott.

For the greater part of the distance between Vera Cruz and the mountainous country, the roads traversing the low level are lined, on either side, by almost impervious thickets of chaparral, with openings, at rare intervals, through which glimpses may be obtained of the lovely sylvan bowers of the *tierra caliente*, spangled with flowers, and overhung with the arching trees loaded down with their abundant foliage, and the gay vines and creepers lovingly entwined about their branches. These thickets are intersected by narrow, blind paths, running hither and thither, and forming a maze as intricate as the windings of the Cretan labyrinth. Leading, as they do, to the haunts of the bandits and guerilleros, they are familiar to those who use them, in the darkest night. They thus serve, both as a covert from which an enemy may be fired on unseen, and as hiding-places in which it is easy to elude pursuit; and had those who frequented them, during the war with the United States, been animated only by that noble and exalted feeling of patriotism, which nerves the arm, and strengthens the heart, the losses of the American army would have been far greater, and more terrible and severe.

Father Jarauta, who seems to have been the leading chieftain among the guerilleros, from Perote to the Gulf, had given orders to his men to shoot every person who carried provisions into Vera Cruz. He had, doubtless, a twofold object in view:—to stop the supplies, and to excite the population to join his rapidly diminishing band. But his plans were soon defeated by the active and vigilant measures of General Patterson. The country between the Jalapa and Orizaba roads, was thoroughly scoured by the Texan rangers, under Colonel Hays, at all times the terror of the guerilleros, and the other volunteer cavalry. A great number of the bandits were killed; their haunts and dépôts were broken up; and large stores of arms and ammunition were captured and destroyed.

Having effectually routed the guerilla bands, for the present, General Patterson left Vera Cruz, to join General Scott, with nearly 4,000 troops. When he reached the National Bridge, he received a message from Father Jarauta, making proposals for a surrender,* which he declined; accompanying his reply, however, with some wholesome advice, counselling him to keep out of reach, or to forsake his occupation, if he hoped to secure favor or commiseration, should the chances of war place him in the power of the American soldiers. The 13th infantry, Colonel Echols, and the light battery of the Maryland and District of Columbia regiment, under Captain Tilghman, which had accompanied General Patterson from Vera Cruz, remained at the Puente Nacional, and the remainder of the column pushed on to Jalapa, whither Colonel Wynkoop had returned from the Plan del Rio, with his command.

While at Jalapa, on the 24th of October, General Patterson caused two Mexican officers, who had been found in command of guerilla parties, in violation of paroles previously given, to be executed. The General was earnestly besought to spare them, by the clergy, and the principal citizens of Jalapa, but refused to pardon, well knowing that the lesson would not be lost on others situated like themselves, many of whom were directly or indirectly connected with the guerilla

* The proposition of Jarauta was perhaps made, on account of the dissensions among the guerilleros. His own immediate band was mostly composed of Spaniards, while Colonel Zenobio commanded a party of native Mexicans. A serious difficulty happened in October, that terminated in a fight between the two bands, in which the Mexicans were sadly beaten

movements.* These officers with two others, were captured on the night of the 19th of October, by Colonel Wynkoop. He had learned that the Indian town of Halcomulco, thirty miles from Jalapa, was a noted haunt of the guerilleros, and set out for that place in the evening with a party of Texan rangers, under Captain Witt. Coming suddenly upon the enemy's pickets he forced them to act as guides, and entered the town. The officers were surprised in their beds; and, having secured his prisoners, Colonel Wynkoop was on his way back to Jalapa before sunrise.

General Cushing was left in command at Jalapa, with the Massachusetts regiment, and a detachment of mounted men; and General Patterson then moved forward towards Mexico, being joined by the 1st Pennsylvania. He arrived at the capital with his reinforcements about the 1st of December—the last of his command reaching the city on the 8th instant.

General Butler reached Vera Cruz, on his way to the head-quarters of the army, on the 17th of November. As soon as his arrangements could be completed, he marched for the capital, with about 5,000 men, who had recently arrived from the United States. Colonel Hughes was now ordered forward to Jalapa with his regiment, and General Cushing, with the Massachusetts volunteers, was directed to proceed to Mexico. At Puebla, General Butler was also reinforced by the column of General Lane; and, on the 19th of December, they joined the main body of the army under General Scott. Towards the close of the month, General

* General Patterson was equally firm where his own men were liable to punishment. On the day previous to the execution of the Mexi can officers, two American teamsters, whom he also refused to pardon were hung for killing a Mexican boy.

Marshall left Vera Cruz with over 1,700 men; his command consisting of the 3rd Tennessee, Colonel Cheatham; a battalion of infantry recruits, regulars and volunteers, under Major Morris, of the 4th artillery; and the Georgia cavalry battalion, Lieutenant Colonel Calhoun. Lieutenant Colonel Miles, of the 5th infantry, followed General Marshall on the 2nd of January, 1848, with 1,500 men, and having overtaken the latter at Jalapa, they proceeded together to the city of Mexico. Shortly after the train under Lieutenant Colonel Miles left Vera Cruz, Lieutenant Walker, of the rifle regiment, in command of the rear-guard of thirty men, was attacked by three or four hundred guerilleros, who killed and wounded ten of his men, and captured three hundred pack mules. Neither train was otherwise seriously molested on the march to the capital. The guerilleros had been terribly cut up, and they only appeared in small parties, their principal depredations being committed on the merchant trains.

Upon his arrival at Queretaro, Peña y Peña issued a proclamation urging Congress to hasten the meeting convoked at that place; as there was danger, on the one hand, of losing their nationality, and, on the other, of the increase of the anarchy and confusion prevailing in every quarter of the republic.* The country was, indeed, in a most distracted condition. The Puros, or anti-sacerdotal party, in Guadalajara, headed by Gomez Farias, had a violent struggle with their opponents, in which the cathedral was sacked, and a number of persons were killed, among whom was General Ampudia, one of the partisans of Farias. Paredes had an interview with Jarauta at Tulancingo, in October, a pro-

* Proclamation of Señor Rosa, Secretary of State, dated October 13th, 1847.

nunciamento was issued, and measures were concerted for the establishment of a monarchy. Santa Anna was quieted for the time, but his friends and followers were still seeking an opportunity to restore him to power. After his defeat at Huamantla, refusing to obey the order requiring him to surrender his command to General Rincon, he directed the greater part of his troops to join General Alvarez in Oajaca, and the remainder to repair to Queretaro, reserving only a small party of hussars as a body-guard. At first he endeavored to make his way out of the country, through the State of Oajaca; but he afterwards returned to his hacienda at Tehuacan, from whence he addressed a protest to the new government, insisting that he had resigned the executive authority temporarily, in order to enable him better to act with the army against the enemy, and a letter to the members of Congress, expressing similar sentiments. He also issued an appeal to the Mexican people, on the 16th of October, complaining of the usage he had received, and declaring that he had done every thing for "the grandeur and glory of Mexico."*

The Mexican Congress finally assembled at Queretaro in November, and on the 11th instant made choice of General Anaya as Provisional President, to serve until the 8th of January following, when the regular term would expire. The inaugural address of General Anaya was not warlike, but was well calculated to soften the asperities of his countrymen; while he declared that he would never "seal the dishonor" of his native land, he pointed them to the fact, which could

* Santa Anna styled himself in his appeal, "Benemerito de la Patria,"—("well deserving of his country.") "I have not spared," said he, at the close of his address, "my blood in achieving that purpose. You know it, and you will do me justice."

not be disguised, that their internal dissensions for the past twenty-five years, had brought on all the troubles and embarrassments under which they now suffered. The reply of Congress was also conciliatory, and a vote was soon after taken, defeating a proposition of Señor Otero, to deprive the Executive of the power to alienate any portion of the territory of the republic, which indicated that the war would soon be brought to a close. The governors of the several states likewise met at Queretaro, and in reply to a circular from the Secretary of State, indicated their willingness to consent to a peace. The leading members of the cabinet, Peña y Peña, Secretary of State, and Mora y Villamil, Minister of War, were open and avowed friends of a cessation of hostilities; and the former manifested a great deal more firmness in maintaining his opinions, than he exhibited as one of General Herrera's advisers.*

The pacific disposition of General Anaya was manifested still further, by the appointment of Señores Cuevas, Conto, and Atristain, as commissioners to treat with Mr. Trist. The authority of the latter had been revoked, in the meantime, by the President of the United States, and instructions had been issued to transmit any proposition for peace that might be received, directly to Washington. The Mexican com-

* There was a cause for this, perhaps, as the power of the army which the federalists seem all along to have dreaded, more than any thing else, was nearly destroyed. The office of General-in-chief, temporarily held by General Gutierrez, was bestowed on General Bustamente, formerly a prominent centralist, but by no means friendly to Santa Anna. On assuming the command of the army, General Bustamente issued an address, in which he avowed his anxious desire to have an opportunity of retrieving the honor of his country. Overtures were held out to him to join Paredes, and others, who were disaffected, in overturning the government, and renewing the war; but he remained faithful to the trust confided to his hands.

missioners were extremely anxious to enter upon negotiations at once, and as they were willing to do so, with a full knowledge of the revocation of Mr. Trist's authority, he decided, under the advice of General Scott, to act in behalf of his government.* The negotiations, however, were continued for several weeks, though with every prospect of a speedy settlement of the difficulties existing between the two countries; the delay being mainly occasioned by the apprehensions of the return of Santa Anna from his retirement, still cherished by the leading federalists, Herrera, Olaguibel, Anaya, and Peña y Peña. General Almonte, long his bosom friend and confidant, had been warmly supported for the office of Provisional President, in opposition to General Anaya, and they were fearful that he might regain the ascendency.† But their fears proved to be unfounded; Santa Anna was completely overwhelmed by his misfortunes; and all the efforts of his friends, whatever may have been their object, were utterly abortive.

The brilliant victories of General Scott, the masterly display of military skill and strategy, exhibited in the reduction of San Juan de Ulua, and in turning the fortifications of Cerro Gordo, El Peñon, and San An-

* Special Message of President Polk, February 22nd, 1848.

† "I had a long conversation with Olaguibel, the governor of Mexico, during which I mentioned the reinforcements which had gone forward. He replied, that it was an act of the Mexican government for which he was not responsible, and then added,—'You ought to know Santa Anna,—he is deceiving you: he wants to make a peace, in order that he may remain at the head of power; but I can assure you there will be no peace until his power and that of the army is destroyed.'"—Extract of a letter from Mexico, dated October 14th, 1847, and published in the "Union."—The movement of troops referred to by the writer of the letter, probably had reference to the concentration of the Mexican forces at Queretaro, a precautionary measure which was very naturally adopted.

tonio, closed with the possession of the Mexican capital. With the reinforcements, the arrival of which has been mentioned, the army at Vera Cruz and Mexico, and the intermediate points, numbered near 30,000 men, of whom about 20,000 were effective. The main column, under the General-in-chief, was increased to not far from 15,000; but, as the Mexican authorities manifested a disposition to treat for peace, he determined not to continue his offensive operations, although his troops were constantly drilled, and every preparation made to fit them for taking the field. Towards the latter part of October, 1847, Generals Quitman and Shields returned to the United States, and General P. F. Smith was appointed governor of Mexico.

On the 25th of November, in pursuance of instructions from home requiring him, as soon as practicable, to raise the means for defraying the expenses of his army, from the territory occupied, General Scott issued an order forbidding the exportation of uncoined bullion from the Mexican ports, until the pleasure of his government should be known, and directing that no rents should be paid for quarters, after the close of the month. On the 13th of December, a further order was issued, which directed all internal taxes, of every description, in the states occupied by the American troops, to be paid over to the officers appointed to receive them, for the support of the army of occupation. Measures were likewise taken to enforce the collection and payment of the taxes, and detachments were ordered to the prominent points in the state and federal district of Mexico, outside the capital. Colonel Withers, of the 9th infantry, with his regiment, a squadron of dragoons, and two pieces of artillery, was ordered to Real del Monte; General Cadwalader was sent to Toluca with his brigade; and Colonel Clarke was afterwards detached to Cuernavaca, in former times the favorite residence of Cortés,* with his brigade, consisting of the 1st and 15th infantry, the Georgia cavalry, and Lieutenant Lovell's light battery.

Occasional disturbances took place in the capital, instigated chiefly by Mexican officers and soldiers, in disguise, and more especially those who were connected with the guerilla bands; but they were promptly put down. Inflammatory articles also appeared in the Mexican journals that were allowed to be published, which were only prevented by the positive orders of General Scott to suppress them, unless a different course was pursued.† On the 10th of January, 1848, he received information that a general rising was in contemplation in the city. During the day previous to the night on which the insurrection was to take place, he directed preparations to be made to prevent an outbreak, and the designs of the enemy were thus frustrated.‡

* Although Cuernavaca is but sixty miles from Mexico, it is surrounded by fields of coffee and sugar-cane, which yield an abundant crop. It is also famous for the splendid groves of mulberry trees in its vicinity. The American artillery occupied the palace of Cortés, now nearly gone to decay. "The Conqueror's palace," says Madame de Calderon, (Life in Mexico, vol. ii. let. 31,) "is a half-ruined barrack, though a most picturesque object, standing on a hill, behind which starts up the great white volcano.'

† Newspapers were established in all the principal towns occupied by the American troops, under their auspices, which exerted a favorable tendency in the restoration of peace. It was a novel idea, which could certainly never have entered the brain of Johannes Faust, that the press and the sword should thus go hand in hand together.

‡ Father Jarauta and General Salazar, the latter so notorious for his cruelty to the Texan prisoners, (See Kendall's Santa Fé Expedition,) were prowling round the city about this time, and were supposed, not without reason, to have been concerned in the contemplated movement.

The guerilleros were not yet entirely quieted, although the vigilance of Colonel Wilson at Vera Cruz, of Colonel Hughes at Jalapa, of Colonel Childs at Puebla, and of Colonel Irwin, who was stationed at the pass of Rio Frio, with the 5th Ohio volunteers, prevented their doing much harm. Near the close of December, 1847, the Mexican spies, under Dominguez, had a brush with a party of cavalry escorting Generals Miñon and Torrejon, between Ojo de Agua and Napoluca; the lancers were dispersed, and the two generals taken prisoners, and delivered to Colonel Childs. On the 1st of January, 1848, Colonel Wynkoop, then in pursuit of General Rea and Padre Jarauta, with a detachment, captured Generals Valencia and Arista. Colonel Hays and his rangers, and the Mexican spy companies, were also constantly on the alert in order to surprise Jarauta; and early in January, the former came unexpectedly on his band, near San Juan, in the valley of Mexico. The guerilleros were routed in an instant. Jarauta himself fell wounded, but was borne off by his men, leaving his horse, lance and cloak, in the hands of the rangers.

Early in the morning of the 18th of January, General Lane left the capital—his men being entirely ignorant of their destination—with two companies of the 3rd dragoons and one of mounted rifles, under Major Polk, of the 3rd dragoons, and four companies of Texan rangers, under Colonel Hays, in all 350 strong. The object of the expedition was the capture of Santa Anna, then understood to be at Tehuacan, rather for the pur-

Imitating the example of his superiors, Jarauta shortly after issued a proclamation to the Mexican people, calling upon them to awake from their lethargy, and to rally around his standard. It does not appear that his exhortations met with a very hearty or unanimous response.

pose of relieving the apprehensions of the Mexican authorities, than of triumphing over a fallen enemy. It was also designed to scour the country in the neighborhood of Orizaba, in search of property taken from the American trains. Proceeding rapidly along the National road, through Puebla and Amasoque, General Lane turned to the left at the latter place, and, passing through rough and unfrequented paths, known only to him and his guide, arrived at a hacienda near Santa Clara, at five o'clock in the morning of the 21st instant, having marched a distance of forty miles, from Puebla, during the previous night. All the Mexicans found on the road, and about the hacienda, were secured, in order to prevent the alarm being communicated, and at sunset the troops were again in the saddle. Tehuacan was still near forty miles distant, and they pressed forward with all speed.

But the precautions of General Lane were rendered useless. Shortly after leaving the hacienda, the party came upon a Mexican gentleman travelling in his coach with a number of servants, under a passport from General Smith, as governor of Mexico. He was allowed to continue his journey unmolested, but through his instrumentality, a message being probably conveyed through some secret though more direct path, Santa Anna was apprised of his danger; and when the Americans entered the town with their jaded horses, at daylight on the 22nd, they found that he had made his escape.* The main object of the expedition was thus

* In a letter to the Minister of War, dated at Cascatlan, February 1st, 1848, Santa Anna says that he was informed of the approach of General Lane, nearly two hours before the latter reached Tehuacan; and while he was engaged in preparing a note, requesting that a passport might be sent to him, to enable him to leave the country. He also

defeated, without fault or neglect on the part of any concerned. General Lane accordingly took possession of the military property of Santa Anna, in the absence of its owner, and on the 23rd instant directed his course towards the beautiful valley and town of Orizaba, which is situated in the centre of a romantic and fertile district, chiefly inhabited, however, by bandits, in time of peace, and guerilleros in time of war. On the 24th, General Lane entered Orizaba, the ayuntamiento of which surrendered the town without resistance. White flags were displayed from every house, as the Americans marched through the streets. Several days were spent here in recovering plundered property, and the command then set out on their return, arriving at the capital on the 10th of February.

It is now time to refer once more to the position of affairs in California and New Mexico.—After the arrival of the regiment of volunteers under Colonel Stevenson,* it was distributed through Upper and Lower California; Colonel Stevenson was stationed at Ciudad de los Angelos, with four companies; Major Hardy, with two companies, at San Francisco; and the other companies were stationed in the valley of the San Joaquim, and at Suters' Fort, on the Rio Sacramento, with the exception of two companies sent by sea, under Lieutenant Colonel Burton, to La Paz.

states, that he took refuge in the town of Teotitlan del Camiro, where there was a force from the state of Oajaca. No further attempt was made to capture him, and he was subsequently permitted to leave Mexico,—embarking at Antigua, just north of Vera Cruz, on the 4th of April, in a Spanish brig, for Kingston, on the island of Jamaica.

* This regiment is sometimes termed the "1st New York Volunteers," and that with the main column of the army, under Colonel Burnett, the "2nd New York Volunteers,"—both regiments having been raised in the State of New York.

The watchfulness of Colonel Mason prevented any further attempts to disturb the tranquillity of Upper California, and in September, 1847, Commodore Shubrick set sail with the greater part of his squadron, for the purpose of capturing, and occupying as far as was practicable, the forts on both sides of the Gulf, not already in possession of the American forces.

On the 20th of October, Guayamas surrendered to Captain Lavallette, who had with him the frigate Congress and sloop of war Portsmouth, after a severe fire, which was continued for nearly an hour, doing considerable damage to the town, and killing and wounding a number of Mexicans. A collector was appointed for the port, but the place was not permanently occupied. The Portsmouth, Commander Montgomery, was left to blockade the port; and the Congress joined Commodore Shubrick, who proceeded to Mazatlan, with the Congress, the razee Independence, the sloop of war Cyane, Commander Du Pont, and the transport Erie, Lieutenant Watson. On his way to Mazatlan, Commodore Shubrick left Lieutenant Heywood at San José, in Lower California, with thirty men and three other officers, together with two nine-pounder guns, to occupy the place.

On the morning of the 10th of November, the American squadron hove in sight of Mazatlan. The town was instantly in commotion, and the greater part of the inhabitants fled into the interior. A large body of the National Guard was stationed at this point, with several pieces of artillery, under Colonel Tellez; but they also withdrew, without offering any opposition; and on the 11th instant Commodore Shubrick landed with a party of sailors and marines, and took possession of the town. The Mexican troops encamped in the vicinity, and several encounters took place, with small loss on either side. The American garrison was continued on shore, and the collection of duties enforced till the close of the war.

The Portsmouth remained but a short time before Guayamas, which continued for several weeks to bo nearly deserted by its inhabitants; and the sloop of war Dale, Commander Selfridge, was subsequently ordered thither. On the 17th of November, fifty sailors, under Lieutenant Smith and Passed Midshipman Duncan, and seventeen marines, under Lieutenant Tansill,—Commander Selfridge heading the party,—landed for the purpose of examining the town and fort. They had proceeded but a short distance from the shore, when they were suddenly attacked by about 400 Mexicans, secreted behind the garden walls and in the houses. A brisk fire was kept up by both parties, until Lieutenant Yard, who had been left in charge of the ship, commenced throwing Paixhan shells into the town. This had the desired effect, and the enemy again abandoned the place to the Americans. Shortly after this affair, an expedition of the officers and men of the Dale, was organized for a march into the interior. They surprised a body of Mexican troops, about three miles from Guayamas, under General Campunazo, and took most of his officers and men prisoners.

After the capture of Mazatlan, the Cyane was ordered to La Paz, and the Portsmouth to San José, both of which posts were threatened by guerilla bands, under their chiefs, Piñada and Mijares. The latter appeared before the works at San José, which merely consisted of two adobé houses, with 150 men and two pieces of cannon. At the commencement of the attack, the guerilla leader was killed, and his men retired from before the post on the arrival of the Portsmouth. Ten more men were added to the command of Lieutenant Heywood; the houses occupied by his force were connected by a high wall, the doors bastioned, and the windows filled in. Piñada was known to be within twenty miles of San José, with from four to five hundred men, but, as every thing appeared quiet, the Portsmouth again set sail for another part of the coast. Lieutenant Colonel Burton was besieged for three weeks by the force under Piñada, when he organized a storming party, under Captain Steele, who drove the enemy from their works, and captured their flag.

The guerilleros, under Piñada, having been driven from La Paz, once more appeared before San José, after the departure of the Portsmouth, and closely invested the place. From the 24th of January, 1848, to the 14th of February, the efforts of the enemy to capture the post, were unintermitting, and a severe fire was constantly kept up. The provisions of the garrison were getting very low, though their courage and determination rose higher as their difficulties increased; they were strictly confined to the cuartel; Passed Midshipman Duncan and six men were taken prisoners, and on the 11th of February Passed Midhipman McLanahan was killed. The water was also cut off, and disease was fast generating. Fortunately, to the great joy of the garrison, Commander Du Pont arrived from La Paz, at sunset on the 14th of February. At daylight on the 15th, he landed with 100 men; Lieutenant Heywood sallied out with his party; and after a short, but well-contested conflict, they effectually routed the enemy, killing and wounding over fifty of their number, and making a great many prisoners.

Commodore Shubrick was now relieved in command of the Pacific Squadron, by Commodore T. Ap Catesby Jones, who arrived in the Ohio, seventy-four. All the principal ports on the coast being at this time, either occupied, or rigorously blockaded, no other event of importance transpired, until the cessation of hostilities.

In the month of August, 1847, General Price, with a portion of his troops, whose terms of service had expired, returned to Missouri, leaving Major Walker in command at Santa Fé. Colonel Newby, of the 6th Illinois, had previously been ordered to New Mexico with his regiment, and was then on the road. He was soon followed by a battalion of Missouri infantry, under Lieutenant Colonel Easton, and the 4th Missouri cavalry, under Colonel Ralls. Another battalion of Missouri volunteers, consisting of cavalry, infantry and artillery, under Lieutenant Colonel Gilpin, was ordered to keep the road open between Fort Leavenworth and Santa Fé—the Indians still continuing their attacks on the American trains.*

General Price returned to Santa Fé in the fall, and directed the troops under his command, about 3,000 in number, to be distributed throughout the valley of the Rio Grande, from Taos to El Paso. Governor Armijo† made no attempt to recover the authority that had

* Still another battalion of Missouri cavalry, under Lieutenant Colonel Powell, was mustered into service, and ordered upon the route to Oregon, to construct a chain of military posts to that territory.

† Governor Armijo was not in very good odor with some of his countrymen, and, in the month of August, he was arrested at Chihuahua, by order of Governor Trias, for indulging too freely in his comments upon the battle of Sacramento.

been wrested from him, and no event of particular moment occurred, until early in February, 1848, when intelligence was received, from various sources, that General Urrea, at the head of a large body of lancers, was moving upon El Paso, where Colonel Ralls was in command, with a part of his regiment. These reports were confirmed by the capture of a small party of Mexicans, near Carrizal, below El Paso; letters announcing the intended march of Urrea being found on their commanding officer. An express was immediately dispatched to General Price, with the information obtained, who left Santa Fé at once, with two companies of the 1st dragoons, under Major Beall; one company of the same regiment, acting as artillery, under Lieutenant Love; Lieutenant Colonel Easton's battalion; and the Santa Fé battalion, under Major Walker. On the 20th of February the command reached El Paso. It was now ascertained that the reported advance of Urrea was unfounded; but General Price also learned, that Governor Trias had collected between 1,500 and 2,000 men, and fourteen pieces of artillery, at Santa Cruz de Rosales, a strongly fortified town, about sixty miles beyond Chihuahua, and determined to march down and attack him.

General Price left El Paso on the 1st of March with 400 men, and arrived at Chihuahua on the 7th, performing the distance of two hundred and eighty-one miles in seven days. After Colonel Doniphan's departure, Chihuahua had been reoccupied by the Mexican authorities, and General Price was met, on his approach, by a civic deputation, who represented that a treaty of peace had been concluded, and requested him not to enter the city. Doubting the information, as he had received no official intelligence of the fact,

General Price entered the town, and on the ensuing day continued his march to Santa Cruz de Rosales where he arrived in the evening. On the morning of the 9th he summoned Governor Trias to surrender The latter refused to comply, stating, also, that it was understood there, that the war had been terminated by a treaty. Considerable parleying ensued, and General Price finally consented to wait for four days, during which time a messenger was expected to return, who had been sent by the governor, to ascertain whether the rumor in regard to a treaty was well founded.

After waiting twice the specified time, and having been joined by a reinforcement of 300 men, whom he had directed to follow him, with the artillery, General Price determined to attack the position, on the morning of the 16th of March. Another demand for a surrender was made, which was rejected, and the action then commenced by a lively cannonade. A good impression having been produced, General Price divided his command into three parties, under Colonel Ralls, Lieutenant Colonel Lane, and Major Walker, who were directed to attack the works from three different positions. The contest was maintained with vigor until eleven o'clock, when it was suspended in consequence of a rumor, which proved to be false, that a body of lancers were moving up in the rear. At three o'clock in the afternoon, the attack was renewed with increased zeal, and continued until sunset, when the Americans had burrowed through the houses to the Plaza; and the Mexicans then surrendered at discretion.

The enemy lost 300 killed and wounded at the storming of Santa Cruz de Rosales, while the American loss was but five killed and twenty wounded.

Governor Trias and forty of his officers, with a num ber of men, were taken prisoners; and 14 pieces of artillery, and 2,000 stands of small arms, were also captured by the Americans. On the 18th of March, General Price returned to Chihuahua, taking with him Governor Trias, and most of the prisoners; and leaving Colonel Ralls to follow him as soon as practicable. The report in relation to the treaty was afterwards ascertained to be correct; and Governor Trias, and his officers and men, were set at liberty, and the captured property restored.

CHAPTER XVIII.

TREATY OF PEACE.

Firmness of the Mexican Administration—Treaty of Peace Concluded—Skirmishes—Expedition of General Lane—Ratification of the Treaty—Evacuation of Mexico by the American Troops—Reflections—The Territory Acquired—Capacity of our Country for War—Conclusion.

It was difficult for the Mexican nation to make the humiliating acknowledgment, even to themselves,—their Castilian pride revolted at the thought,—that they were compelled to sue for peace; that the eagle of Anahuac, breathing a softer, but more enervating atmosphere, was no match for the prouder and hardier bird of the North. But there was no alternative; the Congress, which had taken a recess shortly after the election of General Anaya as Provisional President, reassembled in January, 1848; and a report was then made, in regard to the condition of the army, and the number of troops necessary for the vigorous prosecution of hostilities. It was found that 65,000 men would be required to carry on the war with any prospect of success. To raise this force was impossible, and, were it otherwise, the republic was without the means to pay them. Her forts and arsenals were in possession of the enemy; her military stores and supplies were nearly exhausted; her resources were rapidly diminishing; and the American commander, backed by his victorious soldiers, was already levying heavy contributions upon the country.* Her navy—she had none; and her privateer commissions, and certificates of citizenship, were bandied about in the market, without purchasers or bidders.†

General Anaya's term of office expiring on the 8th of January, he was succeeded by Peña y Peña, as President of the Supreme Court of Justice. There was no change, however, in the determination of those at the head of the government, to conclude a peace. Attempts to incite a revolt were made during the winter, in the states of San Luis, Zacatecas, Guanajuato, Jalisco, and Oajaca, by the Puros and the followers of Santa Anna and Paredes; and, in January, a pronunciamento was issued, at San Luis Potosi, in favor of continuing the war, and against the course pursued by the administration. But the Mexican Executive was firm and decided, and his vigilant measures prevented an outbreak. The negotiations were continued, and on the 2nd of February, 1848, a Treaty of Peace was signed, by the Mexican Commissioners and Mr. Trist, at the city of Guadaloupe Hidalgo.

* General Scott ordered a yearly contribution to be paid by the Mexican States, (New Mexico, California and Yucatan excepted,) amounting in the aggregate, for the year 1848, to $2,745,000, which was nearly quadruple the former annual assessments of the federal government of Mexico.

† Fears were entertained in our principal commercial cities, prior to the commencement of the war, that serious injury would be inflicted on American commerce, in the event of the occurrence of hostilities, by Mexican privateers. "With Mexico," said Mr. Theodore Sedgwick, in his "Thoughts on the Proposed Annexation of Texas," (p. 22, second edition, New York, 1844,)—"with Mexico no glory can be earned, and she has scarcely a dollar afloat,—while the privateers, the legalized pirates of all mankind, would sweep our commerce from the seas." These apprehensions proved to be unfounded, or rather, they failed to be realized.

The provisions of the treaty were very similar to those contained in the projét rejected by the Mexican Commissioners, in obedience to the instructions of Santa Anna, in August, 1847. It was provided that the boundary line between the two republics should commence in the Gulf of Mexico, three leagues from land, opposite the mouth of the Rio Grande, or the deepest channel of the river, if there should be more than one emptying directly into the sea,—running thence up the middle of the river, to the southern boundary of New Mexico—thence along such boundary, to its western termination—thence northerly, along the western boundary of New Mexico, to the first branch, or to the point nearest the first branch, of the river Gila—thence down the Rio Gila to the Rio Colorado—thence, crossing the latter river, and following the division line between Upper and Lower California, to the Pacific ocean, at a point one marine league due south of the southernmost point of the port of San Diego.* It was also provided, that the vessels and citizens of the United States should have the right freely to navigate the Gulf of California, and the Rio Colorado, to and from the territories of said United States;† that the river Gila, and the Rio Grande below the southern boundary of New Mexico, should be common to the citizens and vessels of both republics;‡ and that all places, and forts, with their armaments,§ (the city of Mexico, within the inner

* The guide, fixed by the treaty, for ascertaining the boundaries of New Mexico, is the Map of the United Mexican States, (revised edition, New York, 1847,) published by J. Disturnell; and for determining the southernmost point of the port of San Diego, the plan of the port made in 1782, by Don Juan Pantojer, and published in 1802, at Madrid, in the Atlas to the Voyages of the Schooners Sutil and Mexicana.—Treaty of Peace, Article V.

† Treaty of Peace, Article VI. ‡ Ibid., Article VII.

§ This provision of the treaty occasioned some little difficulty between line of intrenchments, being included in this provision,) occupied by the American troops, and not embraced within the limits of the ceded territory, should be restored.*

It was further agreed, by the treaty, in consideration of the cession of territory before mentioned, that the inhabitants of such territory, choosing to remain after the transfer, should be forever protected in the full enjoyment of their liberty, religion and property, and, as soon as practicable, be admitted to the rights and privileges of citizens of the United States;† and that the United States should pay to Mexico, the sum of fifteen millions of dollars, and assume the claims due her citizens, to an amount not exceeding three and one-fourth millions of dollars—Mexico being entirely released and discharged from the payment of such claims.‡

The Mexican Congress was not in session at the time the treaty was signed, but a number of the members were then at Queretaro, and were consulted in regard to its provisions,—a large majority of them signifying their approbation. "El Progreso," the organ of the revolutionists at Queretaro, violently opposed the treaty; declaring, among other things, that the sum of fifty millions of dollars ought to have been exacted from the United States. Paredes and his adherents likewise attempted another revolution in San Luis;

General Butler, and the Commissioners appointed by the Mexican government to witness the restoration of the forts and armaments. The latter insisted that the heavy guns captured at Contreras and Churubusco should be restored. General Butler referred the matter to the Acting Inspector General, and, upon his report, refused peremptorily to surrender them. The Mexicans finally yielded the point, rather than that the war should be renewed.

* Treaty of Peace, Article IV.

† Ibid., Article IX.

‡ Ibid., Articles XII.—XV.

but General Bustamente immediately moved with a division from Guanajuato, where he had been stationed to keep down the disaffection in that quarter, and arrived at San Luis Potosi on the 27th of March. The revolutionists made attempts to tamper with his fidelity, but finding him firm in his adherence to the administration, they abandoned their projects, for the present.

In the meantime, the American army had made no new movement of importance; except, that in the month of February, Orizaba was occupied by Colonel Bankhead, of the 2nd artillery, with 1,200 men, consisting of the 13th infantry, the Alabama battalion, and a detachment of cavalry. Several skirmishes, however, took place with the guerilleros, who persisted in committing their depredations on the line of the National road.

On the 1st of February, 1848, Captain Lamb, with his company of the 5th Illinois, encountered a Mexican reconnoitering party near Tampico; but at the first discharge, the enemy fled, leaving a number of horses, and their commanding officer and one of his men, in the hands of the Americans. On the 4th instant, Lieutenant Lilly, of the Louisiana cavalry, attacked twice his force, in the neighborhood of Puebla, and soon routed them; killing fifteen of the party, and capturing the remainder, with their arms, horses, and accoutrements. Lieutenant Colonel Biscoe, of the Louisiana rangers, left Vera Cruz, on the 19th of February, for Orizaba, with a detachment of Georgia and Louisiana cavalry. About four o'clock in the afternoon, between forty and fifty guerilleros were discovered in the road, near a place called Matacordera. Captain Wafford, in the advance, with twenty-five of the Georgia men, rushed upon them, when they fell back to a hedge of chaparral, which, in an instant, swarmed with the enemy, estimated to have been from three to four hundred strong. Captain Wafford charged through their line, and then cut his way back. Still, his men were rapidly falling, and must have been completely cut off, had not Lieutenant Colonel Biscoe arrived in time to rescue the party. After he came up with the remainder of his force, the guerilleros were easily driven from the road. In this affair, Lieutenant Henderson, of the Louisiana cavalry, was killed, with four men of the command, and there were twenty wounded.

General Lane,—not inappropriately styled, by his brother officers and soldiers, "the Marion of the army," —set out from the city of Mexico, on the 17th of February, on another secret expedition, with the same command that accompanied him to Tehuacan and Orizaba, in January. Advancing, with the utmost speed, over rough and difficult roads, and along miserable trails, and making frequent rapid night marches, he arrived at Tulancingo, the residence of Paredes, early in the morning of the 21st instant. Paredes was fortunate enough to make his escape a few moments before his house was surrounded. Having rested his men at Tulancingo during the day, General Lane resumed his march on the 22nd, and reached Tehualtaplan, where, as he learned, there were about 1,000 Mexican lancers and guerilleros, under Colonel Montano and Padre Jarauta, at sunrise on the 23rd.

As the Americans entered the town the escopeta balls came whistling about their heads from nearly every house. Headed by General Lane, Colonel Hays and Major Polk, the rangers and dragoons dashed upon the enemy, fighting their way, hand-to-hand, into the houses, and cutting down every man who refused to surrender. A portion of the Mexicans rallied and formed outside the town, but a vigorous charge, led by General Lane and Colonel Hays, quickly put them to rout. Jarauta, who was wounded in the conflict, again escaped; one hundred of the enemy were killed, however, among whom were Colonel Montano, and the bosom friend of Jarauta, Padre Martinez; a still greater number were wounded; and there were fifty taken prisoners. General Lane lost one man killed and four wounded. Quiet was soon restored in the town, after the fighting had ceased, and the Americans returned to the capital, taking with them their prisoners, and a quantity of recovered property that had been plundered from different trains.

General Scott was relieved from duty in Mexico, at his own request, on the 19th of February, when the command was assumed by General Butler. On the 5th of March, a military convention, for the provisional suspension of hostilities, was ratified in the capital, under which the civil authority in most of the towns occupied by the American troops was shortly after surrendered to the officers regularly chosen by the citizens. The guerilleros were now tolerably quiet, though they occasionally attacked the merchant trains. On the 30th of March a train of Mexican merchandise was plundered by a band of marauders, at Paso del Bobo. Colonel Hughes being informed of the transaction, a party of Texan rangers were ordered out from Jalapa, under Captain Daggett, who followed the trail of the guerilleros, and overtook them as they entered the village of Desplobade. But one of the bandits escaped; the remainder, thirteen in number, were captured and shot. This blow was effectual. Towards the latter part of March a large merchant train left Vera Cruz for the city of Mexico, escorted by a mixed command under Lieutenant Colonel Loomis, of the 6th infantry; but they were not molested by the guerilleros.*

The treaty concluded at Guadaloupe Hidalgo was received at Washington, while the American Congress was in session, and in the midst of a discussion on various propositions for a still greater increase of the army. Although the powers of Mr. Trist had been revoked, and he had been recalled, prior to the conclusion of the treaty, President Polk very properly decided to regard his disobedience of orders as a matter resting solely between himself and his government, and therefore communicated the document to the Senate. That body approved the treaty, after making some amendments affecting but slightly the provisions before referred to, on the 10th of March; and on the 30th of May following, the necessary ratifications were exchanged, at Queretaro, by Ambrose H. Sevier, and Nathan Clifford, the Commissioners appointed for that purpose by the American government, and Señor Rosa, Minister of Internal and Foreign Relations of Mexico, —the Mexican Congress having previously ratified the treaty, as amended.

The American troops immediately commenced the evacuation of the Mexican territory. The division of General Worth was the last to leave the capital. On the morning of the 12th of June, it took up the line of march for Vera Cruz. The American flag, after being

* Captain Shover accompanied this train with his battery. On leaving Vera Cruz, he attached a viameter to one of his gun-carriages, by which it appeared that the distance to Mexico was only 252½ miles,—about forty miles less than it has generally been considered.

saluted by the Mexican artillery, in command of General La Vega, was lowered from the National Palace, and the Mexican standard once more ascended in its former place. The latter was saluted, in turn, by the battery of Lieutenant Colonel Duncan, which had been the first to open its thunders on the battle-field of Palo Alto.

The war with Mexico is now ended. Its results, be they for good or for evil, are in progress of accomplishment. To our sister republic, if she regard it aright, this contest may prove a useful lesson. Whether the principle affirmed by the American government, in the annexation of Texas, which, as we have seen, was the original moving cause of the war, though not necessarily so,--that a revolted province, by maintaining a successful rebellion against the authority of the mother country for a period of eight years, acquires the right to be regarded, for all purposes, as an independent nation; whether this be correct, or incorrect—and the time certainly appears reasonable—it cannot be forgotten, that Mexico herself invited hostilities, by a refusal to negotiate. The direct consequence of this refusal was the advance of the American troops to the Rio Grande,—the immediate cause of the war, it is true, but the only mode by which the United States could have asserted her title, when all intercourse with Mexico was suspended, to the territory admitted to be in dispute.—This war, then, will caution Mexico against assuming, on any other occasion, a false attitude at the very commencement of an international difficulty. It will teach her, too, the importance of cultivating harmony at home, and of manifesting and preserving, at all times, good faith in her dealings with other nations.

Clouds and darkness still hover over her lovely valleys and her snow-capped mountains;* yet, blessed, as, we may hope, she will one day be, with a firm, stable, and prudent government, it will be easy for her to redeem the past, and to accomplish a high destiny for the future.

But what have the United States gained by the war? —Its necessary consequence, although not its object, has been, the addition to our territory of a tract of country exceeding 500,000 square miles in extent.† The importance of the Bay of San Francisco, and the other harbors on the Pacific ocean, embraced within the limits of the territory acquired, has been heretofore noticed.‡ Divers opinions are entertained with regard to the value of the acquisition in other respects, and it will, perhaps, be impossible to reconcile them, until its resources, and productive capacity, are fully developed, under the more favorable auspices which always accompany American industry and enterprise.

Recent travellers give no very flattering description

* The result of the canvass of the vote for President, so often postponed, was officially declared soon after the ratification of the treaty. It appeared, as had all along been supposed, that General Herrera had been duly elected. He, at first, declined to serve; but, as Congress refused to accept his resignation, he entered upon the duties of the office. Paredes at once renewed his efforts to excite a revolt. He collected a large force at Guanajuato, in June, 1848, seized the mint, and carefully fortified his position. On the 18th of July, he was attacked by the government troops, under Generals Bustamente, Lombardini, Cortizar, Miñon, and Ortéga. His troops were routed with great loss; most of his fortifications were carried, and he was forced to fly, and secrete himself for safety. Jarauta, the padre and guerillero, was with Paredes, and was captured in the engagement, and instantly shot.

† The area of Upper California is 448,691 square miles, and that of New Mexico, 77,387.

‡ Ante, pp. 123, 124.

of large portions of New Mexico and California;* but, it must be remembered, that mere tourists for pleasure are far from being reliable authorities. The dry sandy plains of New Mexico will never be redeemed, in all probability, from the curse of barrenness; through all time they must continue to appear as they now do—"blasted with antiquity." Yet the territory is not entirely a desert, nor is the Santa Fé trade, which has been of so much profit to some of our western cities, in past years, a mere fiction.† Copper ore abounds in the mountains; coal exists, in large quantities, in the Ratôn range, and at Cerillas and Taos; and there are said to be valuable gold mines south of Santa Fé.‡ The valley of the Rio Grande, from Santa Fé to the southern boundary of New Mexico, throughout its greater extent, is thickly dotted with farm-houses, and lined with fertile fields, with orchards and vineyards; and to the north of Santa Fé, there are extensive pasture lands capable of grazing an immense number of cattle.

Comparatively little information has been so far obtained in regard to the great interior basin of California, lying east of the Sierra Nevada. Between the Sierra and the Pacific, there is a strip of land, from one hundred to one hundred and fifty miles wide, which is nearly all productive. Wheat is grown in abundance in the territory; wine is produced in the valley of the San Gabriel, and there are vineyards, also, in other parts of the country; the hills and plains are covered

* Adventures in Mexico and the Rocky Mountains, by G. F. Ruxton; Scenes in the Rocky Mountains, etc., by a New Englander.

† Gregg's Commerce on the Prairies.

‡ Letter of Señor Manuel Alvarez, late American Consul at Santa Fé, to Hon. J. Houghton.

with sheep and cattle; and large quantities of hides are annually prepared for exportation.* Oranges, limes, figs, olives, grapes, apples, and peaches, grow thriftily, and yield abundantly. The gardens attached to the old Roman mission establishments, at Yerba Buena, San Luis Rey, and San Diego, are fairly choked up, with the fruit-trees and shrubbery, that have been suffered to grow, for many years, unchecked and unpruned. The climate of the territory is mild and equable; the winters are rainy; and, though the summers are dry, there are heavy dews to cool the air and moisten the ground.†

The pecuniary considerations growing out of, or connected with the war, lose much of their importance, however, when we consider its other results. The ability of the country to vindicate her honor and maintain her rights—her great capacity for war, either offensive or defensive,—has been signally demonstrated. The tendency of this will be, to increase, in an eminent degree, the respect and deference paid to our government by other nations. Called upon, at brief notice, to raise and equip a large army,—this was accomplished; and, under such circumstances, we entered into a contest with a people not unpractised in "war's vast art," or unacquainted with the improvements of modern

* Folsom's Mexico in 1842.

† Persons living upon or near the Atlantic are very apt, in instituting a comparison between their own climate and productions, and those of the same latitude on the Pacific coast, to overlook the fact, that isothermal lines, or lines of equal temperature, traverse the surface of the earth with an eccentricity varying very materially from the parallels of latitude. In the valley of the Willamete, which lies above the 45th degree of north latitude, the snow never falls to a greater depth than three or four inches; green peas are eaten at Christmas; the grass grows all winter, and cattle are rarely housed.—Father De Smets' Oregon Missions and Travels over the Rocky Mountains.

science; attacking them, with inferior numbers, in the open field, or assailing them when posted behind fortifications constructed with superior skill, yet ever achieving the same result—a brilliant and glorious victory.

We have shown that, in an emergency, every citizen may become a soldier;—that, at all times, a powerful opponent, in a defensive war, we would be absolutely invincible;—that the military school at West Point has diffused a large amount of valuable informaiion through the land;* and that, while we have officers, whose clear and matchless combinations, and sound and accurate judgments, entitle them to take rank with the Marlboroughs, the Ruperts, and the Fredericks of the past, and the noblest captains of the present age,—we have, also, a citizen soldiery, prompt to obey their country's call, and ready to brave the dangers of war, and the vicissitudes of an unfriendly climate—disregarding, alike, the bolts of their antagonists, and the invisible shafts of man's great enemy.†

* A large number of the officers belonging to the ten new regiments added to the regular army by the act of 1847, were educated at West Point; and there were nine colonels, nine lieutenant colonels, eight majors, and eight captains, of the volunteer regiments, who were graduates of that institution.—Statement G, accompanying the report of Captain Brewerton, of the corps of engineers, superintendent of the Military Academy, to the board of visitors, June, 1847.

† The aggregate loss of the Americans, during the war, in killed and wounded, was about 5,500; of whom probably two thousand were killed on the field of battle, or subsequently died of their wounds. But the ravages of disease were far more appalling. Even in the city of Mexico, there were nearly 1,000 deaths in the army, in a single month,—the climate of the table land being as fatal to the constitutions of the soldiers enlisted in the southern states of the Union, as was the noxious atmosphere of the *tierra caliente*, to those from the northern states. The 1st and 2nd Pennsylvania regiments, which left home 1,800 strong, lost 400 men by disease alone, and a large number were discharged as being unfit for duty, many of whom are supposed to have died. More than

But the unexampled success that has attended our arms in this struggle, should excite no vainglorious spirit, no boastful arrogance, no overweening confidence. Least of all—for this need not be—should it excite a thirst for extended empire. The glowing pages of Solís, the honest enthusiasm of Bernal Diaz, and the truthful eloquence of our own Prescott, may well be admired; but the career of Cortés is none the less unworthy of imitation, because it is adorned, on the pages of history, by the charms of composition, and the graces of intellect. Should a republic, founded as an asylum to which the wronged and the oppressed mght flee for safety—a peaceful refuge from tyranny and wrong—forget its high mission, and seek for glory in foreign conquests, it would, indeed, provoke the scorn and derision of mankind.

War *is* an evil !—Its crimsoned fields, scented with slaughter, and steaming with corruption, speak volumes in its condemnation. Its pride and pomp are based on human misery. The attractions of martial renown are many ; but—alas !—at what an enormous sacrifice are they purchased ! The laurel-wreath of the victor may relieve, but it cannot conceal, the mournful cypress that droops beside it. Scattered all over our fair country, here are monuments, like the tumuli in the church-ards of the Tyrol, evidences of that affection which lings to its object beyond the grave,—of deep, sincere, and heartfelt gratitude ;—yet do they also testify to the suffering and wretchedness that war has occasioned.

one-half of the Georgia infantry battalion died in Mexico, and the 3rd and 4th Tennessee volunteers lost 360 men by death, without having ever been in an engagement. The regular regiments suffered a great deal in this respect, though, being under stricter discipline, in nothing like the same proportion.

As Americans, therefore, sacredly revering the memories of Washington and the heroes of the Revolution, —and in whose minds the names of Jackson, and Harrison, and Brown, are imperishably associated with the plains of Chalmette, the valley of the Thames, and the heights of Niagara,—while we may point with satisfaction, as we ought, to the frowning fortresses, the burning sands, and the lofty mountains of Mexico, as the memorable witnesses of the skill, genius, and gallantry, of Scott and Taylor,—of Worth, and Wool, and Twiggs,—and of the dauntless courage and intrepidity of the brave men whom they led forth to battle,—we should do no injustice to them, none to our national character, by expressing the hope that this may be the last war in which our country shall be engaged, and that, henceforth, all her ways may be ways of pleasantness, and all her paths be peace.

Still, a resort to arms may not always be avoided. The social and political millennium, to which the philanthropist and Christian look forward with eager and anxious expectation, has not yet dawned upon us. The privileges and blessings of peace, desirable as they are, may sometimes be denied. Caution and prudence, united with promptness and determination, will go very far to secure their permanence. "Be just, but fear not!"—should ever be our national maxim.—Firmness is the policy of war, as it is the policy of peace. Justice to our own citizens, in the legislation of the country, will prevent internal feuds and dissensions; and justice to other governments will save us from the manifold evils of war.

So long as this remains the governing principle of our diplomatic intercourse, should collisions unfortunately occur, our soldiers will not forget, in the hour of battle, that he is thrice armed, "who hath his quarrel just." This reflection will be to him both sword and buckler; it will stimulate his zeal, and arouse his courage; it will strengthen his heart, and be a panoply for his protection. By adopting this policy, too, and pursuing it steadily and unerringly, the fire of liberty kindled by our forefathers in this western wilderness, will long be a beacon light to the nations,—not, like the darting meteor, fitful and evanescent, but, as the vestal flame, glowing brighter and purer, ever and forever!

SUPPLEMENTARY NOTE

CONTAINING AN ACCOUNT OF THE

GOLD DISCOVERIES IN CALIFORNIA.

SINCE the publication of the first edition of this history, authentic information has been received of the discovery of vast, and almost incredible mineral wealth, in that portion of California belonging to the United States, under the provisions of the treaty of Guadalupe Hidalgo. If a bare tithe of the accounts daily borne to the Atlantic states prove to be true,—and there is no reason to doubt that they are to a great exten. well-founded,—the *El Dorado*, in quest of which the interior of South America was explored in vain, has been, at length, found amid the swelling slopes and lofty *buttes* of the Sierra Nevada. The remarks, therefore, in the body of this work,* relative to the value of the territory acquired from Mexico, by the terms of the treaty of peace, fall so far short of the reality since the development of its extraordinary resources, that I have thought proper to embody in a supplementary note, all the general and most important facts respecting this discovery.

Vague rumors in regard to the mineral treasures locked up in the volcanic mountain ranges of California,—at certain times attracting greater attention than at others, but never receiving much credit,—have been circulating through the world for centuries. Among the first trophies brought to Cortés, after the conquest of Mexico, in 1521, were samples of Californian pearls; and it was then reported, that gold and gems were to be found in the regions at the north which had not yet been visited by the Europeans. Two expeditions were fitted out by Cortés, in 1532 and 1533, and sent on voyages of discovery to the North-west. The latter crossed the Gulf of California, called by the Spaniards, in honor of the illustrious discoverer, *Mar de Cortés*—the Sea of Cortés—and effected a landing at the modern port of La Paz. Shortly after this, the Conqueror himself embarked with a squadron, and planted a colony at the same place. His attempts to settle the country, however, were unsuccessful, and the colonists eventually returned to Mexico. In 1539, he dispatched another expedition under an officer by the name of Ulloa,

* Ante, p. 500, et seq.

who sailed to the head of the Gulf, doubled the peninsula, and ascended along the western coast, to the twenty-eighth or twenty-ninth degree of north latitude, but was never afterwards heard of.

Nothing daunted by his ill success, Cortés projected still another expedition; but his enterprise was now checked by the viceroy Mendoza, whose mind had been inflamed by the golden reports of an itinerant monk sent to convert the Indians of Sonora, and who had penetrated far into the interior of California. The viceroy claimed the right of discovery, and Cortés appealed to the Emperor. The premature death of Cortés, pending the appeal, put an end to all his ambitious hopes, and, in a considerable degree, to the discoveries which he and others had anticipated.*

Various expeditions were subsequently undertaken, but with little or no success. The energetic spirit of the great adventurer and discoverer had died with him; the glittering realms where gold and precious stones were said to abound in exhaustless profusion, were never reached; and the descendants of the *Conquistadores* were obliged to content themselves with the far less valuable silver mines of Mexico.

The pearl fisheries in the Gulf of California, however, were soon made available, and formal possession of the peninsula was taken by the Spanish authorities, in 1569. Not quite fifty years later, the Jesuits established themselves in the country, and gradually extended their missions to the north. They were, no doubt, aware of the existence of gold and silver in California; yet they dissuaded the Indians from digging after the minerals,—probably for the reason that they did not suppose there could be sufficient quantities found to render the search profitable,—and encouraged them to devote their time to herding cattle and other agricultural pursuits. In 1767, the Jesuits were expelled from the possessions of Spain, and were succeeded, in California, by Franciscan and Dominican friars. Deprived of the fostering care, the energy and industry, of the followers of Ignatius Loyola, the mission establishments began rapidly to decline, and the discoveries which might ultimately have been made under their auspices, were reserved for a more enterprising people than the white inhabitants who now made their way to the Californias.

Adventurers from Mexico, from Spain and the United States, American and European seamen, emigrated thither, and founded settlements on the inner shore of the Gulf, and along the iron-bound coast of the Pacific, from Cape San Lúcas to the Bay of San Francisco.†

* Prescott's Conquest of Mexico, vol. III, p. 333, et seq.—Greenhow's History of Oregon and California, p. 22, et seq.

† The mongrel white population of Upper California was computed, in 1842, to be about 5,000, and the Indians 33,000.

Some few among them appear to have been active and industrious, but the great majority speedily relapsed into habits of indolence and slothfulness. No extraordinary efforts were made to develop the resources of the country; considerable silver was discovered, but as there was no mercury to purify it, that obtained was of an inferior quality, and afforded a trifling profit. A rich mine, called San Antonio, near La Paz, was wrought for several years, and is said to have yielded handsome returns. But the political dissensions that agitated the southern departments of Mexico, were felt in the Californias, perhaps more than all, in the baneful influence which they exerted in repressing the energies of the inhabitants, and curbing the little spirit of enterprise that had previously animated them.

For many years, there was scarcely the least improvement in Upper or Lower California, and if any progress was made, it was at a snail's pace. Hides and tallow formed the principal articles of exportation from the upper province; but the trade was small, and liable to frequent interruptions, by reason of the struggles between the different factions for the ascendancy. Matters remained pretty much in this condition, till after the termination of the war with the United States, and the cession to them of Upper California.

This territory, now belonging to the American Union, embraces an area of 448,961 square miles. It extends along the Pacific coast, from about the thirty-second parallel of north latitude,* a distance of near seven hundred miles, to the forty-second parallel, the southern boundary of Oregon. On the east it is bounded by New Mexico. During the long period which transpired, between its discovery and its cession to the United States, this vast tract of country was frequently visited by men of science from all parts of the world. Repeated examinations were made by learned and enterprising officers and civilians; but none of them discovered the important fact, that the mountain torrents of the Sierra Nevada were constantly pouring down their golden sands into the vallies of the Sacramento and San Joaquim. The glittering particles twinkled beneath their feet in the ravines which they explored, or glistened in the water-courses which they forded,—yet they passed them by unheeded. Not a legend, or tradition, was heard among the white settlers, or the aborigines, that attracted their curiosity. A nation's ransom lay within their grasp, but, strange to say, it escaped their notice,—it flashed and sparkled all in vain.†

The Russian American Company had a large establishment at Ross

* See p. 103, ante.

† A gold *placera* was discovered some years ago near the mission of San Fernando, but it was very little worked, on account of the want of water.

and Rodega, ninety miles north of San Francisco, founded as early as the year 1812; and factories were also established in the territory by the Hudson Bay Company. Their agents and *employés* ransacked the whole country west of the Sierra Nevada, or Snowy Mountains, in search of game. In 1838, Captain Sutter, formerly an officer in the Swiss Guards of Charles X, king of France, emigrated from the state of Missouri to Upper California, and obtained from the Mexican government a conditional grant of thirty leagues square of land, bounded on the west by the Sacramento river. Having purchased the stock, arms, and ammunition, of the Russian establishment, he erected a dwelling and fortification on the left bank of the Sacramento, about fifty miles from its mouth, and near what was termed, in allusion to the new settlers, the American fork. This formed the nucleus of a thriving settlement, to which Captain Sutter gave the name of New Helvetia. It is situated at the head of navigation for vessels on the Sacramento, in latitude 38° 33′ 45″ North, and longitude 121° 20′ 05″ West. During a residence of ten years in the immediate vicinity of the recently discovered *placeras*, or gold regions, Captain Sutter was neither the wiser, nor the richer, for the brilliant treasures that lay scattered around him.*

In the year 1841, careful examinations of the Bay of San Francisco, and of the Sacramento river and its tributaries, were made by Lieutenant Wilkes, the commander of the Exploring Expedition; and a party under Lieutenant Emmons, of the navy, proceeded up the valley of the Willamette, crossed the intervening highlands, and descended the Sacramento. In 1843–4, similar examinations were made by Captain, afterwards Lieutenant-Colonel, Frémont, of the Topographical Engineers, and in 1846, by Major Emory, of the same corps. None of these officers made any discoveries of minerals, although they were led to conjecture, as private individuals who had visited the country had done, from its volcanic formation and peculiar geological features, that they might be found to exist in considerable quantities.†

As is often the case, chance at length accomplished what science had

* Farnham's Adventures in California.—Wilkes' Narrative of the Exploring Expedition.—Frémont's Narrative.

† See Farnham's Adventures, Wilkes' and Frémont's Narratives, and Emory's Report.—In 1846, Eugenio Macnamara, a Catholic priest and missionary, obtained a grant of a large tract of land between the San Joaquim and the Sierra Nevada, the Cosumnés and the Tulares in the vicinity of San Gabriel, from Pio Pico, governor of the Californias, for the purpose of establishing upon it a large colony of Irish Catholics; but the grant was not ratified by the Central Government, and the project was not carried into effect. There is no evidence that Father Macnamara was aware of the existence of gold in the valley of San Joaquim.

failed to do.—In the winter of 1847-8, a Mr. Marshall commenced the construction of a saw-mill for Captain Sutter, on the north branch of the American fork, and about fifty miles above New Helvetia, in a region abounding with pine timber. The dam and race were completed, but on attempting to put the mill in motion, it was ascertained that the tail-race was too narrow to permit the water to escape with perfect freedom. A strong current was then passed in, to wash it wider and deeper, by which a large bed of mud and gravel was thrown up at the foot of the race. Some days after this occurrence, Mr. Marshall observed a number of brilliant particles on this deposit of mud, which attracted his attention. On examining them, he became satisfied that they were gold, and communicated the fact to Captain Sutter. It was agreed between them, that the circumstance should not be made public for the present; but, like the secret of Midas, it could not be concealed. The Mormon emigrants, of whom Mr. Marshall was one, were soon made acquainted with the discovery, and in a few weeks all California was agitated with the startling information.

Business of every kind was neglected, and the ripened grain was left in the fields unharvested. Nearly the whole population of Upper California became infected with the mania, and flocked to the mines. Whalers and merchant vessels entering the ports were abandoned by their crews, and the American soldiers and sailors deserted in scores. Upon the disbandment of Colonel Stevenson's regiment, most of the men made their way to the mineral regions. Within three months after the discovery, it was computed that there were near four thousand persons, including Indians, who were mostly employed by the whites, engaged in washing for gold. Various modes were adopted to separate the metal from the sand and gravel,—some making use of tin-pans; others of close-woven Indian baskets; and others still, of a rude machine, called the cradle, six or eight feet long and mounted on rockers, with a coarse grate, or sieve, at one end, but open at the other. The washings were mainly confined to the low wet grounds, and the margins of the streams, —the earth being rarely disturbed more than eighteen inches below the surface. The value of the gold dust obtained by each man, per day, is said to have ranged from ten to fifty dollars, and sometimes even to have far exceeded that. The natural consequence of this state of things was that the prices of labor, and, indeed, of everything, rose immediately, from ten to twenty fold.*

As may readily be conjectured, every stream and ravine in the valley

* Official Dispatch of Colonel Mason, Commander of the 10th Military Department, August 17, 1848.—Letters of Thomas O. Larkin, U. S. Consul at Monterey, to the Secretary of State, June 1, and June 28, 1848.

of the Sacramento was soon explored. Gold was found on every one of its tributaries; but the richest earth was discovered near the *Rio de las Plumas*, or Feather river,* and its branches, the Yubah and Bear rivers,—and on Weber's creek, a tributary of the American fork. Explorations were also made in the valley of the San Joaquim, which resulted in the discovery of gold on the Cosumnés and other streams, and in the ravines of the Coast Range, west of the valley, as far down as Ciudad de los Angelos.

Sometimes the gold has been found encasing a bright sparkling crystal of quartz, but no accounts have been received up to this date, (January, 1849,) indicating that it has been encountered in its matrix, or the place of its original production. In the "dry diggings," or ravines, it is obtained in grains, averaging from one to two pennyweights,—and one piece has been found weighing thirty-five pennyweights; but in the swamps, and on the margins of streams, it is procured in small flat spangles, six or seven of which are required to make one grain. Specimens of the metal have been assayed at the mint in Philadelphia, under the direction of Professor Patterson, and the average fineness ascertained to be 894 thousandths, being a little below the standard, which is 900, but fully equal to that obtained in the southern States, and nearly as good as the best gold procured in Africa.

In regard to the productiveness of the gold *placeras* of California, it is difficult to make any estimates, or form any conjectures. In a Memorial of the citizens of San Francisco, dated in September, 1848, praying congress to establish a branch mint in the territory, it was estimated that the sum of five and a half millions of dollars would be removed from the mines during the year ending on the 1st of July, 1849. But this calculation was evidently predicated on the number of persons then engaged at the washings. Since that time, there has been a vast influx of *gold-hunters* from Oregon, Mexico, South America, and the Sandwich Islands. Large numbers of citizens of the United States, have also set out for California, by way of Cape Horn, the Panamá route, or overland from Independence. It is, therefore, not improbable that before the close of the year, the population may be trebled, or even quadrupled.

It has been predicted by some, that the washings in California would soon be exhausted, as were those of Brazil, from which ten millions sterling were once annually sent to Europe. The volcanic character of

* Feather river is the first considerable branch of the Sacramento below the *Prairie Buttes*. It has a course of about forty miles, and empties into the main river about fifteen miles above New Helvetia. Though the Sacramento is navigable for vessels, only to that place, boats can pass up one hundred miles further.

the country, and its geological peculiarities, hardly confirm this opinion, although it is by no means improbable. Gold has been found, or there are indications of its existence, at different points along the western base of the Sierra Nevada, for nearly seven hundred miles; and it has been discovered east of the mountains, on the Great Salt Lake, and at various other places in the great interior basin of California. If we may place any reliance upon the inferences fairly deducible from these facts, it may be safely presumed, that the rugged buttresses of the Sierra Nevada contain a vaster deposit of mineral wealth than has yet been found in any other locality in the known world,—in extent and productiveness far excelling the Andes of Peru, the Carpathian range of Hungary, or the Ural mountains of Russia.*

In addition to the gold mines, other important discoveries have been made in Upper California. A rich vein of quicksilver has been opened at New Almadin, near Santa Clara, which, with imperfect machinery, —the heat by which the metal is made to exude from the rock being applied by a very rude process,—yields over thirty per cent. This mine, —one of the principal advantages to be derived from which will be, that the working of the silver mines scattered through the territory must now become profitable,—is superior to those of Almadin in old Spain, and second only to those of Idria, near Trieste, the richest in the world.† It is more than probable, also, that other veins will be opened, as the soil for miles around is highly impregnated with mercury.

Lead mines have likewise been discovered in the neighborhood of Sonoma, and vast beds of iron ore near the American fork, yielding from eighty-five to ninety per cent. Copper, platina, tin, sulphur, zinc, and cobalt, everywhere abound; coal exists in large quantities in the Cascade Range of Oregon, of which the Sierra Nevada is a continuation; and in the vicinity of all this mineral wealth, there are immense quarries of marble and granite, for building purposes.

Colonel Mason expresses the opinion, in his official dispatch, that "there is more gold in the country drained by the Sacramento and San Joaquim rivers, than will pay the cost of the [late] war with Mexico a hundred times over."‡ Should this even prove to be an exaggeration, there can be little reason to doubt, when we take into consideration all

* The peaks of the Sierre Nevada are from ten to fifteen thousand feet above the level of the ocean; the Carpathian mountains seven thousand five hundred feet; and the Ural mountains between four and five thousand feet.

† The mines of Almadin yield only ten per cent; and those at Idria range as high as eighty per cent, although ores containing only one per cent are worked. Specimens of cinnabar from California have been examined at the Philadelphia mint: the red ore yielded over thirty-three per cent, and the yellow ore over fifteen.

‡ Letter to the Secretary of War, dated August 17, 1848.

the mineral resources of the country, that the territory of California is by far the richest acquisition made by this government since its organization.

Additional information, procured since the foregoing remarks were written, seems to confirm the most favorable conjectures which had been formed, with reference to the vastness of the gold deposits on the slopes of the Sierra Nevada, so far as this is possible without a critical examination of every foot of ground containing the precious mineral. Nearly fifty years ago, a somewhat eminent writer and geographer of that day, in an account of Drake's discovery of a portion of California, which he called New Albion, made the following statement:—"The country, too, if we can depend upon what Sir Francis Drake, or his chaplain say, is worth the seeking and the keeping,—since they assert that the land is so rich in gold and silver, that upon the slightest turning it up with a spade or pick-axe, those rich metals plainly appear mixed with the mould. It may be objected that this looks a little fabulous; but to this, two satisfactory answers may be given—the first is, that later discoveries on the same coast confirm the truth of it, which for anything I can see ought to put the fact out of question; but if any doubt should remain, my second answer should overturn these. For I say next, that the country of New Mexico lies directly behind New Albion, on the other side of a narrow bay, and in that country are the mines of Santa Fé, which are allowed to be the richest in the world."*

The glowing accounts of Sir Francis Drake, marvellous as they have hitherto appeared, seem about to be verified. One *placēra* after another, literally overflowing with wealth, has been discovered; and almost countless stores of virgin gold have been exhumed in the *gulches* and *cañons* of California, where it has lain for ages undisturbed.† "But by far the most magnificent discovery," says a recent tourist, "is that recently made upon the *ranche* of Colonel Frémont, on the Mariposa river.‡ It is nothing less than a vein of gold in the solid rock—a *bonâ fide* mine—the first which has been found in California. Whether it was first detected by a party of Sonomans, or by the company which Colonel Frémont organized last spring, and which has since been working in the same locality, is a disputed point, though I believe the credit

* Pinkerton's Voyages, vol. II, p. 172.

† Latterly, it has been rendered more evident that the gold mines of California were worked by the early Spanish settlers, or by the Indians under their direction, as the remains of ancient shafts, and other appearances tending to prove the same fact, have in several instances been discovered.

‡ The Mariposa is one of the tributaries of the San Joaquim.

is due to the latter. At any rate, the gold is there, and in extraordinary abundance. I saw some specimens which were in Colonel Frémont's possession. The stone is a reddish quartz, filled with rich veins of gold, and far surpassing the specimens brought from North Carolina and Georgia. Some stones picked up on the top of the quartz strata, without particular selection, yielded two ounces of gold to every twenty-five pounds. Colonel Frémont informed me that the vein had been traced for more than a mile. The thickness on the surface is two feet, gradually widening as it descends and showing larger particles of gold. The dip downward is only about twenty degrees, so that the mine can be worked with little expense. These are the particulars first given me, when the discovery was announced. Still more astonishing facts have just come to light. A geologist sent out to examine the place, arrived here last night. He reports having traced the vein a distance of two leagues, with an average breadth of one hundred and fifty feet. At one extremity of the mine he found large quantities of native silver, which he calculates will fully pay the expense of setting up machinery and working it. The *ranche* upon which it is situated was purchased by Colonel Frémont in 1846 from Alvarado, former governor of the territory. It was then considered nearly worthless, and Colonel Frémont only took it at the moment of leaving the country, because disappointed in obtaining another property. This discovery has made a great sensation throughout the country; yet it is but the first of many such The Sierra Nevada is pierced in every part with these priceless veins, which will produce gold for centuries after every spot of earth from base to summit shall have been turned over and washed out."*

Almost simultaneously with this discovery, it was ascertained, beyond a reasonable doubt, that the vast plain bounded on the west by the valley of the Sacramento and on the east by the Foot Hills, to which it rises by a gradual ascent, is intersected in every direction by immense strata of quartz, every pound of which will yield from one and a half to two dollars worth of gold. This plain is between five and six hundred miles in length, from forty to sixty miles in breadth, and contains not far from three thousand square miles. It is crossed by the tributaries of the Sacramento and San Joaquim, whose waters have disintegrated the gold from the quartz and deposited it in dust or lumps in their beds. A similar effect, though upon a smaller scale, is produced by each torrent that flows down from the Sierra Nevada during the rainy season. The larger streams that unite with the Sacramento and San Joaquim all have their sources between the Sierra and tho Foot

* Letter of Bayard Taylor to the New York Tribune, October 1, 1849.

Hills, breaking through the latter at an elevation of four thousand feet above the level of the sea.*

During the summer of 1849, this whole auriferous region was examined with great care and accuracy, by the Hon. Thomas Butler King, of Georgia, special agent of the State Department. He spent nearly two months in the gold country, obtained information from every reliable source, explored the valleys or beds of twelve of the tributary streams, and procured a complete collection of specimens of the gold formations, both in union with the quartz and separate from it. His report, made in March, 1850, fully confirms the theory in regard to the extent and richness of the quartz plain.

"The particular specimens which we have seen," says the editor of the Pacific News,† "of these quartz mountain quarries, are in the possession of Mr. Wright, one of the members of Congress elect from California, who will take them on to Washington in the steamer of the 1st of December. They consist, for the most part, of small pieces of quartz rock, generally of a brownish tinge, and, in some instances, presenting the appearance of a slight incipient decay, or decomposition of the rock formation. In all these specimens, the gold points or particles, are very slightly, if at all, visible to the naked eye. The microscope, however, reveals the gold more clearly. Besides these pieces which Mr. Wright has himself selected, with great care, as the fairest average sample of the general appearance of enormous and very numerous veins, or quarries, of quartz, there is also one larger fragment of the same rock, weighing, we should suppose, some ten or twelve pounds, from all parts of which the gold protrudes plainly, in a state almost pure. This single fragment of quartz, which Mr. Wright by no means regards as an average sample of the quarries, but which he pronounces to be the richest rock specimen he has seen, is found, by a most careful specific gravity test, as applied to it by Mr. Wright, to contain pure gold to the amount of about six hundred dollars. This piece of rock, we understand from Mr. Wright, is destined to be laid, (as a memorial from the California mountains, we suppose,) upon the table of the Speaker of the House of Representatives. Its appeal, we think, will be heeded.

"But the interest or importance attaching to this or to any other single and isolated fragment specimen, however peculiar and curious and rich in itself, is very slight, and even inconsiderable, in comparison to that which belongs to the more numerous fragments of quartz, in which very little gold or none, can be discovered by the naked eye,

* Report of Hon. T. B. King, March, 1850.

† November 30, 1849.

and which have been cautiously selected by Mr. Wright on the spot, as the fairest average specimens of whole veins and quarries, said to sweep visibly in sinuous and broken lines through the whole western slope of the Sierra Nevada, and to form vast masses of mountain rock, large enough and numerous enough to freight many times over all the navies and commercial marine of the world. Mr. Wright has spent, he informs us, much of the past season among the mountains, collecting his samples of the quartz in different localities, and subjecting the yield of gold from them, in very many instances, to the most rigorous tests. In all these experiments, Mr. Wright has been guided by the skill and judgment of Mr. Augustus Leland, a gentleman largely conversant with mining operations, and who has been from the first equally interested with Mr. Wright in all the researches which have been made.

"The astonishing result brought out by these investigations is, that in a particular and very extensive vein, four pounds of this rock yielded upon the average eleven dollars worth of pure gold, valued at sixteen dollars to the ounce. That is to say, the yield of gold from these average samples of the rock in this particular vein, is nearly three dollars for each pound of quartz. Mr. Wright exhibited to us two small masses of gold, each about the size and shape of a large musket ball, and both presenting the granulated appearance of gold extracted and collected by the aid of quicksilver. One of these contains about twelve dollars of pure gold, and is the largest yield which has been obtained from four pounds of the rock from the vein in question. The other contains about ten dollars, and is the smallest yield which has been obtained from any of the experiments upon the rock of this vein. We understand that the tests applied have been sometimes the operation of quicksilver, and sometimes the test of the comparative specific gravity of the pure quartz and the gold-bearing quartz. The samples of the rock which Mr. Wright has tested, have been taken from many different veins. In no sample tested, has the yield been less than one dollar to the pound of quartz. The average yield of the different veins has been, as determined by the samples, from one dollar and a half to two dollars, to the pound of rock.

"A single fact will show the unheard of and astonishing character of the results which have been thus arrived at. Mr. Wright informs us that he has recently conversed with an intelligent gentleman, now in this country [California], who has been long conversant, in the capacity of an overseer, with mining operations, as carried on in the quartz veins of Georgia. From this source, Mr Wright learns that a fifteen horse steam power, working twelve stamps, will stamp about a thousand bushels of quartz rock in a day—each bushel of quartz weighing about eighty pounds. If twenty-five cents' worth of gold is yielded from each bushel of eighty pounds, the business is considered a good one in Georgia. If the yield be fifty cents to the bushel, the profit is large. Now the yield of the rock which Mr. Wright has collected and tested, instead of being a quarter of a dollar, or half a dollar to the seventy-five pounds, is, in one great vein, nearly three dollars to one pound. Abate this, in view of possible or probable mistake, or in view of the superior yield of a single richer vein, to an average of two dollars, or of one dollar, or of half a dollar, to the pound, and the result still remains, in every point of view, almost equally unexampled and momentous. The whole question is, does gold-bearing quartz, making any approximation to any such yield, exist in California, in vast and inexhaustible masses? On this main point, the recent investigations of Mr. Wright coincide entirely with the observations and conclusions of Mr. King, and with the testimony of all the explorers of the region with whom we have conversed. They all agree that a large number of veins of quartz permeate visibly the western slope of the Sierra Nevada, running mainly from north to south, and throwing out branches from the main lines, at intervals, in every form, and in all directions. Mr. Wright, we learn, is so well assured of the reality of the results at which he has arrived, that, in connection with his partners, he has already, at a large expense, placed a number of men at work on one of the localities which he has observed, and which he states to be, apparently, scarcely more promising than many others—has sent for a mule load of quartz rock, to take with him to Washington, across the Isthmus—and has already forwarded to the Atlantic side, a large order for machinery suitable for the mining operations which he contemplates.

"In conclusion, we have only to add, that we put forth such statements as these under a full sense of our responsibility to the public. We aver nothing of our own knowledge, for to us this information is as new and as surprising as we are persuaded that it will be to most of our readers, both here and in the Atlantic states. We would say nothing inconsiderately to aggravate the gold mania anywhere. It has already produced, in the gold region of California, and on the routes to it, terrible scenes of individual suffering, disease and death,—scenes before which the boldest spirit may well quail, and from which the hardiest frame may well shrink away. But our information comes to us, at first hand, from sources of unquestionable integrity and intelligence, and appears to be the result of very thorough and deliberate investigation. In its general outlines it has had the full sanction of the most eminent minds among us. It apprises us of a state of facts of the highest importance to California, to the mining interest everywhere, and, in a word, to the whole commercial and financial world. If these facts turn out to have been accurately investigated, and accurately stated, it seems to us that neither in the wet diggings, nor yet in the dry diggings, are the future mining operations of this state to go on; but, on the contrary, in those primeval masses of rock in which the gold was formed, in which it still lies embedded and inexhaustible, of which all the gold, in all its forms, scattered through the ravines and bars of the rivers, is only the inconsiderable chance washings or abrasions, and which the hand even of the most adventurous and intrepid miner among us has yet scarcely touched."

The conclusions which force themselves upon the mind, in view of these new developments, are startling in the extreme. If eye-witnesses, men of intelligence and practical experience, are not grossly deceived in regard to what has fallen under their observation, it can no longer be doubted, that the whole western slope of the Sierra Nevada is one vast field of gold deposited there ages ago by some mighty volcanic cataclysm. Actual demonstration can alone determine how great is its extent, and how rich it is in mineral wealth. It is worse than idle to discuss the probabilities or possibilities. He who attempts to speculate on the subject will only lose himself amid the mazes of conjecture. A few years may suffice to gather the harvest, but it is much more likely to endure for centuries.

Estimated with reference to the future, the *placêras*, or gold diggings, where individual miners have operated, must soon, comparatively speaking, be exhausted; and they do not, therefore, possess so great permanent value. But as the gold-bearing quartz cannot, except in a few instances where it chances to be unusually rich, be profitably worked, without expensive machinery, the use of quicksilver for amalgamation, and the employment of a great number of operatives to secure the benefits and advantages of a subdivision of labor, the *placêras*, for present purposes, seem to possess the most importance. How soon they will be drained of their treasures, it is impossible to say. During the mining season of 1849, there were probably not far from twenty-five thousand persons at work in the diggings, but there is abundant room for thousands upon thousands in addition to that number. The washings on Feather river and some other streams have been measurably exhausted, it is said; but, in many instances, the courses of the rivers have been turned, or their waters dammed up, in order to examine their beds, and valuable deposits of gold have rewarded the persevering efforts of those engaged in the search.

Some of the river bars are found not to contain much gold, but cases of this kind are rare, and in general they have been worked with immense success; the parties concerned realizing from two to ten ounces of gold per day to each man. Besides these deposits in the beds of the streams, there are unquestionably great stores that still remain untouched in the innumerable *cañons* and ravines that intersect the quartz plain; and until all these have been examined there will be room for individual operators. The measure of success will, of course, depend very much on the perseverance and industry of the party himself. He who thinks to escape the curse pronounced upon our first parents, that doomed them and their posterity to unceasing toil and labor, by seeking the golden realms of California, will experience a most bitter disappointment. Speculators, indeed, may amass fortunes in a day, but he who labors in the mines, finds his employment no boyish pastime; and unless inured from childhood to fatigue and hardship, often, very often, he will have cause to regret that he has tasked himself too much, even if he be not forced to lie down and die, unfriended and alone, amid the glittering sands that cannot administer sustenance to his body or comfort to his soul.

Various implements or machines have been invented to separate the gold from the earthy particles with which it is mixed. The rocker, or cradle, continues to be popular with those who are working together in small parties; and in some cases, the earth containing the metal has been scattered upon an inclined plain of rough flat stone, over which the water is gradually poured. By this last method the "soil and gravel are separated and carried off, leaving the gold deposited on the rough plain."* Single individuals, however, prefer a common tin pan, or basin, for washing the gold; and this useful instrument is as popular at the *placēras* of California as is the *gamella*, or round wooden bowl, at the washings of Brazil.

It was for a long time thought impracticable to conduct mining operations during the wet season, or winter months, in consequence of the deep snow, or the swollen character of the mountain torrents when it begins to melt. But during the winter of 1849–50, great numbers of miners remained in the vicinity of the diggings. Having selected a comfortable location, they pitched their tents or erected their cabins, in which they stored a supply of fire-wood and provisions, and at every favorable opportunity emerged from their shelter and resumed their accustomed pursuit.

"Fortune, however, smiles less kindly on those who undergo the greatest fatigue, and perform the severest labor, than upon those who

* Sights in the Gold Region, and Scenes by the Way, p. 221.

profit by their necessities. The toil and sweat of the former often go to enrich the cunning trader and the shrewd speculator. The prices of food and clothing, of luxuries and necessaries, of everything that can please the fancy, or gratify the appetite, are from one to ten hundred per cent. higher than in the Atlantic States; and those engaged in providing supplies for the miners are in a majority of cases accumulating large fortunes. Yet it is to be regretted that the rage for speculation has already extended so widely in the territory, for, though of little importance at the outset, it soon becomes as incapable of control as the raging whirlwind, and, like that, always leaves desolation and ruin in its track. Within a twelvemonth after the first discovery of gold, the credit operations of the citizens of the territory amounted to one hundred millions of dollars, resting for support upon a metallic or specie basis of only ten millions. City and town lots, houses and farming lands, food and raiment, everything that man needs or desires, are the objects of speculation. What will be the result of all this, the future only can determine. Those who keep aloof from the whirlpool, or pause in time, may reap a rich harvest; but if California herself, or the older states in the Union that become too intimately connected with her, are ultimately benefited, it will be an anomaly in the history of the world."

But labor does not go unrewarded in California. If the toil of the miner is severe, the tempting prize at which he aims is often secured. All are not successful; yet those who are temperate, persevering, industrious, and capable of enduring the fatigue, commonly obtain from five to fifteen dollars' worth of gold in a single day. In the numerous towns, also, which have sprung up like mushrooms since the great discovery was made, laborers are ordinarily in great demand, and receive from five to ten dollars per day for their services. Carpenters, and other mechanics whose labor is needed, command from ten to sixteen dollars per day; and at these high prices, if they obtain constant employment, they undoubtedly realize more than those at work in the mines.

The amount of gold procured up to the 1st of January, 1850, was not much short of forty millions of dollars; and it is computed that forty millions more will be obtained by November, 1850, and the further sum of one hundred millions, from the 1st of May, 1851, to the 1st of November, 1852.* Of the sum already procured, about twenty-five millions of dollars have been carried away by foreigners, and the Americans have obtained only fifteen millions. The whole amount of

* Report of Mr. King.

California gold deposited at the United States' mint up to the 1st of March, 1850, was less than ten millions of dollars.

Large as these aggregate sums may appear, when we come to examine into the details, into the mode in which they are made up, we shall find that the average amount of gold so far procured by each person, is less than one thousand dollars. The number of inhabitants of the territory, in April, 1849, was about thirty thousand. Immediately after that time, they began to arrive by ship loads and boat loads, by caravans and by small parties, by hundreds and by thousands; so that at the close of the month of November, 1849, a grand total was presented of at least one hundred thousand souls. Mr. King estimates the population of the territory, in March, 1850, at one hundred and twenty thousand. Of this number at least one hundred thousand are "gold-hunters;" and yet, flattering as is his account of the gold region, he is of opinion that only forty millions of gold will be obtained during the next mining season—an average to each individual of only four hundred dollars. Those who have looked at this subject, undisturbed by the mania which has raged over the whole American continent, cannot fail to have been struck with the remarkable disparity between the few instances of extraordinary good fortune, and the many cases in which there has been nothing to chronicle, but poor success or sad disappointment.

The lessons of experience are alike truthful and valuable; but they are oftentimes learned in sorrow and bitterness. Such may not prove to be the case with the adventurers who have flocked to the golden shores of California; but facts and figures do not warrant the extravagant speculations in which many have indulged. The world may be benefited by the gold discovery; California herself may be benefited, though she may have to pass through many changes and revulsions ere that period arrives; speculators and traders may be benefited; but, judging from the past, the miners themselves, in a majority of cases, will not secure enough to compensate them, at a moderate estimate, for the toils, and trials, and sufferings, they have undergone.

When the gold and silver mines of Mexico and Peru were discovered, an entire revolution was effected in the value of the precious metals. A similar result has been anticipated from the discovery in California. There is, in truth, some reason to apprehend that such an effect will be produced; but it is impossible now to speak with any degree of certainty. The annual average produce of the South American and Mexican mines, from 1800 to 1810, was a little over forty-seven millions of dollars; though subsequent to the latter period, the amount annually procured was reduced to less than twenty millions.* If the annual product of gold in California should continue to be forty or fifty millions of dollars, for several years to come, it must sensibly affect the standard of value.

Up to the 1st day of November, 1849, about five hundred vessels, each containing more or less passengers, besides their crews, had arrived at San Francisco within the year immediately preceding, and it was computed, upon reliable data, that there were then at least two hundred vessels on their way to the same haven, each freighted with scores of adventurers, with bright hopes and aspirations—some foredoomed to disappointment, and others, perhaps, destined to secure a rich reward. Caravans, whose members were counted by thousands, have traversed the arid wastes intervening between the fertile valley of the Mississippi, and the frowning peaks of the Sierra Nevada. Troops of adventurers, also, have crossed the Isthmus, or passed through the Mexican states. The over-crowded hives of other nations have likewise sent forth their thousands to swell the tide of immigration rolling down like an avalanche upon the placéras of California. Danger in every form has been defied. The ocean tempest, and the *vómito* of New Granada, have been passed by unnoticed. Disease and death have followed upon the track of the wayfarer on the desert, with the tenacity of the blood-hound, yet he has never been discouraged or disheartened; and the shriek of the vulture, or the howl of the prairie wolf, has not disturbed his dreams of the golden land which was soon to bless his vision.

From the mongrel and heterogeneous character of the population of California, it would naturally be expected that a great degree of lawlessness and disorder would have been witnessed there, at least during the early stages of the immigration, and the prevalence of the gold excitement. But nothing of the kind, unless it be in a few isolated cases, which should justly be considered as exceptions to the general rule, has taken place. "It is a remarkable fact, and one highly creditable to the immigrants, that the state of society, in the main, has been, and now is, a great deal better than could be looked for among such an incongruous mass. Outrages and excesses have been committed, but they are daily becoming less frequent. For several months the citizens governed themselves, in a degree, by laws arbitrarily adopted, yet which were both appropriate and needful, and usually administered with impartiality and justice. On the 1st day of September, 1849, a convention of delegates elected in the different districts, in pursuance

* Jacob's Historical Inquiry into the Consumption of the Precious Metals, vol. II, p. 267.

of a proclamation of General Riley, then acting as civil and military governor of the territory, assembled at Monterey, and on the 12th day of October following, adopted a state constitution, modelled, in all its general features, after the new constitution of the state of New York; and immediately after the adjournment of that body, all the necessary steps were taken to bring the question of their admission into the confederacy before the national Congress, at its ensuing session." The constitution was duly laid before Congress at that time, by President Taylor, accompanied with an earnest recommendation in favor of the admission of California into the Union.

By the terms of this constitution, the eastern boundary of California is now the 120th meridian, west longitude, which is the only deviation from the boundaries previously described.* The superficial area of the state, within the boundaries as thus altered, "is 155.550 square miles, or 99,552,000 square acres, exclusive of the islands adjacent to her coast."†

One of the most important questions connected with California, in its effect upon the emigration constantly going on from the Atlantic states, is the salubrity of the climate. This has often been questioned, sometimes for apparently very good reasons. But the truth is, that although quite variable, the climate is not unhealthy, and most of the diseases that prevail are not caused directly by its influence. "No climate in the world," says one who speaks from actual observation, and is by no means prejudiced in favor of the country, "can be more healthy, and as a general rule more unpleasant, than that of the coast."‡ "For salubrity," remarks an intelligent traveller, "I do not think there is any climate in the world superior to that of the coast of California. I was in the country nearly a year, exposed much of the time to great hardships and privations, sleeping, for the most part, in the open air, and I never felt while there the first pang of disease, or the slightest indication of bad health. On some portions of the Sacramento and San Joaquim rivers, where vegetation is rank, and decays in the autumn, the malaria produces chills and fever, but generally the attacks are slight, and yield easily to medicine. The atmosphere is so pure and preservative along the coast, that I never saw putrified flesh, although I have seen, in midsummer, dead carcasses lying exposed to the sun and weather for months. They emitted no offensive smell. There is but little disease in the country arising from the climate."§

* Anté, p. 509.

† Memorial of the Senators and Representatives of California to the Congress of the United States, March 1, 1850.

‡ Sights in the Gold Region, etc., p. 217.

§ What I saw in California, p. 451.

"The high and dry character of Upper California," says Lieutenant Revere, "the absence of alluvial bottoms of great extent, the comparative scarcity of timber, and many minor causes which might be enumerated, render Upper California a most healthy country. Most new countries are troubled with ague and fever, and bilious fevers of all varieties; and I am far from saying that California is exempt from them. On the contrary, there is no doubt that large quantities of her quicksilver will be used at home in the shape of calomel, and the demand for quinine will probably be very lively. But these diseases will be contracted chiefly in the low countries and along the valleys of the rivers, while the uplands, which compose the greater part of California, will be as healthy as any part of the world. Men who stand all day long in the mud and water digging for gold under the scorching rays of a summer sun, will be apt to sicken anywhere; and as their operations will be carried on chiefly in the fever and ague, and bilious region, the gold diggers cannot all hope to escape disease. There are seasons when the usually healthy portions of the country become sickly. When the rains come prematurely, and afterwards a 'dry spell' sets in, then the springing vegetation rots, and the miasma arising from that cause sometimes produces disease. But this is of rare occurrence, and it is safe to say that California is quite as healthy as any of our northern states."*

Should the time ever arrive when the mineral wealth of California shall be exhausted, she must still remain rich in agricultural resources. Several years since, a French traveller remarked, that the whole country, lying between the coast of California and the Sierra Nevada, was "of admirable fertility, and perfectly proper for colonization;" and that when it should be settled by an intelligent and laborious population, it would occupy "an elevated rank in the commercial scale."† Probably not more than one fourth of the entire area of the state will ever be useful for agricultural purposes, as two fourths are covered with mountains, and the remaining fourth is a desert waste.‡ But small as the portion adapted to husbandry may appear in the comparison, it will amply reward the labor of the agriculturist. The pasture lands are unsurpassed in the world for verdure and richness. Wild oats grow spontaneously over the plains, and yield an annual crop averaging forty bushels to the acre. With such facilities, cattle and

* Tour of Duty in California, p. 277.

† M. de Mofras' Exploration du Territoire de l'Orégon, des Californies, etc., tom. II, pp. 40, 58.

‡ Memorial of the Senators and Representatives of California.

sheep, in immense quantities, can be raised.* The fertility of the soil in the arable portions, and where irrigation is practicable, is remarkable; eighty bushels of wheat for one is the average yield, and sometimes, though this is not usual, one hundred and twenty have been obtained.†

California, indeed, possesses all the elements of greatness and prosperity. She is rich in her fertile valleys and her grassy slopes; rich in her stores of mineral wealth; rich in her noble bay of San Francisco, "one of the finest, if not the very best harbor, in the world;"‡ and, above all, rich in the hardy, enterprising, and industrious population, which she has received from the older states in the Union, and which will surely make hers a brilliant destiny. It is only necessary to open direct avenues of communication with the valley of the Mississippi, and the Atlantic states, when her capacity and resources will be fully developed; when the rich products of two worlds will be exchanged in her harbors, and her balmy gales be constantly loaded with the fragrance of the spices of the Orient.

* Report of Mr. King.

† Wilkes' Narrative of the Exploring Expedition, vol. V, pp. 158, 159.

‡ Ibid, p. 157.

LIST OF BOOKS

RECENTLY PUBLISHED BY

DERBY & MILLER,

AUBURN, N. Y.

The Life of John Quincy Adams, Sixth President of the United States, by Hon. Wm. H. Seward, U. S. S., with a portrait on steel, 12mo. muslin, gilt backs.

\. 20,000 copies of this popular work have been sold by agents, in the short space of eight months.

There is, indeed, so much to admire throughout the whole work, that were we to enter into anything like an elaborate review, it would require more space than we can spare. * * * * The Life and Public Services of such a man as John Quincy Adams, furnish the very material for such a pen as Gov. Seward's, and we find evidences of his own brilliant intellect impressed upon almost every page and sentence. Preserving the connection of events with almost mathematical nicety, at the same time avoiding everything tedious and prolix. As a writer, it may be doubted whether Gov. Seward has any superiors. * * —*Philadelphia News*, (*Whig.*)

It would be a task of no ordinary difficulty for a contemporary, one who has mingled in the strife and arena of his times, to write an impartial Life of so peculiar and prominent an actor (for half a century) as Mr. Adams. * * Gov. Seward has attempted it, and succeeded in producing an interesting work, characterized by ability and eloquence. * * We consider it worthy of public attention.—*Albany Argus*, (*Dem.*)

We have read this volume with great satisfaction, and hasten to express our thanks to the author; not merely for the pleasures afforded us, but for the services rendered humanity. * * * —*Louisville Examiner*, *Anti-Slavery.*

SEWARD'S LIFE OF JOHN Q. ADAMS.

* * We are glad to see a pretty full account of Mr. Adams' Anti-Slavery efforts in Congress have been given; for, great as his public services were during a long life, his greatest fame with the present and future generations, will rest upon his efforts to break down the Slave power. The great men who eulogized Mr. Adams in Congress and elsewhere, generally passed silently over this part of his life, as if it was something not very creditable to him, and to be talked about as little as possible. Mr. Seward has taken a better view of the subject. We can recommend this biography as being a clear and concise history of Mr. Adams' life. *
* * *Lowell Republican*, (*Free Soil.*)

It is a work well written, prepared evidently with care, conveys an excellent idea of the life and services of that distinguished patriot and statesman. It is well adapted for popular reading, and comes within the means of every citizen. * * And possessing, as it does, a fund of historical and biographical information, of the most interesting description, it will be a desirable book for the library and a welcome companion to any man who cherishes a respect for the memory of Adams. *
* * *Boston Journal.*

* * We have read it and are delighted with the good taste and discrimination with which facts and cotemporary events are brought in to show forth the noble and manly stand of John Quincy Adams. Next to our national pride, that we have such great and good men to adorn the pages of our history, we should glory in having authors like Wm. H. Seward, to chronicle their lives and their deeds. *
* * *Massachusetts Eagle.*

The association of such names as Adams and Seward, one as the subject of the biography, and the other as the biographer, must give to this work an interest which rarely attaches to anything emanating from an American pen. * * *
Washington Advocate.

We would recommend this work to every class of mind — to the vicious, that they may be benefited by the contrast — to the virtuous, that they may be incited to still higher attainments — to the patriot, that the love of country may be renewed in his bosom — to the Christian, that he may see how to honor God in exalted positions — to the young, that they may drink from the pure rill of patriotism, and learn to cherish and protect their privileges — and lastly to the old, that they may yet once more read the lessons of wisdom, as they distilled from the lips of him who was a Nestor among statesmen.— *Wisconsin Chronicle.*

This volume has been now but a few months before the public, during which we understand that some 20,000 copies have been circulated. The fact is sufficient to show that the deceased statesman has found a worthy biographer. Designed for popular use, and prepared from the materials existing in public documents and journals, it is a book, nevertheless, that cannot fail to be read with interest by the scholar as well as the masses. The writer seems imbued with a sincere reverence for the great man whose career he chronicles, and depicts its various eventful incidents with spirit and fidelity. There is no book that we now remember, which presents in the same compass so much that is interesting in our history, during the period of which it treats.— *Washington Republic.*

The Life of Gen. Zachary Taylor, 12th President of the United States, brought down to his inauguration. Steel portrait, 12mo., muslin; a new edition, by H. Montgomery. $1,25.

*** 18,000 of the above work have been sold by us.

"THE LIFE OF GEN. Z. TAYLOR."—*H. Montgomery*, Esq., editor of the Auburn Daily Advertiser, has found leisure, amid the multitude of his engagements, to get up the most respectable looking and carefully prepared biography of the old General we have yet seen. It makes a neat volume, and is printed on excellent paper and new type, and bound in the very best style. It cannot fail to find a tremendous sale; a result due alike to the book itself, and the enterprise of its busy publishers.—*Albany Evening Journal.*

"LIFE OF GENERAL ZACHARY TAYLOR, by *H. Montgomery*," is the latest and most complete of the numerous volumes purporting to be 'Lives' of the General. The author of this work — likewise editor of the Auburn Journal — is already known as a forcible and pleasing writer, handling his subject with a masterly hand; these characteristics are fully developed in the book before us. The stirring incidents of General Taylor's life, and the recent battles on Mexican soil are well portrayed — the very fair and impartial style of narration being a rare quality in depicting battle scenes. The book will repay an attentive perusal.—*N. Y. Tribune.*

THE LIFE OF MAJOR GENERAL ZACHARY TAYLOR. *By H. Montgomery.*— Another and still another "illustrated" Life of the great American, (would that he had as many lives as the publishers give him,) the American whom Carlyle would recognise as "a hero" worthy of his pen's most eloquent recognition; THE MAN OF DUTY in an age of Self. An American in everything; in valor, in strong muscular sense; in simplicity and directness and cordiality of feeling; an American in every thing, save in devotion to our new political God of Expediency.

The volume before us is put forth in Auburn, by the editor of the Auburn Daily Advertiser, whose vigorous, fluent style, and skill in compressing his materials, must make his elegant volume very generally acceptable. Many of the traits ascribed to General Taylor have been assimilated by some of his admirers to the leading military characteristics of Frederick the Great. But, unlike Frederick, Taylor is anything but a martinet in discipline; and, though his movements of small bodies of troops against vast odds, are characterized by the vigorous will and iron determination of Frederick, the arbitrary disposition of the Prussian despot is wholly alien to his tolerant and candid nature. Taylor's affectionate and almost parental relation to his soldiers, perhaps, alone first suggested the parallel, as we find it hinted in the following stanza of some verses upon one of his battles, quoted by Mr. Montgomery:

"'OLD ZACH!' 'OLD ZACH!' the war cry rattles
Among those men of iron tread,
As rung 'OLD FRITZ' in Europe's battles
When thus his host Great Frederick led."

Literary World.